Viking Tales of Old Iceland 3

Original Texts, Translations, and Word Lists

Translated by
Matthew Leigh Embleton

Viking Tales of Old Iceland 3

The Tale of Halldor Snorrason II (*Old Norse*) 3
The Tale of Halldor Snorrason II (*Old Icelandic*) 49
The Tale of Ale-Hood (*Old Norse*) 99
The Tale of Ale-Hood (*Old Icelandic*) 141
The Tale of Thorlief the Earl's Poet (*Old Norse*) 188
The Tale of Thorlief the Earl's Poet (*Old Icelandic*) 238

Cover: Old Norse text over an outline of Iceland. Author's design.

The original Old Norse and Old Icelandic texts are in the public domain.
These translations ©2022 Matthew Leigh Embleton
©2025 Matthew Leigh Embleton (This Edition)

Acknowledgments

I have long been fascinated by languages and history, and I am very grateful to the special people in my life who have supported and encouraged me in my work. Thank you for believing in me. You know who you are.

Introduction

Old Norse is a North Germanic language spoken by inhabitants of Scandinavia from about the 7th to the 15th centuries. Old Icelandic is a variety of Old West Norse that emerged during the Norse settlement of Iceland in the second half of the 9th century. The rich tradition of Icelandic story telling survived by oral tradition over several centuries before being written down in the 13th Century. The Tales of Icelanders are known as Íslendingaþættir. The word 'þáttr' (plural: 'þættir') translates as a strand of rope or a yarn, comparable to the word 'yarn' in English sometimes used to refer to a story.

The texts are presented in Old Norse and Old Icelandic, in their original form, with a literal word-for-word line-by-line translation, and a Modern English translation, all side-by-side. In this way, it is possible to see and feel how the worked and how it has evolved. This book is designed to be of use and interest to anyone with a passion for the Old Norse or Old Icelandic language, Norse history, or languages and history in general.

The Tale of Halldor Snorrason II (*Old Norse*)

Old Norse	Literal	English
1	**1**	**1**
HALLDÓRR Snorrason hafði verit út í Miklagarði með Haraldi, sem áðr er sagt, ok kom í Nóreg með honum austan ór Garðaríki.	Halldor Snorrason had been out in The-Great-City with Harald, as before was said, and came to Norway with him east from Gardariki.	Halldor Snorrason had been to Constantinople with Harald as has been said before, and went east to Norway with him from the Kievan Rus'.
Hafði hann þá mikla sæmð ok virðing af Haraldi konungi.	Had he then much honour and worthiness from Harald the-king.	Then he had much honour and worthiness from king Harald.
Var hann með konungi þenna vetr, er hann sat í Kaupangi.	Was he with the-king that winter, when he stayed at Kaupang.	He was with the king that winter when he stayed a Kaupang in Skiringssal.
En er á leið vetrinn ok vára tók, bjuggu menn kaupferðir sínar snemma, því at náliga hafði engi eða lítill verit skipagangr af Nóregi fyrir sakar ófriðar ok aga þess, sem verit hafði milli Nóregs ok Danmerkr.	And when had passed winter and spring took, preparations people trading-voyages theirs early, because of nearly had none or little been shipping from Norway for the-sake-of hostilities and turbulence those, as had-been had between Norway and Denmark.	And when winter had passed into spring, people began preparations for trading voyages early, because there had been little in the way of trade from Norway because of hostilities and turbulence between Norway and Denmark.
En er á leið várit, fann Haraldr konungr, at Halldórr Snorrason ógladdist mjök.	But when that passed spring, found Harald the-king, that Halldor Snorrason un-glad much.	But when spring had passed, king Harald found Halldor Snorrason very unhappy.
Konungr spurði einn dag, hvat honum bjó í skapi.	The-king asked one day, what he settled in mood.	One day the king asked what had settled in his mood.
Halldórr svarar:	Halldor answered:	Halldor answered:
"Út fýsir mik til Íslands, herra".	"Out desire me to Iceland, lord".	"I desire to travel out to Iceland, lord".
Konungr mælti:	The-king spoke:	The king said:
"Margr myndi þó heimfúsari verit hafa, eða hver eru fararefnin, eða hversu verst fénu?"	"Many would though home-longing being had, but where are travel-goods, or how-so becomes wealth?"	"Many would be longing for home, but where are your travel goods, and how will you spend your wealth?"

The Tale of Halldor Snorrason II (Old Norse)

Old Norse	Literal	English
Hann svarar:	He answered:	He answered:
"Skjótt ætla ek at verja, því at ekki er til nema ígangsklæði mín".	"Swift intend I to spend, because that not have to take travelling-clothes mine".	"Swiftly it seems spent to me, because I don't have any travelling clothes to take".
"Lítt er þá launuð löng þjónusta ok margr háski, ok skal ek fá þér skip ok áhöfnina.	"Little is then repaid long service and many dangers, and shall I pay you a-ship and crew.	"Your long service and all its dangers are little repaid, and I shall buy you a ship and a crew.
Skal faðir þinn sjá mega, at þú hefir mér eigi til engis þjónat".	Shall father yours see may, that you have me not to nothing served".	Your father shall see that you have not served me for nothing".
Halldórr þakkaði konungi gjöfina.	Halldor thanked the-king the-gift.	Halldor thank the king for his gift.
Fám dögum síðar fann Halldórr konung, ok spurði konungr, hversu mjök hann hefði ráðit sér skipverja.	A-few days later found Halldor the-king, and asked the-king, how-so much he had hired for the-crew.	A few days later Halldor found the king and asked him how much of the crew had he hired.
Hann svarar:	He answered:	He answered:
"Allir kaupsveinar hafa sér ráðit áðr skipan, en ek fæ enga menn, ok því ætla ek, at eftir mun verða at vera skip þat, er þér gáfuð mér".	"All trading-men have themselves hired other ships, but I give no men, and therefore suppose I, that remaining should be that becoming the-ship that, is you gave me".	"All the traders have been hired by other ships, but I have got no men, and therefore I suppose that the ship that you gave me should remain".
Konungr mælti:	The-king spoke:	The king spoke:
"Eigi er þá vinveitt gjöfin, ok skulum vit enn bíða, hvat ór ráðist um háseta".	"Not is then favourable gift, and shall with then wait, what from decide about sailors".	"Then it is not a favourable gift, and with that we shall wait to decide about the sailors".
Annan dag eftir var blásit til móts í bænum ok sagt, at konungr vill tala við bæjarmenn ok kaupmenn.	The-next day after was trumpet-blown to meet in the-town and said, that the-king wished-to speak with townspeople and merchants.	The next day the trumpet was blown to meet in the town, and the king said that he wished to speak with the townspeople and the merchants.
Konungr kom seint til mótsins ok sýndist með áhyggjusvip, þá er hann kom.	The-king came late to the-meeting and seemed with worried-face, then as he came.	The king came late to the meeting and seemed to have a worried face when he arrived.
Hann mælti:	He spoke:	He spoke:

The Tale of Halldor Snorrason II (Old Norse)

Old Norse	Literal	English
"Þat heyrum vér sagt, at ófriðr muni kominn í ríki várt austr í Vík.	"This hear we said, that un-peace shall come in kingdom ours east about Vik.	"We hear this, that war shall come to our kingdom east in Vik.
Ræðr Sveinn Danakonungr fyrir Danaher ok vill oss vinna skaða, en vér viljum með engu móti upp gefa vár lönd.	Leading Svein King-of-Denmark for Danish-forces and wishes us to-win-over damages, but we wish-to with none meet up give our land.	King Svein of Denmark is leading the Danish forces and means to win over and damage us, but none of us wish to give up our land.
Fyrir því leggjum vér bann fyrir hvert skip, at ór landi fari, fyrr en ek hefi slíkt sem ek vil af hverju skipi, bæði af liði ok vistum, nema einn knörr, eigi mikill, er á Halldórr Snorrason, skal ganga til Íslands.	For therefore lay we a-ban before each ship, to out-of the-land travel, before that I have such as I wish from each ship, both of men and provisions, except one ship, not great, that of Halldor Snorrason, shall go to Iceland.	Therefore we lay a ban on each ship from travelling out of these lands, until I have what I wish from each ship, men and provisions, except for one small ship of Halldor Snorrason which will go to Iceland.
En þótt yðr þykki þetta nökkut strangt, er áðr hafið búit ferðir yðrar, þá berr oss nauðsyn til slíkra álaga, en betra þætti oss, at um kyrrt væri at sitja ok færi hverr sem vildi".	But though you think this somewhat strange, is before have prepared travel yours, then bears us necessity to such stress, but better seems to-us, that about peace was that settle and travel each as wish".	You will think this somewhat strange, when you have prepared your travel, but it this stress is necessary, and it would be better for us if there was peace and each man could travel wherever he wished.
Eftir þat sleit mótinu.	After that broken-up the-meeting.	After that the meeting was broken up.
Litlu síðar kom Halldórr á konungs fund.	Little afterwards came Halldor to the-king find.	A little afterwards Halldor came to find the king.
Konungr spurði, hvat þá liði um búnaðinn, hvárt hann fengi nökkura háseta.	The-king asked, what then crew about preparations, each he found some crew.	The king asked about what preparations had been made for some crew.
Halldórr svarar:	Halldor answered:	Halldor answered:
"Helzti marga hefi ek nú ráðit, því at miklu fleiri koma nú til mín ok beiða fars en ek mega öllum veita, ok veita menn mér mikinn atgang, at drjúgum eru brotin hús til mín, svá at hvárki nótt né dag hefi ek ró fyrir ákalsi manna her um.	"Rather many have I now hired, because that a-great more came now to me and asked travel than I may all lead, and grant people me much access, that greatly they violated house to me, so that neither night nor day have I rest for calling people here about.	"I have hired rather a lot of men, because a great more came to me and asked to travel than I may lead, and granted much access that my house is violated, so that I have no rest, neither day nor night for these people calling here abouts".

5

The Tale of Halldor Snorrason II (Old Norse)

Old Norse	Literal	English
Konungr mælti:	The-king spoke:	The king spoke:
"Haltu nú þessum hásetum, sem þú hefir tekit, ok sjám enn, hvat í gerist".	"Hold-you now those sailors, that". you have taken, and we-see then, what will be".	"Now keep the sailors that you have hired, and we will see what will happen".
Næsta dag eftir var blásit ok sagt, at konungr vill enn tala við kaupmenn.	Next day after was trumpet-blown and said, the king wished then speak with the-merchants.	The next day, a trumpet was blown, and it was said that the king wished to speak with the merchants.
Nú var eigi sein at konungi til mótsins, því at hann kom í fyrsta lagi.	Now was not late to-come the-king to the-meeting, because that he came to first had.	Now the king was not late in coming to the meeting, because he had arrived first.
Var hann þá blíðligr í yfirbragði.	Was he then happily in complexion.	He was then happy in his complexion.
Hann stóð upp ok mælti:	He stood up and spoke:	He stood up and spoke:
"Nú eru góð tíðendi at segja.	"Now there-are good tidings to say.	"Now there is good news to say.
Þat er ekki nema upplost ok lygi, er þér heyrðuð sagt um ófriðinn fyrra dag.	That is not except false-rumour and lie, that you heard said about un-peace the-first day.	That was nothing except a false rumour and a lie that you heard said about war the other day.
Viljum vér nú leyfa hverju skipi ór landi at fara þangat, sem hverr vill sínu skipi halda.	Wish we now allow each ship out-of lands to travel from-there, as each wishes their ship to-hold.	We now wish to allow each ship out of our lands to travel where they wish with their ships.
Komið aftr at hausti ok færið oss gersimar.	Come back in the-autumn and bring us treasures.	Come back in the autumn, and bring us treasures.
En þér skuluð hafa af oss í mót gæði ok vingan".	But you should have from us in return good-things and friendship".	Then you shall have good things and friendship in return from us".
Allir kaupmenn, er þar váru, urðu þessu fegnir ok báðu hann tala konunga heilstan.	All the-traders, who there were, became this celebrated and bid him speak the-king thanks.	All the traders who were there celebrated at this and spoke thanks to the king.
Fór Halldórr til Íslands um sumarit ok var þann vetr með frændum sínum.	Travelled Halldor to Iceland about summer and was then winter with father his.	Halldor travelled to Iceland around summer and was there with his father for the winter.

The Tale of Halldor Snorrason II (Old Norse)

Old Norse	Literal	English
Hann fór útan eftir um sumarit ok þá enn til hirðar Haralds konungs, ok er svá sagt at Halldórr var þá eigi jafnfylginn konungi sem fyrr, ok sat hann eftir um aftna, þá er konungr gekk at sofa.	He travelled out after about summer and then was to court Harald the-king, and was so said that Halldor was then not equally-following the-king as before, and sat he after about evening, then when the-king went to sleep.	He travelled around summer and was then in the court of king Harald, and so it was said that Halldor was not the same follower of the king that he was before, and he sat up in the evening after the king had gone to sleep.

2

Old Norse	Literal	English
Maðr hét Þórir Englandsfari ok hafði verit inn mesti kaupmaðr ok lengi í siglingum til ýmissa landa ok fært konungi gersimar.	A-man named Thorir England-Traveller and had been the most trading-man and long with sailing to various lands and bringing the-king treasure.	A man was named Thorir the England-Traveller, and he had been the greatest trader and had long sailed to various lands to bring the king treasure.
Þórir var hirðmaðr Haralds konungs ok þá mjök gamall.	Thorir was court-man Harald the-king and then much old.	Thorir was a court man of king Harald and was then very old.
Þórir kom at máli við konung ok mælti:	Thorir came to speak with the-king and spoke:	Thorir came to speak with the king and said:
"Ek er maðr gamall, sem þér vitið, ok mæðumst ek mjök.	"I am a-man old, as you know, and tired I-am much.	"I am an old man as you know, and I am very tired.
Þykkjumst ek nú eigi til færr at fylgja hirðsiðum, minni at drekka eða um aðra hluti, þá sem til heyra.	Think I now not to travel to follow king's-men-customs, mine to drink or about other things, then as to hear.	I now do not think I can follow the customs of the king's men, less drinking or other things which are heard of.
Mun nú annars leita verða, þótt þetta sé bezt ok blíðast, at vera með yðr".	Should now another seek to-be, though it is best and happiest, to be with you".	I should now seek another place to be, though it is best and happiest to be with you".
Konungr svarar:	The-king answered:	The king answered:
"Þar er okkr hægt til órráða, vinr.	"There is our possible to solution, friend.	"There is a possible solution, friend".
Ver með hirðinni ok drekk ekki meira en þú vill, í mínu leyfi".	Be with court and drink not more than you wish, with my leave".	Be with the court and do not drink more than you wish, with my leave".
Bárðr hét maðr upplenzkr, góðr drengr ok ekki gamall.	Bard was-named a-man an-Uplander, good fellow and not old.	There was a man named Bard, an Upplander, a good fellow and not old.

The Tale of Halldor Snorrason II (Old Norse)

Old Norse	Literal	English
Hann var með Haraldi konungi í miklum kærleikum.	He was with Harald the-king in much dearly-loved.	He was with king Harald and much loved by him.
Váru þeir sessunautar, Bárðr, Þórir ok Halldórr.	Were they sitting-together, Bard, Thorir and Halldor.	They were sitting together, Bard, Thorir, and Halldor.
Ok eitt kveld, er konungr gekk þar fyrir, er þeir sátu ok drukku, í því bili gaf Halldórr upp hornit.	And one evening, when the-king went there before, were they sat and drinking, in that moment gave Halldor up the-drinking-horn.	And one evening when the king went before where they sat drinking, in that moment Halldor gave up the drinking horn.
Þat var dýrshorn mikit ok skyggt vel.	It was stag-horn huge and shaded well.	It was a stag horn, and very transparent.
Sá gerla í gegnum, at hann hafði drukkit vel til hálfs við Þóri.	So completely in through, that he had drunk well to half against Thorir.	So completely through, that it could be seen that he had drunk more than half compared to Thorir
En honum gekk seint af at drekka.	Who he went slowly of to drink.	who drank slowly.
Þá mælti konungr:	Then spoke the-king:	Then the king spoke:
"Seint er þó menn at reyna, Halldórr",	"Slow it-is though people to know, Halldor",	"It is slow to get to know Halldor",
segir hann,	said he,	he said,
"er þú níðist á drykkju við gamalmenni ok hleypr at vændiskonum um síðkveldum, en fylgir eigi konungi þínum".	"that you down the drinks against old-men and run to prostitutes about late-evening, while following not king yours".	"that you down the drinks against old men, and run to prostitutes late in the evening, while not following your king".
Halldórr svarar engu, en Bárðr fann, at honum mislíkaði umræða ksonungs.	Halldor answered none, but Bard found, that he misliked discussion the-king's.	Halldor did not answer, but Bard found that he disliked the king's words.
Fór Bárðr þegar um myrgininn snemma á fund konungs.	Went Bard straight-away about morning early to find the-king.	Bard went straight away early in the morning to find the king.
"Þó ert þú nú árrisull, Bárðr",	"Though are you now early-riser, Bard",	"Though you are an early riser, Bard",
segir konungr.	said the-king.	said the king.
"Em ek nú kominn",	"Am I now come",	"And I have now come",

The Tale of Halldor Snorrason II (Old Norse)

Old Norse	Literal	English
kvað Bárðr,	said Bard,	said Bard,
"at ávíta yðr, herra.	"to warn you, lord.	"to warn you lord.
Þér mæltuð illa ok ómakliga í gærkveld til Halldórs, vinar yðvars, er þér kennduð honum, at hann drykki sleitiliga, því at þat var horn Þóris, ok hafði hann unnit ok ætlaði at bera til skapkers, ef eigi drykki Halldórr fyrir hann.	You spoke ill and undeservedly about last-night to Halldor, friend yours, when you taught him, that he drank unfairly, because that it was horn Thorir's, and had he deserved and intended to bear to large-vessel, if not drink Halldor before him.	You spoke badly and unfairly last night to Halldor, your friend, when you told him that he drank unfairly, because it was Thorir's horn, and he deserved and intended to bear a large vessel if Halldor was not drinking before him.
Þat er ok in mesta lygi, er þér mæltuð, at hann færi at léttlætiskonum, en kjósa myndi menn, at hann fylgði þér fastara".	It is also the most lie, that you spoke, that he went to prostitutes, than choose should people, to him follow you more-fixedly".	It is also the greatest lie that you said he went to prostitutes, although people would rather that he followed you more closely".
Konungr svarar ok lét, at þeir myndi semja þetta mál með sér, þá er þeir Halldórr fyndist.	The-king answered and had, that they would negotiate this matter with him, then when they Halldor found.	The king answered that he would negotiate this matter with him when he met Halldor next.
Hittir Bárðr Halldór ok segir honum góð orð konungs til hans ok kvað einsætt vera, at hann léti sér einskis þykkja um vert orðaframkast konungs, ok á Bárðr inn bezta hlut at með þeim.	Found Bard Halldor and said he good words the-king's to him and said clearly being, that he let himself nothing think about worthy outburst the-king's, and this Bard the best part that between them.	Bard found Halldor and told him the king's good words, and that he should let himself think no worth of the king's outburst, and this is how Bard tried to put the best part between them.
Líðr fram at jólum, ok er heldr fátt um með þeim konungi ok Halldóri.	Passed from to Yule, and was rather few about with them the-king and Halldor.	Time passed until Yule, and there was little between the king and Halldor.
Ok er at jólum kemr, þá eru víti upp sögð, sem þar er tízka til.	And when that Yule came, then they-were signalled up told, as there was custom to.	And when Yule came, were they signalled up as was the custom.
Ok einn morgun jólanna er breytt hringingum.	And one morning Yule was changed bell-ringing.	And one morning during Yule, the bell ringing was changed.

The Tale of Halldor Snorrason II (Old Norse)

Old Norse	Literal	English
Gáfu kertisveinar klokkurum fé til at hringja miklu fyrr en vant var, ok varð Halldórr víttr ok fjölði annarra manna, ok settust í hálm um daginn ok skyldu drekka vítin.	Gave court-men clocks payment for to ring much before than expected was, and became Halldor reprimanded and many other people, and sat in the-straw about the-day and should drink penalty.	The court men gave the bell ringers payment to ring the bells much before it was expected, and Halldor was reprimanded along with many other people, who had to sit on the floor in the straw and drink from the penalty horn.
Halldórr sitr í rúmi sínu, ok færa þeir honum eigi at síðr vítit, en hann lézt eigi drekka myndu.	Halldor sat in seat his, and brought they him none the less the-penalty, and he had not drank would.	Halldor sat in his room, and they none the less brought him the penalty horn, and he would not drink from it.
Þeir segja þá konungi til.	They told then the-king about.	They told the king about it.
"Þat mun eigi satt",	"That could not be-true",	"That could not be true",
segir konungr, „ok mun hann við taka, ef ek færi honum",	said the-king, ,and should he with take, if I bring him",	said the king,
- tekr síðan vítishornit ok gengr at Halldóri.	- took then penalty-horn and went to Halldor.	"and he should take it if I bring it to him", and he took the penalty horn and went to Halldor.
Hann stendr upp í móti honum.	He stood up in meeting him.	He stood up upon meeting him.
Konungr biðr hann drekka vítit.	The-king asked him to-drink the-penalty.	The king asked him to drink the penalty.
Halldórr svarar:	Halldor answered:	Halldor answered:
"Ek þykkjumst ekki víttr at heldr, þó at þér setið brögð til hringingar til þess eins at gera mönnum víti".	"I think not penalty to hold, though that you set a-trick to bell-ringing to this alone to do people punishment".	"I don't think to hold the penalty, though you set a trick to the bell ringing only to punish people".
Konungr svarar:	The-king answered:	The king answered:
"Þú munt drekka skulu vítit þó eigi síðr en aðrir menn".	"You must drink should penalty though not less than other people".	"You must drink the penalty no less than other people".
"Vera má þat, konungr",	"Be may that, king",	"That may be, king",
segir Halldórr,	said Halldor,	said Halldor,

The Tale of Halldor Snorrason II (Old Norse)

Old Norse	Literal	English
"at þú komir því á leið, at ek drekka,	"that you come with to pass, that I drink,	"that it shall come to pass that I drink.
en þat kann ek þó segja þér, at eigi myndi Sigurðr sýr fá nauðgat Snorra goða til",	but that know I though say to-you, that not would Sigurd Sow gave force Snorri the-priest to",	But I know to say to you that Sigurd Sow would not have forced Snorri the Priest to",
- ok vill seilast til hornsins, sem hann gerir, ok drekkr af, en konungr reiðist mjök ok gengr til rúms síns.	- and willed to-reach for the-horn, as he went, and drank of, as the-king commanded much and went to room his.	and he reached for the penalty horn, and drank as much as the king commanded, and went to his room.
Ok er kemr inn átti dagr jóla, var mönnum gefinn máli.	And when came the eighth day Yule, were people given payment.	And when the eighth day of Yule came, people were given payment.
Þat var kallat Haraldsslátta.	That was called Harald's-money.	That was called Harald's money.
Var meiri hlutr kopars, þat bezta kosti, at væri helmings silfr.	Was greater part copper, that best benefit, that had half silver.	It was for the greater part copper, and the best of it was half silver.
Ok er Halldórr tók málann, hefir hann í möttulsskauti sínu silfrit ok lítr á ok sýnist eigi skírt málasilfrit, lýstr undir neðan annarri hendi, ok ferr þat allt í hálm niðr.	And when Halldor took payment, had he in cloak-lap his the-silver and looked at and seemed not pure silverware, struck under below other hand, and went it all in straw below.	And when Halldor took the payment, he put the silver in the lap of his cloak, and it seemed not to be pure silver, he swept it down with his other hand and it all went onto the straw on the floor below.
Bárðr mælti, kvað hann illa með fara.	Bard spoke, said he badly with went.	Bard spoke, and said that he was behaving badly:
"Mun konungr þykkjast svívirðr í ok leitat á við hann um málagjöfna".	"Would the-king consider dishonourable of and consider to with him about payment".	"The king would consider this dishonourable, considering with him about payment".
"Ekki má nú fara at slíku",	"Not may now go that such",	"It may not go that way",
segir Halldórr,	said Halldor,	said Halldor,
"litlu hættir nú til".	"little way now to".	"there is little to be done now".

3

Nú er frá því sagt, at þeir búa skip sín eftir jólin.	Now was from of said, that they prepared ships theirs after Yule.	Now it was said that they prepared their ships after Yule.

The Tale of Halldor Snorrason II (Old Norse)

Old Norse	Literal	English
Ætlar konungr suðr fyrir land.	Intended the-king south along the-land.	The king intended to travel south along the land.
Ok er konungr var mjök svá búinn, þá bjóst Halldórr ekki, ok mælti Bárðr:	And when the-king was much so prepared, then readied Halldor not, and spoke Bard:	And when the king was so well prepared, Halldor did not prepare, and Bard said,
"Hví býstu eigi, Halldórr?"	"Why prepared not, Halldor?"	"Why do you not prepare Halldor?"
"Eigi vil ek",	"Not wish I",	"I do not want to,"
segir hann,	said he,	he said,
"ok ekki ætla ek at fara.	"and not intend I to travel.	"and I do not intend to travel.
Sé ek nú, at konungr þokkar ekki mitt mál".	See I now, that the-king favours not my measure".	I see now that the king does not like my case".
Bárðr segir:	Bard said:	Bard said:
"Hann mun þó at vísu vilja, at þú farir".	"He would though that certainly wish, that you travel".	"Though he will want you to travel".
Ferr Bárðr síðan ok hittir konung, segir honum, at Halldórr býst ekki.	Went Bard afterwards and found the-king, said he, that Halldor prepares not.	Afterwards Bad went and found the king, and he told him that Halldor had not prepared,
"Máttu svá ætla, at vandskipaðr mun þér vera stafninn í stað hans".	"May-you so suppose, that difficult would you be the-prow in replace his".	"you may suppose that it would be difficult to replace him in the prow of the ship".
Konungr mælti:	The-king spoke:	The king spoke:
"Seg honum, at ek ætla, at hann skyli mér fylgja, ok þetta er ekki alhugat, fæð sja, er með okkr er um hríð".	"Say to-him, that I intend, that he shall with-me follow, and this is not resolved, sadness see, that with us is about awhile".	"Tell him that I intend that he shall follow with me, and this is not resolved, this sadness that has been seen between us for a while".
Bárðr hittir Halldór ok lætr, at konungr vili enskis kostar láta hans þjónustu, ok þat ræðst ór, at Halldórr ferr, ok halda þeir konungr suðr með landi.	Bard found Halldor and leave, that the-king willed no choice losing his service, and that commanded from, that Halldor went, and held they the-king south along the-land.	Bard found Halldor and put to him that the king gave no choice to lose his service, and that it was a command, and from that Halldor went and they held with the king south along the land.

The Tale of Halldor Snorrason II (Old Norse)

Old Norse	Literal	English
Ok einhverja nótt, er þeir sigldu, þá mælti Halldórr til þess, er stýrði:	And one-such night, that they sailed, then spoke Halldor to that, who steered:	And on one such night the sailed, Halldor spoke to the steersman,
"Lát ýkva",	"Let-it veer",	"let it veer",
segir hann.	said he.	he said.
Konungr mælti til stýrimanns:	The-king spoke to the-steersman:	The king spoke to the steersman,
"Halt svá fram, segir hann.	"Hold so forwards, said he.	"hold straight on", he said.
Halldórr mælti öðru sinni:	Halldor spoke a-second his:	Halldor spoke a second time:
"Lát ýkva".	"Let-it veer".	"Let it veer".
Konungr segir enn á sömu leið.	The-king said then of-the-same way.	The king said the same way.
Halldórr mælti:	Halldor spoke:	Halldor spoke:
"Beint stefnið þér skerit".	"Direction heading you-to a-rock".	"You are heading directly for a rock".
Ok at því varð þeim.	And that accordingly became of-them.	And so it happened of them.
Því næst gekk undan skipinu undirhlutrinn, ok varð þá at flytja til lands með öðrum skipum, ok síðan var skotit landtjald ok bætt at skipinu.	Because next went under the-ship the-under-part, and became then that carried to land with other ships, and afterwards were launched land-tents and repaired the ship.	Because next the underneath of the ship went and it then had to be carried to the land with other ships, and then a land tent was set up, and they ship was repaired.
Við þat vaknar Bárðr, er Halldórr bindr húðfat sitt.	With that awoke Bard, that Halldor tied-up hammock his.	With that Bard awoke to find Halldor tying up his hammock.
Bárðr spyrr, hvat hann ætlast fyrir,	Bard asked, what he intended for,	Bard asked what his intention was.
en Halldórr kvaðst ætla á byrðing, er lá skammt frá þeim, -	then Halldor said intend to merchant-ship, that lay short-distance from them, -	Then Halldor said that he intended to go to a merchant ship that lay a short distance from them,

The Tale of Halldor Snorrason II (Old Norse)

Old Norse	Literal	English
"ok kann vera, at nú leggi sundr reyki vára, ok er þetta fullreynt.	"and can it-be, that now lay separate smoke going, and is that fully-tested.	"and it may be that now our smoke is falling apart, and it has been fully tried".
Ok eigi vil ek, at konungr spilli oftar skipum sínum eða öðrum gersimum mér til svívirðingar ok at mér beri þá verr en áðr".	And not wish I, the king spoil more-often ships his or other treasure me to disgrace and that me bear then worse than before".	And I do not want the king to spoil his ships or other treasures more often to disgrace me, and treat me then worse than before".
"Bíð enn",	"Wait still",	"Still, wait",
segir Bárðr,	said Bard,	said Bard,
"ek vil enn hitta konung.	"I will but find the-king.	"I will just find the king".
Ok er hann kemr, mælti konungr:	And when he came, spoke-to the-king:	And when he came the king spoke:
"Snemma ertu á fótum, Bárðr".	"Soon are-you about feed, Bard".	"You are early on your feet, Bard".
"Svá er nú þörf, herra.	"So is now needed, lord.	"So it is needed now, lord.
Halldórr er í brautbúnaði ok þykkir þú óvingjarnliga til sín gert hafa, ok er nökkut vant at gæta til með ykkr.	Halldor is to away-prepared and thinks you unfriendly to him done have, and is something difficult that take-care to with you-two.	Halldor is preparing to go away and thinks that you have been unfriendly towards him, and it's difficult to keep the peace between you two.
Ætlar hann nú í brott ok ráðast til skips ok fara út til Íslands með reiði, ok ferr þá ómakliga ykkarr skilnaðr,	Intends he now to away and appoint to a-ship and travel out to Iceland with anger, and goes then undeservedly with-you parting,	He now intends to go away and join a ship and travel to Iceland in anger, and that's not a proper way for you to part.
ok þat hygg ek, at varla fáir þú þér annan mann jafntraustan honum".	and it think I, that hardly few you to-you another man equally-trustworthy as-him".	And I think that you will hardly find another man as equally trustworthy as him".
Konungr lét, at þeir myndi enn sættast, ok kvað sér ekki myndu at þessu þykkja.	The-king had, it they would still reconcile, and said himself not would of this think.	The king said that they would still reconcile and said he would not think about it.
Bárðr hittir Halldór ok segir honum vingjarnlig orð konungs.	Bard found Halldor and told him friendly words the-king's.	Bard found Halldor and told him the king's friendly words.
Halldórr svarar:	Halldor answered:	Halldor answered:

The Tale of Halldor Snorrason II (Old Norse)

Old Norse	Literal	English
"Til hvers skal ek honum þjóna lengr, þatki at ek fá mála minn falslaust?"	"To how shall I him serve longer, that-not that I get matter mine without-fraud?"	"Why should I serve him any longer? Let me have my case without fraud".
Bárðr mælti:	Bard spoke:	Bard said,
"Get eigi þess.	"Get not like-this.	"Don't talk like this.
Vel máttu þér þat líka láta, er lendra manna synir hafa, ok ekki fórtu at því með vægð næsta sinni, er þú slótt niðr í hálm silfrinu ok ónýttir,	Well may you that like allow, what is-paid people sons have, and not went-you that therefore with grace next-to yourself, when you struck down into the-straw the-silver and un-used,	Well, you might as well have what the sons of the land have, and you did not do it mercifully the next time you struck the silver down in the straw and wasted it.
ok máttu víst vita, at konungi þykki þat svivirðliga til sín gert".	and may certainly know, that the-king thought that dishonourable to him done".	And you must know that the king considers it disgraceful to do so".
Halldórr svarar:	Halldor answered:	Halldor answered:
"Eigi má ek þat vita, at neitt sinn hafi jafnmjök logizt í um fylgðina mína sem í málagjöfna konungs".	"Not may I that certainly, that nothing he has equally-much cheated in about following mine as in payment the-king's".	"I do not know of having cheated him in my following as much as he has cheated me with the king's payment".
"Satt mun þat vera",	"True would that be",	"That may be true",
segir Bárðr,	said Bard,	said Bard,
"biðleika, enn vil ek hitta konung".	"wait then will I find the-king".	"wait, then I will find the king".
Ok svá gerði hann.	And so did he.	And he did so.
Ok er Bárðr hitti konung, mælti hann:	And when Bard found the-king, spoke he:	And when Bard found the king, he spoke:
"Fá Halldóri mála sinn skíran, því at verðr er hann at hafa".	"Get Halldor payment his cleared, because that worth is he to have".	"Get Halldor his payment cleared, because he is worth having".
Konungr svarar:	The-king answered:	The king answered:

The Tale of Halldor Snorrason II (Old Norse)

Old Norse	Literal	English
"Lízt þér eigi nökkur svá djörfung í at krefja Halldóri annars mála en taka lendra manna synir, með slíkri svívirðing sem hann fór með málanum næstum?"	"Appears to-you not something so bold that to demand Halldor another payment than take payment people's sons, And with such disgrace as he did with payment before?"	"Does it not appear you you somewhat bold to demand Halldor a payment other than people's sons, and with such disgrace as he did with his last payment?"
Bárðr svarar:	Bard answered:	Bard answered:
"Á hitt er at líta, herra, er miklu er meira vert, drengskap hans ok vináttu ykkra, er lengi hefir góð verit, ok þar með stórmennsku þína,	"To find that to look, lord, that much is more worth, honour his and friendship yours, that long has good been, and there with greatness yours,	"The other thing is to look, lord, at who is much more valuable, his boyhood and your friendship that has been good for a long time and thus your greatness.
ok veiztu skap Halldórs ok stirðlæti, ok er þat þinn vegr at gera honum sóma".	and know-you mood Halldor's and hard-temper, and that it your way that to-do him honour".	And we know Halldór's mood and stiffness, and it's your way to do him honor".
Konungr mælti:	The-king spoke:	The king said:
"Fái honum silfrit".	"Give him the-silver".	"Give him the silver".
Var nú svá gert.	Was now so done.	Now this was done.
Kemr Bárðr til Halldórs ok færir honum tólf aura brennda ok mælti:	Came Bard to Halldor and brought him twelve ounces burnt and spoke:	Bard came to Halldor and brought him twelve ounces of refined silver and spoke:
"Sér þú eigi, at þú hefir slíkt, er þú brekar af konungi, ok hann vill, at þú hafir slíkt af honum, sem þú þykkist þurfa".	"See you not, that you have such, that you keep-asking of the-king, and he wishes, that you have such of him, as you think you-need".	"Do you not see that you ask of the king, and he wishes to to have what you think you need, if only you ask for it?"
Halldórr svarar:	Halldor answered:	Halldor answeed:
"Eigi skal ek þó oftar vera á konungsskipinu, ok ef hann vill hafa mitt föruneyti lengr, þá vil ek hafa skip til stjórnar ok eignast þat".	"Not shall I though frequent be in the-king's-ship, and if he wishes to-have my companionship longer, then wish I to-have ship to steer and own it".	"I shall not be on the king's ship more often, and if he wishes to have me in his company any longer, then I wish to have my own ship to steer".
Bárðr svarar:	Bard answered:	Bard answered:

The Tale of Halldor Snorrason II (Old Norse)

Old Norse	Literal	English
"Þat samir eigi, at lendir menn láti skip sín fyrir þér, ok ertu of framgjarn".	"It so not, to landed men have ships theirs for you, and are-you over ambitious".	"It is not so that landed man give up their ships for you, and you are over-ambitious".
Halldórr kvaðst eigi fara myndu elligar.	Halldor said not travelling would otherwise.	Halldor said that he would not travel otherwise.
Bárðr segir konungi, hvers beitt er af Halldórs hendi, –	Bard told the-king, what asked had of Halldor's hand, -	Bard told the king what Halldor had asked for
"ok ef hásetar þess skips eru jafntraustir sem stýrimaðr, þá mun vel hlýða".	"and if sailors these ships were equally-trustworthy as steersman, then would well listen-to".	"and if the sailors of these ships were equally trustworthy as the steersman then they would listen to him well".
Konungr mælti:	The-king spoke:	The king said,
"Þótt þetta þykki framarla mælt vera, þá skal þó af nökkut gera".	"Though this think forward spoken is, then shall though of something do".	"Though this be thought to be far-fetched, something must be done".
Sveinn ór Lyrgju, lendr maðr, stýrði skipi.	Fellow from Lyrgja, land man, steered a-ship.	Svein from Lyrgja, a landed man, steered a ship.
Konungr lét hann kalla á mál við sik.	The-king had him called and conversed with him.	The king had him called and discussed with him.
"Þannug er farit",	"That-way is travelled",	"It is so",
segir konungr,	said the-king,	said the king,
"sem þú veizt, at þú ert maðr stórættaðr.	"that you know, that you are a-man of-high-family.	"that you know that you are a man of great family.
Vil ek fyrir því, at þú sér á mínu skipi, en ek mun þar fá annan mann til skipstjórnar.	Wish I for therefore, that you be on my ship, but I should there get another man to ship-steer.	I want you to be on my ship, but I will get another man to captain it.
Þú ert maðr vizkr, ok vil ek einkum hafa þik við ráð mín".	You are a-man wise, and wish I especially have you with advise me".	You are a man of wisdom and I especially want you with my advice".
Hann segir:	He said:	He said:
"Meir hefir þú aðra menn haft við þínar ráðagerðir hér til, ok til þess em ek litt færr, eða hverjum er þá skipit ætlat?"	"More have you other men had with you advice-giving here to, and to this am I little accomplished, but who is then ship intended?"	"You have had other men with your advice so far and to the point that I can do little, but who is the ship intended for?"

The Tale of Halldor Snorrason II (Old Norse)

Old Norse	Literal	English
"Halldórr Snorrason skal hafa",	"Halldor Snorrason shall have",	"Halldor Snorrason shall have it",
segir konungr.	said the-king.	said the king.
Sveinn segir:	The-fellow said:	Sveinn said:
"Eigi kom mér þat í hug, at þú myndir íslenzkan mann láta taka af mér skipstjórn".	"Not came to-me that to think, that you would Icelander man have take from me ship-steering".	"It never occurred to me that you would choose an Icelander for that, still take me from the captaincy".
Konungr mælti:	The-king spoke:	The king said,
"Hans ætt er eigi verri á Íslandi en þín hér í Nóregi, ok eigi hefir enn alllangt síðan liðit, er þeir váru norrænir, er nú byggja Ísland".	"His ancestry is not worse as Icelander but your forces in Norway, and not has-been but all-long since passed, that they were Norwegians, that now settle Iceland".	"His family is no worse in Iceland than yours here in Norway, and it has not been long since they were Norwegians who now inhabit Iceland".
Nú ferr þat fram, sem konungr vill, at Halldórr tekr við skipi, ok fóru síðan austr til Óslóar, tóku þar veizlur.	Now went that from, as the-king wished, that Halldor took with ship, and travelled afterwards east to Oslo, took there feasts.	Now it went as the king wished, that Halldor took the ship, and travelled afterwards east to Oslo, where they took to feasting.
4	**4**	**4**
Þat er sagt, einnhvern dag, er þeir konungr sátu við drykkju, ok var Halldórr þar í konungs stofunni, at sveinar hans kómu þar, þeir er skipit skyldu varðveita, ok váru allir vátir ok sögðu, at þeir Sveinn höfðu tekit skipit, en rekit þá á kaf.	It was said, one-such day, that there the-king sat with drinking, and was Halldor there in the-king's chamber, the fellows his came there, they were ship should guard-over, and were all wet and said, that they Svein had taken the-ship, and thrown them to overboard.	It was said that one day the king and Halldor sat drinking in the king's chambers, and in came the men who were watching over his ship came in, and they were all wet, and they said that Svein had taken the ship and thrown them overboard.
Halldórr stóð upp ok gekk fyrir konung ok spurði, hvárt hann skyldi eiga skipit ok haldast þat, er konungr hafði mælt.	Halldor stood up and went before the-king and asked, how he should own the-ship and hold that, which the-king had spoken-of.	Halldor stood up and went before the king and asked whether he would own the ship as the king had promised.

The Tale of Halldor Snorrason II (Old Norse)

Old Norse	Literal	English
Konungr svarar ok kvað þat at vísu haldast skyldu, kvaddi síðan hirðina, at þeir skyldi taka sex skip ok fara með Halldóri ok hafa þrenna skipun á hverju.	The-king answered and said that it certainly hold should, called since guardsmen, that they should take six ships and travel with Halldor and have treble crew on each.	The king answered and said that he would keep his promise, and then called to the guardsmen that they should take six ships, travelling with a treble crew on each.
Þeir snúa nú eftir þeim Sveini, ok lætr hann eltast at landi, ok þegar hljóp Sveinn á land upp, en þeir Halldórr tóku skipit ok fóru til konungs.	They turned now after they Svein, and let he chased to land, and there ran Svein on-the land up, and there Halldor took the-ship and went to the-king.	They now turned after Svein and gave him chase ashore, and there Svein ran ashore, but Halldor took the ship and went to the king.
Ok er veizlum var lokit, ferr konungr norðr með landi ok til Þrándheims, er á líðr sumarit.	And when the-feasts were ended, went the-king north along the-land and to Trondheim, where then passed summer.	And when the feasts were over, the king went north along the land, and to Trondheim, when the summer had passed.
Sveinn ór Lyrgju sendi orð konungi, at hann vill gefa upp allt mál um skipit ok leggja á konungs vald, at hann skipi með þeim Halldóri, sem hann vill, ok vildi þó helzt kaupa skipit, ef konungi líkaði.	Svein from Lyrgja sent word to-the-king, that he wished to-give up all matter about the-ship and grant to the-king power, that he ship with them Halldor, as he wished, and wished though rather purchase the-ship, if the-king liked.	Svein of Lyrgja sent word to the king that he wished to give up the whole matter and put it in the king's power, that the ship would be with Halldor as he wished, but would prefer to purchase the ship if it was to the king's liking.
Ok nú er konungr sér þat, at Sveinn skýtr öllu máli undir hans dóm, þá vill hann nú svá til bregða, er báðum mætti líka, falar skipit at Halldóri ok vill, at hann hafi verð sæmiligt, en Sveinn hafi skip, ok kaupir konungr skip, ok á Halldórr við hann um verð, ok gelzt allt upp, nema hálf mörk gulls stendr eftir.	And now as the-king saw that, of Svein launched all matter under his deeming, then wished he now so to foreclose, that both may like, bargain ship that Halldor and wished, that he had worth-the-same, that Svein had ship, and bought the-king the-ship, and that Halldor with him about worth, and paid all up, except half a-mark gold stood behind.	And now the king saw that Svein gave the whole matter up to his judgement, that he now wished to settle the matter to the liking of both parties. The ship was purchased from Halldor and he wished that he had a price the same worth as Svein to have the ship, and the king bought the ship from Halldor, and with him was the price and gold all paid except for half a gold mark left behind.
Heimtir Halldórr lítt, enda galzt þat ekki, ok ferr svá fram um vetrinn.	Got Halldor little, end payment that not, and went so forward about winter.	Halldor did not demand the closure of the payment, and so things went on over the winter.

The Tale of Halldor Snorrason II (Old Norse)

Old Norse	Literal	English
Ok er vára tók, segir Halldórr konungi, at hann vill til Íslands um sumarit, ok kvað sér vel koma, at þá gyldist þat, sem eftir var kaupverðsins.	And as spring took, said Halldor to-the-king, that he wished to Iceland about summer, and said he well come, that then repay that, which remained was ship's-worth.	And as spring came, Halldor said to the king that he wished to travel to Iceland in the summer, and it would be well if he could repay the remainder of the ship's worth.
En konungr ferr heldr undan um gjaldit ok þykkir ekki betr, er hann heimtir, en ekki bannar hann Halldóri útferð, ok býr hann skip sitt um várit í ánni Nið ok leggr út síðan við Bröttueyri.	But the-king went rather from-under about the-payment and seemed not better, that he got, then not ban him Halldor out-travelling, and prepared he ship his about spring in the-river Nid and laid out afterwards with Bratteyar.	But the king escaped the payment, and thought not better that he demanded, but did not ban Halldor from travelling, and he prepared his ship around spring in the river Nid, nd laid out afterwards at Bratteyar.
Ok er þeir váru albúnir ok byrvænligt var, þá gengr Halldórr upp í bæinn með nökkura menn síð um aftan.	And when they were all-prepared and promising-wind were, then going Halldor up out-of town with some men later about evening.	And then they were all prepared and with a promising wind, then Halldor went up in the town with some men later in the evening.
Hann var með vápnum,	He was with weapons,	He was armed with weapons.
gengu þar til, er þau konungr ok dróttning sváfu.	went they to, where then the-king and the-queen slept.	They then went to where the king and queen slept.
Förunautar hans stóðu úti undir loftinu, en hann gengr inn með vápnum sínum, ok verðr glymr ok skark af honum, ok vakna þau konungr við, ok spyrr konungr, hverr brjótist at þeim um nætr.	Companions his stood outside under the-air, then he went inside with weapons his, and came echo and noise of him, and awoke then the-king with, and asked the-king, who breaking in-on them about night.	His companions stood outside, and he went inside and made a noise with his weapons which echoed and woke the king, who asked who was breaking in on them in the night.
"Hér er Halldórr kominn ok búinn til hafs, ok kominn á byrr, ok er nú ráð at gjalda fét".	"Here is Halldor come and prepared to sea, and coming is fair-wind, and is now the-matter to pay wealth".	"Halldor is here, prepared to go to sea, and a fair wind is coming, and now is the matter to settle the payment".
"Ekki má þat nú svá skjótt",	"Not may that now so swiftly",	"Now that may not be done so swiftly",
segir konungr,	said the-king,	said the king,
"ok munum vér greiða fé á morgun".	"and should we assist payment in the-morning".	"and we shall assist with the payment in the morning".

The Tale of Halldor Snorrason II (Old Norse)

Old Norse	Literal	English
"Nú vil ek þegar hafa",	"Now wish I straightaway have",	"Now I wish to have it straight away",
segir Halldórr,	said Halldor,	said Halldor,
"ok munkat ek nú erendlaust fara.	"and shall I now errand-without go.	"and I shall not go without it.
Kann ek ok skap þitt, ok veit ek, hversu þér mun líka þessi för mín ok fjárheimta, hvégi sem þú lætr nú.	Know I also mood yours, and know I, how-so you shall like this going mine and money-insisting, which as you behave now.	I also know your mood, and I know how you would like me to go, and am demanding the money which you will leave now.
Mun ek lítt trúa þér heðan frá, enda er ósýnt, at vit finnimst svá vilgis oft, at mitt sé vænna, ok skal nú neyta þess, ok sé ek, at dróttning hefir hring á hendi því hófi mikinn.	Shall I little believe you hence from, conclude as unseen, that with found so very often, that mine so expected, and shall now use this, and see I, that the-queen has a-ring on hand therefore modest greatly.	I shall not trust you again from now on, it is not clear how often we find that I have the advantage, so I shall now take advantage of this, and I see that the queen has a ring on her hand, which is accordingly greatly modest.
Fá mér þann".	Give me it".	Give it to me".
Konungr svarar:	The-king answered:	The king answered:
"Þá verðum vit fara eftir skálum ok vega hringinn".	"Then worth with going after bowl and weigh the-ring".	"Then it is worth going after the bowls and weighing the ring".
"Ekki þarf þess",	"Not needed is-this",	"That is not needed",
segir Halldórr,	said Halldor,	said Halldor,
"tek ek hann fyrir hlut minn, enda muntu nú ekki prettum við koma at sinni, ok sel fram títt".	"take I it for share mine, and should now not trick with coming this time, and flip forward immediately".	"I will take it for my share, and you shall not try and trick me this time, and give it forward immediately".
Dróttning mælti:	The-queen spoke:	The queen spoke:
"Fá honum hringinn, sem hann beiðir.	"Give him the-ring, as he asks".	"Give him the ring, as he asks".
"Sér þú eigi",	"See you not",	"Do you not see",
segir hon,	said she,	she said,

The Tale of Halldor Snorrason II (Old Norse)

Old Norse	Literal	English
"at hann stendr yfir þér uppi með víghug?" -	"that he stands over you up with killing-mind?" -	"that he stands over you with a mind to kill?"
tekr síðan hringinn ok fær Halldóri.	took then the-ring and brought Halldor.	She then took the ring and brought it to Halldor.
Hann tekr við ok þakkar þeim báðum gjaldit ok biðr þau vel lifa, -	He took with and thanked them both payment and bid them well life, -	He took it and thanked them both for the payment and bid them a good life
"ok munum vér nú skilja",	"and shall we now separate",	"and we shall now separate".
-gengr nú út ok mælti við förunauta sína, biðr þá hlaupa sem tíðast til skipsins, -	-went now out and spoke with companions his, asked them to-run as swiftly to ship, -	He now went out and spoke with his companions, asking them to run swiftly to the ship
"því at ófúss em ek at dveljast lengi í bænum".	"because that unwilling am I to stay long in this-town".	because I am not willing to stay long in this town.
Þeir gera svá, koma á skipit, ok þegar vinda sumir upp segl, sumir eru at báti, sumir heimta upp ákkeri, ok bergst hverr, sem má.	They did so, came to the-ship, and straightaway wind some upped the-sails, some were at the-tow-boat, some drew up the-anchor, and best each, as may.	They did so, and came to the ship and straight away wind came and they upped the sails, some were at the tow boat, and some drew up the anchor, each doing the best they could.
Ok er þeir sigldu út, skorti eigi hornblástr í bænum, ok þat sá þeir síðast, at þrjú langskip váru á floti ok lögðu eftir þeim, en þó berr þá undan ok í haf.	And when they sailed out, shortly one horn-blast from the-city, and this saw they the-last, that three longships were in floating and laid after them, but though carried then under and to sea.	And shortly after they had sailed out, there was a horn blast from the city, and the last thing they saw were three longships floating and laid after them, though then they were carried out to sea.
Skilr þar með þeim, ok byrjaði Halldóri vel út til Íslands, en konungsmenn hurfu aftr, er þeir sá, er Halldór bar undan ok í haf út.	Separated there with them, and began Halldor well out to Iceland, but the-kings-men disappeared after, when they saw, that Halldor bore away-from and to sea out-of.	They separated with them there and Halldor started well out to Iceland, but the king's men turned bak when they saw that Halldor was carried away out to sea.

5

Halldórr Snorrason var mikill maðr vexti ok fríðr sýnum, allra manna styrkastr ok vápndjarfastr.	Halldor Snorrason was a-great man well-built and handsome in-appearance, of-all men strongest and weapons-bold.	Halldor Snorrason was a great man, well built, and handsome in appearance, the strongest of all men, and the best with weapons.

The Tale of Halldor Snorrason II (Old Norse)

Old Norse	Literal	English
Þat vitni bar Haraldr konungr Halldóri, at hann hefði verit með honum allra manna svá, at sízt brygði við váveifliga hluti, hvárt sem at höndum bar mannháska eða fagnaðartíðendi, þá var hann hvárki at glaðari né óglaðari.	That testimony gave Harald the-king Halldor, that he had been with him all men so, that least reacted with unexpected part, which was at hand bringing human-danger or good-news, then was he neither to gladness nor un-gladness.	King Harald gave a testimony of Halldor that of all the men he had been with, that he reacted least to an unexpected lot, which with hand carried danger or good news, he was neither happy nor unhappy.
Eigi neytti hann matar eða drakk eða svaf meira né minna en vanði hans var til, hvárt sem hann mætti blíðu eða stríðu.	Not consumed he food or drank or slept more nor less than custom his was to, each as he might joyful or stressful.	He did not eat or drink or sleep more not less than his custom, whether he was happy or stressful.
Halldórr var maðr fámæltr, stuttorðr, bermæltr, stygglyndr ok ómjúkr, kappgjarn í öllum hlutum, við hvern sem hann átti um.	Halldor was a-man of-few-words, short-worded, outspoken, quick-tempered and un-bending, self-willed in all things, against which as he had about.	Halldor was a man of few words, short, outspoken, quick tempered and ungiving, self-willed about everything that he had.
En þat kom illa við Harald konung, er hann hafði nóga aðra þjónustumenn.	But this came ill with Harald the-king, as he had enough other servants.	But this came badly against king Harald as he had enough other servants.
Kómu þeir því lítt lyndi saman, síðan Haraldr varð konungr í Nóregi.	Came they therefore little temper together, since Harald was king of Norway.	They did not get along well since Haraldur became king of Norway.
En er Halldórr kom til Íslands, gerði hann bú í Hjarðarholti.	But when Halldor came to Iceland, did he settle at Hjardarholt.	But when Halldór came to Iceland he made an estate in Hjarðarholt.
Nökkurum sumrum síðar sendi Haraldr konungr orð Halldóri Snorrasyni, at hann skyldi ráðast enn til hans, ok lét, at eigi skyldi verit hafa hans virðing meiri en þá, ef hann vildi farit hafa, ok engan mann skyldi hann hæra setja í Nóregi ótiginn, ef hann vildi þetta boð þekkjast.	Some summers later sent Harald the-king word-to Halldor Snorrason, that he should arrange then to him, and had, that not should be having his honour more than then, if he willed travel to-sea, and only man should he highest sit in Norway un-high-born, if he wished this invitation accept.	A few summers later, King Harald sent word to Halldor Snorrason that he should appoint him again, and put that his respect would not be greater than that if he wished to travel to sea, and that no man should sit higher than him in Norway if he wished to accept this invitation.
Halldórr svarar svá, er honum kómu þessi orð:	Halldor answered so, as to-him came these words:	Halldor answered when these words came to him:
"Ekki mun ek fara á fund Haralds konungs heðan af.	"Not should I travel to meet Harald the-king from-here of.	"I will not go to King Harald from now on.

The Tale of Halldor Snorrason II (Old Norse)

Old Norse	Literal	English
Mun nú hafa hvárr okkar þat, sem fengit hefir.	Should now have each ours that, which got we-have.	Each of us will now have what he has received.
Mér er kunnigt skaplyndi hans.	To-me it-is known mood-temper his.	His mood is known to me.
Veit ek gerla, at hann myndi þat efna, sem hann hét, at setja engan mann hæra í Noregi en mik, ef ek kæma á hans fund, því at hann myndi mik láta festa á inn hæsta gálga ef hann mætti ráða".	Know I completely, that he should that carry-out, which he promised, to sit no man higher in Norway but me, if I come to him to-meet, therefore that he should me have fasten to the highest gallows if he might prevail".	I know very well that he would do what he promised to put no man higher in Norway than me if I came to meet him, for he would have me fastened to the highest gallows if he could rule it".
Ok er á leið mjök ævi Haralds konungs, þá er sagt, at hann sendi Halldóri orð til, at hann skyldi senda honum melrakkabelgi, vildi gera láta af þeim yfir rekkju sína, því at konungr þóttist þurfa hlýs.	And when had passed much age Harald the-king, then that is-said, that he sent Halldor word to, that he should send him arctic-fox-furs, wished get have of them over bed his, because that the-king thought needed warmth.	And when king Harald became much passed with age, it is said that he sent word to Halldor that he should send him arctic fox furs, he wanted to let them go over his bed because the king thought he needed warmth.
Ok er Halldóri kom sjá orðsending konungs, þá er sagt, at hann skyti því orði við í fyrstu:	And as Halldor came so word-sending the-king, then was said, that he shot accordingly word against at first:	And when Halldor came to see the king's message, it is said that he replied first:
"Eldist árgalinn nú",	"Old-is the-cockerel now",	"The yearling is getting old now",
sagði hann, en sendi honum belgi.	said he, but sent him furs.	he said, but sent him arctic fox furs.
En ekki fundust þeir sjálfir, síðan er þeir skildust í Þrándheimi, þó at þá yrði nökkut með stytti því sinni.	But not met they themselves, afterwards that the separated at Trondheim, though that then became somewhat with short of themselves.	But they did not meet each other since they had separated at Trondheim, though they had taken short leave with each other.
Bjó hann í Hjarðarholti til elli ok varð maðr gamall.	Farmed he in Hjardarholt until old-age and became a-man old.	He lived in Hjarðarholt until old age and became an old man.

Word List (Old Norse to English)

Word List (Old Norse to English)

Old Norse	English

A, a

aðra	other
aðrir	other
af	from, from, of, of
aftan	evening
aftna	evening
aftr	after, back
aga	turbulence
albúnir	all-prepared
alhugat	resolved
allir	all, all
alllangt	all-long
allra	all, of-all
allt	all, all
annan	another, another, the-next
annarra	other
annarri	other
annars	another
at	at, in, in-on, it, of, that, the, this, to, to-come
atgang	access
aura	ounces
austan	east
austr	east

Á, á

á	about, and, as, at, had, in, is, of, on, on-the, that, the, then, this, to
áðr	before, other
áhöfnina	crew
áhyggjusvip	worried-face
ákalsi	calling
ákkeri	the-anchor
álaga	stress
ánni	the-river
árgalinn	the-cockerel
árrisull	early-riser

Old Norse	English
átti	eighth, had
ávíta	warn

Æ, æ

ætla	intend, suppose
ætlaði	intended
ætlar	intended, intends
ætlast	intended
ætlat	intended
ætt	ancestry
ævi	age

B, b

báðu	bid
báðum	both
bæði	both
bæinn	town
bæjarmenn	townspeople
bænum	the-city, the-town, this-town
bætt	repaired
bann	a-ban
bannar	ban
bar	bore, bringing, gave
Bárðr	Bard (name)
báti	the-tow-boat
beiða	asked
beiðir	asks
beint	direction
beitt	asked
belgi	furs
bera	bear
bergst	best
beri	bear
bermæltr	outspoken
berr	bears, carried
betr	better
betra	better
bezt	best
bezta	best

Word List (Old Norse to English)

Old Norse	English
bíð	wait
bíða	wait
biðleika,	wait
biðr	asked, bid
bili	moment
bindr	tied-up
bjó	farmed, settled
bjóst	readied
bjuggu	preparations
blásit	trumpet-blown
blíðast	happiest
blíðligr	happily
blíðu	joyful
boð	invitation
brautbúnaði	away-prepared
bregða	foreclose
brekar	keep-asking
brennda	burnt
breytt	changed
brjótist	breaking
brögð	a-trick
brotin	violated
brott	away
Bröttueyri	Bratteyar (place)
brygði	reacted
bú	settle
búa	prepared
búinn	prepared
búit	prepared
búnaðinn	preparations
byggja	settle
býr	prepared
byrðing	merchant-ship
byrjaði	began
byrr	fair-wind
byrvænligt	promising-wind
býst	prepares
býstu	prepared

D, d

Old Norse	English
dag	day
daginn	the-day
dagr	day
danaher	Danish-forces
danakonungr	king-of-Denmark
Danmerkr	Denmark (place)
djörfung	bold
dögum	days
dóm	deeming
drakk	drank
drekk	drink
drekka	drank, drink, to-drink
drekkr	drank
drengr	fellow
drengskap	honour
drjúgum	greatly
dróttning	the-queen
drukkit	drunk
drukku	drinking
drykki	drank, drink
drykkju	drinking, drinks
dveljast	stay
dýrshorn	stag-horn

E, e

Old Norse	English
eða	but, or
ef	if
efna	carry-out
eftir	after, behind, remained, remaining
eiga	own
eigi	none, not, one
eignast	own
einhverja	one-such
einkum	especially
einn	one
einnhvern	one-such
eins	alone
einsætt	clearly
einskis	nothing
eitt	one
ek	I, I-am
ekki	not
eldist	old-is
elli	old-age
elligar	otherwise
eltast	chased
em	am

Word List (Old Norse to English)

Old Norse	English
en	and, as, But, than, that, then, while, who
enda	and, conclude, end
enga	no
engan	no, only
engi	none
engis	nothing
Englandsfari	England-Traveller (name)
engu	none
enn	but, still, then, was
enskis	no
er	am, as, had, have, is, it-is, that, was, were, what, when, where, which, who
erendlaust	errand-without
ert	are
ertu	are-you
eru	are, there-are, they, they-were, were

F, f

Old Norse	English
fá	gave, get, give, pay
faðir	father
fæ	give
fæð	sadness
fær	brought
færa	brought
færi	bring, travel, went
færið	bring
færir	brought
færr	accomplished, travel
fært	bringing
fagnaðartíðendi	good-news
fái	give
fáir	few
falar	bargain
falslaust	without-fraud
fám	a-few
fámæltr	of-few-words
fann	found
fara	go, going, travel, travelling, went
fararefnin	travel-goods
fari	travel
farir	travel
farit	travel, travelled
fars	travel
fastara	more-fixedly
fátt	few
fé	payment
fegnir	celebrated
fengi	found
fengit	got
fénu	wealth
ferðir	travel
ferr	goes, went
festa	fasten
fét	wealth
finnimst	found
fjárheimta	money-insisting
fjölði	many
fleiri	more
floti	floating
flytja	carried
fór	did, travelled, went
för	going
fórtu	went-you
förunauta	companions
förunautar	companions
föruneyti	companionship
fótum	feed
frá	from
frændum	father
fram	forward, forwards, from
framarla	forward
framgjarn	ambitious
fríðr	handsome
fullreynt	fully-tested
fund	find, meet, to-meet
fundust	met
fylgði	follow
fylgðina	following
fylgir	following
fylgja	follow
fyndist	found
fyrir	along, before, for
fyrr	before
fyrra	the-first

Word List (Old Norse to English)

Old Norse	English
fyrsta	first
fyrstu	first
fýsir	desire

G, g

Old Norse	English
gæði	good-things
gærkveld	last-night
gæta	take-care
gaf	gave
gáfu	gave
gáfuð	gave
gálga	gallows
galzt	payment
gamall	old
gamalmenni	old-men
ganga	go
Garðaríki	Gardariki (place)
gefa	give, to-give
gefinn	given
gegnum	through
gekk	went
gelzt	paid
gengr	going, went
gengu	went
gera	did, do, get, to-do
gerði	did
gerir	went
gerist	be
gerla	completely
gersimar	treasure, treasures
gersimum	treasure
gert	done
get	get
gjalda	pay
gjaldit	payment, the-payment
gjöfin	gift
gjöfina	the-gift
glaðari	gladness
glymr	echo
góð	good
goða	the-priest
góðr	good
greiða	assist

Old Norse	English
gulls	gold
gyldist	repay

H, h

Old Norse	English
hægt	possible
hæra	higher, highest
hæsta	highest
hættir	way
haf	sea
hafa	had, have, having, to-have, to-sea
hafði	had
hafi	had, has
hafið	have
hafir	have
hafs	sea
haft	had
halda	held, to-hold
haldast	hold
hálf	half
Halldór	Halldor (name)
Halldóri	Halldor (name)
Halldórr	Halldor (name)
Halldórs	Halldor (name), Halldor's (name)
hálm	straw, the-straw
halt	hold
haltu	hold-you
hann	he, him, it
hans	him, his
Harald	Harald (name)
Haraldi	Harald (name)
Haraldr	Harald (name)
Haralds	Harald (name)
Haraldsslátta	Harald's-money (name)
háseta	crew, sailors
hásetar	sailors
hásetum	sailors
háski	dangers
hausti	the-autumn
heðan	from-here, hence
hefði	had
hefi	have

Word List (Old Norse to English)

Old Norse	English
hefir	had, has, has-been, have, we-have
heilstan	thanks
heimfúsari	home-longing
heimta	drew
heimtir	got
heldr	hold, rather
helmings	half
helzt	rather
helzti	rather
hendi	hand
her	here
hér	forces, here
herra	lord
hét	named, promised, was-named
heyra	hear
heyrðuð	heard
heyrum	hear
hirðar	court
hirðina	guardsmen
hirðinni	court
hirðmaðr	court-man
hirðsiðum	king's-men-customs
hitt	find
hitta	find
hitti	found
hittir	found
Hjarðarholti	Hjardarholt (place)
hlaupa	to-run
hleypr	run
hljóp	ran
hlut	part, share
hluti	part, things
hlutr	part
hlutum	things
hlýða	listen-to
hlýs	warmth
höfðu	had
hófi	modest
hon	she
höndum	hand
honum	as-him, he, him, to-him
horn	horn
hornblástr	horn-blast
hornit	the-drinking-horn
hornsins	the-horn
hríð	awhile
hring	a-ring
hringingar	bell-ringing
hringingum	bell-ringing
hringinn	the-ring
hringja	ring
húðfat	hammock
hug	think
hurfu	disappeared
hús	house
hvárki	neither
hvárr	each
hvárt	each, how, which
hvat	what
hvégi	which
hver	where
hverju	each
hverjum	who
hvern	which
hverr	each, who
hvers	how, what
hversu	how-so
hvert	each
hví	why
hygg	think

I, i

illa	badly, ill
in	the
inn	inside, the

Í, í

í	about, at, from, in, into, of, out-of, that, to, will, with
ígangsklæði	travelling-clothes
Ísland	Iceland (place)
Íslandi	Icelander (name)
Íslands	Iceland (place)
íslenzkan	Icelander

Word List (Old Norse to English)

Old Norse	English
J, j	
jafnfylginn	equally-following
jafnmjök	equally-much
jafntraustan	equally-trustworthy
jafntraustir	equally-trustworthy
jóla	Yule (name)
jólanna	Yule (name)
jólin	Yule (name)
Jólum	Yule (name)
K, k	
kæma	come
kærleikum	dearly-loved
kaf	overboard
kalla	called
kallat	called
kann	can, know
kappgjarn	self-willed
kaupa	purchase
Kaupangi	Kaupang (place)
kaupferðir	trading-voyages
kaupir	bought
kaupmaðr	trading-man
kaupmenn	merchants, the-merchants, the-traders
kaupsveinar	trading-men
kaupverðsins	ship's-worth
kemr	came
kennduð	taught
kertisveinar	court-men
kjósa	choose
klokkurum	clocks
knörr	ship
kom	came
koma	came, come, coming
komið	come
kominn	come, coming
komir	come
kómu	came
konung	the-king
konunga	the-king
konungi	king, the-king, to-the-king
konungr	king, the-king
konungs	the-king, the-king's
konungsmenn	the-kings-men
konungsskipinu	the-king's-ship
kopars	copper
kostar	choice
kosti	benefit
krefja	demand
ksonungs	the-king's
kunnigt	known
kvað	said
kvaddi	called
kvaðst	said
kveld	evening
kyrrt	peace
L, l	
lá	lay
lætr	behave, leave, let
lagi	had
land	land, the-land
landa	lands
landi	land, lands, the-land
lands	land
landtjald	land-tents
langskip	longships
lát	let-it
láta	allow, have, losing
láti	have
launuð	repaid
leggi	lay
leggja	grant
leggjum	lay
leggr	laid
leið	pass, passed, way
leita	seek
leitat	consider
lendir	landed
lendr	land
lendra	is-paid, payment
lengi	long

Word List (Old Norse to English)

Old Norse	English
lengr	longer
lét	had
léti	let
léttlætiskonum	prostitutes
leyfa	allow
leyfi	leave
lézt	had
liði	crew, men
liðit	passed
líðr	passed
lifa	life
líka	like
líkaði	liked
líta	look
lítill	little
litlu	little
lítr	looked
litt	little
lítt	little
lízt	appears
loftinu	the-air
lögðu	laid
logizt	cheated
lokit	ended
lönd	land
löng	long
lygi	lie
lyndi	temper
Lyrgju	Lyrgja (place)
lýstr	struck

M, m

Old Norse	English
má	may
maðr	a-man, man
mæðumst	tired
mælt	spoken, spoken-of
mælti	spoke, spoke-to
mæltuð	spoke
mætti	may, might, might
mál	conversed, matter, measure
mála	matter, payment, payment
málagjöfna	payment
málann	payment
málanum	payment
málasilfrit	silverware
máli	matter, payment, speak
mann	man
manna	men, people, people's
mannháska	human-danger
marga	many
margr	many
matar	food
máttu	may, may-you
með	along, between, with
mega	may
meir	more
meira	more
meiri	greater, more
melrakkabelgi	arctic-fox-furs
menn	men, people
mér	me, to-me, with-me
mesta	most
mesti	most
mik	me
mikill	a-great, great
mikinn	greatly, much
mikit	huge
mikla	much
Miklagarði	The-Great-City (place)
miklu	a-great, much
miklum	much
milli	between
mín	me, mine
mína	mine
minn	mine
minna	less
minni	mine
mínu	my
mislíkaði	misliked
mitt	mine, my
mjök	much
mönnum	people
morgun	morning, the-morning
mörk	a-mark
mót	return
móti	meet, meeting

Word List (Old Norse to English)

Old Norse	English
mótinu	the-meeting
móts	meet
mótsins	the-meeting
möttulsskauti	cloak-lap
mun	could, shall, should, would
muni	shall
munkat	shall
munt	must
muntu	should
munum	shall, should
myndi	should, would
myndir	would
myndu	would
myrgininn	morning

N, n

Old Norse	English
næst	next
næsta	next, next-to
næstum	before
nætr	night
náliga	nearly
nauðgat	force
nauðsyn	necessity
né	nor
neðan	below
neitt	nothing
nema	except, take
neyta	use
neytti	consumed
Nið	Nid (place)
níðist	down
niðr	below, down
nóga	enough
nökkur	something
nökkura	some
nökkurum	some
nökkut	something, somewhat
norðr	north
Nóreg	Norway (place)
Noregi	Norway (place)
Nóregi	Norway (place)
Nóregs	Norway (place)
norrænir	Norwegians

Old Norse	English
nótt	night
nú	now

O, o

Old Norse	English
of	over
oft	often
oftar	frequent, more-often
ok	also, and
okkar	ours
okkr	our, us
orð	word, words, word-to
orðaframkast	outburst
orði	word
orðsending	word-sending
oss	to-us, us

Ó, ó

Old Norse	English
ófriðar	hostilities
ófriðinn	un-peace
ófriðr	un-peace
ófúss	unwilling
óglaðari	un-gladness
ógladdist	un-glad
ómakliga	undeservedly
ómjúkr	un-bending
ónýttir	un-used
ór	from, out-of
órráða	solution
Ósló	Oslo (place)
ósýnt	unseen
ótiginn	un-high-born
óvingjarnliga	unfriendly

Ö, ö

Old Norse	English
öðru	a-second
öðrum	other
öllu	all
öllum	all

Word List (Old Norse to English)

Old Norse	English
P, p	
prettum	trick
R, r	
ráð	advise, the-matter
ráða	prevail
ráðagerðir	advice-giving
ráðast	appoint, arrange
ráðist	decide
ráðit	hired
ræðr	leading
ræðst	commanded
reiði	anger
reiðist	commanded
rekit	thrown
rekkju	bed
reyki	smoke
reyna	know
ríki	kingdom
ró	rest
rúmi	seat
rúms	room
S, s	
sá	saw, so
sæmð	honour
sæmiligt	the-same
sættast	reconcile
sagði	said
sagt	is-said, said
sakar	the-sake-of
saman	together
samir	so
sat	sat, stayed
satt	be-true, true
sátu	sat, sat
sé	is, see, so
seg	say
segir	said, told
segja	say, told
segl	the-sails
seilast	to-reach
sein	late
seint	late, slow, slowly
sel	flip
sem	as, that, was, which
semja	negotiate
senda	send
sendi	sent
sér	be, for, he, him, himself, saw, see, themselves
sessunautar	sitting-together
setið	set
setja	sit
settust	sat
sex	six
síð	later
síðan	afterwards, since, then
síðar	afterwards, later
síðast	the-last
síðkveldum	late-evening
síðr	less
sigldu	sailed
siglingum	sailing
Sigurðr	Sigurd (name)
sik	him
silfr	silver
silfrinu	the-silver
silfrit	the-silver
sín	him, theirs
sína	his
sínar	theirs
sinn	he, his
sinni	his, themselves, time, yourself
síns	his
sínu	his, their
sínum	his
sitja	settle
sitr	sat
sitt	his
sízt	least
sja	see
sjá	see, so

Word List (Old Norse to English)

Old Norse	English
sjálfir	themselves
sjám	we-see
skaða	damages
skal	shall
skálum	bowl
skammt	short-distance
skap	mood
skapi	mood
skapkers	large-vessel
skaplyndi	mood-temper
skark	noise
skerit	a-rock
skilðust	separated
skilja	separate
skilnaðr	parting
skilr	separated
skip	a-ship, ship, ships, the-ship
skipagangr	shipping
skipan	ships
skipi	a-ship, ship
skipinu	ship, the-ship
skipit	ship, the-ship
skips	a-ship, ships
skipsins	ship
skipstjórn	ship-steering
skipstjórnar	ship-steer
skipum	ships
skipun	crew
skipverja	the-crew
skíran	cleared
skírt	pure
skjótt	swift, swiftly
skorti	shortly
skotit	launched
skulu	should
skuluð	should
skulum	shall
skyggt	shaded
skyldi	should
skyldu	should
skyli	shall
skyti	shot
skýtr	launched
sleit	broken-up
sleitiliga	unfairly

Old Norse	English
slíkra	such
slíkri	such
slíkt	such
slíku	such
slótt	struck
snemma	early, soon
Snorra	Snorri (name)
Snorrason	Snorrason (name)
Snorrasyni	Snorrason (name)
snúa	turned
sofa	sleep
sögð	told
sögðu	said
sóma	honour
sömu	the-same
spilli	spoil
spurði	asked
spyrr	asked
stað	replace
stafninn	the-prow
stefnið	heading
stendr	stands, stood
stirðlæti	hard-temper
stjórnar	steer
stóð	stood
stóðu	stood
stofunni	chamber
stórættaðr	of-high-family
stórmennsku	greatness
strangt	strange
stríðu	stressful
stuttorðr	short-worded
stygglyndr	quick-tempered
stýrði	steered
stýrimaðr	steersman
stýrimanns	the-steersman
styrkastr	strongest
stytti	short
suðr	south
sumarit	summer
sumir	some
sumrum	summers
sundr	separate
svá	so
svaf	slept

Word List (Old Norse to English)

Old Norse	English
sváfu	slept
svarar	answered
sveinar	fellows
Sveini	Svein (name)
sveinn	fellow, Svein (name), the-fellow
svívirðing	disgrace
svivirðliga	dishonourable
svívirðr	dishonourable
sýndist	seemed
synir	sons
sýnist	seemed
sýnum	in-appearance
sýr	Sow

T, t

Old Norse	English
taka	take
tala	speak
tek	take
tekit	taken
tekr	took
tíðast	swiftly
tíðendi	tidings
til	about, for, to, until
títt	immediately
tízka	custom
tók	took
tóku	took
tólf	twelve
trúa	believe

Þ, þ

Old Norse	English
þá	them, then
þætti	seems
þakkaði	thanked
þakkar	thanked
þangat	from-there
þann	it, then
þannug	that-way
þar	there, there, they
þarf	needed
þat	it, that, this
þatki	that-not
þau	them, then, then
þegar	straightaway, straightaway, there
þeim	of-them, them, they
þeir	the, there, they
þekkjast	accept
þenna	that
þér	to-you, you, you-to
þess	is-this, like-this, that, these, this, those
þessi	these, this
þessu	this
þessum	those
þetta	it, that, this
þik	you
þín	your
þína	yours
þínar	you
þinn	your, yours
þínum	yours
þitt	yours
þjóna	serve
þjónat	served
þjónusta	service
þjónustu	service
þjónustumenn	servants
þó	though
þokkar	favours
þörf	needed
Þóri	Thorir (name)
Þórir	Thorir (name), Thorir (name)
Þóris	Thorir's (name)
þótt	though
þóttist	thought
Þrándheimi	Trondheim (place)
Þrándheims	Trondheim (place)
þrenna	treble
þrjú	three
þú	you
þurfa	needed, you-need
því	accordingly, because, of, that, therefore, with
þykki	think, thought

Word List (Old Norse to English)

Old Norse	English
þykkir	seemed, thinks
þykkist	think
þykkja	think
þykkjast	consider
þykkjumst	think

U, u

Old Norse	English
um	about
umræða	discussion
undan	away-from, from-under, under
undir	under
undirhlutrinn	the-under-part
unnit	deserved
upp	up, upped
uppi	up
upplenzkr	an-Upplander
upplost	false-rumour
urðu	became

Ú, ú

Old Norse	English
út	out, out-of
útan	out
útferð	out-travelling
úti	outside

V, v

Old Norse	English
vægð	grace
vændiskonum	prostitutes
vænna	expected
væri	had, was
vakna	awoke
vaknar	awoke
vald	power
vanði	custom
vandskipaðr	difficult
vant	difficult, expected
vápndjarfastr	weapons-bold
vápnum	weapons
var	was, were
vár	our
vára	going, spring
varð	became, was
varðveita	guard-over
várit	spring
varla	hardly
várt	ours
váru	were
vátir	wet
váveifliga	unexpected
vega	weigh
vegr	way
veit	know
veita	grant, lead
veizlum	the-feasts
veizlur	feasts
veizt	know
veiztu	know-you
vel	well
ver	be
vér	we
vera	be, becoming, being, is, it-be
verð	worth
verða	be, to-be
verðr	came, worth
verðum	worth
verit	be, been, being, had-been
verja	spend
verr	worse
verri	worse
verst	becomes
vert	worth, worthy
vetr	winter
vetrinn	winter
vexti	well-built
við	against, with
víghug	killing-mind
Vík	Vik (place)
vil	will, wish
vildi	willed, wish, wished
vilgis	very
vili	willed
vilja	wish
viljum	wish, wish-to

Word List (Old Norse to English)

Old Norse	English
vill	willed, wish, wished, wished-to, wishes
vinar	friend
vináttu	friendship
vinda	wind
vingan	friendship
vingjarnlig	friendly
vinna	to-win-over
vinr	friend
vinveitt	favourable
virðing	honour, worthiness
víst	certainly
vistum	provisions
vísu	certainly
vit	with
vita	certainly, know
víti	punishment, signalled
vitið	know
vítin	penalty
vítishornit	penalty-horn
vítit	penalty, the-penalty
vitni	testimony
víttr	penalty, reprimanded
vizkr	wise

Y, y

yðr	you
yðrar	yours
yðvars	yours
yfir	over
yfirbragði	complexion
ykkarr	with-you
ykkr	you-two
ykkra	yours
yrði	became

Ý, ý

ýkva	veer
ýmissa	various

Word List (English to Old Norse)

Word List (English to Old Norse)

English	Old Norse

A, a

English	Old Norse
a-ban	*bann*
about	*á, í, til, um*
accept	*þekkjast*
access	*atgang*
accomplished	*færr*
accordingly	*því*
advice-giving	*ráðagerðir*
advise	*ráð*
a-few	*fám*
after	*aftr, eftir*
afterwards	*síðan, síðar*
against	*við*
age	*ævi*
a-great	*mikill, miklu*
all	*allir, allir, allra, allt, allt, öllu, öllum*
all-long	*alllangt*
allow	*láta, leyfa*
all-prepared	*albúnir*
alone	*eins*
along	*fyrir, með*
also	*ok*
am	*em, er*
a-man	*maðr*
a-mark	*mörk*
ambitious	*framgjarn*
ancestry	*ætt*
and	*á, en, enda, ok, 0*
anger	*reiði*
another	*annan, annan, annars*
answered	*svarar*
an-Upplander	*upplenzkr*
appears	*lízt*
appoint	*ráðast*
arctic-fox-furs	*melrakkabelgi*
are	*ert, eru*
are-you	*ertu*
a-ring	*hring*
a-rock	*skerit*
arrange	*ráðast*
as	*á, en, er, sem*
a-second	*öðru*
as-him	*honum*
a-ship	*skip, skipi, skips*
asked	*beiða, beitt, biðr, spurði, spyrr*
asks	*beiðir*
assist	*greiða*
at	*á, at, í*
a-trick	*brögð*
away	*brott*
away-from	*undan*
away-prepared	*brautbúnaði*
awhile	*hríð*
awoke	*vakna, vaknar*

B, b

English	Old Norse
back	*aftr*
badly	*illa*
ban	*bannar*
Bard (name)	*Bárðr*
bargain	*falar*
be	*gerist, sér, ver, vera, verða, verit*
bear	*bera, beri*
bears	*berr*
became	*urðu, varð, yrði*
because	*því*
becomes	*verst*
becoming	*vera*
bed	*rekkju*
been	*verit*
before	*áðr, fyrir, fyrr, næstum*
began	*byrjaði*
behave	*lætr*
behind	*eftir*
being	*vera, verit*
believe	*trúa*
bell-ringing	*hringingar, hringingum*
below	*neðan, niðr*
benefit	*kosti*
best	*bergst, bezt, bezta*

Word List (English to Old Norse)

English	*Old Norse*
be-true	*satt*
better	*betr, betra*
between	*með, milli*
bid	*báðu, biðr*
bold	*djörfung*
bore	*bar*
both	*báðum, bæði*
bought	*kaupir*
bowl	*skálum*
Bratteyar (place)	*Bröttueyri*
breaking	*brjótist*
bring	*færi, færið*
bringing	*bar, fært*
broken-up	*sleit*
brought	*fær, færa, færir*
burnt	*brennda*
but	*eða, en, enn*

C, c

English	*Old Norse*
called	*kalla, kallat, kvaddi*
calling	*ákalsi*
came	*kemr, kom, koma, kómu, verðr*
can	*kann*
carried	*berr, flytja*
carry-out	*efna*
celebrated	*fegnir*
certainly	*víst, vísu, vita*
chamber	*stofunni*
changed	*breytt*
chased	*eltast*
cheated	*logizt*
choice	*kostar*
choose	*kjósa*
cleared	*skíran*
clearly	*einsætt*
cloak-lap	*möttulsskauti*
clocks	*klokkurum*
come	*kæma, koma, komið, kominn, komir*
coming	*koma, kominn*
commanded	*ræðst, reiðist*
companions	*förunauta, förunautar*
companionship	*föruneyti*

English	*Old Norse*
completely	*gerla*
complexion	*yfirbragði*
conclude	*enda*
consider	*leitat, þykkjast*
consumed	*neytti*
conversed	*mál*
copper	*kopars*
could	*mun*
court	*hirðar, hirðinni*
court-man	*hirðmaðr*
court-men	*kertisveinar*
crew	*áhöfnina, háseta, liði, skipun*
custom	*tízka, vanði*

D, d

English	*Old Norse*
damages	*skaða*
dangers	*háski*
Danish-forces	*danaher*
day	*dag, dagr*
days	*dögum*
dearly-loved	*kærleikum*
decide	*ráðist*
deeming	*dóm*
demand	*krefja*
Denmark (place)	*Danmerkr*
deserved	*unnit*
desire	*fýsir*
did	*fór, gera, gerði*
difficult	*vandskipaðr, vant*
direction	*beint*
disappeared	*hurfu*
discussion	*umræða*
disgrace	*svívirðing*
dishonourable	*svivirðliga, svívirðr*
do	*gera*
done	*gert*
down	*níðist, niðr*
drank	*drakk, drekka, drekkr, drykki*
drew	*heimta*
drink	*drekk, drekka, drykki*
drinking	*drukku, drykkju*
drinks	*drykkju*

Word List (English to Old Norse)

English	*Old Norse*	English	*Old Norse*
drunk	*drukkit*	follow	*fylgði, fylgja*
		following	*fylgðina, fylgir*

E, e

		food	*matar*
		for	*fyrir, sér, til*
each	*hvárr, hvárt, hverju, hverr, hvert*	force	*nauðgat*
		forces	*hér*
early	*snemma*	foreclose	*bregða*
early-riser	*árrisull*	forward	*fram, framarla*
east	*austan, austr*	forwards	*fram*
echo	*glymr*	found	*fann, fengi, finnimst, fyndist, hitti, hittir*
eighth	*átti*		
end	*enda*	frequent	*oftar*
ended	*lokit*	friend	*vinar, vinr*
England-Traveller (name)	*Englandsfari*	friendly	*vingjarnlig*
		friendship	*vináttu, vingan*
enough	*nóga*	from	*af, af, frá, fram, í, ór*
equally-following	*jafnfylginn*	from-here	*heðan*
equally-much	*jafnmjök*	from-there	*þangat*
equally-trustworthy	*jafntraustan, jafntraustir*	from-under	*undan*
		fully-tested	*fullreynt*
errand-without	*erendlaust*	furs	*belgi*
especially	*einkum*		
evening	*aftan, aftna, kveld*		

G, g

except	*nema*		
expected	*vænna, vant*	gallows	*gálga*
		Gardariki (place)	*Garðaríki*

F, f

		gave	*bar, fá, gaf, gáfu, gáfuð*
		get	*fá, gera, get*
fair-wind	*byrr*	gift	*gjöfin*
false-rumour	*upplost*	give	*fá, fæ, fái, gefa*
farmed	*bjó*	given	*gefinn*
fasten	*festa*	gladness	*glaðari*
father	*faðir, frændum*	go	*fara, ganga*
favourable	*vinveitt*	goes	*ferr*
favours	*þokkar*	going	*fara, för, gengr, vára*
feasts	*veizlur*	gold	*gulls*
feed	*fótum*	good	*góð, góðr*
fellow	*drengr, sveinn*	good-news	*fagnaðartíðendi*
fellows	*sveinar*	good-things	*gæði*
few	*fáir, fátt*	got	*fengit, heimtir*
find	*fund, hitt, hitta*	grace	*vægð*
first	*fyrsta, fyrstu*	grant	*leggja, veita*
flip	*sel*	great	*mikill*
floating	*floti*	greater	*meiri*

Word List (English to Old Norse)

English	*Old Norse*	English	*Old Norse*
greatly	*drjúgum, mikinn*	his	*hans, sína, sinn, sinni, síns, sínu, sínum, sitt*
greatness	*stórmennsku*		
guard-over	*varðveita*		
guardsmen	*hirðina*	Hjardarholt (place)	*Hjarðarholti*
		hold	*haldast, halt, heldr*

H, h

		hold-you	*haltu*
had	*á, átti, er, hafa, hafði, hafi, haft, hefði, hefir, höfðu, lagi, lét, lézt, væri*	home-longing	*heimfúsari*
		honour	*drengskap, sæmð, sóma, virðing*
		horn	*horn*
had-been	*verit*	horn-blast	*hornblástr*
half	*hálf, helmings*	hostilities	*ófriðar*
Halldor (name)	*Halldór, Halldóri, Halldórr, Halldórs*	house	*hús*
		how	*hvárt, hvers*
Halldor's (name)	*Halldórs*	how-so	*hversu*
hammock	*húðfat*	huge	*mikit*
hand	*hendi, höndum*	human-danger	*mannháska*
handsome	*fríðr*		
happiest	*blíðast*		

I, i

happily	*blíðligr*		
Harald (name)	*Harald, Haraldi, Haraldr, Haralds*	I	*ek*
		I-am	*ek*
Harald's-money (name)	*Haraldsslátta*	Iceland (place)	*Ísland, Íslands*
		Icelander	*íslenzkan*
hardly	*varla*	Icelander (name)	*Íslandi*
hard-temper	*stirðlæti*	if	*ef*
has	*hafi, hefir*	ill	*illa*
has-been	*hefir*	immediately	*títt*
have	*er, hafa, hafið, hafir, hefi, hefir, láta, láti*	in	*á, at, í*
		in-appearance	*sýnum*
having	*hafa*	in-on	*at*
he	*hann, honum, sér, sinn*	inside	*inn*
		intend	*ætla*
heading	*stefnið*	intended	*ætlaði, ætlar, ætlast, ætlat*
hear	*heyra, heyrum*		
heard	*heyrðuð*	intends	*ætlar*
held	*halda*	into	*í*
hence	*heðan*	invitation	*boð*
here	*her, hér*	is	*á, er, sé, vera*
higher	*hæra*	is-paid	*lendra*
highest	*hæra, hæsta*	is-said	*sagt*
him	*hann, hans, honum, sér, sik, sín*	is-this	*þess*
		it	*at, hann, þann, þat, þetta*
himself	*sér*		
hired	*ráðit*	it-be	*vera*

Word List (English to Old Norse)

English	*Old Norse*
it-is	*er*

J, j

English	*Old Norse*
joyful	*blíðu*

K, k

English	*Old Norse*
Kaupang (place)	*Kaupangi*
keep-asking	*brekar*
killing-mind	*víghug*
king	*konungi, konungr*
kingdom	*ríki*
king-of-Denmark	*danakonungr*
king's-men-customs	*hirðsiðum*
know	*kann, reyna, veit, veizt, vita, vitið*
known	*kunnigt*
know-you	*veiztu*

L, l

English	*Old Norse*
laid	*leggr, lögðu*
land	*land, landi, lands, lendr, lönd*
landed	*lendir*
lands	*landa, landi*
land-tents	*landtjald*
large-vessel	*skapkers*
last-night	*gærkveld*
late	*sein, seint*
late-evening	*síðkveldum*
later	*síð, síðar*
launched	*skotit, skýtr*
lay	*lá, leggi, leggjum*
lead	*veita*
leading	*ræðr*
least	*sízt*
leave	*lætr, leyfi*
less	*minna, síðr*
let	*lætr, léti*
let-it	*lát*
lie	*lygi*

English	*Old Norse*
life	*lifa*
like	*líka*
liked	*líkaði*
like-this	*þess*
listen-to	*hlýða*
little	*lítill, litlu, litt, lítt*
long	*lengi, löng*
longer	*lengr*
longships	*langskip*
look	*líta*
looked	*lítr*
lord	*herra*
losing	*láta*
Lyrgja (place)	*Lyrgju*

M, m

English	*Old Norse*
man	*maðr, mann*
many	*fjölði, marga, margr*
matter	*mál, mála, máli*
may	*má, mætti, máttu, mega*
may-you	*máttu*
me	*mér, mik, mín*
measure	*mál*
meet	*fund, móti, móts*
meeting	*móti*
men	*liði, manna, menn*
merchants	*kaupmenn*
merchant-ship	*byrðing*
met	*fundust*
might	*mætti, mætti*
mine	*mín, mína, minn, minni, mitt*
misliked	*mislíkaði*
modest	*hófi*
moment	*bili*
money-insisting	*fjárheimta*
mood	*skap, skapi*
mood-temper	*skaplyndi*
more	*fleiri, meir, meira, meiri*
more-fixedly	*fastara*
more-often	*oftar*
morning	*morgun, myrgininn*

Word List (English to Old Norse)

English	*Old Norse*
most	*mesta, mesti*
much	*mikinn, mikla, miklu, miklum, mjök*
must	*munt*
my	*mínu, mitt*

N, n

English	*Old Norse*
named	*hét*
nearly	*náliga*
necessity	*nauðsyn*
needed	*þarf, þörf, þurfa*
negotiate	*semja*
neither	*hvárki*
next	*næst, næsta*
next-to	*næsta*
Nid (place)	*Nið*
night	*nætr, nótt*
no	*enga, engan, enskis*
noise	*skark*
none	*eigi, engi, engu*
nor	*né*
north	*norðr*
Norway (place)	*Nóreg, Noregi, Nóregi, Nóregs*
Norwegians	*norrænir*
not	*eigi, ekki*
nothing	*einskis, engis, neitt*
now	*nú*

O, o

English	*Old Norse*
of	*á, af, af, at, í, því*
of-all	*allra*
of-few-words	*fámæltr*
of-high-family	*stórættaðr*
often	*oft*
of-them	*þeim*
old	*gamall*
old-age	*elli*
old-is	*eldist*
old-men	*gamalmenni*
on	*á*
one	*eigi, einn, eitt*
one-such	*einhverja, einnhvern*
only	*engan*
on-the	*á*
or	*eða*
Oslo (place)	*Ósló*
other	*áðr, aðra, aðrir, annarra, annarri, öðrum*
otherwise	*elligar*
ounces	*aura*
our	*okkr, vár*
ours	*okkar, várt*
out	*út, útan*
outburst	*orðaframkast*
out-of	*í, ór, út*
outside	*úti*
outspoken	*bermæltr*
out-travelling	*útferð*
over	*of, yfir*
overboard	*kaf*
own	*eiga, eignast*

P, p

English	*Old Norse*
paid	*gelzt*
part	*hlut, hluti, hlutr*
parting	*skilnaðr*
pass	*leið*
passed	*leið, liðit, líðr*
pay	*fá, gjalda*
payment	*fé, galzt, gjaldit, lendra, mála, mála, málagjöfna, málann, málanum, máli*
peace	*kyrrt*
penalty	*vítin, vítit, víttr*
penalty-horn	*vítishornit*
people	*manna, menn, mönnum*
people's	*manna*
possible	*hægt*
power	*vald*
preparations	*bjuggu, búnaðinn*
prepared	*búa, búinn, búit, býr, býstu*
prepares	*býst*

Word List (English to Old Norse)

English	*Old Norse*	English	*Old Norse*
prevail	*ráða*	sat	*sat, sátu, sátu, settust, sitr*
promised	*hét*	saw	*sá, sér*
promising-wind	*byrvænligt*	say	*seg, segja*
prostitutes	*léttlætiskonum, vændiskonum*	sea	*haf, hafs*
provisions	*vistum*	seat	*rúmi*
punishment	*víti*	see	*sé, sér, sja, sjá*
purchase	*kaupa*	seek	*leita*
pure	*skírt*	seemed	*sýndist, sýnist, þykkir*
		seems	*þætti*
		self-willed	*kappgjarn*
		send	*senda*
		sent	*sendi*

Q, q

English	*Old Norse*
quick-tempered	*stygglyndr*

R, r

English	*Old Norse*	English	*Old Norse*
ran	*hljóp*	separate	*skilja, sundr*
rather	*heldr, helzt, helzti*	separated	*skilðust, skilr*
reacted	*brygði*	servants	*þjónustumenn*
readied	*bjóst*	serve	*þjóna*
reconcile	*sættast*	served	*þjónat*
remained	*eftir*	service	*þjónusta, þjónustu*
remaining	*eftir*	set	*setið*
repaid	*launuð*	settle	*bú, byggja, sitja*
repaired	*bætt*	settled	*bjó*
repay	*gyldist*	shaded	*skyggt*
replace	*stað*	shall	*mun, muni, munkat, munum, skal, skulum, skyli*
reprimanded	*víttr*	share	*hlut*
resolved	*alhugat*	she	*hon*
rest	*ró*	ship	*knörr, skip, skipi, skipinu, skipit, skipsins*
return	*mót*	shipping	*skipagangr*
ring	*hringja*	ships	*skip, skipan, skips, skipum*
room	*rúms*	ship-steer	*skipstjórnar*
run	*hleypr*	ship-steering	*skipstjórn*
		ship's-worth	*kaupverðsins*
		short	*stytti*
		short-distance	*skammt*
		shortly	*skorti*

S, s

English	*Old Norse*
sadness	*fæð*
said	*kvað, kvaðst, sagði, sagt, segir, sögðu*
sailed	*sigldu*
sailing	*siglingum*
sailors	*háseta, hásetar, hásetum*
short-worded	*stuttorðr*
shot	*skyti*
should	*mun, muntu, munum, myndi, skulu, skuluð, skyldi, skyldu*
signalled	*víti*
Sigurd (name)	*Sigurðr*

Word List (English to Old Norse)

English	Old Norse
silver	*silfr*
silverware	*málasilfrit*
since	*síðan*
sit	*setja*
sitting-together	*sessunautar*
six	*sex*
sleep	*sofa*
slept	*svaf, sváfu*
slow	*seint*
slowly	*seint*
smoke	*reyki*
Snorrason (name)	*Snorrason, Snorrasyni*
Snorri (name)	*Snorra*
so	*sá, samir, sé, sjá, svá*
solution	*órráða*
some	*nökkura, nökkurum, sumir*
something	*nökkur, nökkut*
somewhat	*nökkut*
sons	*synir*
soon	*snemma*
south	*suðr*
Sow	*sýr*
speak	*máli, tala*
spend	*verja*
spoil	*spilli*
spoke	*mælti, mæltuð*
spoken	*mælt*
spoken-of	*mælt*
spoke-to	*mælti*
spring	*vára, várit*
stag-horn	*dýrshorn*
stands	*stendr*
stay	*dveljast*
stayed	*sat*
steer	*stjórnar*
steered	*stýrði*
steersman	*stýrimaðr*
still	*enn*
stood	*stendr, stóð, stóðu*
straightaway	*þegar*
straight-away	*þegar*
strange	*strangt*
straw	*hálm*
stress	*álaga*
stressful	*stríðu*
strongest	*styrkastr*
struck	*lýstr, slótt*
such	*slíkra, slíkri, slíkt, slíku*
summer	*sumarit*
summers	*sumrum*
suppose	*ætla*
Svein (name)	*Sveini, Sveinn*
swift	*skjótt*
swiftly	*skjótt, tíðast*

T, t

English	Old Norse
take	*nema, taka, tek*
take-care	*gæta*
taken	*tekit*
taught	*kennduð*
temper	*lyndi*
testimony	*vitni*
than	*en*
thanked	*þakkaði, þakkar*
thanks	*heilstan*
that	*á, at, en, er, í, sem, þat, þenna, þess, þetta, því*
that-not	*þatki*
that-way	*þannug*
the	*á, at, in, inn, þeir*
the-air	*loftinu*
the-anchor	*ákkeri*
the-autumn	*hausti*
the-city	*bænum*
the-cockerel	*árgalinn*
the-crew	*skipverja*
the-day	*daginn*
the-drinking-horn	*hornit*
the-feasts	*veizlum*
the-fellow	*sveinn*
the-first	*fyrra*
the-gift	*gjöfina*
The-Great-City (place)	*Miklagarði*
the-horn	*hornsins*
their	*sínu*

Word List (English to Old Norse)

English	*Old Norse*	English	*Old Norse*
theirs	sín, sínar	thinks	þykkir
the-king	konung, konunga, konungi, konungr, konungs	this	á, at, þat, þess, þessi, þessu, þetta
		this-town	bænum
the-king's	konungs, ksonungs	Thorir (name)	Þóri, Þórir, Þórir
the-kings-men	konungsmenn	Thorir's (name)	Þóris
the-king's-ship	konungsskipinu	those	þess, þessum
the-land	land, landi	though	þó, þótt
the-last	síðast	thought	þóttist, þykki
them	þá, þau, þeim	three	þrjú
the-matter	ráð	through	gegnum
the-meeting	mótinu, mótsins	thrown	rekit
the-merchants	kaupmenn	tidings	tíðendi
the-morning	morgun	tied-up	bindr
themselves	sér, sinni, sjálfir	time	sinni
then	á, en, enn, síðan, þá, þann, þau, þau	tired	mæðumst
		to	á, at, í, til
the-next	annan	to-be	verða
the-payment	gjaldit	to-come	at
the-penalty	vítit	to-do	gera
the-priest	goða	to-drink	drekka
the-prow	stafninn	together	saman
the-queen	dróttning	to-give	gefa
there	þar, þar, þegar, þeir	to-have	hafa
there-are	eru	to-him	honum
therefore	því	to-hold	halda
the-ring	hringinn	told	segir, segja, sögð
the-river	ánni	to-me	mér
the-sails	segl	to-meet	fund
the-sake-of	sakar	took	tekr, tók, tóku
the-same	sæmiligt, sömu	to-reach	seilast
these	þess, þessi	to-run	hlaupa
the-ship	skip, skipinu, skipit	to-sea	hafa
the-silver	silfrinu, silfrit	to-the-king	konungi
the-steersman	stýrimanns	to-us	oss
the-straw	hálm	to-win-over	vinna
the-tow-boat	báti	town	bæinn
the-town	bænum	townspeople	bæjarmenn
the-traders	kaupmenn	to-you	þér
the-under-part	undirhlutrinn	trading-man	kaupmaðr
they	eru, þar, þeim, þeir	trading-men	kaupsveinar
they-were	eru	trading-voyages	kaupferðir
things	hluti, hlutum	travel	færi, færr, fara, fari, farir, farit, fars, ferðir
think	hug, hygg, þykki, þykkist, þykkja, þykkjumst	travel-goods	fararefnin
		travelled	farit, fór

Word List (English to Old Norse)

English	*Old Norse*	English	*Old Norse*
travelling	*fara*	**W, w**	
travelling-clothes	*ígangsklæði*		
treasure	*gersimar, gersimum*	wait	*bíð, bíða, biðleika,*
treasures	*gersimar*	warmth	*hlýs*
treble	*þrenna*	warn	*ávíta*
trick	*prettum*	was	*enn, er, sem, væri, var, varð*
Trondheim (place)	*Þrándheimi, Þrándheims*	was-named	*hét*
true		way	*hættir, leið, vegr*
trumpet-blown	*blásit*	we	*vér*
turbulence	*aga*	wealth	*fénu, fét*
turned	*snúa*	weapons	*vápnum*
twelve	*tólf*	weapons-bold	*vápndjarfastr*
		we-have	*hefir*
U, u		weigh	*vega*
		well	*vel*
un-bending	*ómjúkr*	well-built	*vexti*
under	*undan, undir*	went	*færi, fara, ferr, fór, gekk, gengr, gengu, gerir*
undeservedly	*ómakliga*		
unexpected	*váveifliga*		
unfairly	*sleitiliga*	went-you	*fórtu*
unfriendly	*óvingjarnliga*	were	*er, eru, var, váru*
un-glad	*ógladdist*	we-see	*sjám*
un-gladness	*óglaðari*	wet	*vátir*
un-high-born	*ótiginn*	what	*er, hvat, hvers*
un-peace	*ófriðinn, ófriðr*	when	*er*
unseen	*ósýnt*	where	*er, hver*
until	*til*	which	*er, hvárt, hvégi, hvern, sem*
un-used	*ónýttir*		
unwilling	*ófúss*	while	*en*
up	*upp, uppi*	who	*en, er, hverjum, hverr*
upped	*upp*	why	*hví*
us	*okkr, oss*	will	*í, vil*
use	*neyta*	willed	*vildi, vili, vill*
		wind	*vinda*
V, v		winter	*vetr, vetrinn*
		wise	*vizkr*
various	*ýmissa*	wish	*vil, vildi, vilja, viljum, vill*
veer	*ýkva*		
very	*vilgis*	wished	*vildi, vill*
Vik (place)	*Vík*	wished-to	*vill*
violated	*brotin*	wishes	*vill*
		wish-to	*viljum*
		with	*í, með, því, við, vit*
		with-me	*mér*

Word List (English to Old Norse)

English	Old Norse
without-fraud	*falslaust*
with-you	*ykkarr*
word	*orð, orði*
words	*orð*
word-sending	*orðsending*
word-to	*orð*
worried-face	*áhyggjusvip*
worse	*verr, verri*
worth	*verð, verðr, verðum, vert*
worthiness	*virðing*
worthy	*vert*
would	*mun, myndi, myndir, myndu*

Y, y

you	*þér, þik, þínar, þú, yðr*
you-need	*þurfa*
your	*þín, þinn*
yours	*þína, þinn, þínum, þitt, yðrar, yðvars, ykkra*
yourself	*sinni*
you-to	*þér*
you-two	*ykkr*
Yule (name)	*jóla, jólanna, jólin, Jólum*

The Tale of Halldor Snorrason II (Old Icelandic)

The Tale of Halldor Snorrason II (*Old Icelandic*)

Old Icelandic	Literal	English
1	**1**	**1**
Halldór Snorrason hafði verið út í Miklagarði með Haraldi sem áður er sagt og kom í Noreg með honum austan úr Garðaríki.	Halldor Snorrason had been out in The-Great-City with Harald as before was said and came to Norway with him east from Gardariki.	Halldor Snorrason had been to Constantinople with Harald as has been said before, and went east to Norway with him from the Kievan Rus'.
Hafði hann þá mikla sæmd og virðing af Haraldi konungi.	Had he then much honour and worthiness from Harald the-king.	Then he had much honour and worthiness from king Harald.
Var hann með konungi þenna vetur er hann sat í Kaupangi.	Was he with the-king that winter when he stayed at Kaupang.	He was with the king that winter when he stayed a Kaupang in Skiringssal.
En er á leið veturinn og vora tók bjuggu menn kaupferðir sínar snemma því að nálega hafði engi eða lítill verið skipagangur af Noregi fyrir sakar ófriðar og aga þess sem verið hafði milli Noregs og Danmerkur.	And when had passed winter and spring took preparations people trading-voyages theirs early because of nearly had none or little been shipping from Norway for the-sake-of hostilities and turbulence those as had-been had between Norway and Denmark.	And when winter had passed into spring, people began preparations for trading voyages early, because there had been little in the way of trade from Norway because of hostilities and turbulence between Norway and Denmark.
En er á leið vorið fann Haraldur konungur að Halldór Snorrason ógladdist mjög.	But when that passed spring found Harald the-king that Halldor Snorrason un-glad much.	But when spring had passed, king Harald found Halldor Snorrason very unhappy.
Konungur spurði einn dag hvað honum bjó í skapi.	The-king asked one day what he settled in mood.	One day the king asked what had settled in his mood.
Halldór svarar:	Halldor answered:	Halldor answered:
"Út fýsir mig til Íslands herra".	"Out desire me to Iceland lord".	"I desire to travel out to Iceland, lord".
Konungur mælti:	The-king spoke:	The king said:
"Margur mundi þó heimfúsari verið hafa eða hver eru fararefni eða hversu verst fénu?"	"Many would though home-longing being had but where are travel-goods or how-so becomes wealth?"	"Many would be longing for home, but where are your travel goods, and how will you spend your wealth?"

The Tale of Halldor Snorrason II (Old Icelandic)

Old Icelandic	Literal	English
Hann svarar:	He answered:	He answered:
"Skjótt ætla eg að verja því að ekki er til nema ígangsklæði mín".	"Swift intend I to spend because that not have to take travelling-clothes mine".	"Swiftly it seems spent to me, because I don't have any travelling clothes to take".
"Lítt er þá launuð löng þjónusta og margur háski og skal eg fá þér skip og áhöfnina.	"Little is then repaid long service and many dangers and shall I pay you a-ship and crew.	"Your long service and all its dangers are little repaid, and I shall buy you a ship and a crew.
Skal faðir þinn sjá mega að þú hefir mér eigi til engis þjónað".	Shall father yours see may that you have me not to nothing served".	Your father shall see that you have not served me for nothing".
Halldór þakkaði konungi gjöfina.	Halldor thanked the-king the-gift.	Halldor thank the king for his gift.
Fám dögum síðar fann Halldór konung og spurði konungur hversu mjög hann hefði ráðið sér skipverja.	A-few days later found Halldor the-king and asked the-king how-so much he had hired for the-crew.	A few days later Halldor found the king and asked him how much of the crew had he hired.
Hann svarar:	He answered:	He answered:
"Allir kaupsveinar hafa sér ráðið áður skipan en eg fæ enga menn og því ætla eg að eftir mun verða að vera skip það er þér gáfuð mér".	"All trading-men have themselves hired other ships but I give no men and therefore suppose I that remaining should be that becoming the-ship that is you gave me".	"All the traders have been hired by other ships, but I have got no men, and therefore I suppose that the ship that you gave me should remain".
Konungur mælti:	The-king spoke:	The king spoke:
"Eigi er þá vinveitt gjöfin og skulum við enn bíða hvað úr ráðist um háseta".	"Not is then favourable gift and shall with then wait what from decide about sailors".	"Then it is not a favourable gift, and with that we shall wait to decide about the sailors".
Annan dag eftir var blásið til móts í bænum og sagt að konungur vill tala við bæjarmenn og kaupmenn.	The-next day after was trumpet-blown to meet in the-town and said that the-king wished-to speak with townspeople and merchants.	The next day the trumpet was blown to meet in the town, and the king said that he wished to speak with the townspeople and the merchants.
Konungur kom seint til mótsins og sýndist með áhyggjusvip þá er hann kom.	The-king came late to the-meeting and seemed with worried-face then as he came.	The king came late to the meeting and seemed to have a worried face when he arrived.
Hann mælti:	He spoke:	He spoke:

The Tale of Halldor Snorrason II (Old Icelandic)

Old Icelandic	Literal	English
"Það heyrum vér sagt að ófriður muni kominn í ríki vort austur í Vík.	"This hear we said that un-peace shall come in kingdom ours east about Vik.	"We hear this, that war shall come to our kingdom east in Vik.
Ræður Sveinn Danakonungur fyrir Danaher og vill oss vinna skaða en vér viljum með engu móti upp gefa vor lönd.	Leading Svein King-of-Denmark for Danish-forces and wishes us to-win-over damages but we wish-to with none meet up give our land.	King Svein of Denmark is leading the Danish forces and means to win over and damage us, but none of us wish to give up our land.
Fyrir því leggjum vér bann fyrir hvert skip að úr landi fari fyrr en eg hefi slíkt sem eg vil af hverju skipi, bæði af liði og vistum, nema einn knörr eigi mikill er á Halldór Snorrason skal ganga til Íslands.	For therefore lay we a-ban before each ship to out-of the-land travel before that I have such as I wish from each ship, both of men and provisions, except one ship not great that of Halldor Snorrason shall go to Iceland.	Therefore we lay a ban on each ship from travelling out of these lands, until I have what I wish from each ship, men and provisions, except for one small ship of Halldor Snorrason which will go to Iceland.
En þótt yður þyki þetta nokkuð strangt er áður hafið búið ferðir yðrar þá ber oss nauðsyn til slíkra álaga en betra þætti oss að um kyrrt væri að sitja og færi hver sem vildi".	But though you think this somewhat strange is before have prepared travel yours then bears us necessity to such stress but better seems to-us that about peace was that settle and travel each as wish".	You will think this somewhat strange, when you have prepared your travel, but it this stress is necessary, and it would be better for us if there was peace and each man could travel wherever he wished.
Eftir það sleit mótinu.	After that broken-up the-meeting.	After that the meeting was broken up.
Litlu síðar kom Halldór á konungs fund.	Little afterwards came Halldor to the-king find.	A little afterwards Halldor came to find the king.
Konungur spurði hvað þá liði um búnaðinn, hvort hann fengi nokkura háseta.	The-king asked what then crew about preparations, each he found some crew.	The king asked about what preparations had been made for some crew.
Halldór svarar:	Halldor answered:	Halldor answered:
"Helsti marga hefi eg nú ráðið því að miklu fleiri koma nú til mín og beiða fars en eg megi öllum veita og veita menn mér mikinn atgang að drjúgum eru brotin hús til mín svo að hvorki nótt né dag hefi eg ró fyrir ákallsi manna hér um".	"Rather many have I now hired because that a-great more came now to me and asked travel than I may all lead and grant people me much access that greatly they violated house to me so that neither night nor day have I rest for calling people here about".	"I have hired rather a lot of men, because a great more came to me and asked to travel than I may lead, and granted much access that my house is violated, so that I have no rest, neither day nor night for these people calling here abouts".

The Tale of Halldor Snorrason II (Old Icelandic)

Old Icelandic	Literal	English
Konungur mælti:	The-king spoke:	The king spoke:
"Haltu nú þessum hásetum sem þú hefir tekið og sjáum enn hvað í gerist".	"Hold-you now those sailors that you have taken and we-see then what will be".	"Now keep the sailors that you have hired, and we will see what will happen".
Næsta dag eftir var blásið og sagt að konungur vill enn tala við kaupmenn.	Next day after was trumpet-blown and said the king wished then speak with the-merchants.	The next day, a trumpet was blown, and it was said that the king wished to speak with the merchants.
Nú var eigi sein aðkoma konungs til mótsins því að hann kom í fyrsta lagi.	Now was not late to-come the-king to the-meeting because that he came to first had.	Now the king was not late in coming to the meeting, because he had arrived first.
Var hann þá blíðlegur í yfirbragði.	Was he then happily in complexion.	He was then happy in his complexion.
Hann stóð upp og mælti:	He stood up and spoke:	He stood up and spoke:
"Nú eru góð tíðindi að segja.	"Now there-are good tidings to say.	"Now there is good news to say.
Það er ekki nema upplost og lygi er þér heyrðuð sagt um ófriðinn fyrra dag.	That is not except false-rumour and lie that you heard said about un-peace the-first day.	That was nothing except a false rumour and a lie that you heard said about war the other day.
Viljum vér nú leyfa hverju skipi úr landi að fara þangað sem hver vill sínu skipi halda.	Wish we now allow each ship out-of lands to travel from-there as each wishes their ship to-hold.	We now wish to allow each ship out of our lands to travel where they wish with their ships.
Komið aftur að hausti og færið oss gersemar.	Come back in the-autumn and bring us treasures.	Come back in the autumn, and bring us treasures.
En þér skuluð hafa af oss í mót gæði og vingan".	But you should have from us in return good-things and friendship".	Then you shall have good things and friendship in return from us".
Allir kaupmenn er þar voru urðu þessu fegnir og báðu hann tala konunga heilastan.	All the-traders who there were became this celebrated and bid him speak the-king thanks.	All the traders who were there celebrated at this and spoke thanks to the king.
Fór Halldór til Íslands um sumarið og var þann vetur með föður sínum.	Travelled Halldor to Iceland about summer and was then winter with father his.	Halldor travelled to Iceland around summer and was there with his father for the winter.

The Tale of Halldor Snorrason II (Old Icelandic)

Old Icelandic	Literal	English
Hann fór utan eftir um sumarið og þá enn til hirðar Haralds konungs og er svo sagt að Halldór var þá eigi jafnfylginn konungi sem fyrr og sat hann eftir um aftna þá er konungur gekk að sofa.	He travelled out after about summer and then was to court Harald the-king and was so said that Halldor was then not equally-following the-king as before and sat he after about evening then when the-king went to sleep.	He travelled around summer and was then in the court of king Harald, and so it was said that Halldor was not the same follower of the king that he was before, and he sat up in the evening after the king had gone to sleep.

2

Old Icelandic	Literal	English
Maður hét Þórir Englandsfari og hafði verið hinn mesti kaupmaður og lengi í siglingum til ýmissa landa og fært konungi gersemar.	A-man named Thorir England-Traveller and had been the most trading-man and long with sailing to various lands and bringing the-king treasure.	A man was named Thorir the England-Traveller, and he had been the greatest trader and had long sailed to various lands to bring the king treasure.
Þórir var hirðmaður Haralds konungs og þá mjög gamall.	Thorir was court-man Harald the-king and then much old.	Thorir was a court man of king Harald and was then very old.
Þórir kom að máli við konung og mælti:	Thorir came to speak with the-king and spoke:	Thorir came to speak with the king and said:
"Eg er maður gamall sem þér vitið og mæðist eg mjög.	"I am a-man old as you know and tired I-am much.	"I am an old man as you know, and I am very tired.
Þykist eg nú eigi til fær að fylgja hirðsiðum, minni að drekka eða um aðra hluti þá sem til heyra.	Think I now not to travel to follow king's-men-customs, mine to drink or about other things then as to hear.	I now do not think I can follow the customs of the king's men, less drinking or other things which are heard of.
Mun nú annars leita verða þótt þetta sé best og blíðast að vera með yður".	Should now another seek to-be though it is best and happiest to be with you".	I should now seek another place to be, though it is best and happiest to be with you".
Konungur svarar:	The-king answered:	The king answered:
"Þar er okkur hægt til úrræða vinur.	"There is our possible to solution friend.	"There is a possible solution, friend".
Ver með hirðinni og drekk ekki meira en þú vilt í mínu leyfi".	Be with court and drink not more than you wish with my leave".	Be with the court and do not drink more than you wish, with my leave".
Bárður hét maður upplenskur, góður drengur og ekki gamall.	Bard was-named a-man an-Upplander, good fellow and not old.	There was a man named Bard, an Upplander, a good fellow and not old.

The Tale of Halldor Snorrason II (Old Icelandic)

Old Icelandic	Literal	English
Hann var með Haraldi konungi í miklum kærleikum.	He was with Harald the-king in much dearly-loved.	He was with king Harald and much loved by him.
Voru þeir sessunautar, Bárður, Þórir og Halldór.	Were they sitting-together, Bard, Thorir and Halldor.	They were sitting together, Bard, Thorir, and Halldor.
Og eitt kveld er konungur gekk þar fyrir er þeir sátu og drukku, í því bili gaf Halldór upp hornið.	And one evening when the-king went there before were they sat and drinking, in that moment gave Halldor up the-drinking-horn.	And one evening when the king went before where they sat drinking, in that moment Halldor gave up the drinking horn.
Það var dýrshorn mikið og skyggt vel.	It was stag-horn huge and shaded well.	It was a stag horn, and very transparent.
Sá gjörla í gegnum að hann hafði drukkið vel til hálfs við Þóri	So completely in through that he had drunk well to half against Thorir	So completely through, that it could be seen that he had drunk more than half compared to Thorir
en honum gekk seint af að drekka.	who he went slowly of to drink.	who drank slowly.
Þá mælti konungur:	Then spoke the-king:	Then the king spoke:
"Seint er þó menn að reyna Halldór",	"Slow it-is though people to know Halldor",	"It is slow to get to know Halldor",
segir hann	said he	he said,
"er þú níðist á drykkju við gamalmenni og hleypur að vændiskonum um síðkveldum en fylgir eigi konungi þínum".	"that you down the drinks against old-men and run to prostitutes about late-evening while following not king yours".	"that you down the drinks against old men, and run to prostitutes late in the evening, while not following your king".
Halldór svarar engu en Bárður fann að honum mislíkaði umræða konungs.	Halldor answered none but Bard found that he misliked discussion the-king's.	Halldor did not answer, but Bard found that he disliked the king's words.
Fór Bárður þegar um myrgininn snemma á fund konungs.	Went Bard straight-away about morning early to find the-king.	Bard went straight away early in the morning to find the king.
"Þó ert þú nú árrisull Bárður",	"Though are you now early-riser Bard",	"Though you are an early riser, Bard",
segir konungur.	said the-king.	said the king.
"Em eg nú kominn",	"Am I now come",	"And I have now come",

The Tale of Halldor Snorrason II (Old Icelandic)

Old Icelandic	Literal	English
kvað Bárður,	said Bard,	said Bard,
"að ávíta yður herra.	"to warn you lord.	"to warn you lord.
Þér mæltuð illa og ómaklega í gærkveld til Halldórs vinar yðvars er þér kennduð honum að hann drykki sleitilega því að það var horn Þóris og hafði hann unnið og ætlaði að bera til skapkers ef eigi drykki Halldór fyrir hann.	You spoke ill and undeservedly about last-night to Halldor friend yours when you taught him that he drank unfairly because that it was horn Thorir's and had he deserved and intended to bear to large-vessel if not drink Halldor before him.	You spoke badly and unfairly last night to Halldor, your friend, when you told him that he drank unfairly, because it was Thorir's horn, and he deserved and intended to bear a large vessel if Halldor was not drinking before him.
Það er og hin mesta lygi er þér mæltuð að hann færi að léttlætiskonum en kjósa mundu menn að hann fylgdi þér fastara".	It is also the most lie that you spoke that he went to prostitutes than choose should people to him follow you more-fixedly".	It is also the greatest lie that you said he went to prostitutes, although people would rather that he followed you more closely".
Konungur svarar og lét að þeir mundu semja þetta mál með sér þá er þeir Halldór fyndust.	The-king answered and had that they would negotiate this matter with him then when they Halldor found.	The king answered that he would negotiate this matter with him when he met Halldor next.
Hittir Bárður Halldór og segir honum góð orð konungs til hans og kvað einsætt vera að hann léti sér einskis þykja um vert orðaframkast konungs og á Bárður hinn besta hlut að með þeim.	Found Bard Halldor and said he good words the-king's to him and said clearly being that he let himself nothing think about worthy outburst the-king's and this Bard the best part that between them.	Bard found Halldor and told him the king's good words, and that he should let himself think no worth of the king's outburst, and this is how Bard tried to put the best part between them.
Líður fram að jólum og er heldur fátt um með þeim konungi og Halldóri.	Passed from to Yule and was rather few about with them the-king and Halldor.	Time passed until Yule, and there was little between the king and Halldor.
Og er að jólum kemur þá eru víti upp sögð sem þar er tíska til.	And when that Yule came then they-were signalled up told as there was custom to.	And when Yule came, were they signalled up as was the custom.
Og einn morgun jólanna er breytt hringingum.	And one morning Yule was changed bell-ringing.	And one morning during Yule, the bell ringing was changed.

The Tale of Halldor Snorrason II (Old Icelandic)

Old Icelandic	Literal	English
Gáfu kertisveinar klokkurum fé til að hringja miklu fyrr en vant var og varð Halldór víttur og fjöldi annarra manna og settust í hálm um daginn og skyldu drekka vítin.	Gave court-men clocks payment for to ring much before than expected was and became Halldor reprimanded and many other people and sat in the-straw about the-day and should drink penalty.	The court men gave the bell ringers payment to ring the bells much before it was expected, and Halldor was reprimanded along with many other people, who had to sit on the floor in the straw and drink from the penalty horn.
Halldór situr í rúmi sínu og færa þeir honum eigi að síður vítið en hann lést eigi drekka mundu.	Halldor sat in seat his and brought they him none the less the-penalty and he had not drank would.	Halldor sat in his room, and they none the less brought him the penalty horn, and he would not drink from it.
Þeir segja þá konungi til.	They told then the-king about.	They told the king about it.
"Það mun eigi satt",	"That could not be-true",	"That could not be true",
segir konungur, "og mun hann við taka ef eg færi honum",	said the-king, "and should he with take if I bring him",	said the king,
tekur síðan vítishornið og gengur að Halldóri.	took then penalty-horn and went to Halldor.	"and he should take it if I bring it to him", and he took the penalty horn and went to Halldor.
Hann stendur upp í móti honum.	He stood up in meeting him.	He stood up upon meeting him.
Konungur biður hann drekka vítið.	The-king asked him to-drink the-penalty.	The king asked him to drink the penalty.
Halldór svarar:	Halldor answered:	Halldor answered:
"Eg þykist ekki víttur að heldur þó að þér setjið brögð til hringinga til þess eins að gera mönnum víti".	"I think not penalty to hold though that you set a-trick to bell-ringing to this alone to do people punishment".	"I don't think to hold the penalty, though you set a trick to the bell ringing only to punish people".
Konungur svarar:	The-king answered:	The king answered:
"Þú munt drekka skulu vítið þó eigi síður en aðrir menn".	"You must drink should penalty though not less than other people".	"You must drink the penalty no less than other people".
"Vera má það konungur",	"Be may that king",	"That may be, king",
segir Halldór,	said Halldor,	said Halldor,

The Tale of Halldor Snorrason II (Old Icelandic)

Old Icelandic	Literal	English
"að þú komir því á leið að eg drekki.	"that you come with to pass that I drink.	"that it shall come to pass that I drink.
En það kann eg þó segja þér að eigi mundi Sigurður sýr fá nauðgað Snorra goða til"	But that know I though say to-you that not would Sigurd Sow gave force Snorri the-priest to",	But I know to say to you that Sigurd Sow would not have forced Snorri the Priest to",
og vill seilast til hornsins sem hann gerir og drekkur af en konungur reiðist mjög og gengur til rúms síns.	and willed to-reach for the-horn as he went and drank of as the-king commanded much and went to room his.	and he reached for the penalty horn, and drank as much as the king commanded, and went to his room.
Og er kemur hinn átti dagur jóla var mönnum gefinn máli.	And when came the eighth day Yule were people given payment.	And when the eighth day of Yule came, people were given payment.
Það var kallað Haraldsslátta.	That was called Harald's-money.	That was called Harald's money.
Var meiri hlutur kopars, það besta kosti að væri helmings silfur.	Was greater part copper, that best benefit that had half silver.	It was for the greater part copper, and the best of it was half silver.
Og er Halldór tók málann hefir hann í möttulsskauti sínu silfrið og lítur á og sýnist eigi skírt málasilfrið, lýstur undir neðan annarri hendi og fer það allt í hálm niður.	And when Halldor took payment had he in cloak-lap his the-silver and looked at and seemed not pure silverware, struck under below other hand and went it all in straw below.	And when Halldor took the payment, he put the silver in the lap of his cloak, and it seemed not to be pure silver, he swept it down with his other hand and it all went onto the straw on the floor below.
Bárður mælti, kvað hann illa með fara:	Bard spoke, said he badly with went:	Bard spoke, and said that he was behaving badly:
"Mun konungur þykjast svívirður í og leitað á við hann um málagjöfina".	"Would the-king consider dishonourable of and consider to with him about payment".	"The king would consider this dishonourable, considering with him about payment".
"Ekki má nú fara að slíku",	"Not may now go that such",	"It may not go that way",
segir Halldór,	said Halldor,	said Halldor,
"litlu hættir nú til".	"little way now to".	"there is little to be done now".

3

Nú er frá því sagt að þeir búa skip sín eftir jólin.	Now was from of said that they prepared ships theirs after Yule.	Now it was said that they prepared their ships after Yule.

The Tale of Halldor Snorrason II (Old Icelandic)

Old Icelandic	Literal	English
Ætlar konungur suður fyrir land.	Intended the-king south along the-land.	The king intended to travel south along the land.
Og er konungur var mjög svo búinn þá bjóst Halldór ekki og mælti Bárður:	And when the-king was much so prepared then readied Halldor not and spoke Bard:	And when the king was so well prepared, Halldor did not prepare, and Bard said,
"Hví býstu eigi Halldór?"	"Why prepared not Halldor?"	"Why do you not prepare Halldor?"
"Eigi vil eg",	"Not wish I",	"I do not want to,"
segir hann,	said he,	he said,
"og ekki ætla eg að fara.	"and not intend I to travel.	"and I do not intend to travel.
Sé eg nú að konungur þokkar ekki mitt mál".	See I now that the-king favours not my measure".	I see now that the king does not like my case".
Bárður segir:	Bard said:	Bard said:
"Hann mun þó að vísu vilja að þú farir".	"He would though that certainly wish that you travel".	"Though he will want you to travel".
Fer Bárður síðan og hittir konung, segir honum að Halldór býst ekki:	Went Bard afterwards and found the-king, said he that Halldor prepares not	Afterwards Bad went and found the king, and he told him that Halldor had not prepared,
"Máttu svo ætla að vandskipaður mun þér vera stafninn í stað hans".	"May-you so suppose that difficult would you be the-prow in replace his".	"you may suppose that it would be difficult to replace him in the prow of the ship".
Konungur mælti:	The-king spoke:	The king spoke:
"Seg honum að eg ætla að hann skuli mér fylgja og þetta er ekki alugað, fæð sjá er með okkur er um hríð".	"Say to-him that I intend that he shall with-me follow and this is not resolved, sadness see that with us is about awhile".	"Tell him that I intend that he shall follow with me, and this is not resolved, this sadness that has been seen between us for a while".
Bárður hittir Halldór og lætur að konungur vilji einskis kostar láta hans þjónustu og það ræðst úr að Halldór fer og halda þeir konungur suður með landi.	Bard found Halldor and leave that the-king willed no choice losing his service and that commanded from that Halldor went and held they the-king south along the-land.	Bard found Halldor and put to him that the king gave no choice to lose his service, and that it was a command, and from that Halldor went and they held with the king south along the land.

The Tale of Halldor Snorrason II (Old Icelandic)

Old Icelandic	Literal	English
Og einhverja nótt er þeir sigldu þá mælti Halldór til þess er stýrði:	And one-such night that they sailed then spoke Halldor to that who steered:	And on one such night the sailed, Halldor spoke to the steersman,
"Lát ýkva",	"Let-it veer",	"let it veer",
segir hann.	said he.	he said.
Konungur mælti til stýrimanns:	The-king spoke to the-steersman:	The king spoke to the steersman,
"Halt svo fram", segir hann.	"Hold so forwards", said he.	"hold straight on", he said.
Halldór mælti öðru sinni:	Halldor spoke a-second his:	Halldor spoke a second time:
"Lát ýkva".	"Let-it veer".	"Let it veer".
Konungur segir enn á sömu leið.	The-king said then of-the-same way.	The king said the same way.
Halldór mælti:	Halldor spoke:	Halldor spoke:
"Beint stefnið þér skerið".	"Direction heading you-to a-rock".	"You are heading directly for a rock".
Og að því varð þeim.	And that accordingly became of-them.	And so it happened of them.
Því næst gekk undan skipinu undirhluturinn og varð þá að flytja til lands með öðrum skipum og síðan var skotið landtjald og bætt að skipinu.	Because next went under the-ship the-under-part and became then that carried to land with other ships and afterwards were launched land-tents and repaired the ship.	Because next the underneath of the ship went and it then had to be carried to the land with other ships, and then a land tent was set up, and they ship was repaired.
Við það vaknar Bárður er Halldór bindur húðfat sitt.	With that awoke Bard that Halldor tied-up hammock his.	With that Bard awoke to find Halldor tying up his hammock.
Bárður spyr hvað hann ætlist fyrir.	Bard asked what he intended for.	Bard asked what his intention was.
En Halldór kvaðst ætla á byrðing er lá skammt frá þeim	Then Halldor said intend to merchant-ship that lay short-distance from them	Then Halldor said that he intended to go to a merchant ship that lay a short distance from them,

The Tale of Halldor Snorrason II (Old Icelandic)

Old Icelandic	Literal	English
"og kann vera að nú leggi sundur reyki vora og er þetta fullreynt.	"and can it-be that now lay separate smoke going and is that fully-tested.	"and it may be that now our smoke is falling apart, and it has been fully tried".
Og eigi vil eg að konungur spilli oftar skipum sínum eða öðrum gersemum mér til svívirðingar og að mér beri þá verr en áður".	And not wish I the king spoil more-often ships his or other treasure me to disgrace and that me bear then worse than before".	And I do not want the king to spoil his ships or other treasures more often to disgrace me, and treat me then worse than before".
"Bíð enn",	"Wait still",	"Still, wait",
segir Bárður,	said Bard,	said Bard,
"eg vil enn hitta konung".	"I will but find the-king".	"I will just find the king".
Og er hann kemur mælti konungur:	And when he came spoke-to the-king:	And when he came the king spoke:
"Snemma ertu á fótum Bárður".	"Soon are-you about feed Bard".	"You are early on your feet, Bard".
"Svo er nú þörf herra.	"So is now needed lord.	"So it is needed now, lord.
Halldór er í brautbúnaði og þykir þú óvingjarnlega til sín gert hafa og er nokkuð vant að gæta til með ykkur.	Halldor is to away-prepared and thinks you unfriendly to him done have and is something difficult that take-care to with you-two.	Halldor is preparing to go away and thinks that you have been unfriendly towards him, and it's difficult to keep the peace between you two.
Ætlar hann nú í brott og ráðast til skips og fara út til Íslands með reiði og fer þá ómaklega ykkar skilnaður.	Intends he now to away and appoint to a-ship and travel out to Iceland with anger and goes then undeservedly with-you parting.	He now intends to go away and join a ship and travel to Iceland in anger, and that's not a proper way for you to part.
Og það hygg eg að varla fáir þú þér annan mann jafntraustan honum".	And it think I that hardly few you to-you another man equally-trustworthy as-him".	And I think that you will hardly find another man as equally trustworthy as him".
Konungur lét að þeir mundu enn sættast og kvað sér ekki mundu að þessu þykja.	The-king had it they would still reconcile and said himself not would of this think.	The king said that they would still reconcile and said he would not think about it.
Bárður hittir Halldór og segir honum vingjarnleg orð konungs.	Bard found Halldor and told him friendly words the-king's.	Bard found Halldor and told him the king's friendly words.
Halldór svarar:	Halldor answered:	Halldor answered:

The Tale of Halldor Snorrason II (Old Icelandic)

Old Icelandic	Literal	English
"Til hvers skal eg honum þjóna lengur? Þatgi að eg fái mála minn falslaust".	"To how shall I him serve longer? That-not that I get matter mine without-fraud".	"Why should I serve him any longer? Let me have my case without fraud".
Bárður mælti:	Bard spoke:	Bard said,
"Get eigi þess.	"Get not like-this.	"Don't talk like this.
Vel máttu þér það líka láta er lendra manna synir hafa og ekki fórstu að því með vægð næsta sinni er þú slóst niður í hálm silfrinu og ónýttir.	Well may you that like allow what is-paid people sons have and not went-you that therefore with grace next-to yourself when you struck down into the-straw the-silver and un-used.	Well, you might as well have what the sons of the land have, and you did not do it mercifully the next time you struck the silver down in the straw and wasted it.
Og máttu víst vita að konungi þykir það svívirðlega til sín gert".	And may certainly know that the-king thought that dishonourable to him done".	And you must know that the king considers it disgraceful to do so".
Halldór svarar:	Halldor answered:	Halldor answered:
"Eigi má eg það vita að neitt sinn hafi jafnmjög logist í um fylgdina mína sem í málagjöfina konungs".	"Not may I that certainly that nothing he has equally-much cheated in about following mine as in payment the-king's".	"I do not know of having cheated him in my following as much as he has cheated me with the king's payment".
"Satt mun það vera",	"True would that be",	"That may be true",
segir Bárður,	said Bard,	said Bard,
"biðleika, enn vil eg hitta konung".	"wait, then will I find the-king".	"wait, then I will find the king".
Og svo gerði hann.	And so did he.	And he did so.
Og er Bárður hitti konung mælti hann:	And when Bard found the-king spoke he:	And when Bard found the king, he spoke:
"Fá Halldóri mála sinn skíran því að verður er hann að hafa".	"Get Halldor payment his cleared because that worth is he to have".	"Get Halldor his payment cleared, because he is worth having".
Konungur svarar:	The-king answered:	The king answered:

The Tale of Halldor Snorrason II (Old Icelandic)

Old Icelandic	Literal	English
"Líst þér eigi nokkur svo djörfung í að krefja Halldóri annars mála en taka lendra manna synir og með slíkri svívirðing sem hann fór með málanum næstum?"	"Appears to-you not something so bold that to demand Halldor another payment than take payment people's sons and with such disgrace as he did with payment before?"	"Does it not appear you you somewhat bold to demand Halldor a payment other than people's sons, and with such disgrace as he did with his last payment?"
Bárður svarar:	Bard answered:	Bard answered:
"Á hitt er að líta herra er miklu er meira vert, drengskap hans og vináttu ykkar er lengi hefir góð verið og þar með stórmennsku þína.	"To find that to look lord that much is more worth, honour his and friendship yours that long has good been and there with greatness yours.	"The other thing is to look, lord, at who is much more valuable, his boyhood and your friendship that has been good for a long time and thus your greatness.
Og veistu skap Halldórs og stirðlæti og er það þinn vegur að gera honum sóma".	And know-you mood Halldor's and hard-temper and that it your way that to-do him honour".	And we know Halldór's mood and stiffness, and it's your way to do him honor".
Konungur mælti:	The-king spoke:	The king said:
"Fáið honum silfrið".	"Give him the-silver".	"Give him the silver".
Var nú svo gert.	Was now so done.	Now this was done.
Kemur Bárður til Halldórs og færir honum tólf aura brennda og mælti:	Came Bard to Halldor and brought him twelve ounces burnt and spoke:	Bard came to Halldor and brought him twelve ounces of refined silver and spoke:
"Sérð þú eigi að þú hefir slíkt er þú brekar af konungi og hann vill að þú hafir slíkt af honum sem þú þykist þurfa?"	"See you not that you have such that you keep-asking of the-king and he wishes that you have such of him as you think you-need?"	"Do you not see that you ask of the king, and he wishes to to have what you think you need, if only you ask for it?"
Halldór svarar:	Halldor answered:	Halldor answeed:
"Eigi skal eg þó oftar vera á konungsskipinu og ef hann vill hafa mitt föruneyti lengur þá vil eg hafa skip til stjórnar og eignast það".	"Not shall I though frequent be in the-king's-ship and if he wishes to-have my companionship longer then wish I to-have ship to steer and own it".	"I shall not be on the king's ship more often, and if he wishes to have me in his company any longer, then I wish to have my own ship to steer".
Bárður svarar:	Bard answered:	Bard answered:

The Tale of Halldor Snorrason II (Old Icelandic)

Old Icelandic	Literal	English
"Það samir eigi að lendir menn láti skip sín fyrir þér og ertu of framgjarn".	"It so not to landed men have ships theirs for you and are-you over ambitious".	"It is not so that landed man give up their ships for you, and you are over-ambitious".
Halldór kvaðst eigi fara mundu ellegar.	Halldor said not travelling would otherwise.	Halldor said that he would not travel otherwise.
Bárður segir konungi hvers beitt er af Halldórs hendi	Bard told the-king what asked had of Halldor's hand	Bard told the king what Halldor had asked for
"og ef hásetar þess skips eru jafntraustir sem stýrimaður þá mun vel hlýða".	"and if sailors these ships were equally-trustworthy as steersman then would well listen-to".	"and if the sailors of these ships were equally trustworthy as the steersman then they would listen to him well".
Konungur mælti:	The-king spoke:	The king said,
"Þótt þetta þyki framarla mælt vera þá skal þó af nakkvað gera".	"Though this think forward spoken is then shall though of something do".	"Though this be thought to be far-fetched, something must be done".
Sveinn úr Lyrgju, lendur maður, stýrði skipi.	Fellow from Lyrgja, land man, steered a-ship.	Svein from Lyrgja, a landed man, steered a ship.
Konungur lét hann kalla á mál við sig.	The-king had him called and conversed with him.	The king had him called and discussed with him.
"Þannug er farið",	"That-way is travelled",	"It is so",
segir konungur,	said the-king,	said the king,
"sem þú veist að þú ert maður stórættaður.	"that you know that you are a-man of-high-family.	"that you know that you are a man of great family.
Vil eg fyrir því að þú sért á mínu skipi en eg mun þar fá annan mann til skipstjórnar.	Wish I for therefore that you be on my ship but I should there get another man to ship-steer.	I want you to be on my ship, but I will get another man to captain it.
Þú ert maður viskur og vil eg einkum hafa þig við ráð mín".	You are a-man wise and wish I especially have you with advise me".	You are a man of wisdom and I especially want you with my advice".
Hann segir:	He said:	He said:
"Meir hefir þú aðra menn haft við þínar ráðagerðir hér til og til þess em eg lítt fær eða hverjum er þá skipið ætlað?"	"More have you other men had with you advice-giving here to and to this am I little accomplished but who is then ship intended?"	"You have had other men with your advice so far and to the point that I can do little, but who is the ship intended for?"

The Tale of Halldor Snorrason II (Old Icelandic)

Old Icelandic	Literal	English
"Halldór Snorrason skal hafa",	"Halldor Snorrason shall have",	"Halldor Snorrason shall have it",
segir konungur.	said the-king.	said the king.
Sveinn segir:	The-fellow said:	Sveinn said:
"Eigi kom mér það í hug að þú mundir íslenskan mann til þess velja en taka mig frá skipstjórn".	"Not came to-me that to think that you would Icelander man to this will then take me from ship-steering".	"It never occurred to me that you would choose an Icelander for that, still take me from the captaincy".
Konungur mælti:	The-king spoke:	The king said,
"Hans ætt er eigi verri á Íslandi en þín hér í Noregi og eigi hefir enn alllangt síðan liðið er þeir voru norrænir er nú byggja Ísland".	"His ancestry is not worse as Icelander but your forces in Norway and not has-been but all-long since passed that they were Norwegians that now settle Iceland".	"His family is no worse in Iceland than yours here in Norway, and it has not been long since they were Norwegians who now inhabit Iceland".
Nú fer það fram sem konungur vill að Halldór tekur við skipi og fóru síðan austur til Óslóar, tóku þar veislur.	Now went that from as the-king wished that Halldor took with ship and travelled afterwards east to Oslo, took there feasts.	Now it went as the king wished, that Halldor took the ship, and travelled afterwards east to Oslo, where they took to feasting.

4

Það er sagt einnhvern dag er þeir konungur sátu við drykkju og var Halldór þar í konungsstofunni að sveinar hans komu þar, þeir er skipið skyldu varðveita, og voru allir votir og sögðu að þeir Sveinn höfðu tekið skipið en rekið þá á kaf.	It was said one-such day that there the-king sat with drinking and was Halldor there in the-king's-chambers the fellows his came there, they were ship should guard-over, and were all wet and said that they Svein had taken the-ship and thrown them to overboard.	It was said that one day the king and Halldor sat drinking in the king's chambers, and in came the men who were watching over his ship came in, and they were all wet, and they said that Svein had taken the ship and thrown them overboard.
Halldór stóð upp og gekk fyrir konung og spurði hvort hann skyldi eiga skipið og haldast það er konungur hafði mælt.	Halldor stood up and went before the-king and asked how he should own the-ship and hold that which the-king had spoken-of.	Halldor stood up and went before the king and asked whether he would own the ship as the king had promised.

The Tale of Halldor Snorrason II (Old Icelandic)

Old Icelandic	Literal	English
Konungur svarar og kvað það að vísu haldast skyldu, kvaddi til síðan hirðina að þeir skyldu taka sex skip og fara með Halldóri og hafa þrenna skipun á hverju.	The-king answered and said that it certainly hold should, called to since guardsmen that they should take six ships and travel with Halldor and have treble crew on each.	The king answered and said that he would keep his promise, and then called to the guardsmen that they should take six ships, travelling with a treble crew on each.
Þeir snúa nú eftir þeim Sveini og lætur hann eltast að landi og þegar hljóp Sveinn á land upp en þeir Halldór tóku skipið og fóru til konungs.	They turned now after they Svein and let he chased to land and there ran Svein on-the land up and there Halldor took the-ship and went to the-king.	They now turned after Svein and gave him chase ashore, and there Svein ran ashore, but Halldor took the ship and went to the king.
Og er veislum var lokið fer konungur norður með landi og til Þrándheims er á líður sumarið.	And when the-feasts were ended went the-king north along the-land and to Trondheim where then passed summer.	And when the feasts were over, the king went north along the land, and to Trondheim, when the summer had passed.
Sveinn úr Lyrgju sendi orð konungi að hann vill gefa upp allt málið og leggja á konungs vald að hann skipi með þeim Halldóri sem hann vill og vildi þó helst kaupa skipið ef konungi líkaði.	Svein from Lyrgja sent word to-the-king that he wished to-give up all matter and grant to the-king power that he ship with them Halldor as he wished and wished though rather purchase the-ship if the-king liked.	Svein of Lyrgja sent word to the king that he wished to give up the whole matter and put it in the king's power, that the ship would be with Halldor as he wished, but would prefer to purchase the ship if it was to the king's liking.
Og nú er konungur sér það að Sveinn skýtur öllu máli undir hans dóm þá vill hann nú svo til bregða er báðum mætti líka, falar skipið að Halldóri og vill að hann hafi verð sæmilegt en Sveinn hafi skip og kaupir konungur skip og á Halldór við hann um verð og gelst allt upp nema hálf mörk gulls stendur eftir.	And now as the-king saw that of Svein launched all matter under his deeming then wished he now so to foreclose that both may like, bargain ship that Halldor and wished that he had worth the-same that Svein had ship and bought the-king the-ship and that Halldor with him about worth and paid all up except half a-mark gold stood behind.	And now the king saw that Svein gave the whole matter up to his judgement, that he now wished to settle the matter to the liking of both parties. The ship was purchased from Halldor and he wished that he had a price the same worth as Svein to have the ship, and the king bought the ship from Halldor, and with him was the price and gold all paid except for half a gold mark left behind.
Heimtir Halldór lítt enda galst það ekki og fer svo fram um veturinn.	Got Halldor little end payment that not and went so forward about winter.	Halldor did not demand the closure of the payment, and so things went on over the winter.

The Tale of Halldor Snorrason II (Old Icelandic)

Old Icelandic	Literal	English
Og er vora tók segir Halldór konungi að hann vill til Íslands um sumarið og kvað sér vel koma að þá gyldist það sem eftir var skipverðsins.	And as spring took said Halldor to-the-king that he wished to Iceland about summer and said he well come that then repay that which remained was ship's-worth.	And as spring came, Halldor said to the king that he wished to travel to Iceland in the summer, and it would be well if he could repay the remainder of the ship's worth.
En konungur fer heldur undan um gjaldið og þykir ekki betur er hann heimtir en ekki bannar hann Halldóri útferð og býr hann skip sitt um vorið í ánni Nið og leggur út síðan við Bröttueyri.	But the-king went rather from-under about the-payment and seemed not better that he got then not ban him Halldor out-travelling and prepared he ship his about spring in the-river Nid and laid out afterwards with Bratteyar.	But the king escaped the payment, and thought not better that he demanded, but did not ban Halldor from travelling, and he prepared his ship around spring in the river Nid, nd laid out afterwards at Bratteyar.
Og er þeir voru albúnir og byrvænlegt var þá gengur Halldór upp í bæinn með nokkura menn síð um aftan.	And when they were all-prepared and promising-wind were then going Halldor up out-of town with some men later about evening.	And then they were all prepared and with a promising wind, then Halldor went up in the town with some men later in the evening.
Hann var með vopnum.	He was with weapons.	He was armed with weapons.
Gengu þar til er þau konungur og drottning sváfu.	Went they to where then the-king and the-queen slept.	They then went to where the king and queen slept.
Förunautar hans stóðu úti undir loftinu en hann gengur inn með vopnum sínum og verður glymur og skark af honum og vakna þau konungur við og spyr konungur hver þar brjótist að þeim um nætur.	Companions his stood outside under the-air then he went inside with weapons his and came echo and noise of him and awoke then the-king with and asked the-king who there breaking in-on them about night.	His companions stood outside, and he went inside and made a noise with his weapons which echoed and woke the king, who asked who was breaking in on them in the night.
"Hér er Halldór kominn og búinn til hafs og kominn á byr og er nú ráð að gjalda féið".	"Here is Halldor come and prepared to sea and coming is fair-wind and is now the-matter to pay wealth".	"Halldor is here, prepared to go to sea, and a fair wind is coming, and now is the matter to settle the payment".
"Ekki má það nú svo skjótt",	"Not may that now so swiftly",	"Now that may not be done so swiftly",
segir konungur,	said the-king,	said the king,
"og munum vér greiða fé á morgun".	"and should we assist payment in the-morning".	"and we shall assist with the payment in the morning".

The Tale of Halldor Snorrason II (Old Icelandic)

Old Icelandic	Literal	English
"Nú vil eg þegar hafa",	"Now wish I straightaway have",	"Now I wish to have it straight away",
segir Halldór,	said Halldor,	said Halldor,
"og munkat eg nú erindlaust fara.	"and shall I now errand-without go.	"and I shall not go without it.
Kann eg og skap þitt og veit eg hversu þér mun líka þessi för mín og fjárheimta hvegi sem þú lætur nú.	Know I also mood yours and know I how-so you shall like this going mine and money-insisting which as you behave now.	I also know your mood, and I know how you would like me to go, and am demanding the money which you will leave now.
Mun eg lítt trúa þér héðan frá enda er ósýnt að við finnumst svo vilgis oft að mitt sé vænna og skal nú neyta þess og sé eg að drottning hefir hring á hendi því hófi mikinn.	Shall I little believe you hence from conclude as unseen that with found so very often that mine so expected and shall now use this and see I that the-queen has a-ring on hand therefore modest greatly.	I shall not trust you again from now on, it is not clear how often we find that I have the advantage, so I shall now take advantage of this, and I see that the queen has a ring on her hand, which is accordingly greatly modest.
Fá mér þann".	Give me it".	Give it to me".
Konungur svarar:	The-king answered:	The king answered:
"Þá verðum við fara eftir skálum og vega hringinn".	"Then worth with going after bowl and weigh the-ring".	"Then it is worth going after the bowls and weighing the ring".
"Ekki þarf þess",	"Not needed is-this",	"That is not needed",
segir Halldór,	said Halldor,	said Halldor,
"tek eg hann fyrir hlut minn enda muntu nú ekki prettunum við koma að sinni og sel fram títt".	"take I it for share mine and should now not trick with coming this time and flip forward immediately".	"I will take it for my share, and you shall not try and trick me this time, and give it forward immediately".
Drottning mælti:	The-queen spoke:	The queen spoke:
		"Give him the ring, as he asks".
"Sérð þú eigi",	"See you not",	"Do you not see",
segir hún,	said she,	she said,

The Tale of Halldor Snorrason II (Old Icelandic)

Old Icelandic	Literal	English
"að hann stendur yfir þér uppi með víghug?"	"that he stands over you up with killing-mind?"	"that he stands over you with a mind to kill?"
Tekur síðan hringinn og fær Halldóri.	Took then the-ring and brought Halldor.	She then took the ring and brought it to Halldor.
Hann tekur við og þakkar þeim báðum gjaldið og biður þau vel lifa	He took with and thanked them both payment and bid them well life	He took it and thanked them both for the payment and bid them a good life
"og munum vér nú skilja".	"and shall we now separate".	"and we shall now separate".
Gengur nú út og mælti við förunauta sína, biður þá hlaupa sem tíðast til skipsins	Went now out and spoke with companions his, asked them to-run as swiftly to ship	He now went out and spoke with his companions, asking them to run swiftly to the ship
"því að ófús em eg að dveljast lengi í bænum".	"because that unwilling am I to stay long in this-town".	because I am not willing to stay long in this town.
Þeir gera svo, koma á skipið og þegar vinda sumir upp segl, sumir eru að báti, sumir heimta upp akkeri og bergst hver sem má.	They did so, came to the-ship and straightaway wind some upped the-sails, some were at the-tow-boat, some drew up the-anchor and best each as may.	They did so, and came to the ship and straight away wind came and they upped the sails, some were at the tow boat, and some drew up the anchor, each doing the best they could.
Og er þeir sigldu út skorti eigi hornblástur í bænum og það sáu þeir síðast að þrjú langskip voru á floti og lögðu eftir þeim en þó ber þá undan og í haf.	And when they sailed out shortly one horn-blast from the-city and this saw they the-last that three longships were in floating and laid after them but though carried then under and to sea.	And shortly after they had sailed out, there was a horn blast from the city, and the last thing they saw were three longships floating and laid after them, though then they were carried out to sea.
Skilur þar með þeim og byrjaði Halldóri vel út til Íslands en konungsmenn hurfu aftur er þeir sáu er Halldór bar undan og í haf út.	Separated there with them and began Halldor well out to Iceland but the-kings-men disappeared after when they saw that Halldor bore away-from and to sea out-of.	They separated with them there and Halldor started well out to Iceland, but the king's men turned bak when they saw that Halldor was carried away out to sea.

5

Halldór Snorrason var mikill maður vexti og fríður sýnum, allra manna styrkastur og vopndjarfastur.	Halldor Snorrason was a-great man well-built and handsome in-appearance, of-all men strongest and weapons-bold.	Halldor Snorrason was a great man, well built, and handsome in appearance, the strongest of all men, and the best with weapons.

The Tale of Halldor Snorrason II (Old Icelandic)

Old Icelandic	Literal	English
Það vitni bar Haraldur konungur Halldóri að hann hefði verið með honum allra manna svo að síst brygði við voveiflega hluti hvort sem að höndum bar mannháska eða fagnaðartíðindi þá var hann hvorki að glaðari né óglaðari.	That testimony gave Harald the-king Halldor that he had been with him all men so that least reacted with unexpected part which was at hand bringing human-danger or good-news then was he neither to gladness nor un-gladness.	King Harald gave a testimony of Halldor that of all the men he had been with, that he reacted least to an unexpected lot, which with hand carried danger or good news, he was neither happy nor unhappy.
Eigi neytti hann matar eða drakk eða svaf meira né minna en vandi hans var til hvort sem hann mætti blíðu eða stríðu.	Not consumed he food or drank or slept more nor less than custom his was to each as he might joyful or stressful.	He did not eat or drink or sleep more not less than his custom, whether he was happy or stressful.
Halldór var maður fámæltur, stuttorður, bermæltur, stygglyndur og ómjúkur, kappgjarn í öllum hlutum við hvern sem hann átti um.	Halldor was a-man of-few-words, short-worded, outspoken, quick-tempered and un-bending, self-willed in all things against which as he had about.	Halldor was a man of few words, short, outspoken, quick tempered and ungiving, self-willed about everything that he had.
En það kom illa við Harald konung er hann hafði nóga aðra þjónustumenn.	But this came ill with Harald the-king as he had enough other servants.	But this came badly against king Harald as he had enough other servants.
Komu þeir því lítt lyndi saman síðan Haraldur varð konungur í Noregi.	Came they therefore little temper together since Harald was king of Norway.	They did not get along well since Haraldur became king of Norway.
En er Halldór kom til Íslands gerði hann bú í Hjarðarholti.	But when Halldor came to Iceland did he settle at Hjardarholt.	But when Halldór came to Iceland he made an estate in Hjarðarholt.
Nokkurum sumrum síðar sendi Haraldur konungur orð Halldóri Snorrasyni að hann skyldi ráðast enn til hans og lét að eigi skyldi verið hafa hans virðing meiri en þá ef hann vildi farið hafa og engan mann skyldi hann hærra setja í Noregi ótiginn ef hann vildi þetta boð þekkjast.	Some summers later sent Harald the-king word-to Halldor Snorrason that he should arrange then to him and had that not should be having his honour more than then if he willed travel to-sea and only man should he highest sit in Norway un-high-born if he wished this invitation accept.	A few summers later, King Harald sent word to Halldor Snorrason that he should appoint him again, and put that his respect would not be greater than that if he wished to travel to sea, and that no man should sit higher than him in Norway if he wished to accept this invitation.
Halldór svarar svo er honum komu þessi orð:	Halldor answered so as to-him came these words:	Halldor answered when these words came to him:
"Ekki mun eg fara á fund Haralds konungs héðan af.	"Not should I travel to meet Harald the-king from-here of.	"I will not go to King Harald from now on.

The Tale of Halldor Snorrason II (Old Icelandic)

Old Icelandic	Literal	English
Mun nú hafa hvor okkar það sem fengið hefir.	Should now have each ours that which got we-have.	Each of us will now have what he has received.
Mér er kunnigt skaplyndi hans.	To-me it-is known mood-temper his.	His mood is known to me.
Veit eg gjörla að hann mundi það efna sem hann hét að setja engan mann hærra í Noregi en mig ef eg kæmi á hans fund því að hann mundi mig láta festa á hinn hæsta gálga ef hann mætti ráða".	Know I completely that he should that carry-out which he promised to sit no man higher in Norway but me if I come to him to-meet therefore that he should me have fasten to the highest gallows if he might prevail".	I know very well that he would do what he promised to put no man higher in Norway than me if I came to meet him, for he would have me fastened to the highest gallows if he could rule it".
Og er á leið mjög ævi Haralds konungs þá er sagt að hann sendi Halldóri orð til að hann skyldi senda honum melrakkabelgi, vildi gera láta af þeim yfir rekkju sína því að konungur þóttist þá þurfa hlýs.	And when had passed much age Harald the-king then that is-said that he sent Halldor word to that he should send him arctic-fox-furs, wished get have of them over bed his because that the-king thought then needed warmth.	And when king Harald became much passed with age, it is said that he sent word to Halldor that he should send him arctic fox furs, he wanted to let them go over his bed because the king thought he needed warmth.
Og er Halldóri kom sjá orðsending konungs þá er sagt að hann skyti því orði við í fyrstu:	And as Halldor came so word-sending the-king then was said that he shot accordingly word against at first:	And when Halldor came to see the king's message, it is said that he replied first:
"Eldist árgalinn nú",	"Old-is the-cockerel now",	"The yearling is getting old now",
sagði hann en sendi honum belgi.	said he but sent him furs.	he said, but sent him arctic fox furs.
En ekki fundust þeir sjálfir síðan er þeir skildust í Þrándheimi þó að þá yrði nokkuð með stytti því sinni.	But not met they themselves afterwards that the separated at Trondheim though that then became somewhat with short of themselves.	But they did not meet each other since they had separated at Trondheim, though they had taken short leave with each other.
Bjó hann í Hjarðarholti til elli og varð maður gamall.	Farmed he in Hjardarholt until old-age and became a-man old.	He lived in Hjarðarholt until old age and became an old man.

Word List (Old Icelandic to English)

Word List (Old Icelandic to English)

Old Icelandic	English

A, a

að	at, in, in-on, it, of, that, the, this, to
aðkoma	to-come
aðra	other
aðrir	other
af	from, from, of, of
aftan	evening
aftna	evening
aftur	after, back
aga	turbulence
akkeri	the-anchor
albúnir	all-prepared
allir	all, all
alllangt	all-long
allra	all, of-all
allt	all, all
alugað	resolved
annan	another, another, the-next
annarra	other
annarri	other
annars	another, another
atgang	access
aura	ounces
austan	east
austur	east, east

Á, á

á	about, and, as, at, had, in, is, of, on, on-the, that, the, then, this, to
áður	before, other
áhöfnina	crew
áhyggjusvip	worried-face
ákallsi	calling
álaga	stress
ánni	the-river
árgalinn	the-cockerel
árrisull	early-riser

Old Icelandic	English
átti	eighth, had
ávíta	warn

Æ, æ

ætla	intend, suppose
ætlað	intended
ætlaði	intended
ætlar	intended, intends
ætlist	intended
ætt	ancestry
ævi	age

B, b

báðu	bid
báðum	both
bæði	both
bæinn	town
bæjarmenn	townspeople
bænum	the-city, the-town, this-town
bætt	repaired
bann	a-ban
bannar	ban
bar	bore, bringing, gave
Bárður	Bard (name)
báti	the-tow-boat
beiða	asked
beint	direction
beitt	asked
belgi	furs
ber	bears, carried
bera	bear
bergst	best
beri	bear
bermæltur	outspoken
best	best
besta	best
betra	better
betur	better
bíð	wait

Word List (Old Icelandic to English)

Old Icelandic	English
bíða	wait
biðleika	wait
biður	asked, bid
bili	moment
bindur	tied-up
bjó	farmed, settled
bjóst	readied
bjuggu	preparations
blásið	trumpet-blown
blíðast	happiest
blíðlegur	happily
blíðu	joyful
boð	invitation
brautbúnaði	away-prepared
bregða	foreclose
brekar	keep-asking
brennda	burnt
breytt	changed
brjótist	breaking
brögð	a-trick
brotin	violated
brott	away
Bröttueyri	Bratteyar (place)
brygði	reacted
bú	settle
búa	prepared
búið	prepared
búinn	prepared
búnaðinn	preparations
byggja	settle
byr	fair-wind
býr	prepared
byrðing	merchant-ship
byrjaði	began
byrvænlegt	promising-wind
býst	prepares
býstu	prepared

D, d

Old Icelandic	English
dag	day
daginn	the-day
dagur	day
danaher	Danish-forces
danakonungur	king-of-Denmark
Danmerkur	Denmark (place)
djörfung	bold
dögum	days
dóm	deeming
drakk	drank
drekk	drink
drekka	drank, drink, to-drink
drekki	drink
drekkur	drank
drengskap	honour
drengur	fellow
drjúgum	greatly
drottning	the-queen
drukkið	drunk
drukku	drinking
drykki	drank, drink
drykkju	drinking, drinks
dveljast	stay
dýrshorn	stag-horn

E, e

Old Icelandic	English
eða	but, or
ef	if
efna	carry-out
eftir	after, behind, remained, remaining
eg	I, I-am
eiga	own
eigi	none, not, one
eignast	own
einhverja	one-such
einkum	especially
einn	one
einnhvern	one-such
eins	alone
einsætt	clearly
einskis	no, nothing
eitt	one
ekki	not
eldist	old-is
ellegar	otherwise
elli	old-age
eltast	chased
em	am

Word List (Old Icelandic to English)

Old Icelandic	English
en	and, as, But, than, that, then, while, who
enda	and, conclude, end
enga	no
engan	no, only
engi	none
engis	nothing
Englandsfari	England-Traveller (name)
engu	none
enn	but, still, then, was
er	am, as, had, have, is, it-is, that, was, were, what, when, where, which, who
erindlaust	errand-without
ert	are
ertu	are-you
eru	are, there-are, they, they-were, were

F, f

Old Icelandic	English
fá	gave, get, give, pay
faðir	father
fæ	give
fæð	sadness
fær	accomplished, brought, travel
færa	brought
færi	bring, travel, went
færið	bring
færir	brought
fært	bringing
fagnaðartíðindi	good-news
fái	get
fáið	give
fáir	few
falar	bargain
falslaust	without-fraud
fám	a-few
fámæltur	of-few-words
fann	found
fara	go, going, travel, travelling, went
fararefni	travel-goods
fari	travel
farið	travel, travelled
farir	travel
fars	travel
fastara	more-fixedly
fátt	few
fé	payment
fegnir	celebrated
féið	wealth
fengi	found
fengið	got
fénu	wealth
fer	goes, went
ferðir	travel
festa	fasten
finnumst	found
fjárheimta	money-insisting
fjöldi	many
fleiri	more
floti	floating
flytja	carried
föður	father
fór	did, travelled, went
för	going
fórstu	went-you
förunauta	companions
förunautar	companions
föruneyti	companionship
fótum	feed
frá	from
fram	forward, forwards, from
framarla	forward
framgjarn	ambitious
fríður	handsome
fullreynt	fully-tested
fund	find, meet, to-meet
fundust	met
fylgdi	follow
fylgdina	following
fylgir	following
fylgja	follow
fyndust	found
fyrir	along, before, for
fyrr	before
fyrra	the-first

Word List (Old Icelandic to English)

Old Icelandic	English	*Old Icelandic*	English
fyrsta	first	*gulls*	gold
fyrstu	first	*gyldist*	repay
fýsir	desire		

G, g

H, h

Old Icelandic	English
gæði	good-things
gærkveld	last-night
gæta	take-care
gaf	gave
gáfu	gave
gáfuð	gave
gálga	gallows
galst	payment
gamall	old
gamalmenni	old-men
ganga	go
Garðaríki	Gardariki (place)
gefa	give, to-give
gefinn	given
gegnum	through
gekk	went
gelst	paid
gengu	went
gengur	going, went
gera	did, do, get, to-do
gerði	did
gerir	went
gerist	be
gersemar	treasure, treasures
gersemum	treasure
gert	done
get	get
gjalda	pay
gjaldið	payment, the-payment
gjöfin	gift
gjöfina	the-gift
gjörla	completely
glaðari	gladness
glymur	echo
góð	good
goða	the-priest
góður	good
greiða	assist

Old Icelandic	English
hægt	possible
hærra	higher, highest
hæsta	highest
hættir	way
haf	sea
hafa	had, have, having, to-have, to-sea
hafði	had
hafi	had, has
hafið	have
hafir	have
hafs	sea
haft	had
halda	held, to-hold
haldast	hold
hálf	half
Halldór	Halldor (name)
Halldóri	Halldor (name)
Halldórs	Halldor (name), Halldor's (name)
hálm	straw, the-straw
halt	hold
haltu	hold-you
hann	he, him, it
hans	him, his
Harald	Harald (name)
Haraldi	Harald (name)
Haralds	Harald (name)
Haraldsslátta	Harald's-money (name)
Haraldur	Harald (name)
háseta	crew, sailors
hásetar	sailors
hásetum	sailors
háski	dangers
hausti	the-autumn
héðan	from-here, hence
hefði	had
hefi	have

Word List (Old Icelandic to English)

Old Icelandic	English
hefir	had, has, has-been, have, we-have
heilastan	thanks
heimfúsari	home-longing
heimta	drew
heimtir	got
heldur	hold, rather
helmings	half
helst	rather
helsti	rather
hendi	hand
hér	forces, here
herra	lord
hét	named, promised, was-named
heyra	hear
heyrðuð	heard
heyrum	hear
hin	the
hinn	the
hirðar	court
hirðina	guardsmen
hirðinni	court
hirðmaður	court-man
hirðsiðum	king's-men-customs
hitt	find
hitta	find
hitti	found
hittir	found
Hjarðarholti	Hjardarholt (place)
hlaupa	to-run
hleypur	run
hljóp	ran
hlut	part, share
hluti	part, things
hlutum	things
hlutur	part
hlýða	listen-to
hlýs	warmth
höfðu	had
hófi	modest
höndum	hand
honum	as-him, he, him, to-him
horn	horn
hornblástur	horn-blast
hornið	the-drinking-horn
hornsins	the-horn
hríð	awhile
hring	a-ring
hringinga	bell-ringing
hringingum	bell-ringing
hringinn	the-ring
hringja	ring
húðfat	hammock
hug	think
hún	she
hurfu	disappeared
hús	house
hvað	what
hvegi	which
hver	each, where, who
hverju	each
hverjum	who
hvern	which
hvers	how, what
hversu	how-so
hvert	each
hví	why
hvor	each
hvorki	neither
hvort	each, how, which
hygg	think

I, i

Old Icelandic	English
illa	badly, ill
inn	inside

Í, í

Old Icelandic	English
í	about, at, from, in, into, of, out-of, that, to, will, with
ígangsklæði	travelling-clothes
Ísland	Iceland (place)
Íslandi	Icelander (name)
Íslands	Iceland (place)
íslenskan	Icelander

Word List (Old Icelandic to English)

Old Icelandic	English

J, j

Old Icelandic	English
jafnfylginn	equally-following
jafnmjög	equally-much
jafntraustan	equally-trustworthy
jafntraustir	equally-trustworthy
jóla	Yule (name)
jólanna	Yule (name)
jólin	Yule (name)
Jólum	Yule (name)

K, k

Old Icelandic	English
kæmi	come
kærleikum	dearly-loved
kaf	overboard
kalla	called
kallað	called
kann	can, know
kappgjarn	self-willed
kaupa	purchase
Kaupangi	Kaupang (place)
kaupferðir	trading-voyages
kaupir	bought
kaupmaður	trading-man
kaupmenn	merchants, the-merchants, the-traders
kaupsveinar	trading-men
kemur	came
kennduð	taught
kertisveinar	court-men
kjósa	choose
klokkurum	clocks
knörr	ship
kom	came
koma	came, come, coming
komið	come
kominn	come, coming
komir	come
komu	came
konung	the-king
konunga	the-king
konungi	king, the-king, to-the-king
konungs	the-king, the-king's
konungsmenn	the-kings-men
konungsskipinu	the-king's-ship
konungsstofunni	the-king's-chambers
konungur	king, the-king
kopars	copper
kostar	choice
kosti	benefit
krefja	demand
kunnigt	known
kvað	said
kvaddi	called
kvaðst	said
kveld	evening
kyrrt	peace

L, l

Old Icelandic	English
lá	lay
lætur	behave, leave, let
lagi	had
land	land, the-land
landa	lands
landi	land, lands, the-land
lands	land
landtjald	land-tents
langskip	longships
lát	let-it
láta	allow, have, losing
láti	have
launuð	repaid
leggi	lay
leggja	grant
leggjum	lay
leggur	laid
leið	pass, passed, way
leita	seek
leitað	consider
lendir	landed
lendra	is-paid, payment
lendur	land
lengi	long
lengur	longer

Word List (Old Icelandic to English)

Old Icelandic	English
lést	had
lét	had
léti	let
léttlætiskonum	prostitutes
leyfa	allow
leyfi	leave
liði	crew, men
liðið	passed
líður	passed
lifa	life
líka	like
líkaði	liked
líst	appears
líta	look
lítill	little
litlu	little
lítt	little
lítur	looked
loftinu	the-air
lögðu	laid
logist	cheated
lokið	ended
lönd	land
löng	long
lygi	lie
lyndi	temper
Lyrgju	Lyrgja (place)
lýstur	struck

M, m

Old Icelandic	English
má	may
maður	a-man, man
mæðist	tired
mælt	spoken, spoken-of
mælti	spoke, spoke-to
mæltuð	spoke
mætti	may, might, might
mál	conversed, matter, measure
mála	matter, payment, payment
málagjöfina	payment
málann	payment
málanum	payment
málasilfrið	silverware
máli	matter, payment, speak
málið	matter
mann	man
manna	men, people, people's
mannháska	human-danger
marga	many
margur	many
matar	food
máttu	may, may-you
með	along, between, with
mega	may
megi	may
meir	more
meira	more
meiri	greater, more
melrakkabelgi	arctic-fox-furs
menn	men, people
mér	me, to-me, with-me
mesta	most
mesti	most
mig	me
mikið	huge
mikill	a-great, great
mikinn	greatly, much
mikla	much
Miklagarði	The-Great-City (place)
miklu	a-great, much
miklum	much
milli	between
mín	me, mine
mína	mine
minn	mine
minna	less
minni	mine
mínu	my
mislíkaði	misliked
mitt	mine, my
mjög	much
mönnum	people
morgun	morning, the-morning
mörk	a-mark
mót	return
móti	meet, meeting

77

Word List (Old Icelandic to English)

Old Icelandic	English
mótinu	the-meeting
móts	meet
mótsins	the-meeting
möttulsskauti	cloak-lap
mun	could, shall, should, would
mundi	should, would
mundir	would
mundu	should, would
muni	shall
munkat	shall
munt	must
muntu	should
munum	shall, should
myrgininn	morning

N, n

Old Icelandic	English
næst	next
næsta	next, next-to
næstum	before
nætur	night
nakkvað	something
nálega	nearly
nauðgað	force
nauðsyn	necessity
né	nor
neðan	below
neitt	nothing
nema	except, take
neyta	use
neytti	consumed
Nið	Nid (place)
níðist	down
niður	below, down
nóga	enough
nokkuð	something, somewhat
nokkur	something
nokkura	some
nokkurum	some
norður	north
Noreg	Norway (place)
Noregi	Norway (place)
Noregs	Norway (place)
norrænir	Norwegians

Old Icelandic	English
nótt	night
nú	now

O, o

of	over
oft	often
oftar	frequent, more-often
og	also, and
okkar	ours
okkur	our, us
orð	word, words, word-to
orðaframkast	outburst
orði	word
orðsending	word-sending
oss	to-us, us

Ó, ó

ófriðar	hostilities
ófriðinn	un-peace
ófriður	un-peace
ófús	unwilling
óglaðari	un-gladness
ógladdist	un-glad
ómaklega	undeservedly
ómjúkur	un-bending
ónýttir	un-used
Ósló	Oslo (place)
ósýnt	unseen
ótiginn	un-high-born
óvingjarnlega	unfriendly

Ö, ö

öðru	a-second
öðrum	other
öllu	all
öllum	all

P, p

Word List (Old Icelandic to English)

Old Icelandic	English
prettunum	trick

R, r

Old Icelandic	English
ráð	advise, the-matter
ráða	prevail
ráðagerðir	advice-giving
ráðast	appoint, arrange
ráðið	hired
ráðist	decide
ræðst	commanded
ræður	leading
reiði	anger
reiðist	commanded
rekið	thrown
rekkju	bed
reyki	smoke
reyna	know
ríki	kingdom
ró	rest
rúmi	seat
rúms	room

S, s

Old Icelandic	English
sá	so
sæmd	honour
sæmilegt	the-same
sættast	reconcile
sagði	said
sagt	is-said, said
sakar	the-sake-of
saman	together
samir	so
sat	sat, stayed
satt	be-true, true
sátu	sat
sáu	saw
sé	is, see, so
seg	say
segir	said, told
segja	say, told
segl	the-sails
seilast	to-reach
sein	late
seint	late, slow, slowly
sel	flip
sem	as, that, was, which
semja	negotiate
senda	send
sendi	sent
sér	for, he, him, himself, saw, themselves
sérð	see
sért	be
sessunautar	sitting-together
setja	sit
setjið	set
settust	sat
sex	six
síð	later
síðan	afterwards, since, then
síðar	afterwards, later
síðast	the-last
síðkveldum	late-evening
síður	less
sig	him
sigldu	sailed
siglingum	sailing
Sigurður	Sigurd (name)
silfrið	the-silver
silfrinu	the-silver
silfur	silver
sín	him, theirs
sína	his
sínar	theirs
sinn	he, his
sinni	his, themselves, time, yourself
síns	his
sínu	his, their
sínum	his
síst	least
sitja	settle
sitt	his
situr	sat
sjá	see, so
sjálfir	themselves

Word List (Old Icelandic to English)

Old Icelandic	English	*Old Icelandic*	English
sjáum	we-see	*slíkra*	such
skaða	damages	*slíkri*	such
skal	shall	*slíkt*	such
skálum	bowl	*slíku*	such
skammt	short-distance	*slóst*	struck
skap	mood	*snemma*	early, soon
skapi	mood	*Snorra*	Snorri (name)
skapkers	large-vessel	*Snorrason*	Snorrason (name)
skaplyndi	mood-temper	*Snorrasyni*	Snorrason (name)
skark	noise	*snúa*	turned
skerið	a-rock	*sofa*	sleep
skildust	separated	*sögð*	told
skilja	separate	*sögðu*	said
skilnaður	parting	*sóma*	honour
skilur	separated	*sömu*	the-same
skip	a-ship, ship, ships, the-ship	*spilli*	spoil
skipagangur	shipping	*spurði*	asked
skipan	ships	*spyr*	asked
skipi	a-ship, ship	*stað*	replace
skipið	ship, the-ship	*stafninn*	the-prow
skipinu	ship, the-ship	*stefnið*	heading
skips	a-ship, ships	*stendur*	stands, stood
skipsins	ship	*stirðlæti*	hard-temper
skipstjórn	ship-steering	*stjórnar*	steer
skipstjórnar	ship-steer	*stóð*	stood
skipum	ships	*stóðu*	stood
skipun	crew	*stórættaður*	of-high-family
skipverðsins	ship's-worth	*stórmennsku*	greatness
skipverja	the-crew	*strangt*	strange
skíran	cleared	*stríðu*	stressful
skírt	pure	*stuttorður*	short-worded
skjótt	swift, swiftly	*stygglyndur*	quick-tempered
skorti	shortly	*stýrði*	steered
skotið	launched	*stýrimaður*	steersman
skuli	shall	*stýrimanns*	the-steersman
skulu	should	*styrkastur*	strongest
skuluð	should	*stytti*	short
skulum	shall	*suður*	south
skyggt	shaded	*sumarið*	summer
skyldi	should	*sumir*	some
skyldu	should	*sumrum*	summers
skyti	shot	*sundur*	separate
skýtur	launched	*svaf*	slept
sleit	broken-up	*sváfu*	slept
sleitilega	unfairly	*svarar*	answered

Word List (Old Icelandic to English)

Old Icelandic	English
sveinar	fellows
Sveini	Svein (name)
sveinn	fellow, Svein (name), the-fellow
svívirðing	disgrace
svívirðlega	dishonourable
svívirður	dishonourable
svo	so
sýndist	seemed
synir	sons
sýnist	seemed
sýnum	in-appearance
sýr	Sow

T, t

Old Icelandic	English
taka	take
tala	speak
tek	take
tekið	taken
tekur	took
tíðast	swiftly
tíðindi	tidings
til	about, for, to, until
tíska	custom
títt	immediately
tók	took
tóku	took
tólf	twelve
trúa	believe

Þ, þ

Old Icelandic	English
þá	them, then
það	it, that, this
þætti	seems
þakkaði	thanked
þakkar	thanked
þangað	from-there
þann	it, then
þannug	that-way
þar	there, there, they
þarf	needed
þatgi	that-not
þau	them, then
þegar	straightaway, straight-away, there
þeim	of-them, them, they
þeir	the, there, they
þekkjast	accept
þenna	that
þér	to-you, you, you-to
þess	is-this, like-this, that, these, this, those
þessi	these, this
þessu	this
þessum	those
þetta	it, that, this
þig	you
þín	your
þína	yours
þínar	you
þinn	your, yours
þínum	yours
þitt	yours
þjóna	serve
þjónað	served
þjónusta	service
þjónustu	service
þjónustumenn	servants
þó	though
þokkar	favours
þörf	needed
Þóri	Thorir (name)
Þórir	Thorir (name), Thorir (name)
Þóris	Thorir's (name)
þótt	though
þóttist	thought
Þrándheimi	Trondheim (place)
Þrándheims	Trondheim (place)
þrenna	treble
þrjú	three
þú	you
þurfa	needed, you-need
því	accordingly, because, of, that, therefore, with
þyki	think

Word List (Old Icelandic to English)

Old Icelandic	English
þykir	seemed, thinks, thought
þykist	think
þykja	think
þykjast	consider

U, u

Old Icelandic	English
um	about
umræða	discussion
undan	away-from, from-under, under
undir	under
undirhluturinn	the-under-part
unnið	deserved
upp	up, upped
uppi	up
upplenskur	an-Upplander
upplost	false-rumour
urðu	became
utan	out

Ú, ú

Old Icelandic	English
úr	from, out-of
úrræða	solution
út	out, out-of
útferð	out-travelling
úti	outside

V, v

Old Icelandic	English
vægð	grace
vændiskonum	prostitutes
vænna	expected
væri	had, was
vakna	awoke
vaknar	awoke
vald	power
vandi	custom
vandskipaður	difficult
vant	difficult, expected
var	was, were
varð	became, was
varðveita	guard-over
varla	hardly
vega	weigh
vegur	way
veislum	the-feasts
veislur	feasts
veist	know
veistu	know-you
veit	know
veita	grant, lead
vel	well
velja	will
ver	be
vér	we
vera	be, becoming, being, is, it-be
verð	worth
verða	be, to-be
verðum	worth
verður	came, worth
verið	be, been, being, had-been
verja	spend
verr	worse
verri	worse
verst	becomes
vert	worth, worthy
vetur	winter
veturinn	winter
vexti	well-built
við	against, with
víghug	killing-mind
Vík	Vik (place)
vil	will, wish
vildi	willed, wish, wished
vilgis	very
vilja	wish
vilji	willed
viljum	wish, wish-to
vill	willed, wished, wished-to, wishes
vilt	wish
vinar	friend
vináttu	friendship
vinda	wind

Word List (Old Icelandic to English)

Old Icelandic	English	*Old Icelandic*	English
vingan	friendship		
vingjarnleg	friendly	*ýkva*	veer
vinna	to-win-over	*ýmissa*	various
vinur	friend		
vinveitt	favourable		
virðing	honour, worthiness		
viskur	wise		
víst	certainly		
vistum	provisions		
vísu	certainly		
vita	certainly, know		
víti	punishment, signalled		
vitið	know		
vítið	penalty, the-penalty		
vítin	penalty		
vítishornið	penalty-horn		
vitni	testimony		
víttur	penalty, reprimanded		
vopndjarfastur	weapons-bold		
vopnum	weapons		
vor	our		
vora	going, spring		
vorið	spring		
vort	ours		
voru	were		
votir	wet		
voveiflega	unexpected		

Y, y

yðrar	yours
yður	you
yðvars	yours
yfir	over
yfirbragði	complexion
ykkar	with-you
ykkra	yours
ykkur	you-two
yrði	became

Ý, ý

Word List (English to Old Icelandic)

Word List (English to Old Icelandic)

English	Old Icelandic

A, a

English	Old Icelandic
a-ban	*bann*
about	*á, í, til, um*
accept	*þekkjast*
access	*atgang*
accomplished	*fær*
accordingly	*því*
advice-giving	*ráðagerðir*
advise	*ráð*
a-few	*fám*
after	*aftur, eftir*
afterwards	*síðan, síðar*
against	*við*
age	*ævi*
a-great	*mikill, miklu*
all	*allir, allir, allra, allt, allt, öllu, öllum*
all-long	*alllangt*
allow	*láta, leyfa*
all-prepared	*albúnir*
alone	*eins*
along	*fyrir, með*
also	*og*
am	*em, er*
a-man	*maður*
a-mark	*mörk*
ambitious	*framgjarn*
ancestry	*ætt*
and	*á, en, enda, og*
anger	*reiði*
another	*annan, annan, annars, annars*
answered	*svarar*
an-Upplander	*upplenskur*
appears	*líst*
appoint	*ráðast*
arctic-fox-furs	*melrakkabelgi*
are	*ert, eru*
are-you	*ertu*
a-ring	*hring*
a-rock	*skerið*
arrange	*ráðast*

English	Old Icelandic
as	*á, en, er, sem*
a-second	*öðru*
as-him	*honum*
a-ship	*skip, skipi, skips*
asked	*beiða, beitt, biður, spurði, spyr*
assist	*greiða*
at	*á, að, í*
a-trick	*brögð*
away	*brott*
away-from	*undan*
away-prepared	*brautbúnaði*
awhile	*hríð*
awoke	*vakna, vaknar*

B, b

English	Old Icelandic
back	*aftur*
badly	*illa*
ban	*bannar*
Bard (name)	*Bárður*
bargain	*falar*
be	*gerist, sért, ver, vera, verða, verið*
bear	*bera, beri*
bears	*ber*
became	*urðu, varð, yrði*
because	*því*
becomes	*verst*
becoming	*vera*
bed	*rekkju*
been	*verið*
before	*áður, fyrir, fyrr, næstum*
began	*byrjaði*
behave	*lætur*
behind	*eftir*
being	*vera, verið*
believe	*trúa*
bell-ringing	*hringinga, hringingum*
below	*neðan, niður*
benefit	*kosti*
best	*bergst, best, besta*

Word List (English to Old Icelandic)

English	*Old Icelandic*	English	*Old Icelandic*
be-true	satt	complexion	yfirbragði
better	betra, betur	conclude	enda
between	með, milli	consider	leitað, þykjast
bid	báðu, biður	consumed	neytti
bold	djörfung	conversed	mál
bore	bar	copper	kopars
both	báðum, bæði	could	mun
bought	kaupir	court	hirðar, hirðinni
bowl	skálum	court-man	hirðmaður
Bratteyar (place)	Bröttueyri	court-men	kertisveinar
breaking	brjótist	crew	áhöfnina, háseta, liði, skipun
bring	færi, færið		
bringing	bar, fært	custom	tíska, vandi
broken-up	sleit		
brought	fær, færa, færir		
burnt	brennda		
but	eða, en, enn		

C, c

D, d

called	kalla, kallað, kvaddi	damages	skaða
calling	ákallsi	dangers	háski
came	kemur, kom, koma, komu, verður	Danish-forces	danaher
		day	dag, dagur
can	kann	days	dögum
carried	ber, flytja	dearly-loved	kærleikum
carry-out	efna	decide	ráðist
celebrated	fegnir	deeming	dóm
certainly	víst, vísu, vita	demand	krefja
changed	breytt	Denmark (place)	Danmerkur
chased	eltast	deserved	unnið
cheated	logist	desire	fýsir
choice	kostar	did	fór, gera, gerði
choose	kjósa	difficult	vandskipaður, vant
cleared	skíran	direction	beint
clearly	einsætt	disappeared	hurfu
cloak-lap	möttulsskauti	discussion	umræða
clocks	klokkurum	disgrace	svívirðing
come	kæmi, koma, komið, kominn, komir	dishonourable	svívirðlega, svívirður
		do	gera
coming	koma, kominn	done	gert
commanded	ræðst, reiðist	down	níðist, niður
companions	förunauta, förunautar	drank	drakk, drekka, drekkur, drykki
companionship	föruneyti	drew	heimta
completely	gjörla	drink	drekk, drekka, drekki, drykki
		drinking	drukku, drykkju
		drinks	drykkju

Word List (English to Old Icelandic)

English	*Old Icelandic*
drunk	*drukkið*

E, e

English	*Old Icelandic*
each	*hver, hverju, hvert, hvor, hvort*
early	*snemma*
early-riser	*árrisull*
east	*austan, austur, austur*
echo	*glymur*
eighth	*átti*
end	*enda*
ended	*lokið*
England-Traveller (name)	*Englandsfari*
enough	*nóga*
equally-following	*jafnfylginn*
equally-much	*jafnmjög*
equally-trustworthy	*jafntraustan, jafntraustir*
errand-without	*erindlaust*
especially	*einkum*
evening	*aftan, aftna, kveld*
except	*nema*
expected	*vænna, vant*

F, f

English	*Old Icelandic*
fair-wind	*byr*
false-rumour	*upplost*
farmed	*bjó*
fasten	*festa*
father	*faðir, föður*
favourable	*vinveitt*
favours	*þokkar*
feasts	*veislur*
feed	*fótum*
fellow	*drengur, sveinn*
fellows	*sveinar*
few	*fáir, fátt*
find	*fund, hitt, hitta*
first	*fyrsta, fyrstu*
flip	*sel*
floating	*floti*

English	*Old Icelandic*
follow	*fylgdi, fylgja*
following	*fylgdina, fylgir*
food	*matar*
for	*fyrir, sér, til*
force	*nauðgað*
forces	*hér*
foreclose	*bregða*
forward	*fram, framarla*
forwards	*fram*
found	*fann, fengi, finnumst, fyndust, hitti, hittir*
frequent	*oftar*
friend	*vinar, vinur*
friendly	*vingjarnleg*
friendship	*vináttu, vingan*
from	*af, af, frá, fram, í, úr*
from-here	*héðan*
from-there	*þangað*
from-under	*undan*
fully-tested	*fullreynt*
furs	*belgi*

G, g

English	*Old Icelandic*
gallows	*gálga*
Gardariki (place)	*Garðaríki*
gave	*bar, fá, gaf, gáfu, gáfuð*
get	*fá, fái, gera, get*
gift	*gjöfin*
give	*fá, fæ, fáið, gefa*
given	*gefinn*
gladness	*glaðari*
go	*fara, ganga*
goes	*fer*
going	*fara, för, gengur, vora*
gold	*gulls*
good	*góð, góður*
good-news	*fagnaðartíðindi*
good-things	*gæði*
got	*fengið, heimtir*
grace	*vægð*
grant	*leggja, veita*
great	*mikill*
greater	*meiri*

Word List (English to Old Icelandic)

English	*Old Icelandic*	English	*Old Icelandic*
greatly	*drjúgum, mikinn*	his	*hans, sína, sinn, sinni, síns, sínu, sínum, sitt*
greatness	*stórmennsku*		
guard-over	*varðveita*		
guardsmen	*hirðina*	Hjardarholt (place)	*Hjarðarholti*
		hold	*haldast, halt, heldur*

H, h

		hold-you	*haltu*
had	*á, átti, er, hafa, hafði, hafi, haft, hefði, hefir, höfðu, lagi, lést, lét, væri*	home-longing	*heimfúsari*
		honour	*drengskap, sæmd, sóma, virðing*
		horn	*horn*
had-been	*verið*	horn-blast	*hornblástur*
half	*hálf, helmings*	hostilities	*ófriðar*
Halldor (name)	*Halldór, Halldóri, Halldórs*	house	*hús*
		how	*hvers, hvort*
Halldor's (name)	*Halldórs*	how-so	*hversu*
hammock	*húðfat*	huge	*mikið*
hand	*hendi, höndum*	human-danger	*mannháska*
handsome	*fríður*		
happiest	*blíðast*		

I, i

happily	*blíðlegur*	I	*eg*
Harald (name)	*Harald, Haraldi, Haralds, Haraldur*	I-am	*eg*
		Iceland (place)	*Ísland, Íslands*
Harald's-money (name)	*Haraldsslátta*	Icelander	*íslenskan*
		Icelander (name)	*Íslandi*
hardly	*varla*	if	*ef*
hard-temper	*stirðlæti*	ill	*illa*
has	*hafi, hefir*	immediately	*títt*
has-been	*hefir*	in	*á, að, í*
have	*er, hafa, hafið, hafir, hefi, hefir, láta, láti*	in-appearance	*sýnum*
		in-on	*að*
		inside	*inn*
having	*hafa*	intend	*ætla*
he	*hann, honum, sér, sinn*	intended	*ætlað, ætlaði, ætlar, ætlist*
heading	*stefnið*	intends	*ætlar*
hear	*heyra, heyrum*	into	*í*
heard	*heyrðuð*	invitation	*boð*
held	*halda*	is	*á, er, sé, vera*
hence	*héðan*	is-paid	*lendra*
here	*hér*	is-said	*sagt*
higher	*hærra*	is-this	*þess*
highest	*hærra, hæsta*	it	*að, hann, það, þann, þetta*
him	*hann, hans, honum, sér, sig, sín*		
himself	*sér*	it-be	*vera*
hired	*ráðið*		

Word List (English to Old Icelandic)

English	*Old Icelandic*
it-is	*er*

J, j

joyful	*blíðu*

K, k

Kaupang (place)	*Kaupangi*
keep-asking	*brekar*
killing-mind	*víghug*
king	*konungi, konungur*
kingdom	*ríki*
king-of-Denmark	*danakonungur*
king's-men-customs	*hirðsiðum*
know	*kann, reyna, veist, veit, vita, vitið*
known	*kunnigt*
know-you	*veistu*

L, l

laid	*leggur, lögðu*
land	*land, landi, lands, lendur, lönd*
landed	*lendir*
lands	*landa, landi*
land-tents	*landtjald*
large-vessel	*skapkers*
last-night	*gærkveld*
late	*sein, seint*
late-evening	*síðkveldum*
later	*síð, síðar*
launched	*skotið, skýtur*
lay	*lá, leggi, leggjum*
lead	*veita*
leading	*ræður*
least	*síst*
leave	*lætur, leyfi*
less	*minna, síður*
let	*lætur, léti*
let-it	*lát*
lie	*lygi*

English	*Old Icelandic*
life	*lifa*
like	*líka*
liked	*líkaði*
like-this	*þess*
listen-to	*hlýða*
little	*lítill, litlu, lítt*
long	*lengi, löng*
longer	*lengur*
longships	*langskip*
look	*líta*
looked	*lítur*
lord	*herra*
losing	*láta*
Lyrgja (place)	*Lyrgju*

M, m

man	*maður, mann*
many	*fjöldi, marga, margur*
matter	*mál, mála, máli, málið*
may	*má, mætti, máttu, mega, megi*
may-you	*máttu*
me	*mér, mig, mín*
measure	*mál*
meet	*fund, móti, móts*
meeting	*móti*
men	*liði, manna, menn*
merchants	*kaupmenn*
merchant-ship	*byrðing*
met	*fundust*
might	*mætti, mætti*
mine	*mín, mína, minn, minni, mitt*
misliked	*mislíkaði*
modest	*hófi*
moment	*bili*
money-insisting	*fjárheimta*
mood	*skap, skapi*
mood-temper	*skaplyndi*
more	*fleiri, meir, meira, meiri*
more-fixedly	*fastara*
more-often	*oftar*
morning	*morgun, myrgininn*

Word List (English to Old Icelandic)

English	Old Icelandic	English	Old Icelandic
most	*mesta, mesti*	one-such	*einhverja, einnhvern*
much	*mikinn, mikla, miklu, miklum, mjög*	only	*engan*
		on-the	*á*
must	*munt*	or	*eða*
my	*mínu, mitt*	Oslo (place)	*Ósló*
		other	*aðra, aðrir, áður, annarra, annarri, öðrum*

N, n

English	Old Icelandic	English	Old Icelandic
		otherwise	*ellegar*
named	*hét*	ounces	*aura*
nearly	*nálega*	our	*okkur, vor*
necessity	*nauðsyn*	ours	*okkar, vort*
needed	*þarf, þörf, þurfa*	out	*út, utan*
negotiate	*semja*	outburst	*orðaframkast*
neither	*hvorki*	out-of	*í, úr, út*
next	*næst, næsta*	outside	*úti*
next-to	*næsta*	outspoken	*bermæltur*
Nid (place)	*Nið*	out-travelling	*útferð*
night	*nætur, nótt*	over	*of, yfir*
no	*einskis, enga, engan*	overboard	*kaf*
noise	*skark*	own	*eiga, eignast*
none	*eigi, engi, engu*		
nor	*né*		
north	*norður*		

P, p

English	Old Icelandic	English	Old Icelandic
Norway (place)	*Noreg, Noregi, Noregs*		
Norwegians	*norrænir*	paid	*gelst*
not	*eigi, ekki*	part	*hlut, hluti, hlutur*
nothing	*einskis, engis, neitt*	parting	*skilnaður*
now	*nú*	pass	*leið*
		passed	*leið, liðið, líður*
		pay	*fá, gjalda*

O, o

English	Old Icelandic	English	Old Icelandic
		payment	*fé, galst, gjaldið, lendra, mála, mála, málagjöfina, málann, málanum, máli*
of	*á, að, af, af, í, því*		
of-all	*allra*		
of-few-words	*fámæltur*		
of-high-family	*stórættaður*	peace	*kyrrt*
often	*oft*	penalty	*vítið, vítin, víttur*
of-them	*þeim*	penalty-horn	*vítishornið*
old	*gamall*	people	*manna, menn, mönnum*
old-age	*elli*		
old-is	*eldist*	people's	*manna*
old-men	*gamalmenni*	possible	*hægt*
on	*á*	power	*vald*
one	*eigi, einn, eitt*	preparations	*bjuggu, búnaðinn*
		prepared	*búa, búið, búinn, býr, býstu*
		prepares	*býst*

Word List (English to Old Icelandic)

English	*Old Icelandic*	English	*Old Icelandic*
prevail	*ráða*	sat	*sat, sátu, settust, situr*
promised	*hét*	saw	*sáu, sér*
promising-wind	*byrvænlegt*	say	*seg, segja*
prostitutes	*léttlætiskonum, vændiskonum*	sea	*haf, hafs*
provisions	*vistum*	seat	*rúmi*
punishment	*víti*	see	*sé, sérð, sjá*
purchase	*kaupa*	seek	*leita*
pure	*skírt*	seemed	*sýndist, sýnist, þykir*
		seems	*þætti*
		self-willed	*kappgjarn*
		send	*senda*
		sent	*sendi*

Q, q

quick-tempered	*stygglyndur*	separate	*skilja, sundur*
		separated	*skildust, skilur*
		servants	*þjónustumenn*
		serve	*þjóna*
		served	*þjónað*

R, r

English	*Old Icelandic*	English	*Old Icelandic*
ran	*hljóp*	service	*þjónusta, þjónustu*
rather	*heldur, helst, helsti*	set	*setjið*
reacted	*brygði*	settle	*bú, byggja, sitja*
readied	*bjóst*	settled	*bjó*
reconcile	*sættast*	shaded	*skyggt*
remained	*eftir*	shall	*mun, muni, munkat, munum, skal, skuli, skulum*
remaining	*eftir*		
repaid	*launuð*	share	*hlut*
repaired	*bætt*	she	*hún*
repay	*gyldist*	ship	*knörr, skip, skipi, skipið, skipinu, skipsins*
replace	*stað*		
reprimanded	*víttur*		
resolved	*alugað*	shipping	*skipagangur*
rest	*ró*	ships	*skip, skipan, skips, skipum*
return	*mót*		
ring	*hringja*	ship-steer	*skipstjórnar*
room	*rúms*	ship-steering	*skipstjórn*
run	*hleypur*	ship's-worth	*skipverðsins*
		short	*stytti*
		short-distance	*skammt*
		shortly	*skorti*
		short-worded	*stuttorður*

S, s

sadness	*fæð*	shot	*skyti*
said	*kvað, kvaðst, sagði, sagt, segir, sögðu*	should	*mun, mundi, mundu, muntu, munum, skulu, skuluð, skyldi, skyldu*
sailed	*sigldu*		
sailing	*siglingum*	signalled	*víti*
sailors	*háseta, hásetar, hásetum*	Sigurd (name)	*Sigurður*

Word List (English to Old Icelandic)

English	*Old Icelandic*	English	*Old Icelandic*
silver	*silfur*	stress	*álaga*
silverware	*málasilfrið*	stressful	*stríðu*
since	*síðan*	strongest	*styrkastur*
sit	*setja*	struck	*lýstur, slóst*
sitting-together	*sessunautar*	such	*slíkra, slíkri, slíkt, slíku*
six	*sex*		
sleep	*sofa*	summer	*sumarið*
slept	*svaf, sváfu*	summers	*sumrum*
slow	*seint*	suppose	*ætla*
slowly	*seint*	Svein (name)	*Sveini, Sveinn*
smoke	*reyki*	swift	*skjótt*
Snorrason (name)	*Snorrason, Snorrasyni*	swiftly	*skjótt, tíðast*
Snorri (name)	*Snorra*		
so	*sá, samir, sé, sjá, svo*		
solution	*úrræða*		

T, t

English	*Old Icelandic*
some	*nokkura, nokkurum, sumir*
something	*nakkvað, nokkuð, nokkur*
somewhat	*nokkuð*
sons	*synir*
soon	*snemma*
south	*suður*
Sow	*sýr*
speak	*máli, tala*
spend	*verja*
spoil	*spilli*
spoke	*mælti, mæltuð*
spoken	*mælt*
spoken-of	*mælt*
spoke-to	*mælti*
spring	*vora, vorið*
stag-horn	*dýrshorn*
stands	*stendur*
stay	*dveljast*
stayed	*sat*
steer	*stjórnar*
steered	*stýrði*
steersman	*stýrimaður*
still	*enn*
stood	*stendur, stóð, stóðu*
straightaway	*þegar*
straight-away	*þegar*
strange	*strangt*
straw	*hálm*

English	*Old Icelandic*
take	*nema, taka, tek*
take-care	*gæta*
taken	*tekið*
taught	*kennduð*
temper	*lyndi*
testimony	*vitni*
than	*en*
thanked	*þakkaði, þakkar*
thanks	*heilastan*
that	*á, að, en, er, í, sem, það, þenna, þess, þetta, því*
that-not	*þatgi*
that-way	*þannug*
the	*á, að, hin, hinn, þeir*
the-air	*loftinu*
the-anchor	*akkeri*
the-autumn	*hausti*
the-city	*bænum*
the-cockerel	*árgalinn*
the-crew	*skipverja*
the-day	*daginn*
the-drinking-horn	*hornið*
the-feasts	*veislum*
the-fellow	*sveinn*
the-first	*fyrra*
the-gift	*gjöfina*
The-Great-City (place)	*Miklagarði*
the-horn	*hornsins*

Word List (English to Old Icelandic)

English	*Old Icelandic*	English	*Old Icelandic*
their	*sínu*	think	*hug, hygg, þyki, þykist, þykja*
theirs	*sín, sínar*	thinks	*þykir*
the-king	*konung, konunga, konungi, konungs, konungur*	this	*á, að, það, þess, þessi, þessu, þetta*
the-king's	*konungs*	this-town	*bænum*
the-king's-chambers	*konungsstofunni*	Thorir (name)	*Þóri, Þórir, Þórir*
the-kings-men	*konungsmenn*	Thorir's (name)	*Þóris*
the-king's-ship	*konungsskipinu*	those	*þess, þessum*
the-land	*land, landi*	though	*þó, þótt*
the-last	*síðast*	thought	*þóttist, þykir*
them	*þá, þau, þeim*	three	*þrjú*
the-matter	*ráð*	through	*gegnum*
the-meeting	*mótinu, mótsins*	thrown	*rekið*
the-merchants	*kaupmenn*	tidings	*tíðindi*
the-morning	*morgun*	tied-up	*bindur*
themselves	*sér, sinni, sjálfir*	time	*sinni*
then	*á, en, enn, síðan, þá, þann, þau*	tired	*mæðist*
		to	*á, að, í, til*
the-next	*annan*	to-be	*verða*
the-payment	*gjaldið*	to-come	*aðkoma*
the-penalty	*vítið*	to-do	*gera*
the-priest	*goða*	to-drink	*drekka*
the-prow	*stafninn*	together	*saman*
the-queen	*drottning*	to-give	*gefa*
there	*þar, þar, þegar, þeir*	to-have	*hafa*
there-are	*eru*	to-him	*honum*
therefore	*því*	to-hold	*halda*
the-ring	*hringinn*	told	*segir, segja, sögð*
the-river	*ánni*	to-me	*mér*
the-sails	*segl*	to-meet	*fund*
the-sake-of	*sakar*	took	*tekur, tók, tóku*
the-same	*sæmilegt, sömu*	to-reach	*seilast*
these	*þess, þessi*	to-run	*hlaupa*
the-ship	*skip, skipið, skipinu*	to-sea	*hafa*
the-silver	*silfrið, silfrinu*	to-the-king	*konungi*
the-steersman	*stýrimanns*	to-us	*oss*
the-straw	*hálm*	to-win-over	*vinna*
the-tow-boat	*báti*	town	*bæinn*
the-town	*bænum*	townspeople	*bæjarmenn*
the-traders	*kaupmenn*	to-you	*þér*
the-under-part	*undirhluturinn*	trading-man	*kaupmaður*
they	*eru, þar, þeim, þeir*	trading-men	*kaupsveinar*
they-were	*eru*	trading-voyages	*kaupferðir*
things	*hluti, hlutum*	travel	*fær, færi, fara, fari, farið, farir, fars, ferðir*

Word List (English to Old Icelandic)

English	*Old Icelandic*
travel-goods	*fararefni*
travelled	*farið, fór*
travelling	*fara*
travelling-clothes	*ígangsklæði*
treasure	*gersemar, gersemum*
treasures	*gersemar*
treble	*þrenna*
trick	*prettunum*
Trondheim (place)	*Þrándheimi, Þrándheims*
true	
trumpet-blown	*blásið*
turbulence	*aga*
turned	*snúa*
twelve	*tólf*

U, u

un-bending	*ómjúkur*
under	*undan, undir*
undeservedly	*ómaklega*
unexpected	*voveiflega*
unfairly	*sleitilega*
unfriendly	*óvingjarnlega*
un-glad	*ógladdist*
un-gladness	*óglaðari*
un-high-born	*ótiginn*
un-peace	*ófriðinn, ófriður*
unseen	*ósýnt*
until	*til*
un-used	*ónýttir*
unwilling	*ófús*
up	*upp, uppi*
upped	*upp*
us	*okkur, oss*
use	*neyta*

V, v

various	*ýmissa*
veer	*ýkva*
very	*vilgis*
Vik (place)	*Vík*
violated	*brotin*

W, w

English	*Old Icelandic*
wait	*bíð, bíða, biðleika*
warmth	*hlýs*
warn	*ávíta*
was	*enn, er, sem, væri, var, varð*
was-named	*hét*
way	*hættir, leið, vegur*
we	*vér*
wealth	*féið, fénu*
weapons	*vopnum*
weapons-bold	*vopndjarfastur*
we-have	*hefir*
weigh	*vega*
well	*vel*
well-built	*vexti*
went	*færi, fara, fer, fór, gekk, gengu, gengur, gerir*
went-you	*fórstu*
were	*er, eru, var, voru*
we-see	*sjáum*
wet	*votir*
what	*er, hvað, hvers*
when	*er*
where	*er, hver*
which	*er, hvegi, hvern, hvort, sem*
while	*en*
who	*en, er, hver, hverjum*
why	*hví*
will	*í, velja, vil*
willed	*vildi, vilji, vill*
wind	*vinda*
winter	*vetur, veturinn*
wise	*viskur*
wish	*vil, vildi, vilja, viljum, vilt*
wished	*vildi, vill*
wished-to	*vill*
wishes	*vill*
wish-to	*viljum*
with	*í, með, því, við*

Word List (English to Old Icelandic)

English	Old Icelandic
with-me	*mér*
without-fraud	*falslaust*
with-you	*ykkar*
word	*orð, orði*
words	*orð*
word-sending	*orðsending*
word-to	*orð*
worried-face	*áhyggjusvip*
worse	*verr, verri*
worth	*verð, verðum, verður, vert*
worthiness	*virðing*
worthy	*vert*
would	*mun, mundi, mundir, mundu*

Y, y

English	Old Icelandic
you	*þér, þig, þínar, þú, yður*
you-need	*þurfa*
your	*þín, þinn*
yours	*þína, þinn, þínum, þitt, yðrar, yðvars, ykkra*
yourself	*sinni*
you-to	*þér*
you-two	*ykkur*
Yule (name)	*jóla, jólanna, jólin, Jólum*

A Word Comparison of Old Norse and Old Icelandic Words

Old Norse	Old Icelandic	English
áðr	áður	before
áðr	áður	other
ætlast	ætlist	intended
ætlat	ætlað	intended
aftr	aftur	after
aftr	aftur	back
ákalsi	ákallsi	calling
ákkeri	akkeri	the-anchor
alhugat	alugað	resolved
at	að	at
at	að	in
at	að	in-on
at	að	it
at	að	of
at	að	that
at	að	the
at	að	this
at	að	to
austr	austur	east
Bárðr	Bárður	Bard (name)
bermæltr	bermæltur	outspoken
berr	ber	bears
berr	ber	carried
betr	betur	better
bezt	best	best
bezta	besta	best
biðleika,	biðleika	wait
biðr	biður	asked
biðr	biður	bid
bindr	bindur	tied-up
blásit	blásið	trumpet-blown
blíðligr	blíðlegur	happily
búit	búið	prepared
byrr	byr	fair-wind
byrvænligt	byrvænlegt	promising-wind
dagr	dagur	day
danakonungr	danakonungur	king-of-Denmark
Danmerkr	Danmerkur	Denmark (place)
drekka	drekki	drink
drekkr	drekkur	drank
drengr	drengur	fellow
dróttning	drottning	the-queen
drukkit	drukkið	drunk
ek	eg	I
ek	eg	I-am
elligar	ellegar	otherwise
enskis	einskis	no
erendlaust	erindlaust	errand-without
fá	fái	get
færr	fær	accomplished
færr	fær	travel
fagnaðartíðendi	fagnaðartíðindi	good-news
fái	fáið	give
fámæltr	fámæltur	of-few-words
fararefnin	fararefni	travel-goods
farit	farið	travel
farit	farið	travelled
fengit	fengið	got
ferr	fer	goes
ferr	fer	went
fét	féið	wealth
finnimst	finnumst	found
fjölði	fjöldi	many
fórtu	fórstu	went-you
frændum	föður	father
fríðr	fríður	handsome
fylgði	fylgdi	follow
fylgðina	fylgdina	following
fyndist	fyndust	found
galzt	galst	payment
gelzt	gelst	paid
gengr	gengur	going
gengr	gengur	went
gerla	gjörla	completely
gersimar	gersemar	treasure
gersimar	gersemar	treasures
gersimum	gersemum	treasure
gjaldit	gjaldið	payment

A Word Comparison of Old Norse and Old Icelandic Words

Old Norse	Old Icelandic	English
gjaldit	gjaldið	the-payment
glymr	glymur	echo
góðr	góður	good
hæra	hærra	higher
hæra	hærra	highest
Halldórr	Halldór	Halldor (name)
Haraldr	Haraldur	Harald (name)
heðan	héðan	from-here
heðan	héðan	hence
heilstan	heilastan	thanks
heldr	heldur	hold
heldr	heldur	rather
helzt	helst	rather
helzti	helsti	rather
her	hér	here
hirðmaðr	hirðmaður	court-man
hleypr	hleypur	run
hlutr	hlutur	part
hon	hún	she
hornblástr	hornblástur	horn-blast
hornit	hornið	the-drinking-horn
hringingar	hringinga	bell-ringing
hvárki	hvorki	neither
hvárr	hvor	each
hvárt	hvort	each
hvárt	hvort	how
hvárt	hvort	which
hvat	hvað	what
hvégi	hvegi	which
hverr	hver	each
hverr	hver	who
in	hin	the
inn	hinn	the
íslenzkan	íslenskan	Icelander
jafnmjök	jafnmjög	equally-much
kæma	kæmi	come
kallat	kallað	called
kaupmaðr	kaupmaður	trading-man
kaupverðsins	skipverðsins	ship's-worth
kemr	kemur	came
kómu	komu	came
konungi	konungs	the-king
konungr	konungur	king
konungr	konungur	the-king
ksonungs	konungs	the-king's
lætr	lætur	behave
lætr	lætur	leave
lætr	lætur	let
leggr	leggur	laid
leitat	leitað	consider
lendr	lendur	land
lengr	lengur	longer
lézt	lést	had
liðit	liðið	passed
líðr	líður	passed
lítr	lítur	looked
litt	lítt	little
lízt	líst	appears
logizt	logist	cheated
lokit	lokið	ended
lýstr	lýstur	struck
maðr	maður	a-man
maðr	maður	man
mæðumst	mæðist	tired
mál	málið	matter
málagjöfna	málagjöfina	payment
málasilfrit	málasilfrið	silverware
margr	margur	many
mega	megi	may
mik	mig	me
mikit	mikið	huge
mjök	mjög	much
myndi	mundi	should
myndi	mundi	would
myndi	mundu	should
myndi	mundu	would
myndir	mundir	would
myndu	mundu	would
nætr	nætur	night
náliga	nálega	nearly
nauðgat	nauðgað	force
niðr	niður	below
niðr	niður	down
nökkur	nokkur	something

A Word Comparison of Old Norse and Old Icelandic Words

Old Norse	Old Icelandic	English	Old Norse	Old Icelandic	English
nökkura	nokkura	some	skerit	skerið	a-rock
nökkurum	nokkurum	some	skilðust	skildust	separated
nökkut	nakkvað	something	skilnaðr	skilnaður	parting
nökkut	nokkuð	something	skilr	skilur	separated
nökkut	nokkuð	somewhat	skipagangr	skipagangur	shipping
norðr	norður	north	skipit	skipið	ship
Nóreg	Noreg	Norway (place)	skipit	skipið	the-ship
			skotit	skotið	launched
Nóregi	Noregi	Norway (place)	skyldi	skyldu	should
Nóregs	Noregs	Norway (place)	skyli	skuli	shall
			skýtr	skýtur	launched
ófriðr	ófriður	un-peace	sleitiliga	sleitilega	unfairly
ófúss	ófús	unwilling	slótt	slóst	struck
ok	og	also	spyrr	spyr	asked
ok	og	and	stendr	stendur	stands
okkr	okkur	our	stendr	stendur	stood
okkr	okkur	us	stóraettaðr	stóraettaður	of-high-family
ómakliga	ómaklega	undeservedly	stuttorðr	stuttorður	short-worded
ómjúkr	ómjúkur	un-bending	stygglyndr	stygglyndur	quick-tempered
ór	úr	from	stýrimaðr	stýrimaður	steersman
ór	úr	out-of	styrkastr	styrkastur	strongest
órráða	úrræða	solution	suðr	suður	south
óvingjarnliga	óvingjarnlega	unfriendly	sumarit	sumarið	summer
prettum	prettunum	trick	sundr	sundur	separate
ráðit	ráðið	hired	svá	svo	so
ræðr	ræður	leading	svivirðliga	svívirðlega	dishonourable
rekit	rekið	thrown			
sá	sáu	saw	svívirðr	svívirður	dishonourable
sæmð	sæmd	honour	tekit	tekið	taken
sæmiligt	sæmilegt	the-same	tekr	tekur	took
sér	sérð	see	þangat	þangað	from-there
sér	sért	be	þat	það	it
setið	setjið	set	þat	það	that
síðr	síður	less	þat	það	this
Sigurðr	Sigurður	Sigurd (name)	þatki	þatgi	that-not
sik	sig	him	þik	þig	you
silfr	silfur	silver	þjónat	þjónað	served
silfrit	silfrið	the-silver	þykki	þyki	think
sitr	situr	sat	þykki	þykir	thought
sízt	síst	least	þykkir	þykir	seemed
sja	sjá	see	þykkir	þykir	thinks
sjám	sjáum	we-see	þykkist	þykist	think

A Word Comparison of Old Norse and Old Icelandic Words

Old Norse	Old Icelandic	English
þykkja	*þykja*	think
þykkjast	*þykjast*	consider
þykkjumst	*þykist*	think
tíðendi	*tíðindi*	tidings
tízka	*tíska*	custom
undirhlutrinn	*undirhluturinn*	the-under-part
unnit	*unnið*	deserved
upplenzkr	*upplenskur*	an-Upplander
útan	*utan*	out
vanði	*vandi*	custom
vandskipaðr	*vandskipaður*	difficult
vápndjarfastr	*vopndjarfastur*	weapons-bold
vápnum	*vopnum*	weapons
vár	*vor*	our
vára	*vora*	going
vára	*vora*	spring
várit	*vorið*	spring
várt	*vort*	ours
váru	*voru*	were
vátir	*votir*	wet
váveifliga	*voveiflega*	unexpected
vegr	*vegur*	way
veizlum	*veislum*	the-feasts
veizlur	*veislur*	feasts
veizt	*veist*	know
veiztu	*veistu*	know-you
verðr	*verður*	came
verðr	*verður*	worth
verit	*verið*	be
verit	*verið*	been
verit	*verið*	being
verit	*verið*	had-been
vetr	*vetur*	winter
vetrinn	*veturinn*	winter
vili	*vilji*	willed
vill	*vilt*	wish
vingjarnlig	*vingjarnleg*	friendly
vinr	*vinur*	friend
vit	*við*	with
vítishornit	*vítishornið*	penalty-horn
vítit	*vítið*	penalty
vítit	*vítið*	the-penalty
víttr	*víttur*	penalty
víttr	*víttur*	reprimanded
vizkr	*viskur*	wise
yðr	*yður*	you
ykkarr	*ykkar*	with-you
ykkr	*ykkur*	you-two

The Tale of Ale-Hood (*Old Norse*)

Old Norse	Literal	English
1	**1**	**1**
Þórhallr hét maðr.	Thorhall was-named a-man.	There was a man named Thorhall.
Hann bjó í Bláskógum á Þórhallsstöðum.	He lived in Blawoods in Thorhallsstead.	He lived in Blawoods in Thorhallsstead.
Hann var vel fjáreigandi ok heldr við aldr, er saga þessi gerðist.	He was well property-owning and rather with age, as story so happened.	He was a wealthy man and rather old when the story happened.
Litill var hann ok ljótr.	Small was he and ugly.	He was small and ugly.
Engi var hann íþróttamaðr; enn þó var hann hagr við járn ok tré.	None was he sports-man; but though was he handy with iron and wood.	He was not a sporty man but he was handy with iron and wood.
Hann hafði þá iðju, at gera öl á þingum, til fjár sér.	He had then occupation, to make ale at assembly, for wealth his.	He had a job making ale at the assembly to earn money
Enn af þeiri iðn varð hann brátt málkunnigr öllu stórmenni, því at þeir keyptu mest munngát.	And of their craft became he soon talking-known all great-men, because that they bought most ale.	and through this he came to talk to and get to know all the important people because they bought the most ale.
Var þá sem oft kann verða, at mungátin eru misjafnt vinsæl, ok svá þeir, er seldu.	Was then so often known was, that ale was uneven-in popularity, and so they, who sold.	As often happens, not everyone liked the ale, or the man who sold it.
Engi var Þórhallr veifiskati kallaðr ok heldr sjúkr.	None was Thorhall spendthrift called and rather stingy.	Thorhall was no spendthrift, and people said he was rather stingy.
Honum váru augu þung oftliga.	His were eyes heavy often.	His eyesight was poor.
Var þat siðr hans, at hafa kofra á höfði, ok jafnan á þingum.	Was it custom him, to have hood on head, and equally at assembly.	Often it was his habit to wear a hood, particularly at the assembly,

The Tale of Ale-Hood (Old Norse)

Old Norse	Literal	English
Enn af því at hann var maðr ekki nafnfrægr, þá gáfu þingmenn honum þat nafn, er við hann festist, at þeir kölluðu hann Ölkofra.	About of since that he was man not named, then gave assembly-men him the name, that with him fastened, that they called him Ale-Hood.	and since people could not remember his name, the assembly people nickhamed him Ale-Hood, and the name stuck.

2

Old Norse	Literal	English
Þat varð til tíðinda eitt haust, at Ölkofri fór í skóg þann, er hann átti, ok ætlaði at brenna kol, sem hann gerði.	It was to news one autumn, that Ale-Hood travelled to forest that, which he had, and intended to burn coal, which he made.	And so it was one autumn that Ale-Hood travelled to the woods where he intended to make charcoal.
Skógr sá var upp frá Hrafnabjörgum ok austr fyrir Lönguhlið.	Forest so was up from Hrafnabjorg and east from Langahlid.	The wood was north of Hrafnabjorg and east of Langahlid.
Hann dvaldist þar nökkura daga ok gerði til kola ok brendi síðan viðinn, ok vakti um nóttina yfir gröfunum.	He dwelled there some days and made to coal and burned since trees, and woke over night over pit.	He stayed there several days and made coal and then prepared the logs and kept watch over the pit.
Enn er á leið nóttina, þá sofnaði hann.	When was during the night, then slept he.	That was during the night, but then he fell asleep
Enn eldr kom upp í gröfunum ok hljóp í limit hjá, ok logaði þat brátt;	But fire came up in pit and ran to foliage beside, and blazed that soon;	and fire flared up in the pit and caught the branches and they were ablaze.
því næst hljóp eldr í skóginn;	then next ran fire to forest;	Then the fire ran through the next wood.
tók þá at brenna.	took then to burn.	It then began to burn.
Þá gerðist á vindr hvass.	Then was the wind sharp.	Then a sharp wind blew.
Nú vaknaði Ölkofri, ok varð því feginn, at hann gæti sér forðat.	Now awoke Ale-Hood, and was then relieved, that he got himself avoided.	Now Ale-Hood awoke and thought he was lucky to have avoided the fire.
Eldrinn hljóp í skóginn;	Fire ran among forest;	The fire ran through the woods.
brann þá skógr fyrst allr, er Ölkofri átti; enn síðan hljóp eldr í þá skóga, er þar váru næstir, ok brunnu skógar víða um hraunit.	burnt so forest first all, that Ale-Hood had; then afterwards ran fire to then forest, that there was nearest, and burned forests widely about lava-fields.	Burnt first were the woods that Ale-Hood owned, then the next woods, then afterwards the fire ran to the woods around the lava fields.

The Tale of Ale-Hood (Old Norse)

Old Norse	Literal	English
Er þar nú kallat á Svíðingi.	That there now called is Svidning.	There it is now called Svidning.
Þar brann skógr sá, er kallaðr var Goðaskógr.	There burned forest that, then called was Godaskogur.	There the wood was burned that was called Goda Wood.
Hann áttu sex goðar.	It had six chieftans.	It belonged to six chieftains.
Einn var Snorri goði, annarr Guðmundr Eyjólfsson, þriði Skafti lög-(sögu)maðr, fjórði Þórkell Geitisson, fimti Eyjólfr son Þórðar gellis, sétti Þórkell trefill Rauða-Bjarnarson.	One was Snorri chieftan, another Gudmund Son-of-Eyjolf, third Skafti law-speaker, fourth Thorkell Son-of-Geiti, fifth Eyjolf son Thord gellir, sixth Thorkell trefill Son-of-Rauda-Bjarn.	One chieftan was Snorri the Priest, another Gudmund Eyjolfson, Skafti the Lawspeaker, Thorkel Geitisson, Eyjolf son of Thord Gellir, and sixth Thorkell Trefill son of Red-Bear.
Þeir höfðu keypt skóga þessa, til þess at hafa til nytja sér á þingi.	They had bought forest then, to this to have to use themselves at assembly.	They had bought the wood for their own use at the assembly.
Eftir kolbrennu þessa reið Ölkofri heim.	After coal-burning this travelled Ale-Hood home.	After this coal burning Ale-Hood travelled home.
Tíðindi þessi spurðust víða um heruð, ok komu fyrst til Skafta þeira manna, er fyrir sköðum höfðu orðit.	News this asked many about district, and came first to Skafti of-the men, who for damage had word.	News about this was learned around the district and came to Skafti, the first of the six men whose woods had been damaged had word.
Um haustit sendi hann orð norðr til Eyjafjarðar með þeim mönnum, er ferð áttu milli heraða, ok lét segja Guðmundi skógabrennuna, ok þat með, at þat mál væri févænligt.	Around autumn sent he word north to Eyjafjord with those men, who travelled directions between districts, and let said Gudmund forest-burning, and with it, that the matter was money-promising.	Around autumn he sent word north to Eyafjord with men who travelled between districts and told Gudmund about the wood burning and with it that the matter could be profitable.
Slík sendiboð fóru ok vestr í heruð til þeira manna, er skóga höfðu átt.	Such sending-asked travelled and west to districts to those men, who forest had owned.	Such errands were travelled to the west, to the districts where the other owners were.
Fóru þá sendiboð um vetrinn eftir milli þeira allra, ok þat með, at goðar þessir sex skyldu hittast á þingi ok vera allir at einu ráði.	Travelled then messenger about winter after between they all, and to among, the chieftans these six should meet at assembly and be all as one counsel.	Messengers travelled through the winter between all six chieftains that they should meet at the assembly and take joint action

The Tale of Ale-Hood (Old Norse)

Old Norse	Literal	English
Enn Skafti skyldi mál til búa, því at hann sat næst.	As Skafti wished matter to settle, since that he sat nearest.	and Skafti would start the matter since he lived nearest.

3

Old Norse	Literal	English
Enn er vár kom, þá reið Skafti til með marga menn ok stefndi Ölkofra um skógabrennuna, ok lét varða skóggangssök.	In the spring came, then rode Skafti to with many men and summons Ale-Hood about forest-burning, and let concerning outlawry.	In the spring, at summons days, Skafti then rode with many men and summoned Ale-Hood for the burning of the wood under threat of outlawry.
Ölkofri var málóði ok heldr stórorðr; lét þess ván, ef vinir hans kœmi til þings, at Skafti mundi eigi jafnstórliga láta.	Ale-Hood was of-strong-language and rather high-sounding; let this wished, if friends his came to assembly, that Skafti would not equally-great leave.	Ale-Hood was swearing and shouting, and said that if his friends came to the assembly that Skafti would not be equally great.
Skafti svarar fá ok reið á brott.	Skafti answered few and rode to away.	Skafti answered little and rode away.
Um sumarit eftir komu þeir goðar sex til þings, er skógana höfðu átt, ok var þat ráðit, at mál skyldi frammi hafa, enn gera fé allmikit; ella hafa sjálfdæmi.	About summer after came chieftans they six to assembly, who forest owned had, and was it decided, the matter should from-forward have, as made fee all-much; otherwise have self-judgement.	In the summer the six chieftains who owned the woods came to the assembly and talked between themselves about the summons, and it was decided that the matter should be heavy damages if they could not have self-judgement.
Ölkofri kom til þings, ok átti munngát at selja.	Ale-Hood came to assembly, and had ale to sell.	Ale-Hood came to the assembly and had ale to sell,
Kom þá til fundar við vini sína, þá sem vanir váru at kaupa öl at honum.	Came then to meet with friends his, then as friends were to buy ale of him.	coming to meet with his friends who bought ale from him.
Hann bað þá liðs, ok bauð þeim öl at selja.	He invited then people, and offered them ale to sell.	He invited people and offered to sell them ale

The Tale of Ale-Hood (Old Norse)

Old Norse	Literal	English
Enn þeir svöruðu allir á einn veg, at þau ein kaup hefði þeir við átzt, at þeim var ekki vilnat í, — sögðu at þeir mundu eigi þeim birni beitast, at deila um mál hans við ofreflismenn slíka; ok vildi engi maðr heita honum liði, ok engi vildi eiga kaup við hann.	But they answered all the one way, that they only bought had they with affection, that they were not willed to, — said that they would not they bear employing, to share about the-matter his with ultra-strong-men such; and willed no man call him help, and none willed have buy with him.	but they all answered the same way, that they had not bought out of affection, and that they were not obliged to him, and they would not seek to get involved in his matter, especially since they were such powerful men, and no one wanted to help or even buy any of his ale.
Þótti honum þá heldr vandast málit.	Seemed to-him then rather difficult matter.	It looked to him that the situation was becoming rather tricky.
Gekk hann þá milli búða, ok fekk þó engi annsvör, þó at hann bæði menn liðs;	Went he then between booths, and got then no answers, though that he asked people help;	He then went among the booths and got no answers to his asking for help.
var þá lokit stórleika hans ok drambi.	Went he then between booths, and got then no answers, though that he asked people help;	He did not have any pride or arrogance left.
Þat var um dag einn, at Ölkofri kom til búðar Þórsteins Síðu-Hallssonar, ok gekk fyrir hann ok bað sér liðs.	That was about day one, that Ale-Hood came to booth Thorstein Son-of-Sidu-Hall, and got before him and asked his help.	It was one day that Ale-Hood came to the booth of Thorstein Hallsson and came before him and asked for his help.
Þórsteinn veitti honum slík annsvör sem aðrir.	Thorstein granted him such answer as others.	Thorstein gave him the same answer as the others.

4 | # 4 | # 4

Old Norse	Literal	English
Maðr er nefndr Broddi Bjarnason, mágr Þórsteins.	Man was named Broddi Bjarnason, brother-in-law Thorstein's.	There was a man camed Broddi Bjarnarson, Thorstein's brother-in-law.
Hann sat hit næsta honum.	He sat then next-to him.	He was sitting next to him.
Broddi var þá á tvítugs aldri.	Broddi was then about twenty aged.	Broddi was then aged about twenty.
Ölkofri gekk út með búðinni, þá er Þórsteinn hafði synjat honum liðs.	Ale-Hood went out-of among booths, then as Thorstein had refused him help.	Ale-Hood went out of the booth as Thorstein had refused to help him.

The Tale of Ale-Hood (Old Norse)

Old Norse	Literal	English
Broddi mælti þá:	Broddi said then:	Broddi then said:
"Svá lízt mér, mágr, sem þessi maðr sé ekki vel til skógarmanns feldr, ok er þat litilræði at sekja hann, þeim er miklir þykkjast menn fyrir sér.	"So like to-me, brother-in-law, that this man should not well to outlawry fall, and was it little-advised that seek him, they that great consider people therefore themselves.	"It seems to be brother-in-law that this man should not be an outlaw and it was mean-spirited that they seek this for him, those who consider themselves so important.
Nú er þér drengskapr, mágr, at veita þeim lið, er þíns liðs þarfnast".	Now is that word-of-honour, brother-in-law, that grant them help, that your assistance as-needed".	Now it would be honourable, brother-in-law, that we give him help and you appear as counsel".
Þórsteinn svarar:	Thorstein answered:	Thorstein answered:
"Veittú honum lið, ef þú ert allfúss til, enn veita mun ek þér gengi til þess sem annars".	"Grant him assistance, if you are all-happy to, and grant should i to-you going to this as others".	"Give him help if you are happy to, and I shall give you assistance on this path as I do others".
Broddi mælti þá við mann einn, at ganga skyldi eftir Ölkofra;	Broddi spoke then with man one, that go should after Ale-Hood;	Broddi spoke with a man and asked him to go after Ale-Hood.
sá gerði svá, — gekk út, ok þar hjá búðarveggnum hitti hann Ölkofra.	so done so, — went out, and there beside booth-walls found he Ale-Hood.	So it was done, he went out and there beside the booth walls he found Ale-Hood.
Stóð hann þar ok grét aumliga.	Stood he there and wept abjectly.	He was stood there weeping abjectly.
Þessi maðr bað hann ganga inn í búðina ok taka af sér ópit, "ok eigi skaltú snökta, er þú kemr til Þórsteins".	This man invited him to-go in to booth and take of him open, "and not shall-you sob, as you come to Thorstein".	The man invited him to go into the booth and stop himself shrieking "and don't be sobbing when you come to Thorstein".
Ölkofri varð grátfeginn ok gerði svá.	Ale-Hood became weeping-for-joy and did so.	Ale-Hood started weeping with joy and did so.
Enn er þeir komu fyrir Þórstein, þá tók Broddi til orða:	Then as they came before Thorstein, then took Broddi to words:	Then as they came before Thorstein then Broddi started to speak:
"Svá þykkir mér sem Þórsteinn vili þér lið veita, ok þykkir honum þetta klengisök vera;	"So seems to me Thorstein willing to-you assistance know, and seems to-him that small-blame be;	"So it seems to me Thorstein is willing to help you, and it seems to him that there is small blame.

The Tale of Ale-Hood (Old Norse)

Old Norse	Literal	English
máttir þú eigi gæta skóga þeira, er þú attir".	may you not guarded forest theirs, when you burned".	You may not have been able to guard against their woods burning when your own had burned down.
Ölkofri mælti:	Ale-Hood said:	Ale-Hood said:
"Hverr er sjá hinn sæli maðr, er nú mælir við mik?"	"Who is this the good man, that now speaks with me?"	"Who is this good man that now speaks with me?"
"Broddi heiti ek", segir hann.	"Broddi named i", said he.	"I am named Broddi", he said.
Þá mælti Ölkofri:	Then spoke Ale-Hood:	Then Ale-Hood spoke:
"Hvárt er hér Broddi Bjarnason?"	"Which is here Broddi Bjarnason?"	"He who is named Broddi Bjarnarson?"
"Svá er", segir Broddi.	"So is", said Broddi.	"So it is", said Broddi.
"Bæði er", kvað Ölkofri, "at þú ert göfigligri at sjá enn aðrir menn, enda áttu til þess varit".	"Both are", said Ale-Hood, "that you are nobler to this than other people, in-the-end have to this defend".	"Both are", said Ale-Hood, "that you are nobler to see than other men, in-the-end to your family's worth",
Fór hann þar mörgum orðum um, ok gerist þá hraustr í máli.	For he there many words about, and was then brave to speak.	and he went on to speak many words about it and became braver.
"Hitt er nú til", kvað Þórsteinn, "ef þú ert allfúss til, Broddi, at veita honum nökkut lið, er þó lofar hann þik svá mjök".	"Find i now to", said Thorstein, "if you are all-happy to, Broddi, to grant him some assistance, as though praises he you so much".	"Now I find towards", said Thorstein, "if you are happy to give him some assistance since he praises you so much".
Broddi stóð þá upp ok margt manna með honum.	Broddi stood then up and many men with him.	Broddi then stood up, and with many many with him.
Gekk hann út ór búðinni.	Went he from out-of booth.	He went out of his booth.
Hafði Broddi þá Ölkofra á einmæli ok ræddi við hann.	He Drew then Ale-Hood to one-talk and discussed with him.	He then took Ale-Hood to talk privately and discuss with him.
Síðan ganga þeir upp á völluna;	Afterwards went they up to plains;	Afterwards they went up to the assembly plains.
var þar fyrir margt manna.	were there before many men.	There were many men before them.

The Tale of Ale-Hood (Old Norse)

Old Norse	Literal	English
Höfðu þeir þá verit í lögréttu.	Had they then been at law-assembly.	They had been at the law-assembly.
5	**5**	**5**
Enn er aðrir menn höfðu í brott gengit, þá sátu þeir eftir Guðmundr ok Skafti, ok rœddu um lög.	And as other men had to away walked, then sat they behind Gudmund and Skafti, and discussed about law.	As the other men left, there sat behind Gudmund and Skafti discussing law.
Broddi ok förunautar hans reikuðu um völluna, enn Ölkofri gekk í lögréttuna.	Broddi and companions his roamed about plains, but Ale-Hood went to law-assembly.	Broddi and his companions walked about the assembly plains but Ale-Hood went to the law-assembly.
Hann fell til jarðar allr, ok kraup til fóta þeim ok mælti:	He fell to earth all, and kneeled about feet them and said:	He fell to the ground and kneeled at their feet among them and said:
"Sæll er ek orðinn, er ek hefi ykkr fundit, hina dýrligu menn ok höfðingja mína, eðr munu þit nökkut vilja mér hjálpa, hinir góðu menn, þótt ek sé ómakligr; því at ek verð nú allr fyrir borði, nema þit dugit mér".	"Happy am i become, that i have you found, then dearly men and chieftans mine, but shall you some wish to-me help, other good men, though i so uncomfortable; because that i deserve not all before borne, take you enough of-me".	"I am happy to have found you my dear men and chieftains, but should some of you wish to help me, good people, though I do not deserve it, I am uncomfortable because now I will be all before the table unless enough of you are with me?"
Seint er at telja öll orð Ölkofra, þau er hann mælti, ok lét hann sem aumligast á allan hátt.	Late is to tell all words Ale-hood's, his that he spoke, and let him as miserable in every way.	It would take too long to tell all of Ale-Hood's words that he spoke as he was miserable in every way.
Þá mælti Guðmundr til Skafta:	Then said Gudmund to Skafti:	Then Gudmund said to Skafti:
"Allvesalliga lætr þessi maðr".	"Miserable behaviour this man".	"What miserable behaviour from this man".
Skafti svarar:	Skafti answered:	Skafti answered:

The Tale of Ale-Hood (Old Norse)

Old Norse	Literal	English
"Hvar er nú, Ölkofri, stórlæti þitt? Ólíkligt þótti mér í vár, þá er vér fórum stefnuför, at sá mundi þinn hinn bezti kostr, at leggja málit undir mik; eðr hversu drjúgir verða þeir þér nú í liðveizlunni, höfðingjarnir, er þú hœttir mér í vár?"	"Where is now, Ale-Hood, pride yours Unlike seem you as spring, then as we travelled summons, to-you so could you the best choice, to allow the-matter under me; but how substantial were they to-you now the supportive, chieftans, that you mannered to-me about spring?"	"Where is your pride now Ale-Hood? You seem different from the spring when we travelled to summon you, so you could make the best choice to have the matter judged by me, but how substantial have you found the supportive chieftains that you threatened me with in the spring?"
Ölkofri svarar:	Ale-Hood said:	Ale-Hood said:
"Œrr var ek þá, ok þó verr, er ek vilda þat eigi, at þú dœmdir um mitt mál, enda gettú eigi höfðingja, því at þeir eru órhjarta allir, þegar þeir sjá ykkr at koma.	"Awed was i then, and though worse, am i willed it not, to you deem about my matter, in-the-end getting no chieftans, because that they were un-hearted all, as-soon-as they saw you that came.	"I was awed then, and worse that I willed it not to be judged by you in the matter, getting no chieftains in the end because they were disheartened as soon as they saw that you had come.
Sæll væra ek þá, ef ek næða því, at koma undir ykkr mínu máli.	Happy would-be i then, if i neared therefore, to come under you my matter.	How happy I would be if I could be nearer to my matter coming under you.
Eigi á ek nökkura ván þess, enn várkunn er þér, Skafti minn, at þú hafir mér svá reiðst, at nú sé þess engi kostr.	But to i some hope this, then pity i that, Skafti mine, that you have to-me such counsel, that now see this none choice.	But what hope is there of this? Then it is a pity that you have given me such counsel that I now see this is not a choice.
Var ek þá fól ok afglapi, er ek neitaða gerð þinni.	Was i then fool and simpleton, that i refusal made yours.	I was then a fool and a simpleton to refuse your offer
Enn ek þori eigi at sjá þá grimmu menn, er þegar munu drepa mik, ef þit hjálpit mér eigi við".	That i greater-part not to saw then grim men, that straight-away will kill me, if you help me not with".	that I saw no greater part then, the terrible men that will kill me straight away if you do not help me with this".
Hann mælti oft hit sama; sagði ok at hann þóttist sæll, ef þeir skyldi dœma hans mál.	He spoke often the same; said and that he thought happy, if they should deem his matter.	He often said the same things, saying that he thought he would be happy if they should judge the matter.
"Þykki mér þar mitt fé bezt komit, er þit hafit".	"Think i that my money best comes, that you have".	"I think that my money would be best if you have it".
Guðmundr mælti til Skafta:	Gudmund said to Skafti:	Gudmund spoke to Skafti:

The Tale of Ale-Hood (Old Norse)

Old Norse	Literal	English
"Ekki ætla ek þenna vel til sektar fallinn, eðr mun eigi hitt heldr ráð, at vér gerim hann feginn, ok látim hann kjósa menn til gerðar þessar.	"Not intend i that well to guilt fall, but should not find rather advice, to we being he relieved, and let he choose people to do this.	"I don't suppose it will be well if he falls guilty, and should it not rather be the decision left with him to choose people to do this? Though I know not how others alike is this matter agreed with him".
Þó veit ek eigi, hversu hinum líkar, er eigu þetta mál við hann".	Though know i not, how-so others alike, is said-of this matter with him".	Though I don't know how others are alike in this matter being agreed with him".
"Nú þá, hinir góðu menn", segir Ölkofri, "veitit mér þá nökkurn dugnað eftir".	"Now then, other good men", said Ale-Hood, "know i then someone assistance after".	"Now then other good men", said Ale-Hood, "I know then that you will give me some assistance after".
Skafti mælti:	Skafti said:	Skafti said:
"Undir mér er lykt máls þessa, því at ek fer með sökina.	"Under me is conclusion matter this, therefore that i go with seeking.	"Under me is the judgement of this matter, therefore I will seek to resolve it.
Munum vér til þess hætta, Ölkofri, at vit Guðmundr gerim um ok lúkim málinu.	Should on to this end, Ale-Hood, that with Gudmund be about and conclude case.	So to that end, Ale-Hood, the case will be concluded with Gudmund.
Get ek, at þér muni þat duga við fullting okkart".	Get i, that you would that help with assistance ours".	That is how it would help you with our assistance".

6

Þá stóð Ölkofri upp, ok takast þeir siðan í hendr.	Then stood Ale-Hood up, and took them then in hand.	Then Ale-Hood stood up and took them then in hand.
Nefndi Ölkofri þegar vátta, hveru at öðrum, ok er váttnefna kom upp, þá drifu menn at.	Named Ale-Hood then witness, each to others, and as witnesses came up, then flocked many to.	Ale-Hood then named each of his witnesses, and many people crowded around.
Nefndi Ölkofri fyrst Brodda ok föruneyti hans.	Named Ale-Hood first Brodda and companions his.	Ale-Hood named Broddi and his companions.
Skafti mælti:	Skafti spoke:	Skafti spoke:

The Tale of Ale-Hood (Old Norse)

Old Norse	Literal	English
"Sökunautr várr biðr okkr Guðmund til gerðar um mál þetta, enn þó at vit hafim þat staðfest með oss, er skaða höfum fengit, at sjálfdœmi skyldi fyrir koma, þá viljum vit Guðmundr þat nú veita honum, at vit gerim heldr um enn aðrir, ef Þórhallr vill þat kjörit hafa.	"Defendant our invited us Gudmund to do about matter this, and though that we have that confirmed with us, that damages have got, to self-judgement should by coming, then will we Gudmund that now provide him, to with doing rather of the others, if Thorhall wishes that choice have.	"The defendant has invited Gudmund and myself to do about this matter, and though we have confirmed that those who suffered the loss are to accept self-judgement, Gudmund and I are willing to grant Ale-Hood this much, that we two rather than any other men shall decide the matter if Thorhall agrees.
Skulu þér þess nefndir váttar, at fyrir mál þetta skal fé gera enn eigi mannsektir.	Should you this name witnesses, as for the-matter that shall money make about only fines.	You should stand witness for the matter that only damages shall be awarded.
Ek handsala niðrfall at sökum þeim, er ek stefnda í vár".	I confirm dropping the blame those, that i summonsed in spring".	I confirm that I drop the charge for which I summoned him in the spring.
Síðan slitu þeir handlaginu.	After dissolved they handshake.	Then they dissolved with a handshake.
Þá mælti Skafti við Guðmund:	Then spoke Skafti with Gudmund:	Then Skafti spoke with Gudmund.
"Því mun eigi vel, at vit lúkim þessu af?"	"Why should not well, that we conclude this of?"	"Why don't we conclude this?"
"Vel má þat", segir Guðmundr.	"Well may that", said Gudmund.	"That may well be", said Gudmund.
Ölkofri mælti:	Ale-Hood spoke:	Ale-Hood spoke:
"Ekki skulu þit hrapa því svá, því at er ekki ráðinn í, at kjósa ykkr, heldr enn aðra menn".	"Not should you hurry therefore so, for that am not decided of, to choose you, rather than other people".	"You should not be in such a hurry, because I have not decided if I choose you or rather someone else".
Guðmundr mælti:	Gudmund spoke:	Gudmund spoke:
"Svá var skilt, at vér skyldim gera, nema þú kjörir heldr þá aðra, er þetta mál eigu með okkr".	"So was divided, that we should do, taking your choice rather then others, that this matter have with us".	"It was so agreed that Skafti and I would decide rather than others who would have this matter with us".
Ölkofri mælti:	Ale-Hood said:	Ale-Hood said:

The Tale of Ale-Hood (Old Norse)

Old Norse	Literal	English
"Því neitaða ek alla tíma, at þeir skyldi gera; enn svá var skilit í handlaginu, at ek skylda kjósa tvá menn til, þá er ek vilda".	"Since refused i all time, that they should do; about so was divided at agreement, that i should choose two men for, then as i willed".	"I never agreed at the time that these men should decide, it was agreed at the handshake that I could choose any two men I wanted".
Þá var leitat um handsals-vætti.	Then was sought about agreement.	Then the agreement was sought about the assembly,
Enn þingmenn Guðmundar ok Skafta deildust allmjök at, hversu skilit var; enn Broddi ok förunautar hans skáru skýrt ór, at svá hefði skilit verit sem Ölkofri sagði, at hann skyldi kjósa menn til gerðar.	The assembly Gudmund and Skafti judged all-greatly that, how understood was; that Broddi and companions his cut clear of, that so had understood been which Ale-Hood said, that he should choose man to do.	Gudmund and Skafti disagreed greatly about how it had been agreed, but Broddi and his companions were clear about how it was understood, as Ale-Hood had said, that he could choose the men to decide.
Þá mælti Skafti:	Then spoke Skafti:	Then Skafti Spoke:
"Hvaðan rann sjá alda undir? Ok sé ek, at þú heldr nökkuru rakkara halanum, enn fyrir stundu áðan.	"Where runs this wave from-beneath And see i, that you rather somewhat bolder tail-wagging, than before awhile earlier.	"Where runs this wave from beneath you Ale-Hood? I see that you are wagging your tail more boldy than before,
Eðr hverja menn muntú kjósa til gerðar?"	But what men should choose to do?"	and which men do you choose to decide?
Ölkofri mælti:	Ale-Hood spoke:	Ale-Hood spoke:
"Ekki skal lengi at því hyggja.	"Not shall longer to for think.	"I shall think on it no longer.
Ek kýs Þórstein Hallsson ok Brodda Bjarnason mág hans, ok ætla ek, at þá sé málit betr komit, enn þit gerit um".	I choose Thorstein Hallsson and Brodda Bjarnason brother-in-law his, and intend i, that then so matter better comes, than you make about".	I choose Thorstein Hallsson and his brother-in-law Broddi Bjarnarson, and I suppose that the matter will be better than if undertaken by you".
Skafti sagði, at hann ætlaði, at þat mál væri vel komit, þótt þeir gerði um,	Skafti said, to him intended, that this matter would-be well coming, though they made about,	Skafti said to him that he supposed that this matter would be in good hands if they undertook it.
því at málaefni vár eru brýn ok góð; enn þeir eru svá vitrir, at þeir munu sjá kunna, hversu þungs þú ert af verðr.	as the matters are they urgent and good; and they are so wise, that they should this know, how-so heavily you are of worth.	"As the case is urgent and just and they are wise men, they should know how heavily you shall be dealt with".

The Tale of Ale-Hood (Old Norse)

Old Norse	Literal	English
Ölkofri gekk þá í lið Brodda, ok fóru menn heim til búða.	Ale-Hood went then with company Brodda's, and travelled men home to booths.	Ale-Hood went then with Brodda's company and the men travelled home to their booths.

7

Eftir um daginn skyldi upp segja sætt.	Later in the-day should up said settlement.	Later in the day the verdict was to be announced.
Báru þeir þá ráð sín saman Þórsteinn ok Broddi.	Bore they then matter theirs together Thorstein and Broddi.	Thorstein and Broddi started to consider the matter.
Vildi Þórsteinn meira gera; enn Broddi kvað þat skýrst, at gera svá sem hann vildi, ok segja þá sjálfr sátt upp.	Willed Thorstein more to-do; than Broddi said it clarified, to be so as he willed, and say then himself settlement up.	Thorstein wanted more of a settlement than Broddi did, and it was agreed that it would be as he said.
Broddi bað hann kjósa, hvárt er hann vildi:	Broddi asked him choose, either as he willed:	Broddi invited him to choose either as he wished,
segja sjálfr sátt upp, eðr sitja fyrir svörum, ef nökkurir menn yrði til, at leita á gerðina.	say yourself settlement up, or sit before answers, if some men be to, the objection to make.	to decide the settlement or sit in judgement and answer any objections.
Þórsteinn lézt heldr vilja segja sátt upp, enn skifta hnœfilyrðum við þá goðana.	Thorstein let rather willed say settlement up, than exchange blows with then chieftans.	Thorstein said that he would rather give the judgement than exchange blows with the chieftains.
Síðan sagði Þórsteinn, at Ölkofri skyldi eigi lengi þurfa síns hluta at bíða; kvað þá skyldu gjaldast féit allt at Lögbergi.	Since said Thorstein, that Ale-Hood should not long need his lot to wait; said then should pay fee altogether at Law-Rock.	Then Thorstein said that Ale-Hood would not need to wait long, saying that then the payment of a fee should be made altogether at the law rock.
Síðan gengu þeir til Lögbergs.	Then went they to Law-Rock.	Then they went to the law rock.
Enn er lokit var þar lögskil at mæla, þá spurði Þórsteinn Hallsson, hvárt goðar þeir væri at Lögbergi, er mál áttu at kæra við Ölkofra.	And when ended were there legal-settlement to matters, then asked Thorstein Hallsson, whether chieftans they were at Law-Rock, that matter had to accuse with Ale-Hood.	And when the other legal settlements were done, Thorstein Halsson asked whether the chieftains who had brought the accusation against Ale-Hood were present:
"Mér er svá sagt, at vit Broddi skylim gera um mál þat.	"To-me is so said, that with Broddi should make about matter that.	"It has been said to me that Broddi and I shall settle the matter.

The Tale of Ale-Hood (Old Norse)

Old Norse	Literal	English
Munum vit nú upp lúka gerðinni, ef þér vilit til hlýða".	Should with now up finish make, if you will to listen".	We shall deliver the conclusion if you are ready to listen".
Þeir sögðust góðs at vænta, er þeir mundu ráttlátir í gerðinni.	They said good to expect, that they would right-like to make.	They said they expected the decision would be just.
Þá mælti Þórsteinn:	Then spoke Thorstein:	Then Thorstein spoke:
"Svá lízt okkr á, sem lítils sé fyrir vert um skóga yðra félaga;	"So beholding ours is, that little being for worth about forest yours companions;	"So is our finding that your wood and that of your companions is of little worth.
váru þeir félitlir ok fjarlægir yðr til gagns.	were they fee-little and financial yours little benefit.	They were worth very little financially for you to benefit.
Var eigingirni í mikil þeira manna, er góðs áttu kost, ok kalla þat með eign sinni annarri.	Was selfish that much these men, the chieftans had benefit, and call that with may opinion another.	It was a great selfishness that these chieftains had benefitted from this property in this way,
Enn hann mátti eigi ábyrgjast yðvarn skóg, er hann brendi sinn skóg, ok eru slíkt váðaverk.	That he may not guarantee your forest, that he burned his forest, and are such accidents.	and another opinion is that he could not have guaranteed to save your woods once his had burned, and it is therefore as such an accident.
Enn fyrir því, at þat er í gerð lagt, þá skal gera nökkut fyrir.	But for because, that it is to made laid, then shall be-done something for.	But because this settlement is to be made then something shall be done.
Þér sex menn hafit átt skógana.	Then six men have had forests.	These six men who own the woods.
Nú viljum vit gera sex álnir hverjum yðrum, ok skal þat gjaldast hér þegar".	Now will we make six measures each yours, and shall that be-paid here straightaway".	Now we will award six measures, one for each of you that shall be paid here immediately".
Broddi hafði við búizt, ok stikat vaðmál í sundr, ok kastar hann sérhverjum stúf til þeira ok mælti:	Broddi had with prepared, and stitched homespun-cloth to asunder, and cast he theirs stump to them and said:	Broddi had prepared and stitched a homespun cloth and cast each strip down to them and said:
"Slikt kalla ek arga skatt".	"Such call i a-dog's tax".	I call this a tribute to the dastardly.
Skafti svarar:	Skafti said:	Skafti said:

The Tale of Ale-Hood (Old Norse)

Old Norse	Literal	English
"Auðsætt er þat, Broddi, at þú ert fúss til at eiga illt við oss.	"Obvious is it, Broddi, that you are willing to that have ill with us.	"It is obvious Broddi that you wish to have bad will with us.
Hefir þú mjök stungizt til þessa máls, ok ferr þú lítt þverr á fœti at fjandskap við oss;	Have you much wounded about this matter, and go you little around on foot to fiend-ship with us;	You have made a great wound in this matter, and you do not tip-toe around making enemies of us.
kann vera at oss falli önnur mál léttra".	can be that ours fall another matter easier".	It can be that other law suits will be resolved more easily".
Broddi svarar:	Broddi answered:	Broddi answered:
"Þurfu muntú þess Skafti, at taka meira á öðrum sakferlum, ef skerða skal í þat skarð, er Ormr frændi þinn reytti af þér, fyrir mansöngsdrápu, er þú ortir um konu hans.	"Need should this Skafti, to take more of other lawsuits, if action shall to that gap, that Orm kinsmen yours tried of you, for love-song-poem, that you worded about wife his.	You need to make more money from other law suits, Skafti, to make up for the damages your kinsman Orm got from you for the love-poem you composed about his wife.
Var þat illa gert, enda var þat illa goldit".	Was that ill done, in-the-end was that ill paid".	Was that bad will all paid in the end?"
Þá mælti Þórkell trefill:	Then spoke Thorkell trefill:	Then Thorkell Trefill spoke:
"Allmjök missýnist slíkum manni sem Broddi er;	"All-much mistake such man as Broddi that;	"That was very much a mistake from such a man as Broddi.
hann vill hafa vináttu Ölkofra, eðr nökkurar mútugjafir, ok kaupa svá, at gera sér at óvinum slíka menn, sem hann hefir í fangi".	he will have friendship Ale-hood's, or some bribes, and bought so, that made his to un-friends such men, as he has to enemies".	That he will have Ale-Hood's friendship, or his bribes, so that he makes his opponents into enemies".
Broddi svarar:	Broddi said:	Broddi said:
"Ekki er þat missýni, at halda einurð sinni, þótt mannamunr sé með yðr Ölkofra;	"Not is that mistake, to hold determined his, thought integrity as with yours Ale-Hood;	"It is no mistake to hold with determination to your integrity, yours or Ale-Hood's.

The Tale of Ale-Hood (Old Norse)

Old Norse	Literal	English
enn hitt var glámsýni í vár, er þú reitt til várþings, at þú varaðist eigi þat, er Steingrimr hafði stóðhest selfeitan, ek lagðist hann upp at baki þér; enn merin sú, er þú reitt var mögr, ok fell hún undir þér ok hefi ek eigi spurt til sanns, hverjum þá slöðraði; enn hitt sá menn, at þú vart lengi fastr, því at hestrinn lagði fœtrna fram yfir kápuna".	but find then big-mistake in spring, when you rode to local-assembly, that you warned not-of it, that Steingrim had stallion fat, and laid he up to back you; as mare yours, were you riding was skinny, and fell she under you also have i not asked about the-truth, whether then trailing-behind; about found this people, that you were long fastened, with the horse laid feet from across cloak".	But you yourself made a big mistake in the spring when you rode to a local assembly, you were not aware of the fat stallion that Steingrim had until he was laid up to your backside, and you were riding that skinny mare as she fell under you, and I have never learned the truth whether those trailing behind you found that you were long fastened with the horse with his feet laid across your cloak".
Eyjólfr Þórðarson mælti:	Eyjolf Thordarson spoke:	Eyjolf Thordarson spoke:
"Þat er satt at segja, at sjá maðr hefir allmjök dregit bust ór nefi oss, enda mælir rán ok regin við oss á svá gert ofan".	"It is true to say, that this man has all-much drawn cheated from noses ours, in-the-end talking robbery and ruling with us by saying done over".	"It is true that this man has cheated us out of our reward in front of our noses, and heaping abuse over us".
Broddi svarar:	Broddi said:	Broddi said:
"Eigi hefi ek dregit bust ór nefi yðr.	"Not have i drawn cheated of noses yours.	"I have not cheated you of your noses.
Þá var dregin bust ór nefi þér, er þú fórt norðr til Skagafjarðar ok stalt öxnum frá Þórkeli Eirekssyni; enn Goðdala-Starri reið eftir þér, ok sáttu þá eftirförina, er þér varut komnir í Vatnsdal.	Then were drawn cheated of nose you, as you travelled north to Skagafjord and stealing oxen from Thorkell Eriksson; and Guddala-Starri rode after you, and saw-you then after-travelling, that you were coming to Vatnsdal.	You were cheated of your nose as you travelled north to Skagafjord stealing oxen from Thorkell Eriksson and Guddala-Starri rode after you, and then you reached Vatnsdal.
Varðtú þá svá hræddr, at þú brátt þér í merarlíki, ok váru slíkt firn mikil; enn þeir Starri ráku aftr öxnina, ok var þat satt, at hér dró bust ór nefi þér".	Were-you then so scared, that you transformed you to mare-like, and were so awful much; that they Starri drove back oxen, and was that true, that he drew cheated of nose you".	You were so scared that you turned yourself into a mare, an awful thing to do, and Starri drove the oxen back, so it is true, he cheated your nose".
Þá mælti Snorri goði:	Then spoke Snorri chieftan:	Then Snorri the chieftain spoke:

The Tale of Ale-Hood (Old Norse)

Old Norse	Literal	English
"Allt er oss annat tiltœkilegt, enn deila hér illyrðum við Brodda; enn þat er líkast, at vér gerim oss minnisamt um fjandskap þenna, er Broddi lýsír við oss, ef vér komumst í fœri".	"All are we other available, than sharing here malice with Broddi; but it is likely, that we make us memorable about fiend-ship this, that Broddi declared with us, if we come to opportunity".	We would all rather be unavailable than here sharing malice with Broddi, but it is likely that we shall have it remembered what fiendship Broddi has shown us, and how it has come to be.
Broddi svarar:	Broddi said:	Broddi said:
"Um snýr þú þá sœmdunum, Snorri, ef þú leggr allan hug á at hefna mér, enn þú hefnir eigi föður þíns".	"Around turned you then honour, Snorri, if you lay all mind to that revenge to-me, than you avenge not father yours".	"Your honour is turned around then, Snorri, if you put your mind to revenge that instead of avenging your father".
Þá mælti Þórkell Geitisson:	Then spoke Thorkell Geitisson:	Then Thorkell Geitisson spoke:
"Þetta er líkast, at þú hafir þat helzt af nafni því, er þú ert eftir heitinn, at hann vildi hvers manns hlut óhœfan af sér verða láta, ok þat annat at menn þoli eigi, ok liggir þú drepinn, er stundir líða".	"It is likely, that you have that held of the-name of, that you are after named, that he wills each man's lot trouble of himself being let, and that other of men tolerate not, and laying you killed, be awhile passed".	It is likely, that all you have held of the name your father gave to you, is to make trouble with every man, other men will not tolerate it and you may be killed after a while.
Broddi svarar:	Broddi said:	Broddi said:
"Engi vegr er okkr i, frændi, at yppa hér fyrir alþýðu ógæfu frænda várra; enn ekki skal þat dylja, er margir vitu, at Brodd-Helgi var veginn.	"No way is ours of, kinsmen, that up here before the-people un-giving kinsmen talking-loudly; about not shall this disguise, that many knowing, that Brodd-Helgi was killed.	"There is no way to gain anything, kinsmen, by talking loudly, this shall not disguise that many know that Brodd-Helgi was killed.
Var mér ok þat sagt, at faðir þinn tœki ofarliga til þeira launanna; enn hitt ætla ek, ef þú leitar at, at þú munir fingrum kenna þat, er faðir minn markaði þik í Böðvarsdal".	Was i and that told, that father yours took high-up to their loans; but find suppose i, if you seek that, as you should fingers know that, was father mine marked you in Bodvarsdale".	I was told that your father paid the highest price, but I suppose that if you find your fingers, then they will find where my father marked you at Bodvarsdale".
Eftir þat skildust þeir, ok gengu heim til búða.	After that separated they, and none home to booths.	After that they separated and went back home to their booths.
Er nú Ölkofri ór sögunni.	Is now Ale-Hood out-of the-saga.	Ale-Hood is now out of the saga.

The Tale of Ale-Hood (Old Norse)

Old Norse	Literal	English
# 8	# 8	# 8
Annan dag eftir gekk Broddi til búðar Þorkels Geitissonar ok inn í búðina, ok kastaði orðum á Þorkel.	Next day after went Broddi to booth Thorkell Geitisson's and in to booth, and cast words to Thorkell.	The next day afterwards Broddi went to Thorkell Geitisson's booth and exchanged words with Thorkell.
Hann svarar fá, ok var hinn reiðasti.	He answered few, and was the most-angry.	He answered little and was very angry.
Broddi mælti:	Broddi spoke:	Broddi spoke:
"Því er ek hér kominn, frændi, at ek sá missmíði á því, er ek talaða við þik.	"For am i here coming, kinsman, that i saw mistake in what, was i said with you.	"For I have come here, kinsman, because I saw a mistake in what I said to you.
Vil ek þess biðja, at þú virðir mér þat til berusku ok óvizku, en látum eigi frændsemi okkra at verri.	Will i this ask, that you value me that to childishness and unwise, but let-us not kinship ours to worsen.	I wish to ask you, though you find me given to childishness, and unwise, let our kinship not worsen.
Er hér sverð búit, er ek vil gefa þér;	Is here sword to-settle, that i will give to-you;	Here is a sword that I will give to you to settle.
vil ek, at þat fylgi, at þá farir at heimboði til mín í sumar, ok skal því lýsa, at eigi skulu betri gripir í minni eigu enn þeir, er þú skalt þiggja".	will i, to this follow, that you travel to home-booth to mine in summer, and shall that show, that none shall better treasures of mine own than this, that you shall receive".	I would like to follow this by inviting you to travel to my home booth in summer, and I will show you that I have no treasures finer than the ones that you shall receive here".
Þorkell tók þessu þakksamliga; sagði, at hann var þess fúss, at þeir gerði góða sína frændsemi.	Thorkell took these thankfully; said, that he was this willing, that they made good their kinship.	Thorkell took this gladly, and said that he was willing to make good their kinship.
Gekk þá Broddi heim.	Went then Broddi home.	Broddi then went home.
Þat var aftaninn fyrir þinglausnir, at Broddi gekk vestr yfir á; enn við brúarsporðinn hittust þeir Guðmundr, ok varð ekki at kveðjum.	That was back for assembly-ending, that Broddi went west over river; and with footbridge found they Gudmund, and were not to greet.	It was the last day of the assembly that Broddi went west over the river, and at a footbridge he met Gudmund, and neither greeted the other.
Ok er þeir skildust, þá veik Guðmundr aftr ok mælti:	And as they separated, then gave Gudmund back and said:	And as they passed each other Gudmund looked back and said:

The Tale of Ale-Hood (Old Norse)

Old Norse	Literal	English
"Hverja leið skaltu ríða af þingi, Broddi?" Hann sneri aftr ok mælti:	"What way shall-you ride from assembly, Broddi?" He turned back and said:	Which way will you ride back from the Assembly, Broddi?
"Ef þér er forvitni á því, þá mun ek ríða um Kjöl til Skagafjarðar; þá til Eyjafjarðar, þaðan Ljósavatnsskarð, ok svá til Mývatns, ok síðan Möðrudalsheiði".	"If you are curious of then, there shall i ride about Kjol to Skagafjord; then to Eyjafjord, from-there Ljosavatnsskard, and so to Mywater, and after Morudale-moor".	He turned back and said: "If you are curious then I shall ride around Kjol to Skagafjord, then to Eyafjord, and from there to Ljosavatnsskard and so on to Mywater, and after that Morudale-Moor".
Guðmundr mælti:	Gudmund said:	Gudmind said:
"Efn orð þín, ok ríð Ljósavatnsskarð".	"Carry-out words yours, and ride Ljosavatnsskard".	Carry out your words and ride through Ljosavatnsskard.
Broddi svarar:	Broddi said:	Broddi said:
"Efna skal þat; eðr ætlar þú, Guðmundr, at verja mér skarðit? Allmjök eru þér þá mislagðar hendr, ef þú varðar mér Ljósavatnsskarð, svá at ek mega þar eigi fara með förunautum mínum, enn þú varðar þat eigi, hit litla skarðit, sem er milli þjóa þér, svá at ámælilaust sé".	"Carry-out shall that; but intend you, Gudmund, to guard me the-pass All-greatly are you then misplaced hand, if you guard me Ljosavatnsskard, such that i may there not travel with companions mine, as you guarded that not, the little gap, as that between buttocks yours, so as without-reproach be".	"I shall carry that out, but do you intend to guard against me passing? You are greatly mistaken if you try to stop me at Ljosavatnsskard with my companions, as you failed to guard the little gap in your backside so as to be without reproach".
Skildist þeir við svá búit ok spurðust þessi orð um allt þingit.	Separated they with so settled and asked these words about all assembly.	They separated and these words were learnt by all who were at the assembly.
Enn er Þórkell Geitisson varð þess víss, þá gekk hann til fundar við Brodda, ok bað at hann skyldi ríða Sandleið, eðr ella hit eystra.	When that Thorkell Geitisson was this aware, then went he to meet with Brodda, and bid that he should ride Sandy-road, or otherwise the east.	When Thorkell Geitisson was aware of this, he went to meet with Broddi and invited that he "should ride on the sandy road or to the east".
Broddi svarar:	Broddi said:	Broddi said:
"Ek mun ríða þá leið, er ek hefi sagt Guðmundi, því at hann mun virða mér til hugleysis, ef ek fer eigi svá".	"I would ride then way, that i have said Gudmund, because that he should worth me to cowardice, if i travel not so".	I should ride the way that I told Gudmund I would, because otherwise he shall value me as a coward if I do not.

The Tale of Ale-Hood (Old Norse)

Old Norse	Literal	English
Þórkell mælti; "Vit munum þá ríða báðir saman, frændi, ok flokkr okkarr litill".	Thorkell said; "With should then ride both together, kinsman, and band ours little".	Thorkell said: "We should both ride together then, kinsman, and our little band".
Broddi sagði, at honum þætti sœmd í föruneyti hans, ok lézt þat gjarna vilja.	Broddi said, that he thought honour to companions his, and burden that remove would.	Broddi said that he thought it a great honour to ride with him and his companions, and it would remove a burden.
Síðan ríða þeir Þórkell ok Broddi báðir saman með flokka sína norðr Öxnadalsheiði.	Afterwards rode they Thorkell and Broddi both together with band his north Oxnadale-moor.	Afterwards Thorkell and Broddi together with his band rode north to Oxnadale-Moor.
Váru þeir í einni ferð ok Einarr Eyjólfsson, mágr Þórkels.	Was they on one journey and Einar Eyjolfsson, brother-in-law Thorkell.	It was on the journey that Thorkell's father-in-law Einar Eyjolfsson joined them.
Riðu þeir Broddi ok Þórkell til Þverár, með Einari, ok váru þar um nótt.	Rode they Broddi and Thorkell to Thverriver, with Einar, and were there about night.	Broddi and Thorkell rode to Thverriver with Einar and stayed there for the night.
Síðan reið Einarr á leið með þeim með fjölmenni mikit, ok skildust eigi fyrr enn við Skjálfandafljót.	After riding Einar the way with them with followers many, and separated not before about with Skjalfandi-River.	Afterwards Einar and his many followers rode with them, and they did not separate until they reached Skjalfandi River.
Enn þeir Þórkell ok Broddi léttu eigi sinni ferð, fyrr enn þeir komu austr í Vápnafjörð til búa sinna.	About them Thorkell and Broddi relieved not their journey, before that they came east to Vopnafjord to homes theirs.	Einar then rode home and then Thorkell and Broddi did not rest their journey until they came east to Vapnfjord to their homes.
Þat sumar fór Þórkell at heimboði til Brodda frænda síns, ok þá bar allgóðar gjafir.	That summer travelled Thorkell to home-booth to Broddi kinsman his, and then there all-good gifts.	That summer Thorkell travelled to the home-booth of his kinsman Broddi and then accepted all good gifts.
Höfðu þeir þá hina bezta frændsemi með vináttu, ok helzt þat meðan þeir lifðu.	Had they then the best kinship with friendship, and held that long-as they lived.	They then had the best kinship as long as they lived.
Ok lýkr þar sögu Ölkofra.	And ends here the-saga Ale-Hood.	And here ends the saga of Ale-Hood.

Word List (Old Norse to English)

Word List (Old Norse to English)

Old Norse	English

A, a

aðra	other, others
aðrir	other, others
af	from, of, of
afglapi	simpleton
aftaninn	back
aftr	back
alda	wave
aldr	age
aldri	aged
alla	all
allan	all, every
allfúss	all-happy, all-happy
allgóðar	all-good
allir	all, all
allmikit	all-much
allmjök	all-greatly, all-greatly, all-much, all-much
allr	all, all
allra	all
allt	all, all, altogether
allvesalliga	miserable
alþýðu	the-people
annan	next
annarr	another
annarri	another
annars	others
annat	other, other
annsvör	answer, answers
arga	a-dog's
at	as, as, at, at, of, of, that, that, the, the, to, to, to-you
attir	burned
auðsætt	obvious
augu	eyes
aumliga	abjectly
aumligast	miserable
austr	east, east

Á, á

á	about, at, by, during, in, is, of, on, river, the, to
ábyrgjast	guarantee
áðan	earlier
álnir	measures
ámælilaust	without-reproach
átt	had, owned
átti	had
áttu	directions, had, have
átzt	affection

Æ, æ

ætla	intend, suppose
ætlaði	intended
ætlar	intend

B, b

bað	asked, bid, invited
báðir	both
bæði	asked, both
baki	back
báru	bore
bauð	offered
beitast	employing
berusku	childishness
betr	better
betri	better
bezt	best
bezta	best
bezti	best
bíða	wait
biðja	ask
biðr	invited
birni	bear
Bjarnason	Bjarnason (name)
bjó	lived
Bláskógum	Blawoods (place)
Böðvarsdal	Bodvarsdale (place)

119

Word List (Old Norse to English)

Old Norse	English
borði	borne
brann	burned, burnt
brátt	soon, transformed
brendi	burned
brenna	burn
Brodda	Brodda (name), Brodda's (name), Broddi (name)
Brodd-Helgi	Brodd-Helgi (name)
Broddi	Broddi (name), drew
brott	away
brúarsporðinn	footbridge
brunnu	burned
brýn	urgent
búa	homes, settle
búða	booths
búðar	booth
búðarveggnum	booth-walls
búðina	booth
búðinni	booth, booths
búit	settled, to-settle
búizt	prepared
bust	cheated

D, d

Old Norse	English
dag	day
daga	days
daginn	the-day
deila	share, sharing
deildust	judged
dœma	deem
dœmdir	deem
drambi	arrogance
dregin	drawn
dregit	drawn
drengskapr	word-of-honour
drepa	kill
drepinn	killed
drifu	flocked
drjúgir	substantial
dró	drew
duga	help
dugit	enough
dugnað	assistance
dvaldist	dwelled
dylja	disguise
dýrligu	dearly

E, e

Old Norse	English
eðr	but, or
ef	if
efn	carry-out
efna	carry-out
eftir	after, behind, later
eftirförina	after-travelling
eiga	have
eigi	but, no, none, not, not-of, only
eigingirni	selfish
eign	may
eigu	have, own, said-of
ein	only
Einari	Einar (name)
Einarr	Einar (name)
einmæli	one-talk
einn	one
einni	one
einu	one
einurð	determined
Eirekssyni	Eriksson (name)
eitt	one
ek	and, i
ekki	not
ekkí	not
eldr	fire
eldrinn	fire
ella	otherwise
en	but
enda	in-the-end
engi	no, none
enn	about, and, as, but, in, than, that, the, then, when
er	am, are, as, be, i, is, that, the, then, was, were, when, which, who
ert	are

Word List (Old Norse to English)

Old Norse	English
eru	are, they, was, were
Eyjafjarðar	Eyjafjord (place)
Eyjólfr	Eyjolf (name)
Eyjólfsson	Eyjolfsson (name), son-of-Eyjolf (name)
eystra	east

F, f

Old Norse	English
fá	few
faðir	father
falli	fall
fallinn	fall
fangi	enemies
fara	travel
farir	travel
fastr	fastened
fé	fee, money
feginn	relieved
féit	fee
fekk	got
félaga	companions
feldr	fall
félitlir	fee-little
fell	fell
fengit	got
fer	go, travel
ferð	journey, travelled
ferr	go
festist	fastened
févænligt	money-promising
fimti	fifth
fingrum	fingers
firn	awful
fjandskap	fiend-ship
fjár	wealth
fjáreigandi	property-owning
fjarlægir	financial
fjölmenni	followers
fjórði	fourth
flokka	band
flokkr	band
föður	father
fœri	opportunity
fœti	foot
fœtrna	feet
fól	fool
fór	for, travelled
forðat	avoided
fórt	travelled
fóru	travelled
fórum	travelled
förunautar	companions
förunautum	companions
föruneyti	companions
forvitni	curious
fóta	feet
frá	from
frænda	kinsman, kinsmen
frændi	kinsman, kinsmen
frændsemi	kinship
fram	from
frammi	from-forward
fullting	assistance
fundar	meet
fundit	found
fúss	willing
fylgi	follow
fyrir	before, by, for, from, therefore
fyrr	before
fyrst	first

G, g

Old Norse	English
gæta	guarded
gæti	got
gáfu	gave
gagns	benefit
ganga	go, to-go, went
gefa	give
Geitisson	Geitisson (name), son-of-Geiti (name)
Geitissonar	Geitisson's (name)
gekk	got, went
gellis	gellir
gengi	going
gengit	walked
gengu	none, went

Word List (Old Norse to English)

Old Norse	English
gera	be, be-done, do, made, make, to-do
gerð	made
gerðar	do
gerði	did, done, made
gerðina	make
gerðinni	make
gerðist	happened, was
gerim	be, being, doing, make
gerist	was
gerit	make
gert	done
get	get
gettú	getting
gjafir	gifts
gjaldast	be-paid, pay
gjarna	remove
glámsýni	big-mistake
góð	good
góða	good
goðana	chieftans
goðar	chieftans, they
Goðaskógr	Godaskogur (place)
Goðdala-Starri	Guddala-Starri (name)
goði	chieftan
góðs	chieftans, good
góðu	good
göfigligri	nobler
goldit	paid
grátfeginn	weeping-for-joy
grét	wept
grimmu	grim
gripir	treasures
gröfunum	pit
Guðmund	Gudmund (name)
Guðmundar	Gudmund (name)
Guðmundi	Gudmund (name)
Guðmundr	Gudmund (name)

H, h

Old Norse	English
hætta	end
hafa	have
hafði	had, he
hafim	have
hafir	have
hafit	have
hagr	handy
halanum	tail-wagging
halda	hold
Hallsson	Hallsson (name)
handlaginu	agreement, handshake
handsala	confirm
handsals-vætti	agreement
hann	he, him, it
hans	him, his
hátt	way
haust	autumn
haustit	autumn
hefði	had
hefi	have
hefir	has, have
hefna	revenge
hefnir	avenge
heim	home
heimboði	home-booth
heita	call
heiti	named
heitinn	named
heldr	rather
helzt	held
hendr	hand
hér	he, here
heraða	districts
heruð	district, districts
hestrinn	horse
hét	was-named
hina	the, then
hinir	other
hinn	the
hinum	others
hit	the, then
hitt	find, found
hittast	meet
hitti	found
hittust	found
hjá	beside
hjálpa	help

Word List (Old Norse to English)

Old Norse	English
hjálpit	help
hljóp	ran
hlut	lot
hluta	lot
hlýða	listen
hnœfilyrðum	blows
hœttir	mannered
höfði	head
höfðingja	chieftans
höfðingjarnir	chieftans
höfðu	had, owned
höfum	have
honum	he, him, his, to-him
hræddr	scared
Hrafnabjörgum	Hrafnabjorg (place)
hrapa	hurry
hraunit	lava-fields
hraustr	brave
hug	mind
hugleysis	cowardice
hún	she
hvaðan	where
hvar	where
hvárt	either, whether, which
hvass	sharp
hverja	what
hverjum	each, whether
hverr	who
hvers	each
hversu	how, how-so
hveru	each
hyggja	think

I, i

Old Norse	English
i	of, to
iðju	occupation
iðn	craft
illa	ill
illt	ill
illyrðum	malice
inn	in

Í, í

Old Norse	English
í	about, among, as, at, in, of, on, that, the, to, with
íþróttamaðr	sports-man

J, j

Old Norse	English
jafnan	equally
jafnstórliga	equally-great
jarðar	earth
járn	iron

K, k

Old Norse	English
kæra	accuse
kalla	call
kallaðr	called
kallat	called
kann	can, known
kápuna	cloak
kastaði	cast
kastar	cast
kaup	bought, buy
kaupa	bought, buy
kemr	come
kenna	know
keypt	bought
keyptu	bought
Kjöl	Kjol (place)
kjörir	choice
kjörit	choice
kjósa	choose
klengisök	small-blame
kœmi	came
kofra	hood
kol	coal
kola	coal
kolbrennu	coal-burning
kölluðu	called
kom	came
koma	came, come, coming
kominn	coming
komit	comes, coming

Word List (Old Norse to English)

Old Norse	English
komnir	coming
komu	came
komumst	come
konu	wife
kost	benefit
kostr	choice
kraup	kneeled
kunna	know
kvað	said
kveðjum	greet
kýs	choose

L, l

Old Norse	English
lætr	behaviour
lagði	laid
lagðist	laid
lagt	laid
láta	leave, let
látim	let
látum	let-us
launanna	loans
leggja	allow
leggr	lay
leið	the, way
leita	objection
leitar	seek
leitat	sought
lengi	long, longer
lét	let
léttra	easier
léttu	relieved
lézt	burden, let
lið	assistance, company, help
líða	passed
liði	help
liðs	assistance, help, people
liðveizlunni	supportive
lifðu	lived
liggir	laying
líkar	alike
líkast	likely
limit	foliage

Old Norse	English
litill	little, small
litilræði	little-advised
lítils	little
litla	little
lítt	little
lízt	beholding, like
Ljósavatnsskarð	Ljosavatnsskard (place)
ljótr	ugly
lofar	praises
lög	law
lög-(sögu)maðr	law-speaker
logaði	blazed
Lögbergi	Law-Rock (place)
Lögbergs	Law-Rock (place)
lögréttu	law-assembly
lögréttuna	law-assembly
lögskil	legal-settlement
lokit	ended
Lönguhlið	Langahlid (place)
lúka	finish
lúkim	conclude
lýkr	ends
lykt	conclusion
lýsa	show
lýsír	declared

M, m

Old Norse	English
má	may
maðr	a-man, man
mæla	matters
mælir	speaks, talking
mælti	said, spoke
mág	brother-in-law
mágr	brother-in-law
mál	matter, matter, the-matter
málaefni	matters
máli	matter, speak
málinu	case
málit	matter, the-matter
málkunnigr	talking-known
málóði	of-strong-language
máls	matter

Word List (Old Norse to English)

Old Norse	English
mann	man
manna	men
mannamunr	integrity
manni	man
manns	man's
mannsektir	fines
mansöngsdrápu	love-song-poem
marga	many
margir	many
margt	many
markaði	marked
mátti	may
máttir	may
með	among, it, with
meðan	long-as
mega	may
meira	more
menn	man, many, men, people
mér	i, me, of-me, to, to-me, you
merarlíki	mare-like
merin	mare
mest	most
mik	me
mikil	much
mikit	many
miklir	great
milli	between
mín	mine
mína	mine
minn	mine
minni	mine
minnisamt	memorable
mínu	my
mínum	mine
misjafnt	uneven-in
mislagðar	misplaced
missmíði	mistake
missýni	mistake
missýnist	mistake
mitt	my
mjök	much
Möðrudalsheiði	Morudale-moor (place)
mögr	skinny
mönnum	men
mörgum	many
mun	shall, should, would
mundi	could, would
mundu	would
mungátin	ale
muni	would
munir	should
munngát	ale
muntú	should
munu	shall, should, will
munum	should
mútugjafir	bribes
Mývatns	Mywater (place)

N, n

Old Norse	English
næða	neared
næst	nearest, next
næsta	next-to
næstir	nearest
nafn	name
nafnfrægr	named
nafni	the-name
nefi	nose, noses
nefndi	named
nefndir	name
nefndr	named
neitaða	refusal, refused
nema	take, taking
niðrfall	dropping
nökkura	some
nökkurar	some
nökkurir	some
nökkurn	someone
nökkuru	somewhat
nökkut	some, something
norðr	north
nótt	night
nóttina	night
nú	not, now
nytja	use

O, o

Word List (Old Norse to English)

Old Norse	English
ofan	over
ofarliga	high-up
ofreflismenn	ultra-strong-men
oft	often
oftliga	often
ok	also, and
okkarr	ours
okkart	ours
okkr	ours, us
okkra	ours
orð	word, words
orða	words
orðinn	become
orðit	word
orðum	words
ormr	orm
ortir	worded
oss	ours, us, we

Ó, ó

Old Norse	English
ógæfu	un-giving
óhœfan	trouble
ólíkligt	unlike
ómakligr	uncomfortable
ópit	open
ór	from, of, out-of
órhjarta	un-heartened
óvinum	un-friends
óvizku	unwise

Ö, ö

Old Norse	English
öðrum	other, others
öl	ale
Ölkofra	Ale-Hood (name), Ale-hood's (name)
Ölkofri	Ale-Hood (name)
öll	all
öllu	all
önnur	another
Öxnadalsheiði	Oxnadale-moor (place)
öxnina	oxen
öxnum	oxen

Œ, œ

Old Norse	English
œrr	awed

R, r

Old Norse	English
ráð	advice, matter
ráði	counsel
ráðinn	decided
ráðit	decided
ræddi	discussed
rakkara	bolder
ráku	drove
rán	robbery
rann	runs
ráttlátir	right-like
Rauða-Bjarnarson	son-of-Rauda-Bjarn (name)
regin	ruling
reið	riding, rode, travelled
reiðasti	most-angry
reiðst	counsel
reikuðu	roamed
reitt	riding, rode
reytti	tried
ríð	ride
riða	ride, rode
ríða	ride
riðu	rode
rœddu	discussed

S, s

Old Norse	English
sá	saw, so, that, this
sæli	good
sæll	happy
sætt	settlement
saga	story
sagði	said
sagt	said, told

Word List (Old Norse to English)

Old Norse	English	Old Norse	English
sakferlum	lawsuits	sjúkr	stingy
sama	same	skaða	damages
saman	together	Skafta	Skafti (name)
sandleið	sandy-road	Skafti	Skafti (name)
sanns	the-truth	Skagafjarðar	Skagafjord (place)
sat	sat	skal	shall
satt	TRUE	skalt	shall
sátt	settlement	skaltu	shall-you
sáttu	saw-you	skaltú	shall-you
sátu	sat	skarð	gap
sé	as, be, being, see, should, so	skarðit	gap, the-pass
segir	said	skáru	cut
segja	said, say	skatt	tax
seint	late	skerða	action
sekja	seek	skifta	exchange
sektar	guilt	skildist	separated
seldu	sold	skildust	separated
selfeitan	fat	skilit	divided, understood
selja	sell	skilt	divided
sem	as, me, so, that, which	Skjálfandafljót	Skjalfandi-River (place)
sendi	sent	sköðum	damage
sendiboð	messenger, sending-asked	skóg	forest
		skóga	forest
sér	him, himself, his, themselves	skógabrennuna	forest-burning
		skógana	forest, forests
sérhverjum	theirs	skógar	forests
sétti	sixth	skógarmanns	outlawry
sex	six	skóggangssök	outlawry
siðan	then	skóginn	forest
síðan	after, afterwards, since, then	skógr	forest
		skulu	shall, should
siðr	custom	skylda	should
Síðu-Hallssonar	son-of-Sidu-Hall (name)	skyldi	should, wished
		skyldim	should
sín	theirs	skyldu	should
sína	his, their	skylim	should
sinn	his	skýrst	clarified
sinna	theirs	skýrt	clear
sinni	his, opinion, their	slík	such
síns	his	slíka	such
sitja	sit	slikt	such
sjá	saw, this	slíkt	so, such
sjálfdæmi	self-judgement	slíkum	such
sjálfdœmi	self-judgement	slitu	dissolved
sjálfr	himself, yourself	slóðraði	trailing-behind

Word List (Old Norse to English)

Old Norse	English
sneri	turned
snökta	sob
Snorri	Snorri (name)
snýr	turned
sœmd	honour
sœmdunum	honour
sofnaði	slept
sögðu	said
sögðust	said
sögu	the-saga
sögunni	the-saga
sökina	seeking
sökum	blame
sökunautr	defendant
son	son
spurði	asked
spurðust	asked
spurt	asked
staðfest	confirmed
stalt	stealing
Starri	Starri (name)
stefnda	summonsed
stefndi	summons
stefnuför	summons
Steingrimr	Steingrim (name)
stikat	stitched
stóð	stood
stóðhest	stallion
stórlæti	pride
stórleika	pride
stórmenni	great-men
stóroroðr	high-sounding
stúf	stump
stundir	awhile
stundu	awhile
stungizt	wounded
sú	yours
sumar	summer
sumarit	summer
sundr	asunder
svá	saying, so, such
svarar	answered, said
sverð	sword
Svíðingi	Svidning (place)
svöruðu	answered
svörum	answers
synjat	refused

T, t

Old Norse	English
taka	take
takast	took
talaða	said
telja	tell
tíðinda	news
tíðindi	news
til	about, for, little, to
tiltœkilegt	available
tíma	time
tœki	took
tók	took
tré	wood
trefill	trefill
tvá	two
tvítugs	twenty

Þ, þ

Old Norse	English
þá	so, then, there, you
þaðan	from-there
þakksamliga	thankfully
þann	that
þar	here, that, there
þarfnast	as-needed
þat	it, that, the, this, to, with
þau	his, they
Þórðarson	Thordarson (name)
Þörkels	Thorkell (name)
þegar	as-soon-as, straightaway, straight-away, then
þeim	them, they, those
þeir	chieftans, them, they, this
þeira	of-the, their, theirs, them, these, they, those
þeiri	their
þenna	that, this

Word List (Old Norse to English)

Old Norse	English
þér	that, then, to-you, you, yours
þess	this
þessa	then, this
þessar	this
þessi	so, these, this
þessir	these
þessu	these, this
þetta	it, that, this
þiggja	receive
þik	you
þín	yours
þingi	assembly
þingit	assembly
þinglausnir	assembly-ending
þingmenn	assembly, assembly-men
þings	assembly
þingum	assembly
þinn	you, yours
þinni	yours
þíns	your, yours
þit	you
þitt	yours
þjóa	buttocks
þó	then, though
þœtti	thought
þoli	tolerate
Þórðar	Thord (name)
Þórhallr	Thorhall (name)
Þórhallsstöðum	Thorhallsstead (place)
þori	greater-part
Þórkel	Thorkell (name)
Þórkeli	Thorkell (name)
Þórkell	Thorkell (name)
Þórkels	Thorkell (name)
Þórstein	Thorstein (name)
Þórsteinn	Thorstein (name)
Þórsteins	Thorstein (name), Thorstein's (name)
þótt	though, thought
þótti	seem, seemed
þóttist	thought
þriði	third
þú	you, your
þung	heavy
þungs	heavily
þurfa	need
þurfu	need
Þverár	Thverriver (place)
þverr	around
því	as, because, for, of, since, that, then, therefore, what, why, with
þykki	think
þykkir	seems
þykkjast	consider

U, u

Old Norse	English
um	about, around, in, of, over
undir	from-beneath, under
upp	up

Ú, ú

Old Norse	English
út	from, out, out-of

V, v

Old Norse	English
váðaverk	accidents
vaðmál	homespun-cloth
vænta	expect
væra	would-be
væri	was, were, would-be
vaknaði	awoke
vakti	woke
ván	hope, wished
vandast	difficult
vanir	friends
Vápnafjörð	Vopnafjord (place)
var	then, was, were
vár	are, spring
varaðist	warned
varð	became, was, were
varða	concerning
varðar	guard, guarded

Word List (Old Norse to English)

Old Norse	English
varðtú	were-you
varit	defend
várkunn	pity
várr	our
várra	talking-loudly
vart	were
várþings	local-assembly
váru	was, were
varut	were
Vatnsdal	Vatnsdal (place)
vátta	witness
váttar	witnesses
váttnefna	witnesses
veg	way
veginn	killed
vegr	way
veifiskati	spendthrift
veik	gave
veit	know
veita	grant, know, provide
veitit	know
veitti	granted
veittú	grant
vel	well
vér	on, we
vera	be
verð	deserve
verða	being, was, were
verðr	worth
verit	been
verja	guard
verr	worse
verri	worsen
vert	worth
vestr	west
vetrinn	winter
við	with
víða	many, widely
viðinn	trees
vil	will
vilda	willed
vildi	willed, wills
vili	willing
vilit	will
vilja	willed, wish, would
viljum	will
vill	will, wishes
vilnat	willed
vináttu	friendship
vindr	wind
vini	friends
vinir	friends
vinsæl	popularity
virða	worth
virðir	value
víss	aware
vit	we, with
vitrir	wise
vitu	knowing
völluna	plains

Y, y

Old Norse	English
yðr	yours
yðra	yours
yðrum	yours
yðvarn	your
yfir	across, over
ykkr	you
yppa	up
yrði	be

Word List (English to Old Norse)

Word List (English to Old Norse)

English	Old Norse	English	Old Norse

A, a

about	á, á, á, á, á	accuse	kæra
at	á, á, á, á	allow	leggja
age	aldr	alike	líkar
aged	aldri	a-man	maðr
all	alla, allan, allan, allfúss, allfúss, allgóðar, allir, allir, allmikit, allmjök, allmjök	ale	mungátin, munngát, mútugjafir
		awed	œrr
		also	ok
		Ale-Hood (name)	Ölkofra, Ölkofra
all-happy	allfúss, allfúss	Ale-hood's (name)	Ölkofra
all-good	allgóðar	advice	ráð
all-much	allmikit, allmjök, allmjök	afterwards	síðan
		action	skerða
all-greatly	allmjök, allmjök	awhile	stundir, stundu
altogether	allt	asunder	sundr
another	annarr, annarri, annsvör	answered	svarar, svöruðu
		as-needed	þarfnast
answer	annsvör	as-soon-as	þegar
answers	annsvör, arga	assembly	þingi, þingit, þinglausnir, þingmenn, þingmenn
a-dog's	arga		
as	at, at, at, at, átt, átti, attir, áttu	assembly-ending	þinglausnir
		assembly-men	þingmenn
affection	átzt	around	þverr, því
abjectly	aumliga	available	tiltœkilegt
asked	bað, bað, bað, báðir, bæði	accidents	váðaverk
		awoke	vaknaði
ask	biðja	aware	víss
away	brott	across	yfir
arrogance	drambi		
assistance	dugnað, dvaldist, dylja, dýrligu		

B, b

after	eftir, eftir	by	á, á
after-travelling	eftirförina	back	aftaninn, aftr, aldr
and	ek, ek, eldr	burned	attir, áttu, áttu, áttu
am	er	bid	bað
are	er, er, er, er	both	báðir, bæði
awful	firn	bore	báru
avoided	forðat	better	betr, betri
agreement	handlaginu, handlaginu	best	bezt, bezta, bezti
		bear	birni
autumn	haust, haustit	Bjarnason (name)	Bjarnason
avenge	hefnir	Blawoods (place)	Bláskógum
among	í, í		

Word List (English to Old Norse)

English	Old Norse
Bodvarsdale (place)	*Böðvarsdal*
borne	*borði*
burnt	*brann*
burn	*brenna*
Brodda (name)	*Brodda*
Brodda's (name)	*Brodda*
Broddi (name)	*Brodda, Brodd-Helgi*
Brodd-Helgi (name)	*Brodd-Helgi*
booths	*búða, búðar*
booth	*búðar, búðarveggnum, búðina*
booth-walls	*búðarveggnum*
but	*eðr, ef, efn, efna*
behind	*eftir*
be	*er, er, er, ert, eru, Eyjafjarðar*
band	*flokka, flokkr*
before	*fyrir, fyrir*
benefit	*gagns, ganga*
be-done	*gera*
being	*gerim, gerim, gerim*
be-paid	*gjaldast*
big-mistake	*glámsýni*
beside	*hjá*
blows	*hnœfilyrðum*
brave	*hraustr*
bought	*kaup, kaup, kaupa, kaupa*
buy	*kaup, kaupa*
behaviour	*lætr*
burden	*lézt*
beholding	*lízt*
blazed	*logaði*
brother-in-law	*mág, mágr*
between	*milli*
bribes	*mútugjafir*
become	*orðinn*
bolder	*rakkara*
blame	*sökum*
buttocks	*þjóa*
because	*því*
became	*varð*
been	*verit*

C, c

English	Old Norse
childishness	*berusku*
cheated	*bust*
carry-out	*efn, efna*
companions	*félaga, feldr, félitlir, fell*
curious	*forvitni*
chieftans	*goðana, goðar, Goðaskógr, Goðdala-Starri, goði, góðs*
chieftan	*goði*
confirm	*handsala*
call	*heita, helzt*
cowardice	*hugleysis*
craft	*iðn*
called	*kallaðr, kallat, kann*
can	*kann*
cloak	*kápuna*
cast	*kastaði, kastar*
come	*kemr, kenna, keypt*
choice	*kjörir, kjörit, kjósa*
choose	*kjósa, kœmi*
came	*kœmi, kofra, kol, kola*
coal	*kol, kola*
coal-burning	*kolbrennu*
coming	*koma, kominn, komit, komit*
comes	*komit*
company	*lið*
conclude	*lúkim*
conclusion	*lykt*
case	*málinu*
could	*mundi*
counsel	*ráði, ráðinn*
custom	*siðr*
cut	*skáru*
clarified	*skýrst*
clear	*skýrt*
confirmed	*staðfest*
consider	*þykkjast*
concerning	*varða*

D, d

Word List (English to Old Norse)

English	*Old Norse*
during	*á*
directions	*áttu*
drew	*broddi, brott*
day	*dag*
days	*daga*
deem	*dœma, dœmdir*
drawn	*dregin, dregit*
dwelled	*dvaldist*
disguise	*dylja*
dearly	*dýrligu*
determined	*einurð*
do	*gera, gera*
did	*gerði*
done	*gerði, gerði*
doing	*gerim*
districts	*heraða, heruð*
district	*heruð*
declared	*lýsír*
dropping	*niðrfall*
decided	*ráðinn, ráðit*
discussed	*ræddi, rakkara*
drove	*ráku*
damages	*skaða*
divided	*skilit, skilt*
damage	*sköðum*
dissolved	*slitu*
defendant	*sökunautr*
difficult	*vandast*
defend	*varit*
deserve	*verð*

E, e

English	*Old Norse*
earlier	*áðan*
every	*allan*
eyes	*augu*
east	*austr, austr, bað*
employing	*beitast*
enough	*dugit*
Einar (name)	*Einari, Einarr*
Eriksson (name)	*Eirekssyni*
Eyjafjord (place)	*Eyjafjarðar*
Eyjolf (name)	*Eyjólfr*
Eyjolfsson (name)	*Eyjólfsson*
enemies	*fangi*
end	*hætta*
either	*hvárt*
each	*hverjum, hvers, hversu*
equally	*jafnan*
equally-great	*jafnstórliga*
earth	*jarðar*
easier	*léttra*
ended	*lokit*
ends	*lýkr*
exchange	*skifta*
expect	*vænta*

F, f

English	*Old Norse*
from	*af, aftaninn, aftr, aldr, aldri, alla*
footbridge	*brúarsporðinn*
flocked	*drifu*
fire	*eldr, eldrinn*
few	*fá*
father	*faðir, falli*
fall	*falli, fallinn, fangi*
fastened	*fastr, fé*
fee	*fé, fé*
fee-little	*félitlir*
fell	*fell*
fifth	*fimti*
fingers	*fingrum*
fiend-ship	*fjandskap*
financial	*fjarlægir*
followers	*fjölmenni*
fourth	*fjórði*
foot	*fœti*
feet	*fœtrna, fól*
fool	*fól*
for	*fór, forðat, förunautar, förunautum*
from-forward	*frammi*
found	*fundit, fylgi, fyrir, fyrir*
follow	*fylgi*
first	*fyrst*
find	*hitt*
foliage	*limit*

Word List (English to Old Norse)

English	Old Norse	English	Old Norse
finish	*lúka*	grant	*veita, veita*
fines	*mannsektir*	granted	*veitti*
fat	*selfeitan*		
forest	*skóg, skóga, skógabrennuna, skógana, skógana*		

H, h

English	Old Norse
forest-burning	*skógabrennuna*
forests	*skógana, skógar*
from-there	*þaðan*
from-beneath	*undir*
friends	*vanir, vár, varð*
friendship	*vináttu*

English	Old Norse
had	*átt, átti, attir, áttu, áttu, áttu*
have	*áttu, átzt, augu, aumliga, aumligast, austr, austr, bað, bað, bað*
homes	*búa*
help	*duga, dugit, dugnað, dvaldist, dylja, dýrligu*
happened	*gerðist*
he	*hafði, hafim, hafir, hafit*

G, g

English	Old Norse
guarantee	*ábyrgjast*
got	*fekk, félaga, feldr, félitlir*
go	*fer, ferð, ferr*
guarded	*gæta, gæti*
gave	*gáfu, gagns*
give	*gefa*
Geitisson (name)	*Geitisson*
Geitisson's (name)	*Geitissonar*
gellir	*gellis*
going	*gengi*
get	*get*
getting	*gettú*
gifts	*gjafir*
good	*góð, góða, goðana, goðar, Goðaskógr*
Godaskogur (place)	*Goðaskógr*
Guddala-Starri (name)	*Goðdala-Starri*
grim	*grimmu*
Gudmund (name)	*Guðmund, Guðmundar, Guðmundi, Guðmundr*
greet	*kveðjum*
great	*miklir*
guilt	*sektar*
gap	*skarð, skarðit*
great-men	*stórmenni*
greater-part	*þori*
guard	*varðar, varðar*

English	Old Norse
handy	*hagr*
hold	*halda*
Hallsson (name)	*Hallsson*
handshake	*handlaginu*
him	*hann, hann, hans, hans*
his	*hans, haust, haustit, hefði, hefi, hefir, hefir, hefnir*
has	*hefir*
home	*heim*
home-booth	*heimboði*
held	*helzt*
hand	*hendr*
here	*hér, heraða*
horse	*hestrinn*
head	*höfði*
Hrafnabjorg (place)	*Hrafnabjörgum*
hurry	*hrapa*
how	*hversu*
how-so	*hversu*
hood	*kofra*
high-up	*ofarliga*
happy	*sæll*
himself	*sér, sér*
honour	*sœmd, sœmdunum*
high-sounding	*stórorðr*
heavy	*þung*
heavily	*þungs*

Word List (English to Old Norse)

English	Old Norse
homespun-cloth	*vaðmál*
hope	*ván*

I, i

English	Old Norse
in	*á, á, ábyrgjast, áðan, ætla*
is	*á, ábyrgjast*
intend	*ætla, ætlaði*
intended	*ætlaði*
invited	*bað, báðir*
if	*ef*
i	*ek, eldr, eldrinn*
in-the-end	*enda*
it	*hann, hans, hans, haust*
ill	*illa, illt*
iron	*járn*
integrity	*mannamunr*

J, j

English	Old Norse
judged	*deildust*
journey	*ferð*

K, k

English	Old Norse
kill	*drepa*
killed	*drepinn, drifu*
kinsman	*frænda, frænda*
kinsmen	*frænda, frændi*
kinship	*frændsemi*
known	*kann*
know	*kenna, keypt, keyptu, Kjöl, kjörir*
Kjol (place)	*Kjöl*
kneeled	*kraup*
knowing	*vitu*

L, l

English	Old Norse
lived	*bjó, Bláskógum*
later	*eftir*
lot	*hlut, hluta*
listen	*hlýða*
lava-fields	*hraunit*
laid	*lagði, lagðist, lagt*
leave	*láta*
let	*láta, látim, látum, launanna*
let-us	*látum*
loans	*launanna*
lay	*leggr*
long	*lengi*
longer	*lengi*
laying	*liggir*
likely	*líkast*
little	*litill, litilræði, lítils, litla, lítt*
little-advised	*litilræði*
like	*lízt*
Ljosavatnsskard (place)	*Ljósavatnsskarð*
law	*lög*
law-speaker	*lög-(sögu)maðr*
Law-Rock (place)	*Lögbergi, Lögbergs*
law-assembly	*lögréttu, lögréttuna*
legal-settlement	*lögskil*
Langahlid (place)	*Lönguhlið*
love-song-poem	*mansöngsdrápu*
long-as	*meðan*
lawsuits	*sakferlum*
late	*seint*
local-assembly	*várþings*

M, m

English	Old Norse
miserable	*allvesalliga, álnir*
measures	*álnir*
may	*eign, eigu, Einari, Einarr, einurð*
money	*fé*
money-promising	*févænligt*
meet	*fundar, fundit*
made	*gera, gera, gerð*
make	*gera, gerð, gerðar, gerði, gerði*

Word List (English to Old Norse)

English	Old Norse
mannered	*hœttir*
mind	*hug*
malice	*illyrðum*
man	*maðr, mæla, mág, mágr*
matters	*mæla, mág*
matter	*mál, mál, málaefni, máli, málinu, málit*
men	*manna, mannamunr, manni*
man's	*manns*
many	*marga, margir, margt, markaði, mátti, máttir, með*
marked	*markaði*
more	*meira*
me	*mér, merarlíki, merin*
mare-like	*merarlíki*
mare	*merin*
most	*mest*
much	*mikil, mikit*
mine	*mín, mína, minn, minni, minnisamt*
memorable	*minnisamt*
my	*mínu, mínum*
misplaced	*mislagðar*
mistake	*missmíði, missýni, missýnist*
Morudale-moor (place)	*Möðrudalsheiði*
Mywater (place)	*Mývatns*
most-angry	*reiðasti*
messenger	*sendiboð*

N, n

English	Old Norse
next	*annan, annars*
no	*eigi, eigi*
none	*eigi, eigi, eigi*
not	*eigi, eigi, eigi, eigingirni*
not-of	*eigi*
nobler	*göfigligri*
named	*heiti, heitinn, heldr, hét, hina*
neared	*næða*
nearest	*næst, næst*
next-to	*næsta*
name	*nafn, nafnfrægr*
nose	*nefi*
noses	*nefi*
north	*norðr*
night	*nótt, nóttina*
now	*nú*
need	*þurfa, þurfu*
news	*tíðinda, tíðindi*

O, o

English	Old Norse
of	*á, á, á, á, á, aðra, aðra, aðrir, aðrir, ætla*
on	*á, á, á*
other	*aðra, aðra, aðrir, aðrir, ætla, af*
others	*aðra, aðrir, aðrir, ætla, af*
owned	*átt, auðsætt*
obvious	*auðsætt*
offered	*bauð*
or	*eðr*
only	*eigi, eigingirni*
own	*eigu*
one-talk	*einmæli*
one	*einn, einni, einu, eitt*
otherwise	*ella*
opportunity	*fœri*
occupation	*iðju*
objection	*leita*
of-strong-language	*málóði*
of-me	*mér*
over	*ofan, ofreflismenn, oft*
often	*oft, oftliga*
ours	*okkarr, okkart, okkr, okkr, okkra*
open	*ópit*
out-of	*ór, orð*
orm	*ormr*
Oxnadale-moor (place)	*Öxnadalsheiði*
oxen	*öxnina, öxnum*
opinion	*sinni*
outlawry	*skógarmanns, skóggangssök*

Word List (English to Old Norse)

English	*Old Norse*
of-the	*þeira*
out	*út*
our	*várr*

P, p

English	*Old Norse*
prepared	*búizt*
property-owning	*fjáreigandi*
pay	*gjaldast*
paid	*goldit*
pit	*gröfunum*
passed	*líða*
people	*liðs, liðveizlunni*
praises	*lofar*
pride	*stórlæti, stórleika*
pity	*várkunn*
provide	*veita*
popularity	*vinsæl*
plains	*völluna*

R, r

English	*Old Norse*
river	*á*
relieved	*feginn, fer*
remove	*gjarna*
revenge	*hefna*
rather	*heldr*
ran	*hljóp*
refusal	*neitaða*
refused	*neitaða, nema*
robbery	*rán*
runs	*rann*
right-like	*ráttlátir*
ruling	*regin*
riding	*reið, reið*
rode	*reið, reið, reikuðu, reitt*
roamed	*reikuðu*
ride	*ríð, riða, riða*
receive	*þiggja*

S, s

English	*Old Norse*
suppose	*ætla*
simpleton	*afglapi*
soon	*brátt*
settle	*búa*
settled	*búit*
share	*deila*
sharing	*deila*
substantial	*drjúgir*
selfish	*eigingirni*
said-of	*eigu*
son-of-Eyjolf (name)	*Eyjólfsson*
son-of-Geiti (name)	*Geitisson*
scared	*hræddr*
she	*hún*
sharp	*hvass*
sports-man	*íþróttamaðr*
small-blame	*klengisök*
said	*kvað, leið, leið, leita, leitar, leitat, léttu, líða, liðs, liðveizlunni*
seek	*leitar, leitat*
sought	*leitat*
supportive	*liðveizlunni*
small	*litill*
show	*lýsa*
speaks	*mælir*
spoke	*mælti*
speak	*máli*
skinny	*mögr*
shall	*mun, mun, mun, mundi, mundu*
should	*mun, mun, mundi, mundu, muni, munir, muntú, munu, munu, munu, munum, næða*
some	*nökkura, nökkurar, nökkurir, nökkurn*
someone	*nökkurn*
somewhat	*nökkuru*
something	*nökkut*
son-of-Rauda-Bjarn (name)	*Rauða-Bjarnarson*
saw	*sá, sá*
so	*sá, sá, sá, sætt, saga, sagði, sagt*
settlement	*sætt, saga*
story	*saga*

Word List (English to Old Norse)

English	*Old Norse*	English	*Old Norse*
same	*sama*	seem	*þótti*
sandy-road	*sandleið*	seemed	*þótti*
sat	*sat, satt*	seems	*þykkir*
saw-you	*sáttu*	spring	*vár*
see	*sé*	spendthrift	*veifiskati*
say	*segja*		
sold	*seldu*		
sell	*selja*		
sent	*sendi*		
sending-asked	*sendiboð*		
sixth	*sétti*		
six	*sex*		
since	*síðan, síðan*		
son-of-Sidu-Hall (name)	*Síðu-Hallssonar*		

T, t

English	*Old Norse*
the	*á, á, aðra, aðra, aðrir, aðrir, ætla, af, af, afglapi, alda*
to	*á, aðra, aðra, aðrir, aðrir, ætla, af, af*
the-people	*alþýðu*
that	*at, at, at, at, at, at, at, átt, auðsætt, bauð, bíða, brátt, brátt, brýn*
to-you	*at, átt*
transformed	*brátt*
to-settle	*búit*
the-day	*daginn*
than	*enn*
then	*enn, enn, er, er, er, er, er, er, er, er, eru, eru, eru*
they	*eru, eru, eru, Eyjólfsson, fara, farir*
travel	*fara, farir, feginn*
travelled	*ferð, fjár, fjáreigandi, fœri, fór, fórt*
therefore	*fyrir, ganga*
to-go	*ganga*
to-do	*gera*
treasures	*gripir*
tail-wagging	*halanum*
to-him	*honum*
think	*hyggja, i*
talking	*mælir*
the-matter	*mál, máli*
talking-known	*málkunnigr*
to-me	*mér*
the-name	*nafni*
take	*nema, nema*
taking	*nema*
trouble	*óhœfan*
tried	*reytti*

English	*Old Norse*
sit	*sitja*
self-judgement	*sjálfdæmi, sjálfdœmi*
stingy	*sjúkr*
Skafti (name)	*Skafta, Skafti*
Skagafjord (place)	*Skagafjarðar*
shall-you	*skaltu, skaltú*
separated	*skildist, skildust*
Skjalfandi-River (place)	*Skjálfandafljót*
such	*slík, slíka, slikt, slíkt, slíkt, slíkum*
sob	*snökta*
Snorri (name)	*Snorri*
slept	*sofnaði*
seeking	*sökina*
son	*son*
stealing	*stalt*
Starri (name)	*Starri*
summonsed	*stefnda*
summons	*stefndi, stefnuför*
Steingrim (name)	*Steingrimr*
stitched	*stikat*
stood	*stóð*
stallion	*stóðhest*
stump	*stúf*
summer	*sumar, sumarit*
saying	*svá*
sword	*sverð*
Svidning (place)	*Svíðingi*
straightaway	*þegar*
straight-away	*þegar*

138

Word List (English to Old Norse)

English	Old Norse
this	sá, sætt, saga, sagði, sagt, sagt, sama, saman, sandleið, sanns, sat
told	sagt
together	saman
the-truth	sanns
true	
themselves	sér
theirs	sérhverjum, sétti, sex, siðan
their	sína, sinna, sinni, sinni
the-pass	skarðit
tax	skatt
trailing-behind	slöðraði
turned	sneri, snökta
the-saga	sögu, sögunni
took	takast, talaða, telja
tell	telja
there	þá, þá
thankfully	þakksamliga
Thordarson (name)	Þórðarson
Thorkell (name)	Þorkels, þegar, þegar, þegar, þeim
them	þeim, þeim, þeim
those	þeim, þeir
these	þeira, þeira, þeira, þeiri
though	þó, þœtti
thought	þœtti, þoli, Þórðar
tolerate	þoli
Thord (name)	Þórðar
Thorhall (name)	Þórhallr
Thorhallsstead (place)	Þórhallsstöðum
Thorstein (name)	Þórstein, Þórsteinn, Þórsteins
Thorstein's (name)	Þórsteins
third	þriði
Thverriver (place)	Þverár
time	tíma
trefill	trefill
two	tvá
twenty	tvítugs
talking-loudly	várra
trees	viðinn

U, u

English	Old Norse
urgent	brýn
ugly	ljótr
uneven-in	misjafnt
use	nytja
ultra-strong-men	ofreflismenn
un-giving	ógæfu
us	okkr, okkra
unlike	ólíkligt
uncomfortable	ómakligr
un-heartened	órhjarta
un-friends	óvinum
unwise	óvizku
understood	skilit
under	undir
up	upp, út

V, v

English	Old Norse
Vopnafjord (place)	Vápnafjörð
Vatnsdal (place)	Vatnsdal
value	virðir

W, w

English	Old Norse
wave	alda
without-reproach	ámælilaust
wait	bíða
word-of-honour	drengskapr
when	enn, er
was	er, er, er, er, er, eru, eru, eru, Eyjólfsson
were	er, er, er, er, eru, eru, eru, Eyjólfsson, fara
which	er, er, eru
who	er, eru
wealth	fjár
willing	fúss, fyrir
went	ganga, Geitisson, gekk
walked	gengit
weeping-for-joy	grátfeginn

Word List (English to Old Norse)

English	*Old Norse*	English	*Old Norse*
wept	*grét*	you	*mér, misjafnt, mögr, mun, mun, mun, mundi, mundu*
way	*hátt, hefna, heiti, heitinn*		
was-named	*hét*	yourself	*sjálfr*
where	*hvaðan, hvar*	yours	*sú, sumar, sumarit, svá, svá, svá, svarar, sverð, Svíðingi, synjat*
whether	*hvárt, hvárt*		
what	*hverja, hverjum*		
with	*í, iðju, íþróttamaðr, klengisök, konu, kvað*	your	*þíns, þíns, þit*
wife	*konu*		
would	*mun, mundi, mundu, muni, munir*		
will	*munu, munum, næða, næst, næst*		
word	*orð, orð*		
words	*orð, orða, orðit*		
worded	*ortir*		
we	*oss, óvinum, óvizku*		
wished	*skyldi, skyldim*		
wounded	*stungizt*		
why	*því*		
wood	*tré*		
would-be	*væra, væri*		
woke	*vakti*		
warned	*varaðist*		
were-you	*varðtú*		
witness	*vátta*		
witnesses	*váttar, váttnefna*		
well	*vel*		
worth	*verðr, verr, verri*		
worse	*verr*		
worsen	*verri*		
west	*vestr*		
winter	*vetrinn*		
widely	*víða*		
willed	*vilda, vildi, vildi, vili*		
wills	*vildi*		
wish	*vilja*		
wishes	*vill*		
wind	*vindr*		
wise	*vitrir*		

Y, y

The Tale of Ale-Hood (Old Icelandic)

The Tale of Ale-Hood (*Old Icelandic*)

Old Icelandic	Literal	English
1	**1**	**1**
Þórhallur hét maður.	Thorhall was-named a-man.	There was a man named Thorhall.
Hann bjó í Bláskógum á Þórhallsstöðum.	He lived in Blawoods in Thorhallsstead.	He lived in Blawoods in Thorhallsstead.
Hann var vel fjáreigandi og heldur við aldur er saga sjá gerðist.	He was well property-owning and rather with age as story so happened.	He was a wealthy man and rather old when the story happened.
Lítill var hann og ljótur.	Small was he and ugly.	He was small and ugly.
Engi var hann íþróttamaður en þó var hann hagur við járn og tré.	None was he sports-man but though was he handy with iron and wood.	He was not a sporty man but he was handy with iron and wood.
Hann hafði þá iðju að gera öl á þingum til fjár sér	He had then occupation to make ale at assembly for wealth his	He had a job making ale at the assembly to earn money
en af þessi iðn varð hann brátt málkunnigur öllu stórmenni því að þeir keyptu mest mungát.	and of this craft became he soon talking-known all great-men because that they bought most ale.	and through this he came to talk to and get to know all the important people because they bought the most ale.
Var þá sem oft kann verða að mungátin eru misjafnt vinsæl og svo þeir er seldu.	Was then so often known was that ale was uneven-in popularity and so they who sold.	As often happens, not everyone liked the ale, or the man who sold it.
Engi var Þórhalldur veifiskati kallaður og heldur sínkur.	None was Thorhall spendthrift called and rather stingy.	Thorhall was no spendthrift, and people said he was rather stingy.
Honum voru augu þung.	His were eyes heavy.	His eyesight was poor.
Oftlega var það siður hans að hafa kofra á höfði og jafnan á þingum	Often was it custom him to have hood on head and equally at assembly	Often it was his habit to wear a hood, particularly at the assembly,

The Tale of Ale-Hood (Old Icelandic)

Old Icelandic	Literal	English
en af því að hann var maður ekki nafndrægur þá gáfu þingmenn honum það nafn er við hann festist að þeir kölluðu hann Ölkofra.	about of since that he was man not named then gave assembly-men him the name that with him fastened that they called him Ale-Hood.	and since people could not remember his name, they assembly people nickhamed him Ale-Hood, and the name stuck.
Það varð til tíðinda eitt haust að Ölkofri fór í skóg þann er hann átti og ætlaði að brenna kol sem hann gerði.	It was to news one autumn that Ale-Hood travelled to forest that which he had and intended to burn coal which he made.	And so it was one autumn that Ale-Hood travelled to the woods where he intended to make charcoal.
Skógur sá var upp frá Hrafnabjörgum og austur frá Lönguhlíð.	Forest so was up from Hrafnabjorg and east from Langahlid.	The wood was north of Hrafnabjorg and east of Langahlid.
Hann dvaldist þar nokkura daga og gerði til kola og brenndi síðan viðinn og vakti um nótt yfir gröfunum.	He dwelled there some days and made to coal and burned since trees and woke over night over pit.	He stayed there several days and made coal and then prepared the logs and kept watch over the pit.
En er leið á nóttina þá sofnaði hann	When was during the night then slept he	That was during the night, but then he fell asleep
en eldur kom upp í gröfunum og hljóp í limið hjá og logaði það brátt.	but fire came up in pit and ran to foliage beside and blazed that soon.	and fire flared up in the pit and caught the branches and they were ablaze.
Því næst hljóp eldur í skóginn.	Then next ran fire to forest.	Then the fire ran through the next wood.
Tók hann þá að brenna.	Took it then to burn.	It then began to burn.
Þá gerist á vindur hvass.	Then was the wind sharp.	Then a sharp wind blew.
Nú vaknaði Ölkofri og varð því feginn að hann gæti sér forðað.	Now awoke Ale-Hood and was then relieved that he got himself avoided.	Now Ale-Hood awoke and thought he was lucky to have avoided the fire.
Eldurinn hljóp í skóginn.	Fire ran among forest.	The fire ran through the woods.
Brann sá skógur fyrst allur er Ölkofri átti en síðan hljóp eldur í þá skóga er þar voru næstir og brunnu skógar víða um hraunið.	Burnt so forest first all that Ale-Hood had then afterwards ran fire to then forest that there was nearest and burned forests widely about lava-fields.	Burnt first were the woods that Ale-Hood owned, then the next woods, then afterwards the fire ran to the woods around the lava fields.

The Tale of Ale-Hood (Old Icelandic)

Old Icelandic	Literal	English
Er þar nú kallað á Sviðningi.	That there now called is Svidning.	There it is now called Svidning.
Þar brann skógur sá er kallaður var Goðaskógur.	There burned forest that then called was Godaskogur.	There the wood was burned that was called Goda Wood.
Hann áttu sex goðar.	It had six chieftans.	It belonged to six chieftains.
Einn var Snorri goði, annar Guðmundur Eyjólfsson, þriðji Skafti lögmaður, fjórði Þorkell Geitisson, fimmti Eyjólfur son Þórðar gellis, sétti Þorkell trefill Rauða-Bjarnarson.	One was Snorri chieftan, another Gudmund Son-of-Eyjolf, third Skafti law-speaker, fourth Thorkell Son-of-Geiti, fifth Eyjolf son Thord gellir, sixth Thorkell trefill Son-of-Rauda-Bjarn.	One chieftan was Snorri the Priest, another Gudmund Eyjolfson, Skafti the Lawspeaker, Thorkel Geitisson, Eyjolf son of Thord Gellir, and sixth Thorkell Trefill son of Red-Bear.
Þeir höfðu keypt skóga þá til þess að hafa til nytja sér á þingi.	They had bought forest then to this to have to use themselves at assembly.	They had bought the wood for their own use at the assembly.
Eftir kolbrennu þessa fór Ölkofri heim.	After coal-burning this travelled Ale-Hood home.	After this coal burning Ale-Hood travelled home.
En tíðindi þessi spurðust víða um héruð og komu fyrst til Skafta þeirra mann er fyrir sköðum höfðu orðið.	About news this asked many about district and came first to Skafti of-the men who for damage had word.	News about this was learned around the district and came to Skafti, the first of the six men whose woods had been damaged had word.
Um haustið sendi hann orð norður til Eyjafjarðar með þeim mönnum er ferð áttu milli héraða og lét segja Guðmundi skógabrennuna og það með að það mál var févænlegt.	Around autumn sent he word north to Eyjafjord with those men who travelled directions between districts and let said Gudmund forest-burning and with it that the matter was money-promising.	Around autumn he sent word north to Eyafjord with men who travelled between districts and told Gudmund about the wood burning and with it that the matter could be profitable.
Slík erindi fóru og vestur í héruð til þeirra manna er skóga höfðu átt.	Such errand travelled and west to districts to those men who forest had owned.	Such errands were travelled to the west, to the districts where the other owners were.
Fóru þá sendiboð um veturinn eftir milli þeirra allra og það með að goðar þeir sex skyldu hittast á þingi og vera allir að einu ráði	Travelled then messenger about winter after between they all and to among the chieftans they six should meet at assembly and be all as one counsel	Messengers travelled through the winter between all six chieftains that they should meet at the assembly and take joint action
en Skafti skyldi mál til búa því að hann sat næst.	as Skafti wished matter to settle since that he sat nearest.	and Skafti would start the matter since he lived nearest.

The Tale of Ale-Hood (Old Icelandic)

Old Icelandic	Literal	English
En er vor kom og stefnudagar þá reið Skafti til með marga menn og stefndi Ölkofra um skógabrennuna og lét varða skóggang.	In the spring came and policy-days then rode Skafti to with many men and summons Ale-Hood about forest-burning and let concerning outlawry.	In the spring, at summons days, Skafti then rode with many men and summoned Ale-Hood for the burning of the wood under threat of outlawry.
Ölkofri var málóði og heldur stórorðu, lét þess von ef vinir hans kæmu til þings að Skafti mundi eigi jafnstórlega láta.	Ale-Hood was of-strong-language and rather high-sounding, let this wished if friends his came to assembly that Skafti would not equally-great leave.	Ale-Hood was swearing and shouting, and said that if his friends came to the assembly that Skafti would not be equally great.
Skafti svaraði fá og reið á brott.	Skafti answered few and rode to away.	Skafti answered little and rode away.
Um sumarið eftir komu goðar þeir sex til þings er skóga höfðu átt og höfðu brátt stefnu sín á milli og var það ráðið að mál skyldi fram hafa en gera fé allmikið ella hafa sjálfdæmi.	About summer after came chieftans they six to assembly who forest owned had and had soon summons they about between and was it decided the matter should from-forward have as made fee all-much otherwise have self-judgement.	In the summer the six chieftains who owned the woods came to the assembly and talked between themselves about the summons, and it was decided that the matter should be heavy damages if they could not have self-judgement.
Ölkofri kom til þings og átti mungát að selja,	Ale-Hood came to assembly and had ale to sell,	Ale-Hood came to the assembly and had ale to sell,
kom þá til fundar við vini sína þá sem vanir voru að kaupa öl að honum.	came then to meet with friends his then as friends were to buy ale of him.	coming to meet with his friends who bought ale from him.
Hann bað þá liðs og bauð þeim öl að selja	He invited then people and offered them ale to sell	He invited people and offered to sell them ale
en þeir svöruðu allir á einn veg að þau ein kaup hefðu þeir við ást að þeim var ekki vilnað í, sögðu að þeir mundu eigi þeim birni beitast að deila um mál hans við ofureflismenn slíka og vildi engi maður heita honum liði og engi vildi eiga kaup við hann.	but they answered all the one way that they only bought had they with affection that they were not willed to, said that they would not they bear employing to share about the-matter his with ultra-strong-men such and willed no man call him help and none willed have buy with him.	but they all answered the same way, that they had not bought out of affection, and that they were not obliged to him, and they would not seek to get involved in his matter, especially since they were such powerful men, and no one wanted to help or even buy any of his ale.

The Tale of Ale-Hood (Old Icelandic)

Old Icelandic	Literal	English
Þótti honum þá heldur vandast málið.	Seemed to-him then rather difficult matter.	It looked to him that the situation was becoming rather tricky.
Gekk hann þá milli búða og fékk þá engi andsvör þótt hann bæði menn liðs.	Went he then between booths and got then no answers though he asked people help.	He then went among the booths and got no answers to his asking for help.
Var þá lokið stórleika hans og drambi.	Was then ended pride his and arrogance.	He did not have any pride or arrogance left.
Það var um dag einn að Ölkofri kom til búðar Þorsteins Síðu-Hallssonar og fekk fyrir hann og bað sér liðs.	That was about day one that Ale-Hood came to booth Thorstein Son-of-Sidu-Hall and got before him and asked his help.	It was one day that Ale-Hood came to the booth of Thorstein Hallsson and came before him and asked for his help.
Þorsteinn veitti honum slík andsvör sem aðrir.	Thorstein granted him such answer as others.	Thorstein gave him the same answer as the others.

2

Maður er nefndur Broddi Bjarnason, mágur Þorsteins.	Man was named Broddi Bjarnason, brother-in-law Thorstein's.	There was a man camed Broddi Bjarnarson, Thorstein's brother-in-law.
Hann sat hið næsta honum.	He sat then next-to him.	He was sitting next to him.
Broddi var þá á tvítugsaldri.	Broddi was then about twenty-aged.	Broddi was then aged about twenty.
Ölkofri gekk út með búðinni þá er Þorsteinn hafði synjað honum liðs.	Ale-Hood went out-of among booths then as Thorstein had refused him help.	Ale-Hood went out of the booth as Thorstein had refused to help him.
Broddi mælti þá:	Broddi said then:	Broddi then said:
"Svo líst mér mágur sem þessi maður muni ekki vel til skógarmanns felldur og er það lítilræði að sekja hann þeim er miklir þykjast fyrir sér.	"So like to-me brother-in-law that this man should not well to outlawry fall and was it little-advised that seek him they that great consider therefore themselves.	"It seems to be brother-in-law that this man should not be an outlaw and it was mean-spirited that they seek this for him, those who consider themselves so important.
Nú er það drengskapur mágur að veita honum lið og mun þér það sýnast ráð".	Now is that word-of-honour brother-in-law that grant him help and should you that appear counsel".	Now it would be honourable, brother-in-law, that we give him help and you appear as counsel".

The Tale of Ale-Hood (Old Icelandic)

Old Icelandic	Literal	English
Þorsteinn svarar:	Thorstein answered:	Thorstein answered:
"Veittu honum lið ef þú ert allfús til en veita mun eg þér brautargengi til þess sem annars".	"Grant him assistance if you are all-happy to and grant should i to-you path-assistance to this as others".	"Give him help if you are happy to, and I shall give you assistance on this path as I do others".
Broddi mælti við mann einn að ganga skyldi eftir Ölkofra.	Broddi spoke with man one that go should after Ale-Hood.	Broddi spoke with a man and asked him to go after Ale-Hood.
Sá gerði svo, gekk út og þar hjá búðarvegginum hitti hann Ölkofra.	So done so, went out and there beside booth-walls found he Ale-Hood.	So it was done, he went out and there beside the booth walls he found Ale-Hood.
Stóð hann þar og grét aumlega.	Stood he there and wept abjectly.	He was stood there weeping abjectly.
Þessi maður bað hann ganga inn í búðina og taka af sér ópið "og eigi skaltu snökta er þú kemur til Þorsteins".	This man invited him to-go in to booth and take of him open "and not shall-you sob as you come to Thorstein".	The man invited him to go into the booth and stop himself shrieking "and don't be sobbing when you come to Thorstein".
Ölkofri varð grátfeginn og gerði svo.	Ale-Hood became weeping-for-joy and did so.	Ale-Hood started weeping with joy and did so.
En er þeir komu fyrir Þorstein þá tók Broddi til orða:	Then as they came before Thorstein then took Broddi to words:	Then as they came before Thorstein then Broddi started to speak:
"Svo þykir mér sem Þorsteinn vilji þér lið veita og þykir honum þetta klengisök vera.	"So seems to me Thorstein willing to-you assistance know and seems to-him that small-blame be.	"So it seems to me Thorstein is willing to help you, and it seems to him that there is small blame.
Máttir þú eigi gæta skóga þeirra er þú brenndir þann er þú áttir".	May you not guarded forest theirs when you burned then that you had".	You may not have been able to guard against their woods burning when your own had burned down.
Ölkofri mætli:	Ale-Hood said:	Ale-Hood said:
"Hver er sjá hinn sæli maður er nú mælir við mig?" "Broddi heiti ég", segir hann.	"Who is this the good man that now speaks with me?" "Broddi named i", said he.	"Who is this good man that now speaks with me?"
"Hver er sjá hinn sæli maður er nú mælir við mig?" "Broddi heiti ég", segir hann.	"Who is this the good man that now speaks with me?" "Broddi named i", said he.	"I am named Broddi", he said.

The Tale of Ale-Hood (Old Icelandic)

Old Icelandic	Literal	English
Þá mælti Ölkofri:	Then spoke Ale-Hood:	Then Ale-Hood spoke:
"Hvert er hér Broddi Bjarnason?"	"Which is here Broddi Bjarnason?"	"He who is named Broddi Bjarnarson?"
"Svo er", segir Broddi.	"So is", said Broddi.	"So it is", said Broddi.
"Bæði er", kvað Ölkofri, "að þú ert göfulegri að sjá en aðrir menn enda áttu til þess varið",	"Both are", said Ale-Hood, "that you are nobler to this than other people in-the-end have to this defend",	"Both are", said Ale-Hood, "that you are nobler to see than other men, in-the-end to your family's worth",
for hann þar mörgum orðum um og gerist þá hraustur í máli.	for he there many words about and was then brave to speak.	and he went on to speak many words about it and became braver.
"Hitt er nú til", kvað Þorsteinn, "ef þú ert allfús til Broddi að veita honum nokkuð lið er þó lofar hann þig svo mjög".	"Find i now to", said Thorstein, "if you are all-happy to Broddi to grant him some assistance as though praises he you so much".	"Now I find towards", said Thorstein, "if you are happy to give him some assistance since he praises you so much".
Broddi stóð þá upp og mart manna með honum.	Broddi stood then up and many men with him.	Broddi then stood up, and with many many with him.
Gekk hann út úr búðinni.	Went he from out-of booth.	He went out of his booth.
Hann brá þá Ölkofra á einmæli og ræddi við hann.	He drew then Ale-Hood to one-talk and discussed with him.	He then took Ale-Hood to talk privately and discuss with him.
Síðan ganga þeir upp á völluna.	Afterwards went they up to plains.	Afterwards they went up to the assembly plains.
Var þar fyrir mart manna.	Were there before many men.	There were many men before them.
Höfðu þeir þá verið í lögréttu.	Had they then been at law-assembly.	They had been at the law-assembly.
En er aðrir menn höfðu í brott gengið þá sátu þeir eftir Guðmundur og Skafti og ræddu um lög.	And as other men had to away walked then sat they behind Gudmund and Skafti and discussed about law.	As the other men left, there sat behind Gudmund and Skafti discussing law.

The Tale of Ale-Hood (Old Icelandic)

Old Icelandic	Literal	English
Broddi og förunautar hans reikuðu um völluna en Ölkofri gekk í lögréttuna.	Broddi and companions his roamed about plains but Ale-Hood went to law-assembly.	Broddi and his companions walked about the assembly plains but Ale-Hood went to the law-assembly.
Hann féll til jarðar allur og kraup til fóta með þeim og mælti:	He fell to earth all and kneeled about feet among them and said:	He fell to the ground and kneeled at their feet among them and said:
"Sæll er eg orðinn er eg hefi ykkur fundið hina dýrlegu menn og höfðingja mína eða munuð þið nokkuð vilja mér hjálpa hinir góðu menn þót eg sé ómaklegur því að eg verð nú allur fyrir borði nema þið dugið mér?"	"Happy am i become that i have you found then dearly men and chieftans mine but shall you some wish to-me help other good men though i so uncomfortable because that i deserve not all before borne take you enough of-me?"	"I am happy to have found you my dear men and chieftains, but should some of you wish to help me, good people, though I do not deserve it, I am uncomfortable because now I will be all before the table unless enough of you are with me?"
Seint er að telja öll orð Ölkofra þau er hann mælti og lét hann ssem aumlegast á allan hátt.	Late is to tell all words Ale-hood's his that he spoke and let him as miserable in every way.	It would take too long to tell all of Ale-Hood's words that he spoke as he was miserable in every way.
Þá mætli Guðmundur til Skafta:	Then said Gudmund to Skafti:	Then Gudmund said to Skafti:
"Allvesallega lætur þessi maður".	"Miserable behaviour this man".	"What miserable behaviour from this man".
Skafti svarar:	Skafti answered:	Skafti answered:
"Hvar er nú Ölkofri stórlæti þitt? Ólíklegt þótti þér í vor þá er vér fórum stefnuför að sá mundi þinn hinn besti kostur að leggja málið undir mig eða hversu drjúgir verða þeir þér nú í liðveilsunni höfðingjarnir er þú hættir mér í vor?"	"Where is now Ale-Hood pride yours Unlike seem you as spring then as we travelled summons to-you so could you the best choice to allow the-matter under me but how substantial were they to-you now the supportive chieftans that you mannered to-me about spring?"	"Where is your pride now Ale-Hood? You seem different from the spring when we travelled to summon you, so you could make the best choice to have the matter judged by me, but how substantial have you found the supportive chieftains that you threatened me with in the spring?"
Ölkofri segir:	Ale-Hood said:	Ale-Hood said:

The Tale of Ale-Hood (Old Icelandic)

Old Icelandic	Literal	English
"Ær var eg þá og þó verr er eg vildi það eigi að þú dæmdir um mitt mál enda gettu eigi höfðingja því að þeir eru örhjarta allir þegar þeir sjá ykkur að koma.	"Awed was i then and though worse am i willed it not to you deem about my matter in-the-end getting no chieftans because that they were unheartened all as-soon-as they saw you that came.	"I was awed then, and worse that I willed it not to be judged by you in the matter, getting no chieftains in the end because they were disheartened as soon as they saw that you had come.
Sæll væri eg þá ef eg næði því að koma undir ykkur mínu máli.	Happy would-be i then if i neared therefore to come under you my matter.	How happy I would be if I could be nearer to my matter coming under you.
Eða á eg nokkura von þess? En vorkunn er það Skafti minn að þú hafir mér svo reiðst að nú sé þess engi kostur.	But to i some hope this Then pity i that Skafti mine that you have to-me such counsel that now see this none choice.	But what hope is there of this? Then it is a pity that you have given me such counsel that I now see this is not a choice.
Var eg þá fól og afglapi er eg neitaði gerð þinni	Was i then fool and simpleton that i refusal made yours	I was then a fool and a simpleton to refuse your offer
en eg þori eigi að sjá þá grimmu menn er þegar munu drepa mig ef þið hjálpið mér eigi við".	that i greater-part not to saw then grim men that straightaway will kill me if you help me not with".	that I saw no greater part then, the terrible men that will kill me straight away if you do not help me with this".
Hann mælti oft hið sama, sagði svo að hann þóttist sæll ef þeir skyldu dæma hans mál:	He spoke often the same, said so that he thought happy if they should deem his matter:	He often said the same things, saying that he thought he would be happy if they should judge the matter.
"Þykir mér það mitt fé best komið er þið hafið".	"Think i that my money best comes that you have".	"I think that my money would be best if you have it".
Guðmundur mælti til Skafta:	Gudmund said to Skafti:	Gudmund spoke to Skafti:
"Ekki ætla eg þenna vel til sektar fallinn eða mun eigi hitt heldur ráð að við gerum hann feginn og látum hann kjósa menn til gerðar þessar?	"Not intend i that well to guilt fall but should not find rather advice to with being he relieved and let he choose people to do this	"I don't suppose it will be well if he falls guilty, and should it not rather be the decision left with him to choose people to do this? Though I know not how others alike is this matter agreed with him".
Þó veit eg eigi hversu hinum líkar er þetta mál eiga við hann".	Though know i not how-so others alike is this matter said-of with him".	Though I don't know how others are alike in this matter being agreed with him".

The Tale of Ale-Hood (Old Icelandic)

Old Icelandic	Literal	English
"Nú þá hinir góðu menn", segir Ölkofri, *"veitið mér þá nokkurn dugnað eftir"*.	"Now then other good men", said Ale-Hood, "know i then someone assistance after".	"Now then other good men", said Ale-Hood, "I know then that you will give me some assistance after".
Skafti mælti:	Skafti said:	Skafti said:
"Undir mér er lykt máls þessa því að eg fer með sókina.	"Under me is conclusion matter this therefore that i go with seeking.	"Under me is the judgement of this matter, therefore I will seek to resolve it.
Munum við til þess hætta Ölkofri að við Guðmundur gerum um og lúkum málinu.	Should on to this end Ale-Hood that with Gudmund be about and conclude case.	So to that end, Ale-Hood, the case will be concluded with Gudmund.
Get eg að þér muni það duga við fullting okkart".	Get i that you would that help with assistance ours".	That is how it would help you with our assistance".
Þá stóð Ölkofri upp og takast þeir síðan í hendur.	Then stood Ale-Hood up and took them then in hand.	Then Ale-Hood stood up and took them then in hand.
Nefndi Ölkofri þegar votta hvern að öðrum og er vottnefna kom upp þá drifu menn að.	Named Ale-Hood then witness each to others and as witnesses came up then flocked many to.	Ale-Hood then named each of his witnesses, and many people crowded around.
Nefndi Ölkofri fyrst Brodda og förunauta hans.	Named Ale-Hood first Brodda and companions his.	Ale-Hood named Broddi and his companions.
Skafti mælti:	Skafti spoke:	Skafti spoke:
"Sökunautur vor biður okkur Guðmund til gerðar um mál þetta en þó að vér höfum það staðfest með oss er skaða höfum fengið að sjálfdæmi skyldi fyrir koma þá viljum við Guðmundur það nú veita honum að við gerum heldur um en aðrir ef Þórhallur vill það kjörið hafa.	"Defendant our invited us Gudmund to do about matter this and though that we have that confirmed with us that damages have got to self-judgement should by coming then will we Gudmund that now provide him to with doing rather of the others if Thorhall wishes that choice have.	"The defendant has invited Gudmund and myself to do about this matter, and though we have confirmed that those who suffered the loss are to accept self-judgement, Gudmund and I are willing to grant Ale-Hood this much, that we two rather than any other men shall decide the matter if Thorhall agrees.
Skuluð þér þess nefndir vottar að fyrir mál þetta skal fé gera en eigi mannsektir.	Should you this name witnesses as for the-matter that shall money make about only fines.	You should stand witness for the matter that only damages shall be awarded.

The Tale of Ale-Hood (Old Icelandic)

Old Icelandic	Literal	English
Eg handsala niðurfall að sökum þeim er eg stefndi í vor".	I confirm dropping the blame those that i summonsed in spring".	I confirm that I drop the charge for which I summoned him in the spring.
Síðan slitu þeir handlaginu.	After dissolved they handshake.	Then they dissolved with a handshake.
Þá mælti Skafti við Guðmund:	Then spoke Skafti with Gudmund:	Then Skafti spoke with Gudmund.
"Hví mun eigi vel að við lúkum þessu af?"	"Why should not well that we conclude this of?"	"Why don't we conclude this?"
"Vel má það", segir Guðmundur.	"Well may that", said Gudmund.	"That may well be", said Gudmund.
Ölkofri mælti:	Ale-Hood spoke:	Ale-Hood spoke:
"Ekki skuluð þið hrapa því svo því að eg er ekki ráðinn í að kjósa ykkur heldur en aðra menn".	"Not should you hurry therefore so for that i am not decided of to choose you rather than other people".	"You should not be in such a hurry, because I have not decided if I choose you or rather someone else".
Guðmundur mælti:	Gudmund spoke:	Gudmund spoke:
"Svo var skilt að við skyldum gera nema þú kjörir heldur þá aðra er þetta mál eiga með okkur".	"So was divided that we should do taking your choice rather then others that this matter have with us".	"It was so agreed that Skafti and I would decide rather than others who would have this matter with us".
Ölkofri segir:	Ale-Hood said:	Ale-Hood said:
"Því neitaði eg allan tíma að þeir skyldu gera en svo var skilið í handlagi að eg skyldi kjósa tvo menn til þá er eg vildi".	"Since refused i all time that they should do about so was divided at agreement that i should choose two men for then as i willed".	"I never agreed at the time that these men should decide, it was agreed at the handshake that I could choose any two men I wanted".
Þá var leitað um handsalsvætti	Then was sought about agreement	Then the agreement was sought about the assembly,

The Tale of Ale-Hood (Old Icelandic)

Old Icelandic	Literal	English
en þingmenn Guðmundar og Skafta deildust allmjög að hversu skilið var en Broddi og förunautar hans skáru skýrt úr að svo hafði skilið verið sem Ölkofri sagði að hann skyldi kjósa menn til gerðar.	the assembly Gudmund and Skafti judged all-greatly that how understood was that Broddi and companions his cut clear of that so had understood been which Ale-Hood said that he should choose man to do.	Then the agreement was sought about the assembly, Gudmund and Skafti disagreed greatly about how it had been agreed, but Broddi and his companions were clear about how it was understood, as Ale-Hood had said, that he could choose the men to decide.
Þá mælti Skafti:	Then spoke Skafti:	Then Skafti Spoke:
"Hvaðan rann sjá alda undir Ölkofri? Sé eg að þú heldur nokkuru rakkara halanum en fyrir stundu áðan	"Where runs this wave from-beneath Ale-Hood See i that you rather somewhat bolder tail-wagging than before awhile earlier	"Where runs this wave from beneath you Ale-Hood? I see that you are wagging your tail more boldy than before,
eða hverja menn muntu kjósa til gerðar?"	but what men should choose to do?"	and which men do you choose to decide?
Ölkofri mælti:	Ale-Hood spoke:	Ale-Hood spoke:
"Ekki skal lengi að því hyggja.	"Not shall longer to for think.	"I shall think on it no longer.
Eg kýs Þorstein Hallsson og Brodda Bjarnason mág hans og ætla eg að þá sé málið beutr komið en þið gerið um".	I choose Thorstein Hallsson and Brodda Bjarnason brother-in-law his and intend i that then so matter better comes than you make about".	I choose Thorstein Hallsson and his brother-in-law Broddi Bjarnarson, and I suppose that the matter will be better than if undertaken by you".
Skafti sagði að hann ætlaði að það mál væri vel komið þótt þeir gerðu um	Skafti said to him intended that this matter would-be well coming though they made about	Skafti said to him that he supposed that this matter would be in good hands if they undertook it.
því að málaefni voru eru brýn og góð en þeir eru svo vitrir að þeir munu sjá kunna hversu þungs þú ert af verður.	as the matters are they urgent and good and they are so wise that they should this know how-so heavily you are of worth.	"As the case is urgent and just and they are wise men, they should know how heavily you shall be dealt with".
Ölkofri gekk þá í lið Brodda og fóru menn heim til búða.	Ale-Hood went then with company Brodda's and travelled men home to booths.	Ale-Hood went then with Brodda's company and the men travelled home to their booths.

The Tale of Ale-Hood (Old Icelandic)

Old Icelandic	Literal	English
# 3	# 3	# 3
Eftir um daginn skyldi upp segja sætt.	Later in the-day should up said settlement.	Later in the day the verdict was to be announced.
Báru þeir þá ráð sín saman Þorsteinn og Broddi.	Bore they then matter theirs together Thorstein and Broddi.	Thorstein and Broddi started to consider the matter.
Vildi Þorsteinn meira gera en Broddi kvað það skýrst að gera svo sem hann vildi og segja þá sjálfur sátt upp.	Willed Thorstein more to-do than Broddi said it clarified to be so as he willed and say then himself settlement up.	Thorstein wanted more of a settlement than Broddi did, and it was agreed that it would be as he said.
Broddi bað hann kjósa hvort er hann vildi,	Broddi asked him choose either as he willed,	Broddi invited him to choose either as he wished,
segja sátt upp eða sitja fyrir svörum ef nokkurir menn yrðu til að leiða á gerðina.	say settlement up or sit before answers if some men be to the objection to make.	to decide the settlement or sit in judgement and answer any objections.
Þorsteinn lést heldur vilja segja sátt upp en skipta hnæfilyrðum við þá goðana.	Thorstein let rather willed say settlement up than exchange blows with then chieftans.	Thorstein said that he would rather give the judgement than exchange blows with the chieftains.
Síðan sagði Þorsteinn að Ölkofri skyldi eigi lengi þurfa síns hluta að bíða, kvað þá skyldu gjaldast féið allt að Lögbergi.	Since said Thorstein that Ale-Hood should not long need his lot to wait, said then should pay fee altogether at Law-Rock.	Then Thorstein said that Ale-Hood would not need to wait long, saying that then the payment of a fee should be made altogether at the law rock.
Síðan gengu þeir til Lögbergs.	Then went they to Law-Rock.	Then they went to the law rock.
En er lokið var þar lögskil að mæla þá spurði Þorsteinn Hallsson hvort goðar þeir væru að Lögbergi er mál áttu að kæra við Ölkofra:	And when ended were there legal-settlement to matters then asked Thorstein Hallsson whether chieftans they were at Law-Rock that matter had to accuse with Ale-Hood:	And when the other legal settlements were done, Thorstein Halsson asked whether the chieftains who had brought the accusation against Ale-Hood were present:
"Mér er svo sagt að við Broddi skulum gera um mál það.	"To-me is so said that with Broddi should make about matter that.	"It has been said to me that Broddi and I shall settle the matter.
Munum við nú upp lúka gerðinni ef þér viljið til hlýða".	Should with now up finish make if you will to listen".	We shall deliver the conclusion if you are ready to listen".

The Tale of Ale-Hood (Old Icelandic)

Old Icelandic	Literal	English
Þeir sögðust góðs að vænta að þeir mundu réttlátir í gerðinni.	They said good to expect that they would right-like to make.	They said they expected the decision would be just.
Þá mælti Þorsteinn:	Then spoke Thorstein:	Then Thorstein spoke:
"Svo líst okkur á sem lítils sé fyrir vert um skóga yðra félaga.	"So beholding ours is that little being for worth about forest yours companions.	"So is our finding that your wood and that of your companions is of little worth.
Voru þeir félitlir og fjárlægir yður itl gagns.	Were they fee-little and financial yours little benefit.	They were worth very little financially for you to benefit.
Var eigngirni mikil í þeim mönnum er góðs áttu kost og kalla það meigu sinni annarri	Was selfish great that these men the chieftans had benefit and call that may opinion another	It was a great selfishness that these chieftains had benefitted from this property in this way,
en hann mátti eigi ábyrgjast yðvarn skóg er hann brenndi sinn skóg og eru slíkt voðaverk.	that he may not guarantee your forest that he burned his forest and are such accidents.	and another opinion is that he could not have guaranteed to save your woods once his had burned, and it is therefore as such an accident.
En fyrir því að það er í gerð lagt þá skal gera nokkuð fyrir.	But for because that it is to made laid then shall be-done something for.	But because this settlement is to be made then something shall be done.
Þér sex menn hafið átt skógana.	Then six men have had forests.	These six men who own the woods.
Nú viljum vér gera sex alnar hverjum yðrum og skal það gjaldast hér þegar".	Now will we make six measures each yours and shall that be-paid here straightaway".	Now we will award six measures, one for each of you that shall be paid here immediately".
Broddi hafði búist og stikað vaðmál í sundur og kastar hann þá sér hverjum stúf til þeirra og mælti:	Broddi had prepared and stitched homespun-cloth to asunder and cast he then theirs each stump to them and said:	Broddi had prepared and stitched a homespun cloth and cast each strip down to them and said:
"Slíkt kalla eg argaskatt".	"Such call i cowardly".	I call this a tribute to the dastardly.
Skafti segir:	Skafti said:	Skafti said:
"Auðsætt er það Broddi að þú ert fús til að eiga illt við oss.	"Obvious is it Broddi that you are willing to that have ill with us.	"It is obvious Broddi that you wish to have bad will with us.

The Tale of Ale-Hood (Old Icelandic)

Old Icelandic	Literal	English
Hefir þú mjög stungist til þessa máls og ferð þú lítt þverafæti að fjandskap við oss.	Have you much wounded about this matter and go you little foot-around to fiend-ship with us.	You have made a great wound in this matter, and you do not tip-toe around making enemies of us.
Kann vera að oss falli önnur mál lettara".	Can be that ours fall another matter easier".	It can be that other law suits will be resolved more easily".
Broddi svarar:	Broddi answered:	Broddi answered:
"Þurfa muntu þess Skafti að taka meira á öðrum sakferlum ef skríða skal í það skarð er Ormur frændi þinn reytti af þér fyrir mansöngsdrápu er þú ortir um konu hans.	"Need should this Skafti to take more of other lawsuits if action shall to that gap that Orm kinsmen yours tried of you for love-song-poem that you worded about wife his.	You need to make more money from other law suits, Skafti, to make up for the damages your kinsman Orm got from you for the love-poem you composed about his wife.
Var það illa gert enda var það illa goldið"	Was that ill done in-the-end was that ill paid?"	Was that bad will all paid in the end?"
Þá mælti Þorkell trefill:	Then spoke Thorkell trefill:	Then Thorkell Trefill spoke:
"Allmjög missýnist slíkum manni sem Broddi er.	"All-much mistake such man as Broddi that.	"That was very much a mistake from such a man as Broddi.
Hann vill hafa vináttu Ölkofra eða nokkurar mútugjafir og kaupa svo að gera sér að óvinum slíka menn sem hann hefir í fangi".	He will have friendship Ale-hood's or some bribes and bought so that made his to un-friends such men as he has to enemies".	That he will have Ale-Hood's friendship, or his bribes, so that he makes his opponents into enemies".
Broddi segir:	Broddi said:	Broddi said:
"Ekki er það missýni að halda einurð sinni þótt mannamunur sé með yður Ölkofra.	"Not is that mistake to hold determined his thought integrity as with yours Ale-Hood.	"It is no mistake to hold with determination to your integrity, yours or Ale-Hood's.

The Tale of Ale-Hood (Old Icelandic)

Old Icelandic	Literal	English
En hitt var glámsýni í vor er þú reiðst til vorþings að þú varaðist eigi það er Steingrímur hafði stóðhest selfeitan og lagðist hann upp að baki þér en merin sú er þú reiðst var mögur og féll hún undir þér og hefi eg eigi spurt til sanns hverjum þá slauðraði en hitt sáu menn að þú varst lengi fastur því að hesturinn lagði fæturna fram yfir kápuna".	But find then big-mistake in spring when you rode to local-assembly that you warned not-of it that Steingrim had stallion fat and laid he up to back you as mare yours were you riding was skinny and fell she under you also have i not asked about the-truth whether then trailing-behind about found this people that you were long fastened with the horse laid feet from across cloak".	But you yourself made a big mistake in the spring when you rode to a local assembly, you were not aware of the fat stallion that Steingrim had until he was laid up to your backside, and you were riding that skinny mare as she fell under you, and I have never learned the truth whether those trailing behind you found that you were long fastened with the horse with his feet laid across your cloak".
Eyjólfur Þórðarson mætli:	Eyjolf Thordarson spoke:	Eyjolf Thordarson spoke:
"Það er satt að segja að sjá maður hefur allmjög dregið burst úr nefi oss enda mælir rán og regin við oss á sogört ofan".	"It is true to say that this man has all-much drawn cheated from noses ours in-the-end talking robbery and ruling with us by saying over".	"It is true that this man has cheated us out of our reward in front of our noses, and heaping abuse over us".
Broddi segir:	Broddi said:	Broddi said:
"Eigi hefi eg dregið burst úr nefi yður.	"Not have i drawn cheated of noses yours.	"I have not cheated you of your noses.
Þá var dregin burst úr nefi þér er þú fórst norðu til Skagafjarðar og stalst öxnum frá Þorkeli Eiríkssyni en Guðdala-Starri reið eftir þér og sástu þá eftirförina er þér voruð komnir í Vatnsdal.	Then were drawn cheated of nose you as you travelled north to Skagafjord and stealing oxen from Thorkell Eriksson and Guddala-Starri rode after you and saw-you then after-travelling that you were coming to Vatnsdal.	You were cheated of your nose as you travelled north to Skagafjord stealing oxen from Thorkell Eriksson and Guddala-Starri rode after you, and then you reached Vatnsdal.
Varðstu þá svo hræddur að þú brást þér í merarlíki og voru slíkt firn mikil en þeir Starri ráku aftur öxnina og var það satt að hann dró burst úr nefi þér".	Were-you then so scared that you transformed you to mare-like and were so awful much that they Starri drove back oxen and was that true that he drew cheated of nose you".	You were so scared that you turned yourself into a mare, an awful thing to do, and Starri drove the oxen back, so it is true, he cheated your nose".
Þá mælti Snorri goði:	Then spoke Snorri chieftan:	Then Snorri the chieftain spoke:

The Tale of Ale-Hood (Old Icelandic)

Old Icelandic	Literal	English
"Allt er oss annað tiltækilegra en deila hér illyrðum við Brodda en það er líkast að vér gerum oss minnisamt um fjandskap þenna er Broddi lýsir við oss ef vér komumst í færi".	"All are we other available than sharing here malice with Broddi but it is likely that we make us memorable about fiend-ship this that Broddi declared with us if we come to opportunity".	We would all rather be unavailable than here sharing malice with Broddi, but it is likely that we shall have it remembered what fiendship Broddi has shown us, and how it has come to be.
Broddi segir:	Broddi said:	Broddi said:
"Um snýrð þú þá sæmdunum Snorri ef þú leggur allan hug á að hefna mér en þú hefnir eigi föður þíns".	"Around turned you then honour Snorri if you lay all mind to that revenge to-me than you avenge not father yours".	"Your honour is turned around then, Snorri, if you put your mind to revenge that instead of avenging your father".
Þá mælti Þorkell Geitisson:	Then spoke Thorkell Geitisson:	Then Thorkell Geitisson spoke:
"Þetta er líkast að þú hafir það helst af nafni því er þú ert eftir heitinn að hann vildi hvers manns hlut óhæfan af sér verða láta og það annað að menn þoli eigi og liggir þú drepinn er stundir líða".	"It is likely that you have that held of-the-name of that you are after named that he wills each man's lot trouble of himself being let and that other of men tolerate not and laying you killed be awhile passed".	It is likely, that all you have held of the name your father gave to you, is to make trouble with every man, other men will not tolerate it and you may be killed after a while.
Broddi segir:	Broddi said:	Broddi said:
"Engi vegur er okkur í frændi að yppa hér fyrir alþýðu ógæfu frænda vorra en ekki skal þess dylja er margir vita að Brodd-Helgi var veginn.	"No way is ours of kinsmen that up here before the-people un-giving kinsmen talking-loudly about not shall this disguise that many knowing that Brodd-Helgi was killed.	"There is no way to gain anything, kinsmen, by talking loudly, this shall not disguise that many know that Brodd-Helgi was killed.
Var mér og það sagt að faðir þinn tæki ofarlega til þeirra launanna en hitt ætla eg ef þú leitar að er þú munir fingrum kenn það er faðir minn markaði þig í Böðvarsdal".	Was i and that told that father yours took high-up to their loans but find suppose i if you seek that as you should fingers know that was father mine marked you in Bodvarsdale".	I was told that your father paid the highest price, but I suppose that if you find your fingers, then they will find where my father marked you at Bodvarsdale".
Eftir það skildust þeir og engu heim til búðar.	After that separated they and none home to booths.	After that they separated and went back home to their booths.
Er nú Ölkofri úr sögunni.	Is now Ale-Hood out-of the-saga.	Ale-Hood is now out of the saga.

The Tale of Ale-Hood (Old Icelandic)

Old Icelandic	Literal	English
# 4	# 4	# 4
Annan dag eftir gekk Broddi til búðar Þorkels Geitssonar og inn í búðina og kastaði orðum á Þorkel.	Next day after went Broddi to booth Thorkell Geitsson's and into booth and cast words to Thorkell.	The next day afterwards Broddi went to Thorkell Geitisson's booth and exchanged words with Thorkell.
Hann svaraði fá og var hinn reiðasti.	He answered few and was the most-angry.	He answered little and was very angry.
Broddi mælti:	Broddi spoke:	Broddi spoke:
"Því er eg hér kominn frændi að eg sá missmíð á því er eg talaði við þig.	"For am i here coming kinsman that i saw mistake in what was i said with you.	"For I have come here, kinsman, because I saw a mistake in what I said to you.
Vil eg þess biðja að þú virðir mér það til bernsku og ólvisku en látum eigi frændsemi okkar að verri.	Will i this ask that you value me that to childishness and unwise but let-us not kinship ours to worsen.	I wish to ask you, though you find me given to childishness, and unwise, let our kinship not worsen.
Er hér sverð búið er eg vil gefa þér.	Is here sword to-settle that i will give to-you.	Here is a sword that I will give to you to settle.
Vil eg að það fylgi að þú farir að heimboði til mín í sumar og skal það lýsa að eigi skulu betri gripir í minni eigu en þeir er þú skalt þiggja".	Will i to this follow that you travel to home-booth to mine in summer and shall that show that none shall better treasures of mine own than this that you shall receive".	I would like to follow this by inviting you to travel to my home booth in summer, and I will show you that I have no treasures finer than the ones that you shall receive here".
Þorkell tók þessu þakksamlega, sagði að hann var þess fús að þeir gerðu góða sína frændsemi.	Thorkell took these thankfully, said that he was this willing that they made good their kinship.	Thorkell took this gladly, and said that he was willing to make good their kinship.
Gekk þá Broddi heim.	Went then Broddi home.	Broddi then went home.
Það var aftaninn fyrir þinglausnir að Broddi gekk vestur yfir á en við brúarsporðinn hittast þeir Guðmundur og varð ekki að kveðjum.	That was back for assembly-ending that Broddi went west over river and with footbridge found they Gudmund and were not to greet.	It was the last day of the assembly that Broddi went west over the river, and at a footbridge he met Gudmund, and neither greeted the other.
Og er þeir skildust þá veik Guðmundur aftur og mælti:	And as they separated then gave Gudmund back and said:	And as they passed each other Gudmund looked back and said:

The Tale of Ale-Hood (Old Icelandic)

Old Icelandic	Literal	English
"Hverja leið skaltu ríða af þingi Broddi?" Hann sneri aftur og mælti:	"What way shall-you ride from assembly Broddi?" He turned back and said:	Which way will you ride back from the Assembly, Broddi?
"Ef þér er forvitni á því mun eg ríða um Kjöl til Skagafjarðar, þá til Eyjafjarðar, þaðan Ljósavatnsskarð og svo til Mývatns og síðan Möðrudalsheiði".	"If you are curious of then shall i ride about Kjol to Skagafjord, then to Eyjafjord, from-there Ljosavatnsskard and so to Mywater and after Morudale-moor".	He turned back and said: "If you are curious then I shall ride around Kjol to Skagafjord, then to Eyafjord, and from there to Ljosavatnsskard and so on to Mywater, and after that Morudale-Moor".
Guðmundur mælti:	Gudmund said:	Gudmind said:
"Efn orð þín og ríð Ljósavatnsskarð".	"Carry-out words yours and ride Ljosavatnsskard".	Carry out your words and ride through Ljosavatnsskard.
Broddi segir:	Broddi said:	Broddi said:
"Efna skal það eða ætlar þú Guðmundur að verja mér skarðið? Allmjög eru þér þá mislagðar hendur ef þú varðar mér Ljósavatnsskarð svo að eg megi þar eigi fara með förunautum mínum en þú varðar það eigi hið litla skarð sem er í milli þjóa þér svo að ámælislaust sé".	"Carry-out shall that but intend you Gudmund to guard me the-pass All-greatly are you then misplaced hand if you guard me Ljosavatnsskard such that i may there not travel with companions mine as you guarded that not the little gap as that in between buttocks yours so as without-reproach be".	"I shall carry that out, but do you intend to guard against me passing? You are greatly mistaken if you try to stop me at Ljosavatnsskard with my companions, as you failed to guard the little gap in your backside so as to be without reproach".
Skildust þeir við svo búið og spurðust þessi orð um allt þingið.	Separated they with so settled and asked these words about all assembly.	They separated and these words were learnt by all who were at the assembly.
En er Þorkell Geitsson varð þessa vís þá gekk hann til fundar við Brodda og bað að hann skyldi ríða Sandleið eða ella hið eystra".	When that Thorkell Geitisson was this aware then went he to meet with Brodda and bid that he should ride Sandy-road or otherwise the east".	When Thorkell Geitisson was aware of this, he went to meet with Broddi and invited that he "should ride on the sandy road or to the east".
Broddi segir:	Broddi said:	Broddi said:
"Eg mun ríða þá leið er eg hefi sagt Guðmundi því að hann mun virða mér til hugleysis ef eg fer eigi svo".	"I would ride then way that i have said Gudmund because that he should worth me to cowardice if i travel not so".	I should ride the way that I told Gudmund I would, because otherwise he shall value me as a coward if I do not.

The Tale of Ale-Hood (Old Icelandic)

Old Icelandic	Literal	English
Þorkell mælti: "Við munum þá ríða báðir saman frændi og flokkur okkar lítill".	Thorkell said: "With should then ride both together kinsman and band ours little".	Thorkell said: "We should both ride together then, kinsman, and our little band".
Broddi sagði að honum þótti sæmd í föruneyti hans og lést það fjarna vilja.	Broddi said that he thought honour to companions his and burden that remove would.	Broddi said that he thought it a great honour to ride with him and his companions, and it would remove a burden.
Síðan ríða þeir Þorkell og Broddi báðir saman með flokka sína norður Öxnadalsheiði.	Afterwards rode they Thorkell and Broddi both together with band his north Oxnadale-moor.	Afterwards Thorkell and Broddi together with his band rode north to Oxnadale-Moor.
Voru þeir í einni ferð og Einar Eyjólfsson mágur Þorkels.	Was they on one journey and Einar Eyjolfsson brother-in-law Thorkell.	It was on the journey that Thorkell's father-in-law Einar Eyjolfsson joined them.
Riðu þeir Broddi og Þorkell til Þverár með Einari og voru þar um nótt.	Rode they Broddi and Thorkell to Thverriver with Einar and were there about night.	Broddi and Thorkell rode to Thverriver with Einar and stayed there for the night.
Síðan reið Einar á leið með þeim með fjölmenni mikið og skildust eigi fyrr en við Skjálfandafljót.	After riding Einar the way with them with followers many and separated not before about with Skjalfandi-River.	Afterwards Einar and his many followers rode with them, and they did not separate until they reached Skjalfandi River.
Reið þá Einar heim en þeir Þorkell og Broddi léttu eigi sinni ferð fyrr en þeir komu austur í Vopnafjörð til búa sinna.	Rode then Einar home about them Thorkell and Broddi relieved not their journey before that they came east to Vopnfjord to homes theirs.	Einar then rode home and then Thorkell and Broddi did not rest their journey until they came east to Vapnfjord to their homes.
Það sumar fór Þorkell að heimboði til Brodda frænda síns og þá þar allgóðar gjafir.	That summer travelled Thorkell to home-booth to Broddi kinsman his and then there all-good gifts.	That summer Thorkell travelled to the home-booth of his kinsman Broddi and then accepted all good gifts.
Höfðu þeir þá hina bestu frændsemi með vináttu og hélst það meðan þeir lifðu.	Had they then the best kinship with friendship and held that long-as they lived.	They then had the best kinship as long as they lived.
Og lýkur þar sögu Ölkofra.	And ends here the-saga Ale-Hood.	And here ends the saga of Ale-Hood.

Word List (Old Icelandic to English)

Old Icelandic	English

A, a

Old Icelandic	English
að	as, at, of, that, the, to, to-you
aðra	other, others
aðrir	other, others
af	from, of, of
afglapi	simpleton
aftaninn	back
aftur	back
alda	wave
aldur	age
allan	all, all, every
allfús	all-happy, all-happy
allgóðar	all-good
allir	all, all
allmikið	all-much
allmjög	all-greatly, all-greatly, all-much, all-much
allra	all
allt	all, all, altogether
allur	all, all
allvesallega	miserable
alnar	measures
alþýðu	the-people
andsvör	answer, answers
annað	other, other
annan	next
annar	another
annarri	another
annars	others
argaskatt	cowardly
auðsætt	obvious
augu	eyes
aumlega	abjectly
aumlegast	miserable
austur	east, east

Á, á

Old Icelandic	English
á	about, at, by, in, is, of, on, river, the, to
ábyrgjast	guarantee
áðan	earlier
ámælislaust	without-reproach
ást	affection
átt	had, had, owned
átti	had
áttir	had
áttu	directions, had, have

Æ, æ

Old Icelandic	English
ær	awed
ætla	intend, suppose
ætlaði	intended
ætlar	intend

B, b

Old Icelandic	English
bað	asked, bid, invited
báðir	both
bæði	asked, both
baki	back
báru	bore
bauð	offered
beitast	employing
bernsku	childishness
best	best
besti	best
bestu	best
betri	better
beutr	better
bíða	wait
biðja	ask
biður	invited
birni	bear
Bjarnason	Bjarnason (name)
bjó	lived
Bláskógum	Blawoods (place)
Böðvarsdal	Bodvarsdale (place)
borði	borne
brá	drew
brann	burned, burnt
brást	transformed

Word List (Old Icelandic to English)

Old Icelandic	English
brátt	soon
brautargengi	path-assistance
brenna	burn
brenndi	burned
brenndir	burned
Brodda	Brodda (name), Brodda's (name), Broddi (name)
Brodd-Helgi	Brodd-Helgi (name)
Broddi	Broddi (name)
brott	away
brúarsporðinn	footbridge
brunnu	burned
brýn	urgent
búa	homes, settle
búða	booths
búðar	booth, booths
búðarvegginum	booth-walls
búðina	booth
búðinni	booth, booths
búið	settled, to-settle
búist	prepared
burst	cheated

D, d

Old Icelandic	English
dæma	deem
dæmdir	deem
dag	day
daga	days
daginn	the-day
deila	share, sharing
deildust	judged
drambi	arrogance
dregið	drawn
dregin	drawn
drengskapur	word-of-honour
drepa	kill
drepinn	killed
drifu	flocked
drjúgir	substantial
dró	drew
duga	help
dugið	enough
dugnað	assistance
dvaldist	dwelled
dylja	disguise
dýrlegu	dearly

E, e

Old Icelandic	English
eða	but, or
ef	if
efn	carry-out
efna	carry-out
eftir	after, behind, later
eftirförina	after-travelling
eg	i
eiga	have, said-of
eigi	no, none, not, not-of, only
eigngirni	selfish
eigu	own
ein	only
Einar	Einar (name)
Einari	Einar (name)
einmæli	one-talk
einn	one
einni	one
einu	one
einurð	determined
Eiríkssyni	Eriksson (name)
eitt	one
ekki	not
eldur	fire
eldurinn	fire
ella	otherwise
en	about, and, as, but, in, than, that, the, then, when
enda	in-the-end
engi	no, none
engu	none
er	am, are, as, be, i, is, that, the, then, was, were, when, which, who
erindi	errand
ert	are
eru	are, they, was, were

Word List (Old Icelandic to English)

Old Icelandic	English
Eyjafjarðar	Eyjafjord (place)
Eyjólfsson	Eyjolfsson (name), son-of-Eyjolf (name)
Eyjólfur	Eyjolf (name)
eystra	east

É, é

ég	i

F, f

fá	few
faðir	father
færi	opportunity
fæturna	feet
falli	fall
fallinn	fall
fangi	enemies
fara	travel
farir	travel
fastur	fastened
fé	fee, money
feginn	relieved
féið	fee
fekk	got
fékk	got
félaga	companions
félitlir	fee-little
féll	fell
félldur	fall
fengið	got
fer	go, travel
ferð	go, journey, travelled
festist	fastened
févænlegt	money-promising
fimmti	fifth
fingrum	fingers
firn	awful
fjandskap	fiend-ship
fjár	wealth
fjáreigandi	property-owning
fjárlægir	financial
fjarna	remove
fjölmenni	followers
fjórði	fourth
flokka	band
flokkur	band
föður	father
fól	fool
for	for
fór	travelled
forðað	avoided
fórst	travelled
fóru	travelled
fórum	travelled
förunauta	companions
förunautar	companions
förunautum	companions
föruneyti	companions
forvitni	curious
fóta	feet
frá	from
frænda	kinsman, kinsmen
frændi	kinsman, kinsmen
frændsemi	kinship
fram	from, from-forward
fullting	assistance
fundar	meet
fundið	found
fús	willing
fylgi	follow
fyrir	before, by, for, therefore
fyrr	before
fyrst	first

G, g

gæta	guarded
gæti	got
gáfu	gave
gagns	benefit
ganga	go, to-go, went
gefa	give
Geitisson	Geitisson (name), son-of-Geiti (name)
Geitsson	Geitisson (name)
Geitssonar	Geitisson's (name)

Word List (Old Icelandic to English)

Old Icelandic	English
gekk	went
gellis	gellir
gengið	walked
gengu	went
gera	be, be-done, do, made, make, to-do
gerð	made
gerðar	do
gerði	did, done, made
gerðina	make
gerðinni	make
gerðist	happened
gerðu	made
gerið	make
gerist	was
gert	done
gerum	be, being, doing, make
get	get
gettu	getting
gjafir	gifts
gjaldast	be-paid, pay
glámsýni	big-mistake
góð	good
góða	good
goðana	chieftans
goðar	chieftans
Goðaskógur	Godaskogur (place)
goði	chieftan
góðs	chieftans, good
góðu	good
göfulegri	nobler
goldið	paid
grátfeginn	weeping-for-joy
grét	wept
grimmu	grim
gripir	treasures
gröfunum	pit
Guðdala-Starri	Guddala-Starri (name)
Guðmund	Gudmund (name)
Guðmundar	Gudmund (name)
Guðmundi	Gudmund (name)
Guðmundur	Gudmund (name)

H, h

Old Icelandic	English
hætta	end
hættir	mannered
hafa	have
hafði	had
hafið	have
hafir	have
hagur	handy
halanum	tail-wagging
halda	hold
Hallsson	Hallsson (name)
handlagi	agreement
handlaginu	handshake
handsala	confirm
handsalsvætti	agreement
hann	he, him, it
hans	him, his
hátt	way
haust	autumn
haustið	autumn
hefðu	had
hefi	have
hefir	has, have
hefna	revenge
hefnir	avenge
hefur	has
heim	home
heimboði	home-booth
heita	call
heiti	named
heitinn	named
heldur	rather
helst	held
hélst	held
hendur	hand
hér	here
héraða	districts
héruð	district, districts
hesturinn	horse
hét	was-named
hið	the, then
hina	the, then
hinir	other
hinn	the

164

Word List (Old Icelandic to English)

Old Icelandic	English
hinum	others
hitt	find, found
hittast	found, meet
hitti	found
hjá	beside
hjálpa	help
hjálpið	help
hljóp	ran
hlut	lot
hluta	lot
hlýða	listen
hnæfilyrðum	blows
höfði	head
höfðingja	chieftans
höfðingjarnir	chieftans
höfðu	had, owned
höfum	have
honum	he, him, his, to-him
hræddur	scared
Hrafnabjörgum	Hrafnabjorg (place)
hrapa	hurry
hraunið	lava-fields
hraustur	brave
hug	mind
hugleysis	cowardice
hún	she
hvaðan	where
hvar	where
hvass	sharp
hver	who
hverja	what
hverjum	each, whether
hvern	each
hvers	each
hversu	how, how-so
hvert	which
hví	why
hvort	either, whether
hyggja	think

I, i

Old Icelandic	English
iðju	occupation
iðn	craft
illa	ill
illt	ill
illyrðum	malice
inn	in
inn´í	into
itl	little

Í, í

Old Icelandic	English
í	about, among, as, at, in, of, on, that, the, to, with
íþróttamaður	sports-man

J, j

Old Icelandic	English
jafnan	equally
jafnstórlega	equally-great
jarðar	earth
járn	iron

K, k

Old Icelandic	English
kæmu	came
kæra	accuse
kalla	call
kallað	called
kallaður	called
kann	can, known
kápuna	cloak
kastaði	cast
kastar	cast
kaup	bought, buy
kaupa	bought, buy
kemur	come
kenn	know
keypt	bought
keyptu	bought
Kjöl	Kjol (place)
kjörið	choice
kjörir	choice
kjósa	choose
klengisök	small-blame
kofra	hood

Word List (Old Icelandic to English)

Old Icelandic	English
kol	coal
kola	coal
kolbrennu	coal-burning
kölluðu	called
kom	came
koma	came, come, coming
komið	comes, coming
kominn	coming
komnir	coming
komu	came
komumst	come
konu	wife
kost	benefit
kostur	choice
kraup	kneeled
kunna	know
kvað	said
kveðjum	greet
kýs	choose

L, l

Old Icelandic	English
lætur	behaviour
lagði	laid
lagðist	laid
lagt	laid
láta	leave, let
látum	let, let-us
launanna	loans
leggja	allow
leggur	lay
leið	during, way
leiða	objection
leitað	sought
leitar	seek
lengi	long, longer
lést	burden, let
lét	let
lettara	easier
léttu	relieved
lið	assistance, company, help
líða	passed
liði	help
liðs	help, people
liðveilsunni	supportive
lifðu	lived
liggir	laying
líkar	alike
líkast	likely
limið	foliage
líst	beholding, like
lítill	little, small
lítilræði	little-advised
lítils	little
litla	little
lítt	little
Ljósavatnsskarð	Ljosavatnsskard (place)
ljótur	ugly
lofar	praises
lög	law
logaði	blazed
Lögbergi	Law-Rock (place)
Lögbergs	Law-Rock (place)
lögmaður	law-speaker
lögréttu	law-assembly
lögréttuna	law-assembly
lögskil	legal-settlement
lokið	ended
Lönguhlíð	Langahlid (place)
lúka	finish
lúkum	conclude
lykt	conclusion
lýkur	ends
lýsa	show
lýsir	declared

M, m

Old Icelandic	English
má	may
maður	a-man, man
mæla	matters
mælir	speaks, talking
mælti	said, spoke
mætli	said, spoke
mág	brother-in-law
mágur	brother-in-law
mál	matter, the-matter
málaefni	matters

Word List (Old Icelandic to English)

Old Icelandic	English
máli	matter, speak
málið	matter, the-matter
málinu	case
málkunnigur	talking-known
málóði	of-strong-language
máls	matter
mann	man, men
manna	men
mannamunur	integrity
manni	man
manns	man's
mannsektir	fines
mansöngsdrápu	love-song-poem
marga	many
margir	many
markaði	marked
mart	many
mátti	may
máttir	may
með	among, it, with
meðan	long-as
megi	may
meigu	may
meira	more
menn	man, many, men, people
mér	i, me, of-me, to, to-me
merarlíki	mare-like
merin	mare
mest	most
mig	me
mikið	many
mikil	great, much
miklir	great
milli	between
mín	mine
mína	mine
minn	mine
minni	mine
minnisamt	memorable
mínu	my
mínum	mine
misjafnt	uneven-in
mislagðar	misplaced
missmíð	mistake
missýni	mistake
missýnist	mistake
mitt	my
mjög	much
Möðrudalsheiði	Morudale-moor (place)
mögur	skinny
mönnum	men
mörgum	many
mun	shall, should, would
mundi	could, would
mundu	would
mungát	ale
mungátin	ale
muni	should, would
munir	should
muntu	should
munu	should, will
munuð	shall
munum	should
mútugjafir	bribes
Mývatns	Mywater (place)

N, n

Old Icelandic	English
næði	neared
næst	nearest, next
næsta	next-to
næstir	nearest
nafn	name
nafndrægur	named
nafni	the-name
nefi	nose, noses
nefndi	named
nefndir	name
nefndur	named
neitaði	refusal, refused
nema	take, taking
niðurfall	dropping
nokkuð	some, something
nokkura	some
nokkurar	some
nokkurir	some
nokkurn	someone
nokkuru	somewhat
norðu	north

Word List (Old Icelandic to English)

Old Icelandic	English
norður	north
nótt	night
nóttina	night
nú	not, now
nytja	use

O, o

Old Icelandic	English
ofan	over
ofarlega	high-up
oft	often
oftlega	often
ofureflismenn	ultra-strong-men
og	also, and
okkar	ours
okkart	ours
okkra	ours
okkur	ours, us
orð	word, words
orða	words
orðið	word
orðinn	become
orðum	words
ormur	orm
ortir	worded
oss	ours, us, we

Ó, ó

Old Icelandic	English
ógæfu	un-giving
óhæfan	trouble
ólíklegt	unlike
ómaklegur	uncomfortable
ópið	open
óvinum	un-friends
ósisku	unwise

Ö, ö

Old Icelandic	English
öðrum	other, others
öl	ale
Ölkofra	Ale-Hood (name), Ale-hood's (name)
Ölkofri	Ale-Hood (name)
öll	all
öllu	all
önnur	another
örhjarta	un-heartened
Öxnadalsheiði	Oxnadale-moor (place)
öxnina	oxen
öxnum	oxen

R, r

Old Icelandic	English
ráð	advice, counsel, matter
ráði	counsel
ráðið	decided
ráðinn	decided
ræddi	discussed
ræddu	discussed
rakkara	bolder
ráku	drove
rán	robbery
rann	runs
Rauða-Bjarnarson	son-of-Rauda-Bjarn (name)
regin	ruling
reið	riding, rode
reiðasti	most-angry
reiðst	counsel, riding, rode
reikuðu	roamed
réttlátir	right-like
reytti	tried
ríð	ride
ríða	ride, rode
riðu	rode

S, s

Old Icelandic	English
sá	saw, so, that
sæli	good
sæll	happy
sæmd	honour
sæmdunum	honour
sætt	settlement

Word List (Old Icelandic to English)

Old Icelandic	English
saga	story
sagði	said
sagt	said, told
sakferlum	lawsuits
sama	same
saman	together
sandleið	sandy-road
sanns	the-truth
sástu	saw-you
sat	sat
satt	TRUE
sátt	settlement
sátu	sat
sáu	this
sé	as, be, being, see, so
segir	said
segja	said, say
seint	late
sekja	seek
sektar	guilt
seldu	sold
selfeitan	fat
selja	sell
sem	as, me, so, that, which
sendi	sent
sendiboð	messenger
sér	him, himself, his, theirs, themselves
sétti	sixth
sex	six
síðan	after, afterwards, since, then
Síðu-Hallssonar	son-of-Sidu-Hall (name)
siður	custom
sín	theirs, they
sína	his, their
sínkur	stingy
sinn	his
sinna	theirs
sinni	his, opinion, their
síns	his
sitja	sit
sjá	saw, so, this
sjálfdæmi	self-judgement
sjálfur	himself
skaða	damages
Skafta	Skafti (name)
Skafti	Skafti (name)
Skagafjarðar	Skagafjord (place)
skal	shall
skalt	shall
skaltu	shall-you
skarð	gap
skarðið	the-pass
skáru	cut
skildust	separated
skilið	divided, understood
skilt	divided
skipta	exchange
Skjálfandafljót	Skjalfandi-River (place)
sköðum	damage
skóg	forest
skóga	forest
skógabrennuna	forest-burning
skógana	forests
skógar	forests
skógarmanns	outlawry
skóggang	outlawry
skóginn	forest
skógur	forest
skríða	action
skulu	shall
skuluð	should
skulum	should
skyldi	should, wished
skyldu	should
skyldum	should
skýrst	clarified
skýrt	clear
slauðraði	trailing-behind
slík	such
slíka	such
slíkt	so, such
slíkum	such
slitu	dissolved
sneri	turned
snökta	sob
Snorri	Snorri (name)
snýrð	turned

Word List (Old Icelandic to English)

Old Icelandic	English
sofnaði	slept
sögðu	said
sögðust	said
sogört	saying
sögu	the-saga
sögunni	the-saga
sökina	seeking
sökum	blame
sökunautur	defendant
son	son
spurði	asked
spurðust	asked
spurt	asked
ssem	as
staðfest	confirmed
stalst	stealing
Starri	Starri (name)
stefndi	summons, summonsed
stefnu	summons
stefnudagar	policy-days
stefnuför	summons
Steingrímur	Steingrim (name)
stikað	stitched
stóð	stood
stóðhest	stallion
stórlæti	pride
stórleika	pride
stórmenni	great-men
stórorðu	high-sounding
stúf	stump
stundir	awhile
stundu	awhile
stungist	wounded
sú	yours
sumar	summer
sumarið	summer
sundur	asunder
svaraði	answered
svarar	answered
sverð	sword
Sviðningi	Svidning (place)
svo	so, such
svöruðu	answered
svörum	answers
sýnast	appear
synjað	refused

T, t

Old Icelandic	English
tæki	took
taka	take
takast	took
talaði	said
telja	tell
tíðinda	news
tíðindi	news
til	about, for, to
tiltækilegra	available
tíma	time
tók	took
tré	wood
trefill	trefill
tvítugsaldri	twenty-aged
tvo	two

Þ, þ

Old Icelandic	English
þá	then
það	it, that, the, this, to, with
þaðan	from-there
þakksamlega	thankfully
þann	that, then
þar	here, there
þau	his, they
þegar	as-soon-as, straightaway, straight-away, then
þeim	them, these, they, those
þeir	them, they, this
þeirra	of-the, their, theirs, them, they, those
þenna	that, this
þér	then, to-you, you, yours
þess	this
þessa	this
þessar	this
þessi	these, this

Word List (Old Icelandic to English)

Old Icelandic	English
þessu	these, this
þetta	it, that, this
þið	you
þig	you
þiggja	receive
þín	yours
þingi	assembly
þingið	assembly
þinglausnir	assembly-ending
þingmenn	assembly, assembly-men
þings	assembly
þingum	assembly
þinn	you, yours
þinni	yours
þíns	yours
þitt	yours
þjóa	buttocks
þó	though
þoli	tolerate
Þórðar	Thord (name)
Þórðarson	Thordarson (name)
Þórhalldur	Thorhall (name)
Þórhallsstöðum	Thorhallsstead (place)
Þórhallur	Thorhall (name)
þori	greater-part
Þorkel	Thorkell (name)
Þorstein	Thorstein (name)
Þorsteinn	Thorstein (name)
Þorsteins	Thorstein (name), Thorstein's (name)
þót	though
þótt	though, thought
þótti	seem, seemed, thought
þóttist	thought
þriðji	third
þú	you, your
þung	heavy
þungs	heavily
þurfa	need
þverafæti	foot-around
Þverár	Thverriver (place)
því	as, because, for, of, since, then, therefore, what, with
þykir	seems, think
þykjast	consider

U, u

Old Icelandic	English
um	about, around, in, of, over
undir	from-beneath, under
upp	up

Ú, ú

Old Icelandic	English
úr	from, of, out-of
út	from, out, out-of

V, v

Old Icelandic	English
vaðmál	homespun-cloth
vænta	expect
væri	would-be
væru	were
vaknaði	awoke
vakti	woke
vandast	difficult
vanir	friends
var	then, was, were
varaðist	warned
varð	became, was, were
varða	concerning
varðar	guard, guarded
varðstu	were-you
varið	defend
varst	were
Vatnsdal	Vatnsdal (place)
veg	way
veginn	killed
vegur	way
veifiskati	spendthrift
veik	gave
veit	know

Word List (Old Icelandic to English)

Old Icelandic	English	*Old Icelandic*	English
veita	grant, know, provide	*vorþings*	local-assembly
veitið	know	*voru*	are, was, were
veitti	granted	*voruð*	were
veittu	grant	*votta*	witness
vel	well	*vottar*	witnesses
vér	we	*vottnefna*	witnesses
vera	be		
verð	deserve	## Y, y	
verða	being, was, were		
verður	worth	*yðra*	yours
verið	been	*yðrum*	yours
verja	guard	*yður*	yours
verr	worse	*yðvarn*	your
verri	worsen	*yfir*	across, over
vert	worth	*ykkur*	you
vestur	west	*yppa*	up
veturinn	winter	*yrðu*	be
við	on, we, with		
víða	many, widely		
viðinn	trees		
vil	will		
vildi	willed, wills		
vilja	willed, wish, would		
vilji	willing		
viljið	will		
viljum	will		
vill	will, wishes		
vilnað	willed		
vináttu	friendship		
vindur	wind		
vini	friends		
vinir	friends		
vinsæl	popularity		
virða	worth		
virðir	value		
vís	aware		
vita	knowing		
vitrir	wise		
voðaverk	accidents		
völluna	plains		
von	hope, wished		
Vopnafjörð	Vopnafjord (place)		
vor	our, spring		
vorkunn	pity		
vorra	talking-loudly		

Word List (English to Old Icelandic)

Word List (English to Old Icelandic)

English	Old Icelandic	English	Old Icelandic

A, a

about	á, á, á, á, á	alike	líkar
at	á, á, á	a-man	maður
as	að, að, áðan, ær, ætla, ætlaði, ætlar, af	ale	mungát, mungátin, mútugjafir
awed	ær	also	og
age	aldur	Ale-Hood (name)	Ölkofra, Ölkofra
all	allan, allan, allan, allfús, allfús, allgóðar, allir, allir, allmikið, allmjög, allmjög	Ale-hood's (name)	Ölkofra
		advice	ráð
		afterwards	síðan
		action	skríða
all-happy	allfús, allfús	awhile	stundir, stundu
all-good	allgóðar	asunder	sundur
all-much	allmikið, allmjög, allmjög	answered	svaraði, svarar, svöruðu
all-greatly	allmjög, allmjög	appear	sýnast
altogether	allt	as-soon-as	þegar
answer	andsvör	assembly	þingi, þingið, þinglausnir, þingmenn, þingmenn
answers	andsvör, annar		
another	annar, annarri, argaskatt		
		assembly-ending	þinglausnir
affection	ást	assembly-men	þingmenn
abjectly	aumlega	available	tiltækilegra
asked	bað, bað, bað, báðir, bæði	around	um
		awoke	vaknaði
ask	biðja	aware	vís
away	brott	accidents	voðaverk
arrogance	drambi	across	yfir
assistance	dugnað, dvaldist, dylja		

B, b

after	eftir, eftir	by	á, á
after-travelling	eftirförina	back	aftaninn, aftur, aldur
and	en, en	bid	bað
am	er	both	báðir, bæði
are	er, er, er, er	bore	báru
awful	firn	best	best, besti, bestu
avoided	forðað	better	betri, beutr
agreement	handlagi, handlaginu	bear	birni
autumn	haust, haustið	Bjarnason (name)	Bjarnason
avenge	hefnir	Blawoods (place)	Bláskógum
among	í, í	Bodvarsdale (place)	Böðvarsdal
accuse	kæra	borne	borði
allow	leggja	burned	brann, brann, brenna, brenndi

173

Word List (English to Old Icelandic)

English	*Old Icelandic*	English	*Old Icelandic*
burnt	*brann*	cowardly	*argaskatt*
burn	*brenna*	childishness	*bernsku*
Brodda (name)	*Brodda*	cheated	*burst*
Brodda's (name)	*Brodda*	carry-out	*efn, efna*
Broddi (name)	*Brodda, Brodd-Helgi*	companions	*félaga, félitlir, féll, felldur, fengið*
Brodd-Helgi (name)	*Brodd-Helgi*	curious	*forvitni*
booths	*búða, búðar, búðar*	chieftans	*goðana, goðar, Goðaskógur, goði, góðs*
booth	*búðar, búðar, búðarvegginum*	chieftan	*goði*
booth-walls	*búðarvegginum*	confirm	*handsala*
but	*eða, ef*	call	*heita, helst*
behind	*eftir*	cowardice	*hugleysis*
be	*er, er, er, erindi, ert, eru*	craft	*iðn*
band	*flokka, flokkur*	came	*kæmu, kæra, kalla, kallað*
before	*fyrir, fyrir*	called	*kallað, kallaður, kann*
benefit	*gagns, ganga*	can	*kann*
be-done	*gera*	cloak	*kápuna*
being	*gerum, gerum, gerum*	cast	*kastaði, kastar*
be-paid	*gjaldast*	come	*kemur, kenn, keypt*
big-mistake	*glámsýni*	choice	*kjörið, kjörir, kjósa*
beside	*hjá*	choose	*kjósa, kofra*
blows	*hnæfilyrðum*	coal	*kol, kola*
brave	*hraustur*	coal-burning	*kolbrennu*
bought	*kaup, kaup, kaupa, kaupa*	coming	*koma, komið, komið, kominn*
buy	*kaup, kaupa*	comes	*komið*
behaviour	*lætur*	company	*lið*
burden	*lést*	conclude	*lúkum*
beholding	*líst*	conclusion	*lykt*
blazed	*logaði*	case	*málinu*
brother-in-law	*mág, mágur*	could	*mundi*
between	*milli*	counsel	*ráð, ráð, ráði*
bribes	*mútugjafir*	custom	*siður*
become	*orðinn*	cut	*skáru*
bolder	*rakkara*	clarified	*skýrst*
blame	*sökum*	clear	*skýrt*
buttocks	*þjóa*	confirmed	*staðfest*
because	*því*	consider	*þykjast*
became	*varð*	concerning	*varða*
been	*verið*		

C, c

D, d

Word List (English to Old Icelandic)

English	*Old Icelandic*
directions	áttu
drew	brá, brann
deem	dæma, dæmdir
day	dag
days	daga
drawn	dregið, dregin
dwelled	dvaldist
disguise	dylja
dearly	dýrlegu
determined	einurð
do	gera, gera
did	gerði
done	gerði, gerði
doing	gerum
districts	héraða, héruð
district	héruð
during	leið
declared	lýsir
dropping	niðurfall
decided	ráðið, ráðinn
discussed	ræddi, ræddu
drove	ráku
damages	skaða
divided	skilið, skilt
damage	sköðum
dissolved	slitu
defendant	sökunautur
difficult	vandast
defend	varið
deserve	verð

E, e

English	*Old Icelandic*
earlier	áðan
every	allan
eyes	augu
east	austur, austur, bað
employing	beitast
enough	dugið
Einar (name)	Einar, Einari
Eriksson (name)	Eiríkssyni
errand	erindi
Eyjafjord (place)	Eyjafjarðar
Eyjolfsson (name)	Eyjólfsson
Eyjolf (name)	Eyjólfur
enemies	fangi
end	hætta
each	hverjum, hvern, hvers
either	hvort
equally	jafnan
equally-great	jafnstórlega
earth	jarðar
easier	lettara
ended	lokið
ends	lýkur
exchange	skipta
expect	vænta

F, f

English	*Old Icelandic*
from	af, aftaninn, aftur, aldur, allan
footbridge	brúarsporðinn
flocked	drifu
fire	eldur, eldurinn
few	fá
father	faðir, fæturna
feet	fæturna, falli
fall	falli, fallinn, fangi
fastened	fastur, fé
fee	fé, fé
fee-little	félitlir
fell	féll
fifth	fimmti
fingers	fingrum
fiend-ship	fjandskap
financial	fjárlægir
followers	fjölmenni
fourth	fjórði
fool	fól
for	for, forðað, förunauta, förunautar
from-forward	fram
found	fundið, fylgi, fyrir, fyrir
follow	fylgi
first	fyrst
find	hitt
foliage	limið
finish	lúka

Word List (English to Old Icelandic)

English	*Old Icelandic*	English	*Old Icelandic*
fines	*mannsektir*	granted	*veitti*
fat	*selfeitan*		
forest	*skóg, skóga, skógabrennuna, skógana*		

H, h

English	*Old Icelandic*
forest-burning	*skógabrennuna*
forests	*skógana, skógar*
from-there	*þaðan*
foot-around	*þverafæti*
from-beneath	*undir*
friends	*vanir, varð, varða*
friendship	*vináttu*

English	*Old Icelandic*
had	*átt, átt, átti, áttir, áttu, áttu, áttu, augu*
have	*áttu, augu, aumlega, aumlegast, austur, austur, bað, bað*
homes	*búa*
help	*duga, dugið, dugnað, dvaldist, dylja, dýrlegu*
happened	*gerðist*
handy	*hagur*
hold	*halda*
Hallsson (name)	*Hallsson*
handshake	*handlaginu*
he	*hann, hann*
him	*hann, hann, hans, hans*
his	*hans, haust, haustið, hefðu, hefi, hefir, hefir, hefnir*
has	*hefir, hefir*
home	*heim*
home-booth	*heimboði*
held	*helst, hélst*
hand	*hendur*
here	*hér, héraða*
horse	*hesturinn*
head	*höfði*
Hrafnabjorg (place)	*Hrafnabjörgum*
hurry	*hrapa*
how	*hversu*
how-so	*hversu*
hood	*kofra*
high-up	*ofarlega*
happy	*sæll*
honour	*sæmd, sæmdunum*
himself	*sér, sér*
high-sounding	*stórorðu*
heavy	*þung*
heavily	*þungs*
homespun-cloth	*vaðmál*
hope	*von*

G, g

English	*Old Icelandic*
guarantee	*ábyrgjast*
got	*fekk, fékk, félaga, félitlir*
go	*fer, ferð, ferð*
guarded	*gæta, gæti*
gave	*gáfu, gagns*
give	*gefa*
Geitisson (name)	*Geitisson, Geitsson*
Geitisson's (name)	*Geitssonar*
gellir	*gellis*
get	*get*
getting	*gettu*
gifts	*gjafir*
good	*góð, góða, goðana, goðar, Goðaskógur*
Godaskogur (place)	*Goðaskógur*
grim	*grimmu*
Guddala-Starri (name)	*Guðdala-Starri*
Gudmund (name)	*Guðmund, Guðmundar, Guðmundi, Guðmundur*
greet	*kveðjum*
great	*mikil, mikil*
guilt	*sektar*
gap	*skarð*
great-men	*stórmenni*
greater-part	*þori*
guard	*varðar, varðar*
grant	*veita, veita*

Word List (English to Old Icelandic)

English	Old Icelandic	English	Old Icelandic
		little	itl, jafnan, jafnstórlega, jarðar, járn

I, i

in	á, á, ábyrgjast, að, að
is	á, ábyrgjast
intend	ætla, ætlaði
intended	ætlaði
invited	bað, báðir
if	ef
i	eg, ég, eiga, Einar
in-the-end	enda
it	hann, hans, hans, haust
ill	illa, illt
into	inn´i
iron	járn
integrity	mannamunur

J, j

judged	deildust
journey	ferð

K, k

kill	drepa
killed	drepinn, drifu
kinsman	frænda, frænda
kinsmen	frænda, frændi
kinship	frændsemi
known	kann
know	kenn, keypt, keyptu, Kjöl, kjörið
Kjol (place)	Kjöl
kneeled	kraup
knowing	vita

L, l

lived	bjó, Bláskógum
later	eftir
lot	hlut, hluta
listen	hlýða
lava-fields	hraunið
laid	lagði, lagðist, lagt
leave	láta
let	láta, látum, látum, launanna
let-us	látum
loans	launanna
lay	leggur
long	lengi
longer	lengi
laying	liggir
likely	líkast
like	líst
little-advised	lítilræði
Ljosavatnsskard (place)	Ljósavatnsskarð
law	lög
Law-Rock (place)	Lögbergi, Lögbergs
law-speaker	lögmaður
law-assembly	lögréttu, lögréttuna
legal-settlement	lögskil
Langahlid (place)	Lönguhlíð
love-song-poem	mansöngsdrápu
long-as	meðan
lawsuits	sakferlum
late	seint
local-assembly	vorþings

M, m

miserable	allvesallega, alnar
measures	alnar
money	fé
money-promising	févænlegt
meet	fundar, fundið
made	gera, gera, gerð, gerðar
make	gera, gerð, gerðar, gerði, gerði
mannered	hættir
mind	hug
malice	illyrðum
may	má, maður, maður, mæla, mág

Word List (English to Old Icelandic)

English	*Old Icelandic*
man	*maður, mæla, mág, mágur*
matters	*mæla, mág*
matter	*mál, málaefni, máli, málið, málinu*
men	*mann, manna, mannamunur, manni*
man's	*manns*
many	*marga, margir, markaði, mart, mátti, máttir, með*
marked	*markaði*
more	*meira*
me	*mér, merarlíki, merin*
mare-like	*merarlíki*
mare	*merin*
most	*mest*
much	*mikil, miklir*
mine	*mín, mína, minn, minni, minnisamt*
memorable	*minnisamt*
my	*mínu, mínum*
misplaced	*mislagðar*
mistake	*missmíð, missýni, missýnist*
Morudale-moor (place)	*Möðrudalsheiði*
Mywater (place)	*Mývatns*
most-angry	*reiðasti*
messenger	*sendiboð*

N, n

English	*Old Icelandic*
next	*annan, annars*
no	*eigi, eigi*
none	*eigi, eigi, eigi*
not	*eigi, eigi, eigi*
not-of	*eigi*
nobler	*göfulegri*
named	*heiti, heitinn, heldur, hét, hið*
neared	*næði*
nearest	*næst, næst*
next-to	*næsta*
name	*nafn, nafndrægur*
nose	*nefi*
noses	*nefi*
north	*norðu, norður*
night	*nótt, nóttina*
now	*nú*
need	*þurfa*
news	*tíðinda, tíðindi*

O, o

English	*Old Icelandic*
of	*á, á, á, á, á, að, að, að*
on	*á, á, á*
other	*aðra, aðra, aðrir, aðrir, ætla, af*
others	*aðra, aðrir, aðrir, ætla, af*
owned	*átt, auðsætt*
obvious	*auðsætt*
offered	*bauð*
or	*eða*
only	*eigi, eigngirni*
own	*eigu*
one-talk	*einmæli*
one	*einn, einni, einu, eitt*
otherwise	*ella*
opportunity	*færi*
occupation	*iðju*
objection	*leiða*
of-strong-language	*málóði*
of-me	*mér*
over	*ofan, oft, oftlega*
often	*oft, oftlega*
ours	*okkar, okkart, okkra, okkur, okkur*
open	*ópið*
orm	*ormur*
Oxnadale-moor (place)	*Öxnadalsheiði*
oxen	*öxnina, öxnum*
opinion	*sinni*
outlawry	*skógarmanns, skóggang*
of-the	*þeirra*
out-of	*úr, út*
out	*út*
our	*vor*

Word List (English to Old Icelandic)

English	*Old Icelandic*

P, p

English	*Old Icelandic*
path-assistance	*brautargengi*
prepared	*búist*
property-owning	*fjáreigandi*
pay	*gjaldast*
paid	*goldið*
pit	*gröfunum*
passed	*líða*
people	*liðs, liðveilsunni*
praises	*lofar*
policy-days	*stefnudagar*
pride	*stórlæti, stórleika*
provide	*veita*
popularity	*vinsæl*
plains	*völluna*
pity	*vorkunn*

R, r

English	*Old Icelandic*
river	*á*
relieved	*feginn, fer*
remove	*fjarna*
revenge	*hefna*
rather	*heldur*
ran	*hljóp*
refusal	*neitaði*
refused	*neitaði, nema*
robbery	*rán*
runs	*rann*
ruling	*regin*
riding	*reið, reið*
rode	*reið, reiðst, reiðst, reikuðu*
roamed	*reikuðu*
right-like	*réttlátir*
ride	*ríð, ríða*
receive	*þiggja*

S, s

English	*Old Icelandic*
suppose	*ætla*
simpleton	*afglapi*
soon	*brátt*
settle	*búa*
settled	*búið*
share	*deila*
sharing	*deila*
substantial	*drjúgir*
said-of	*eiga*
selfish	*eigngirni*
son-of-Eyjolf (name)	*Eyjólfsson*
son-of-Geiti (name)	*Geitisson*
scared	*hræddur*
she	*hún*
sharp	*hvass*
sports-man	*íþróttamaður*
small-blame	*klengisök*
said	*kvað, leið, leiða, leitað, leitar, léttu, líða, liðs, liðveilsunni, lítill*
sought	*leitað*
seek	*leitar, léttu*
supportive	*liðveilsunni*
small	*lítill*
show	*lýsa*
speaks	*mælir*
spoke	*mælti, mætli*
speak	*máli*
skinny	*mögur*
shall	*mun, mun, mun, mundi, mundu*
should	*mun, mun, mundi, mundu, muni, muni, munir, muntu, munu, munu, munuð*
some	*nokkuð, nokkuð, nokkura, nokkurar*
something	*nokkuð*
someone	*nokkurn*
somewhat	*nokkuru*
son-of-Rauda-Bjarn (name)	*Rauða-Bjarnarson*
saw	*sá, sá*
so	*sá, sá, sætt, saga, sagði, sagt*

Word List (English to Old Icelandic)

English	Old Icelandic
settlement	*sætt, saga*
story	*saga*
same	*sama*
sandy-road	*sandleið*
saw-you	*sástu*
sat	*sat, satt*
see	*sé*
say	*segja*
sold	*seldu*
sell	*selja*
sent	*sendi*
sixth	*sétti*
six	*sex*
since	*síðan, síðan*
son-of-Sidu-Hall (name)	*Síðu-Hallssonar*
stingy	*sínkur*
sit	*sitja*
self-judgement	*sjálfdæmi*
Skafti (name)	*Skafta, Skafti*
Skagafjord (place)	*Skagafjarðar*
shall-you	*skaltu*
separated	*skildust*
Skjalfandi-River (place)	*Skjálfandafljót*
such	*slík, slíka, slíkt, slíkt, slíkum*
sob	*snökta*
Snorri (name)	*Snorri*
slept	*sofnaði*
saying	*sogört*
seeking	*sökina*
son	*son*
stealing	*stalst*
Starri (name)	*Starri*
summons	*stefndi, stefndi, stefnu*
summonsed	*stefndi*
Steingrim (name)	*Steingrímur*
stitched	*stikað*
stood	*stóð*
stallion	*stóðhest*
stump	*stúf*
summer	*sumar, sumarið*
sword	*sverð*
Svidning (place)	*Sviðningi*
straightaway	*þegar*
straight-away	*þegar*
seem	*þótti*
seemed	*þótti*
seems	*þykir*
spendthrift	*veifiskati*
spring	*vor*

T, t

English	Old Icelandic
the	*á, á, að, að, að, að, að, aðra, aðra*
to	*á, að, að, að, að, að*
that	*að, að, að, að, aðra, aðra, aðrir, aðrir, ætla, af*
to-you	*að, aðra*
the-people	*alþýðu*
transformed	*brást*
to-settle	*búið*
the-day	*daginn*
than	*en*
then	*en, en, engi, engi, engu, er, er, er, er, er, er*
they	*eru, eru, eru, Eyjólfsson, færi, fara*
travel	*fara, farir, feginn*
travelled	*ferð, fjár, fjáreigandi, fjarna, fór*
therefore	*fyrir, ganga*
to-go	*ganga*
to-do	*gera*
treasures	*gripir*
tail-wagging	*halanum*
to-him	*honum*
think	*hyggja, í*
talking	*mælir*
the-matter	*mál, máli*
talking-known	*málkunnigur*
to-me	*mér*
the-name	*nafni*
take	*nema, nema*
taking	*nema*
trouble	*óhæfan*
tried	*reytti*
told	*sagt*

Word List (English to Old Icelandic)

English	Old Icelandic
together	saman
the-truth	sanns
true	
this	sáu, sé, sé, segir, segja, segja, sekja, seldu, selja, sem, sem
theirs	sér, sér, sétti, sex
themselves	sér
their	sína, sínkur, sinna
the-pass	skarðið
trailing-behind	slauðraði
turned	sneri, snökta
the-saga	sögu, sögunni
took	tæki, taka, takast
tell	telja
thankfully	þakksamlega
there	þar
them	þeim, þeim, þeim
these	þeim, þeim, þeim
those	þeim, þeir
though	þó, þoli, Þórðar
tolerate	þoli
Thord (name)	Þórðar
Thordarson (name)	Þórðarson
Thorhall (name)	Þórhalldur, Þórhallsstöðum
Thorhallsstead (place)	Þórhallsstöðum
Thorkell (name)	Þorkel
Thorstein (name)	Þorstein, Þorsteinn, Þorsteins
Thorstein's (name)	Þorsteins
thought	þótt, þótti, þótti
third	þriðji
Thverriver (place)	Þverár
time	tíma
trefill	trefill
twenty-aged	tvítugsaldri
two	tvo
trees	viðinn
talking-loudly	vorra

U, u

English	Old Icelandic
urgent	brýn
ugly	ljótur
uneven-in	misjafnt
use	nytja
ultra-strong-men	ofureflismenn
un-giving	ógæfu
us	okkur, ólíklegt
unlike	ólíklegt
uncomfortable	ómaklegur
un-heartened	örhjarta
un-friends	óvinum
unwise	ósvisku
understood	skilið
under	undir
up	upp, úr

V, v

English	Old Icelandic
Vatnsdal (place)	Vatnsdal
value	virðir
Vopnafjord (place)	Vopnafjörð

W, w

English	Old Icelandic
wave	alda
without-reproach	ámælislaust
wait	bíða
word-of-honour	drengskapur
when	en, engi
was	er, er, er, er, er, eru, eru
were	er, er, er, er, eru, eru, eru, Eyjólfsson, færi
which	er, er, eru
who	er, eru
wealth	fjár
willing	fús, fyrir
went	ganga, Geitisson, gekk
walked	gengið
weeping-for-joy	grátfeginn
wept	grét
way	hátt, hefna, heiti, heitinn
was-named	hét

Word List (English to Old Icelandic)

English	Old Icelandic	English	Old Icelandic
where	*hvaðan, hvar*	yours	*sú, sumar, sumarið, sverð, Sviðningi, svo, svo, synjað, tæki, taka*
what	*hverja, hverjum*		
whether	*hverjum, hvert*		
why	*hví*	you	*þér, þér, þess, þessa, þessar, þessi*
with	*í, iðju, íþróttamaður, klengisök, konu*		
wife	*konu*	your	*þú, þurfa*
would	*mun, mundi, mundu, muni, muni*		
will	*munu, munuð, munum, næði, næst*		
word	*orð, orð*		
words	*orð, orða, orðið*		
worded	*ortir*		
we	*oss, óvinum, ósvisku*		
wished	*skyldi, skyldu*		
wounded	*stungist*		
wood	*tré*		
would-be	*væri*		
woke	*vakti*		
warned	*varaðist*		
were-you	*varðstu*		
well	*vel*		
worth	*verður, verr, verri*		
worse	*verr*		
worsen	*verri*		
west	*vestur*		
winter	*veturinn*		
widely	*víða*		
willed	*vildi, vildi, vilja*		
wills	*vildi*		
wish	*vilja*		
wishes	*vill*		
wind	*vindur*		
wise	*vitrir*		
witness	*votta*		
witnesses	*vottar, vottnefna*		

Y, y

A Word Comparison of Old Norse and Old Icelandic Words

A Word Comparison of Old Norse and Old Icelandic Words

Old Norse	Old Icelandic	English
aftr	aftur	back
aldr	aldur	age
alla	allan	all
allfúss	allfús	all-happy
allmikit	allmikið	all-much
allmjök	allmjög	all-greatly
Allmjök	allmjög	all-much
allr	allur	all
Allvesalliga	allvesallega	miserable
álnir	alnar	measures
ámælilaust	ámælislaust	without-reproach
annarr	annar	another
annat	annað	other
annsvör	andsvör	answer
annsvör	andsvör	answers
at	að	as
at	að	at
at	að	of
at	að	that
at	að	the
at	að	to
at	að	to-you
átzt	ást	affection
aumliga	aumlega	abjectly
aumligast	aumlegast	miserable
austr	austur	east
berusku	bernsku	childishness
betr	beutr	better
bezt	best	best
bezta	bestu	best
bezti	besti	best
biðr	biður	invited
brátt	brást	transformed
brendi	brenndi	burned
Broddi	brá	drew
búða	búðar	booths
búðarvegginum	búðarvegginum	booth-walls
búit	búið	settled
búit	búið	to-settle
búizt	búist	prepared
bust	burst	cheated
dœma	dæma	deem
dœmdir	dæmdir	deem
dregit	dregið	drawn
drengskapr	drengskapur	word-of-honour
dugit	dugið	enough
dýrligu	dýrlegu	dearly
eðr	eða	but
eðr	eða	or
Eigi	eða	but
eigingirni	eigngirni	selfish
eigu	eiga	have
Einarr	einar	Einar (name)
Eirekssyni	eiríkssyni	Eriksson (name)
ek	eg	I
ek	ég	I
ek	og	and
ekkí	ekki	not
eldr	eldur	fire
Eldrinn	eldurinn	fire
Enn	en	about
Enn	en	and
Enn	en	as
enn	en	but
Enn	en	in
enn	en	than
Enn	en	that
enn	en	the
enn	en	then
Enn	en	when
er	að	that
Eyjólfr	eyjólfur	Eyjolf (name)
fastr	fastur	fastened
féit	féið	fee
fekk	fékk	got
feldr	felldur	fall
fell	féll	fell
fengit	fengið	got
ferr	ferð	go

A Word Comparison of Old Norse and Old Icelandic Words

Old Norse	Old Icelandic	English	Old Norse	Old Icelandic	English
févænligt	févænlegt	money-promising	handsalsvætti	handsalsvætti	agreement
fimti	fimmti	fifth	haustit	haustið	autumn
fjarlægir	fjárlægir	financial	hefði	hafði	had
flokkr	flokkur	band	hefði	hefðu	had
føri	færi	opportunity	hefir	hefur	has
føtrna	fæturna	feet	heldr	heldur	rather
Fór	for	for	helzt	helst	held
forðat	forðað	avoided	helzt	hélst	held
fórt	fórst	travelled	hendr	hendur	hand
föruneyti	förunauta	companions	hér	hann	he
frammi	fram	from-forward	heraða	héraða	districts
fundit	fundið	found	heruð	héruð	district
fúss	fús	willing	heruð	héruð	districts
fyrir	frá	from	hestrinn	hesturinn	horse
Geitisson	geitsson	Geitisson (name)	hit	hið	the
Geitissonar	geitssonar	Geitisson's (name)	hit	hið	then
			hittust	hittast	found
gekk	fekk	got	hjálpit	hjálpið	help
gengit	gengið	walked	hnœfilyrðum	hnæfilyrðum	blows
gerði	gerðu	made	hœttir	hættir	mannered
gerðist	gerist	was	hræddr	hræddur	scared
gerim	gerum	be	hraunit	hraunið	lava-fields
gerim	gerum	being	hraustr	hraustur	brave
gerim	gerum	doing	Hvárt	hvert	which
gerim	gerum	make	hvárt	hvort	either
gerit	gerið	make	hvárt	hvort	whether
gettú	gettu	getting	Hverr	hver	who
gjarna	fjarna	remove	hveru	hvern	each
goðar	þeir	they	i	í	of
Goðaskógr	goðaskógur	Godaskogur (place)	i	í	to
Goðdala-Starri	guðdala-starri	Guddala-Starri (name)	íþróttamaðr	íþróttamaður	sports-man
göfigligri	göfulegri	nobler	jafnstórliga	jafnstórlega	equally-great
goldit	goldið	paid	kallaðr	kallaður	called
Guðmundr	guðmundur	Gudmund (name)	kallat	kallað	called
			kemr	kemur	come
Hafði	hann	he	kenna	kenn	know
hafim	höfum	have	kjörit	kjörið	choice
hafit	hafið	have	kœmi	kæmu	came
hagr	hagur	handy	komit	komið	comes
handlaginu	handlagi	agreement	komit	komið	coming
			kostr	kostur	choice
			lætr	lætur	behaviour

A Word Comparison of Old Norse and Old Icelandic Words

Old Norse	Old Icelandic	English	Old Norse	Old Icelandic	English
látim	látum	let	mögr	mögur	skinny
leggr	leggur	lay	munngát	mungát	ale
leið	á	the	muntú	muntu	should
leita	leiða	objection	munu	munuð	shall
leitat	leitað	sought	næða	næði	neared
léttra	lettara	easier	nafnfrægr	nafndrægur	named
lézt	lést	burden	nefndr	nefndur	named
lézt	lést	let	neitaða	neitaði	refusal
liðveizlunni	liðveilsunni	supportive	neitaða	neitaði	refused
limit	limið	foliage	niðrfall	niðurfall	dropping
litill	lítill	little	nökkura	nokkura	some
Litill	lítill	small	nökkurar	nokkurar	some
litilræði	lítilræði	little-advised	nökkurir	nokkurir	some
lízt	líst	beholding	nökkurn	nokkurn	someone
lízt	líst	like	nökkuru	nokkuru	somewhat
ljótr	ljótur	ugly	nökkut	nokkuð	some
lög-(sögu)maðr	lögmaður	law-speaker	nökkut	nokkuð	something
			norðr	norðu	north
lokit	lokið	ended	norðr	norður	north
Lönguhlið	lönguhlíð	Langahlid (place)	nóttina	nótt	night
			Œrr	ær	awed
lúkim	lúkum	conclude	ofarliga	ofarlega	high-up
lýkr	lýkur	ends	ofreflismenn	ofureflismenn	ultra-strong-men
lýsír	lýsir	declared			
maðr	maður	a-man	oftliga	oftlega	often
maðr	maður	man	óhœfan	óhæfan	trouble
mælti	mætli	said	ok	og	also
mælti	mætli	spoke	ok	og	and
mælti	segir	said	okkarr	okkar	ours
mágr	mágur	brother-in-law	okkr	okkur	ours
málit	málið	matter	okkr	okkur	us
málit	málið	the-matter	Ólíkligt	ólíklegt	unlike
málkunnigr	málkunnigur	talking-known	ómakligr	ómaklegur	uncomfortable
manna	mann	men			
manna	mönnum	men	ópit	ópið	open
mannamunr	mannamunur	integrity	ór	úr	from
margt	mart	many	ór	úr	of
mega	megi	may	ór	úr	out-of
mér	þér	you	orðit	orðið	word
mik	mig	me	órhjarta	örhjarta	un-heartened
mikit	mikið	many	Ormr	ormur	orm
missmíði	missmíð	mistake	óvizku	ósvisku	unwise
mjök	mjög	much	ráðit	ráðið	decided

185

A Word Comparison of Old Norse and Old Icelandic Words

Old Norse	Old Icelandic	English
ráttlátir	réttlátir	right-like
reið	fór	travelled
reitt	reiðst	riding
reitt	reiðst	rode
riða	ríða	ride
riða	ríða	rode
rœddu	ræddu	discussed
sá	sáu	this
sáttu	sástu	saw-you
sé	muni	should
sem	ssem	as
sérhverjum	sér	theirs
siðan	síðan	then
siðr	siður	custom
sjálfdœmi	sjálfdæmi	self-judgement
sjálfr	sjálfur	himself
sjúkr	sínkur	stingy
skaltú	skaltu	shall-you
skarðit	skarð	gap
skarðit	skarðið	the-pass
skerða	skríða	action
skifta	skipta	exchange
Skildist	skildust	separated
skilit	skilið	divided
skilit	skilið	understood
skógana	skóga	forest
skóggangssök	skóggang	outlawry
Skógr	skógur	forest
Skulu	skuluð	should
skylda	skyldi	should
skyldi	skyldu	should
skyldim	skyldum	should
skylim	skulum	should
Slikt	slíkt	such
slöðraði	slauðraði	trailing-behind
snýr	snýrð	turned
sœmd	sæmd	honour
sœmdunum	sæmdunum	honour
Sökunautr	sökunautur	defendant
stalt	stalst	stealing
stefnda	stefndi	summonsed
Steingrimr	steingrímur	Steingrim (name)
stikat	stikað	stitched
stórorðr	stórorðu	high-sounding
stungizt	stungist	wounded
sumarit	sumarið	summer
sundr	sundur	asunder
svá	sogört	saying
svá	svo	so
svá	svo	such
svarar	segir	said
svarar	svaraði	answered
Svíðingi	sviðningi	Svidning (place)
synjat	synjað	refused
talaða	talaði	said
þá	sá	so
þá	þú	you
þakksamliga	þakksamlega	thankfully
þar	það	that
þat	það	it
þat	það	that
þat	það	the
þat	það	this
þat	það	to
þat	það	with
þat	þess	this
Þðrðarson	þórðarson	Thordarson (name)
Þðrkels	þorkels	Thorkell (name)
þeira	þeim	these
þeira	þeirra	of-the
þeira	þeirra	their
þeira	þeirra	theirs
þeira	þeirra	them
þeira	þeirra	they
þeira	þeirra	those
þér	það	that
þess	þessa	this
þessa	þá	then
þik	þig	you
þingit	þingið	assembly

A Word Comparison of Old Norse and Old Icelandic Words

Old Norse	Old Icelandic	English
þit	þið	you
þó	þá	then
þó	þótt	though
þœtti	þótti	thought
Þórhallr	þórhalldur	Thorhall (name)
Þórhallr	þórhallur	Thorhall (name)
Þórkel	þorkel	Thorkell (name)
Þórkeli	þorkeli	Thorkell (name)
Þórkell	þorkell	Thorkell (name)
Þórkels	þorkels	Thorkell (name)
Þórstein	þorstein	Thorstein (name)
Þórsteinn	þorsteinn	Thorstein (name)
Þórsteins	þorsteins	Thorstein (name)
Þórsteins	þorsteins	Thorstein's (name)
þótt	þót	though
þriði	þriðji	third
Þurfu	þurfa	need
Því	hví	why
því	það	that
Þykki	þykir	think
þykkir	þykir	seems
þykkjast	þykjast	consider
til	itl	little
tiltœkilegt	tiltækilegra	available
tœki	tæki	took
tvá	tvo	two
váðaverk	voðaverk	accidents
væra	væri	would-be
væri	væru	were
væri	var	was
ván	von	hope
ván	von	wished
Vápnafjörð	vopnafjörð	Vopnafjord (place)
vár	vor	spring
vár	voru	are
Varðtú	varðstu	were-you
varit	varið	defend
várkunn	vorkunn	pity
várr	vor	our
várra	vorra	talking-loudly
vart	varst	were
várþings	vorþings	local-assembly
váru	voru	was
váru	voru	were
varut	voruð	were
vátta	votta	witness
váttar	vottar	witnesses
váttnefna	vottnefna	witnesses
vegr	vegur	way
veitit	veitið	know
Veittú	veittu	grant
vér	við	on
vér	við	we
verðr	verður	worth
verit	verið	been
vestr	vestur	west
vetrinn	veturinn	winter
vilda	vildi	willed
vili	vilji	willing
vilit	viljið	will
vilnat	vilnað	willed
vindr	vindur	wind
víss	vís	aware
vit	vér	we
vit	við	we
vit	við	with
vitu	vita	knowing
yðr	yður	yours
ykkr	ykkur	you
yrði	yrðu	be

The Tale of Thorlief the Earl's Poet (*Old Norse*)

Old Norse	Literal	English
1	**1**	**1**
Nú skal segja þann œvintýr er gerðist á ofanverðum dögum Hákonar Hlaðajarls, í hverjum kynstrum, göldrum og gerningum hann varð forsmáðr og mjǫk at verðugu, því at hans mannillska og guðníðingskapr varð mörgum manni til mikils þunga og óbœtilegs skaða andar og líkama.	Now shall say then adventure that happened in the-uppermost days Hakon Earl-Of-Lade, about who's strange, magical-arts and witchcraft he was shamed and much to honour, because that he man-evil and idol-worship became many people to much heavy and un-redeemable damage soul and body.	Now shall be told the adventure that happened in the early days of Hakon the earl of Lade, about his strange magic and witchcraft which greatly shamed his honour, because this evil man and his idolatry became a heavy burden to many people, and caused irreparable harm to soul and body.
Varð honum þat sem margan tímir at þá er hegningartíminn er kominn er eigi hœgt undan at komast því at þat er óvinarins náttúra at þann manninn sem hann þykist fullkomið vald á eiga og önga von á til guðs blekkir hann fyrst og blygðar með krókóttum kyndugskap sinna bölvaðra slœgða í framleiðslu hans ljótu lífsdaga en at þrotnum hans stundlegum lífstíma verðr hann drekktr í dökkri dýflissu dálegra kvala með eymd og ánauð utan enda.	Became to-him that as many time that then was punishment-time was came that not possible out-of to come because that it was the-enemy's nature that then people which he thought full-coming power that not and none hope of to God deceived he first and shame with devious cunning his cursed slyness in causing his ghastly life-days then that waning his temporary lifetime became he drowned in dark dungeon harmful torment with misery and enslavement without end.	It befell him, as it does to many, when the time of punishment came, he could not come out of it, as it was the devil's nature to deceive people who he thinks he has full power over, and who has no hope of God's mercy. First comes shame with devious cunning and cursed slyness, causing a ghastly life, and in the waning of his temporary life, he is drowned in the dark dungeon of harmful torment, with misery and enslavement without end.
2	**2**	**2**
Þá bjó Ásgeir rauðfeldr á Brekku í Svarfaðardal.	Then lived Asgeir Red-Cloak at Brekka in Svarfardal.	Then Asgeir Red-Cloak lived at Brekka in Svafardal.
Hann var ríkr maðr og stórœttaðr.	He was powerful man and great-family.	He was a powerful man from a great family.
Þórhildr hét kona hans.	Thorhild named wife his.	His wife was named Thorhild.
Hún var vitr kona og vinsœl og skörungr mikill.	She was wise woman and popular and noble much.	She was a very wise, popular, and noble woman.

The Tale of Thorlief the Earl's Poet (Old Norse)

Old Norse	Literal	English
Þau áttu þrjá syni og voru allir efnilegir.	They had three sons and were all promising.	They had three sons, all of whom were promising.
Ólafr hét son þeirra hinn elsti og var kallaðr völubrjótr, annar Helgi hinn frœkni og koma þeir báðir meir við aðrar sögr en þessa.	Olaf named son theirs the eldest and was called knuckle-breaker, another Helgi the brave and came they both more with other sagas than this.	Their eldest son was named Olaf, who was called 'knuckle-breaker', the second son was called Helgi the brave, and they appear in other sagas than this one.
Þorleifr hét hinn yngsti son þeirra.	Thorleif named the youngest son theirs.	Their youngest son was named Thorleif.
Hann var snemma gildr og gervilegr og hinn mesti atgervimaðr um íþróttir.	He was early-age capable and talented and the most accomplished-man at skilled.	He was fully capable at an early age, an accomplished man and skilful.
Hann var skáld gott.	He was a-poet good.	He was a good poet
Hann var á fóstri með Miðfjarðar-Skeggja móðrbróðr sínum at Reykjum í Miðfirði þar til er hann var átján vetra gamall.	He was in fostered with Midfjorder-Skeggi mother's-brother his at Reykir in Midfjord there until that he was eighteen winters old.	He was brought up with his uncle Midfjorder-Skeggi at Reykir in Midfjord there until he was eighteen years old.
Skeggi unni mikið Þorleifi og lagði við hann ástfóstr.	Skeggi loved much Thorleif and had with him foster-care.	Skeggi loved Thorleif very much and brought him up with care.
Þat töluðu menn at Skeggi mundi fleira kenna Þorleifi í frœðum fornlegum en aðrir mundu vita.	This told people that Skeggi would more teach Thorleif in instruction ancient-ways than others would know.	People said that Skeggi would teach Thorleif more about the ways of magic than others would know.
Þá fór Þorleifr heim til föðr síns.	Then went Thorleif home to father his.	Then Thorleif went home to his father.
Hann vó Klaufa böggva með fulltingi Ólafs bróðr síns en til eftirmáls eftir Klaufa var Karl hinn rauði og gekk svo fast at at Þorleifr varð útlœgr og ger í burt úr Svarfaðardal.	He killed Klaufi the-mauler with assistance Olaf's brother his and to after-the-case after Klaufi was Karl the Red and went so closed it that Thorleif became outlaw and made to away from-out-of Svarfardal.	He killed Klaufi the mauler with the help of his brother Olaf, and in the following legal case was Karl the Red, and so it concluded that Thorleif became an outlaw and banished from Svafardal.
Ljótólfr goði hafði fylgt Yngvildi fagurkinn systr Þorleifs.	Ljotolf chieftain had followed Yngvild Fair-Cheek sister Thorleif's.	Ljotolf the chieftain lived with Yngvild the fair-cheek, Thorleif's sister.

The Tale of Thorlief the Earl's Poet (Old Norse)

Old Norse	Literal	English
Hann kom Þorleifi í skip á Gáseyri.	He came Thorleif to ship at Gaseyri.	He brought Thorleif to a ship at Gaseyri.
Þorleifr varð afturreka.	Thorleif became back-driven.	But Thorleif was driven back.
Hann var um veturinn á laun ýmist með Ljótólfi goða eða Ásgeiri föðr sínum.	He was about winter in secrecy either with Ljotolf the-chieftain or Asgeir father his.	During the winter he was hiding with Ljotolf the chieftain or his father Asgeir.
Nam hann þá at föðr sínum marga fornfrœði því at hann var sagðr margkunnandi.	Took he then to father his many ancient-ways because that he was said many-known.	He then took to learning many of the ancient ways, as it is said that he knew many things.
Var þá Þorleifr nítján vetra.	Was then Thorleif nineteen winters.	Thorleif was then nineteen winters old.
Karl leitaði fast eftir um Þorleif og urðu þar um veturinn margir atburðir, þeir er frásagnar eru verðir sem segir í Svarfdœla sögu.	Karl sought closely after about Thorleif and became there about winter many events, they are from-told are will-be as said in Svarfardal saga.	Karl looked closely for Thorleif, and from there came many events, which are told in Svafardal Saga.
Um vorið eftir fór Þorleifr vestr til Skeggja fóstra síns og frænda og biðr hann ásjá og umráða með sér um þessi mál.	About spring after travelled Thorleif west to Skeggi foster-father his and kinsmen and asked him assistance and about-advice with him about this matter.	About the following spring, Thorleif travelled west to Skeggi his foster father and kinsman, and asked for his help and guidance in this matter.
Og með styrk og ráðum Miðfjarðar-Skeggja og Ljótólfs goða fer Þorleifr og kaupir sér skip at kaupmönnum er uppi stóð í Blönduósi og rœðr háseta til og fór síðan heim á Brekku og hitti föðr sinn og móðr og beiddist af þeim fararefna og fékk svo mikinn fjárhlut sem honum þótti sér þarfa og at vordögum lét hann varning sinn til skips binda og fór í brott af Brekku alfari og bat vel fyrir föðr sínum og móðr og Miðfjarðar-Skeggja fóstra sínum.	And with support and advice Midfjorder-Skeggi and Ljotolf the-chieftain went Thorleif and bought himself a-ship from trading-men that up stood in Blonduos and hired first-mate for and travelled afterwards home to Brekka and met father his and mother and asked of them travel-goods and got so much fee-lot as he thought he-himself needed and to spring-days had he wares his to ship bound and travelled to away from Brekka for-good and bid well for father his and mother and Midfjorder-Skeggi foster-father his.	And with the support and advice of Midfjorder-Skeggi and Ljotolf the chieftain, Thorleif went and bought himself a ship from merchants up in Blonduos, and hired a first mate for it. After that he then travelled home to Brekka and met his father and mother, asking for wares and travel goods, and he got as much money as he thought he needed. In the first days of spring he brought his wares to his ship, bound them up, and travelled away from Brekka once and for all, wishing his father and mother well, and Midfjorder-Skeggi, his foster father.

The Tale of Thorlief the Earl's Poet (Old Norse)

Old Norse	Literal	English
3	**3**	**3**
Nú lœtr Þorleifr í haf og byrjar honum vel og kemr skipi sínu í Vík austr.	Now left Thorleif to sea and fair-wind he-had well and came ship his into Vik east.	Now Thorleif set out to sea and got a fair wind, and his ship came to Vik in the east.
Hákon Hlaðajarl var þá í Víkinni.	Hakon Earl-Of-Lade was then in The-bay.	Hakon was the earl of Lade at Vik.
Þorleifr gekk á land og lét ryðja skip sitt.	Thorleif went to the-land and had cleared ship his.	Thorleif went to land and had is ship unloaded.
Hann hitti jarlinn og kvaddi hann.	He met the-earl and greeted him.	He met the earl and greeted him.
Jarl tók honum vel og spurði hann at nafni, œtt og kynferði en Þorleifr sagði honum.	The-earl received him well and asked him of name, ancestors and kinsmen-origins and Thorleif told him.	The earl received him well and asked his name, ancestry, and origins, and Thorleif told him.
Jarl spurði og margra tíðinda af Íslandi en Þorleifr sagði honum ofléttlega.	The-earl asked of much news of Iceland and Thorleif told him willingly.	The earl asked for much news of Iceland, and Thorleif told him.
Þá sagði jarl:	Then said the-earl:	Then the earl said:
"Svo er orðið Þorleifr at vér viljum hafa sölr af þér og hásetum þínum".	"So has become Thorleif that we wish-to have sale of you and crew yours".	"So it is, Thorleif, that we wish to buy some things from you and your crew".
Þorleifr svarar:	Thorleif answered:	Thorleif answered:
"Vér höfum lítinn varninginn herra en oss eru þó aðrir kaupunautar hentugri og munuð þér láta oss sjálfráða vera at selja þeim góss vort og peninga sem oss líkar".	"We have little wares lord and us we-are though other customers more-convenient and shall you allow us ourselves-decide being for to-sell them belongings ours and money as we like".	"We have little in the way of wares, my lord, and we need more useful customers, and you shall allow us to decide for ourselves who to sell our belongings to as we like".
Jarli þótti hann þykklega svara og mislíkaði orð hans mjǫk og skildu við svo búið.	Earl thought he arrogantly answered and misliked words his much and parted with so settled.	The earl thought he had answered arrogantly, and disliked his words, and with that they parted.

The Tale of Thorlief the Earl's Poet (Old Norse)

Old Norse	Literal	English
Þorleifr fór nú til manna sinna og svaf af um nóttina og um morguninn rís hann upp og fer í kaupstaðinn og fréttist fyrir um góða kaupunauta og kaupslagar við þá um daginn.	Thorleif travelled now to men his and slept of about the-night and about morning rose he up and travelled to market-town and sought for about food customers and bargaining with then about the-day.	Thorleif went back to his men and slept through the night, and in the morning he got up and travelled to town and sought good customers, and bargained with them throughout the day.
Og er jarl spurði þat fór hann með fjölmenni til skips Þorleifs og lét taka þar menn alla og binda.	And when the-earl learned that travelled he with following-men to ships Thorleif's and had took there men all and tied-up.	And when the earl learned of this, he travelled with his followers to Thorleif's ship and took all the men and had them tied up.
Síðan rændi hann þar fjárhlut öllum og kastaði á sinni eign en lét brenna skipið at köldum kolum.	Afterwards robbed he there financial-share of-all and cast about himself owning and had burnt the-ship to cold coals.	Afterwards he robbed them of all their wealth and took it for himself, and had the ship burnt to coals.
Og eftir þetta lét hann skjóta ásum milli búðanna og lét þar hengja við alla förunauta Þorleifs.	And after this had he launched poles between booths and had them hanged with all companions Thorleif's.	After this he had poles raised between booths and had all of Thorleif's companions hanged.
Síðan fór jarl í brott og hans menn og tók at sér varning þann er Þorleifr hafði átt og skipti upp með sínum mönnum.	Afterwards travelled the-earl to away and his men and took then for-himself wares then that Thorleif had had and exchanged up with his men.	Afterwards the earl went away with his men, taking all the wares and dividing it among his men.
En um kveldið er Þorleifr kom heim og ætlaði at vitja manna sinna sem hann gerði sá hann vegsummerki hversu við hans félaga hafði farið verið og þóttist vita at Hákon jarl mundi þessu vonda verki valdið hafa og spyr nú eftir þessum tíðindum glögglega.	Then about evening when Thorleif came home and intended to know men his what he had-done saw he traces how-so with his companions had gone been and thought certainly that Hakon earl would this wicked work caused had and learned now after this news clearly.	In the evening when Thorleif came home and looked for his men as usual, he saw traces of what had happened with his companions, and thought certainly that Earl Hakon caused this evil deed, and afterwards he learned the full news clearly.
Og er hann hafði þessi tíðindi sannlega spurt þá kvat hann vísu:	And when he had this news truly learned then spoke he this-verse:	And when he learned the news, then he spoke this verse:
Hrollir hugr minn illa. Hefir drengr skaða fengið sé ég á sléttri eyri, svarri, báts og knarrar.	Shivering heart mine badly. Have men damage caught see i this levelled sand, grave, boats and merchant-ships.	My heart shivers badly. Men have caught damage, I see this levelled sand, grave, both ship and boat.

The Tale of Thorlief the Earl's Poet (Old Norse)

Old Norse	Literal	English
Hinn er upp réð brenna öldu fíl fyrir skaldi, hver veit nema kol knarrar köld fýsi mig gjalda.	Those are up ruled burned wave elephant before the-poet, who knows except the-coals of-the-ship cold desire shall-i repay.	Those that ruled to burn the elephant of the waves, who knows except the coals of the ship cold desire I to repay.

4

Svo er sagt at eftir þenna atburð kom Þorleifr sér í skip með kaupmönnum og sigldu suðr til Danmerkr og fór hann á fund Sveins konungs og var með honum um veturinn.	So it-is said that after those events came Thorleif himself in a-ship with trading-men and sailed south to Denmark and travelled he to meet Svein the-king and was with him about winter.	It is said that after this Thorleif went on a ship with trading-men and sailed south to Denmark, and he travelled to meet king Svein and stayed with him over the winter.
En er hann hafði þar eigi lengi verið var þat einn dag at Þorleifr gekk fyrir konung og beiddi hann hlýða kvœði því er hann hafði ort um hann.	Then when he had there not long been was it one day that Thorleif went before the-king and asked him to-hear poem since that he had worded about him.	Then when he had not long been there, one day Thorleif went before the king and asked hi to hear a poem that he had composed about him.
Konungr spurði hvort hann vœri skáld.	The-king asked whether he was a-poet.	The king asked whether he was a poet.
Þorleifr svarar:	Thorleif answered:	Thorleif answered:
"Þat er eftir því sem þér viljið dœmt hafa herra er þér heyrið".	"It is after therefore which to-you will deem have lord when you hear".	"That is for you to judge, lord, when you have heard it".
Konungr bat hann þá fram flytja.	The-king asked him then from to-carry.	The king then asked him to perform.
Þorleifr kvat þá fertuga drápu og er þetta stef í:	Thorleif spoke then forty phrases and is this stave in:	Thorleif spoke forty verses and among them is this stave:
Oft með œrnri giftu öðlings himins röðla Jóta gramr hinn ítri Englandi roðið branda.	Often with merry luck noble heaven's wheel Jutland warrior the high-born England reddened swords.	Often with merry luck from noble heaven's wheel the high-born Jutland warrior reddened swords in England.
Konungr lofaði mjök kvœðið og allir þeir er heyrðu og sögðu bœði vel kveðið og skörulega fram flutt.	The-king praised much the-poem and all they who heard and said both well spoken and boldly forward performed.	The king praised the poem very much, and all those who heard it said it was both well spoken and boldly performed.

The Tale of Thorlief the Earl's Poet (Old Norse)

Old Norse	Literal	English
Konungr gaf Þorleifi at kvæðislaunum hring þann er stóð mörk og þat sverð er til kom hálf mörk gulls og bat hann lengi með sér vera.	The-king gave Thorleif to poem's-reward a-ring then was stood a-mark and with a-sword was to come half a-mark of-gold and invited him long with him to-be.	The king gave Thorleif a reward for the poem, a ring that was worth a mark of gold, and a sword worth half a mark of gold, and he invited him to stay with him.
Þorleifr gekk til sœtis og þakkaði vel konungi.	Thorleif went to sit and thanked well the-king.	Thorleif took his place and thanked the king well.
Og leið svo fram nokkura hríð og ekki lengi áðr en Þorleifr ógladdist svo mjǫk at hann gáði varla undir drykkjuborð at ganga eða samsœtis við sína bekkjunauta.	And passed so from some awhile and not long before that Thorleif un-gladdened so much that he cared scarcely up-to drinking-tables and went either banquet with himself bench-fellows.	And so it passed, and it was not long before Thorleif became so unhappy that he scarcely cared to go to the drinking tables to feast or talk with his bench mates.
Finnr konungr þetta bráðlega og lætr kalla Þorleif fyrir sig og mælti:	Found the-king this quickly and had called Thorleif before him and spoke:	The king soon noticed this and had Thorleif called before him, and asked:
"Hvat veldr ógleði þinni er þú gáir varla at halda háttum við oss?"	"What brought-about un-gladness yours that you care scarcely to hold custom with us?"	"What has brought about your unhappiness, that you hardly keep to our customs?"
Þorleifr svarar:	Thorleif answered:	Thorleif answered:
"Þat munuð þér heyrt hafa herra at sá er skyldr at leysa annars vandrœði er at spyr".	"That should you heard have lord that so who should to solve another's difficulty who that asks".	"You must have heard, lord, that he who asks another's difficulty should solve it for him".
"Segðu fyrst",	"Say-you first",	"Tell it first",
segir konungr.	said the-king.	said the king.
Þorleifr svarar:	Thorleif answered:	Thorleif answered:
"Eg hefi kveðið vísr nokkurar í vetr er eg kalla Konrvísr er eg hefi ort um Hákon jarl því at jarl er kona kenndr í skáldskap.	"If have poem verses some in winter that i call Woman-Verses that i have worded about Hakon earl because that the-earl is a-woman known in poetry.	"I have composed some verses in the winter, that I call Women Verses, that I composed about Earl Hakon, because the earl is called a woman in poetry.

The Tale of Thorlief the Earl's Poet (Old Norse)

Old Norse	Literal	English
Nú ógleðr mig þat herra ef eg fœ eigi orlof af yðr at fara til Noregs og fœra jarli kvœðið".	Now un-glad me that lord if i get not leave of yours to travel to Norway and bring the-earl the-poem".	I will be unhappy, lord, if I do not get your leave to travel to Norway to bring the earl the poem".
"Þú skalt at vísu fá orlof",	"You shall this certainly get leave",	"You shall certainly have leave",
segir konungr, "og skaltu þó heita oss áðr at koma aftr til vor þat fljótasta sem þú getr því at vér viljum þín ekki missa sakir íþrótta þinna".	said the-king, "and shall-you though promise us return to come after to spring the soonest as you get therefore that we wish your not miss sake skills yours".	said the king, "and you shall promise to return to us soon after spring, because we do not wish to miss your skills".
Þorleifr hét því og fékk sér nú farning og fór norðr í Noreg og linnir eigi fyrr en hann kemr í Þrándheim.	Thorleif promised accordingly and got himself now passage and travelled north to Norway and stopped not before that he came to Trondheim.	Thorleif promised accordingly and now got himself passage to travel north to Norway, and did not stop until he came to Trondheim.
Þá sat Hákon jarl á Hlöðum.	Then sat Hakon earl at Lade.	Then Hakon sat in residence at Lade.
Þorleifr býr sér nú stafkarls gervi og bindr sér geitarskegg og tók sér eina stóra hít og lét koma undir stafkarls gervina og bjó svo um at öllum skyldi sýnast sem hann œti þann kost er hann kastaði í hítina því at gíman hennar var uppi við munn honum undir geitarskegginu.	Thorleif prepared himself now as-a-beggar character and bound himself goat-beard and took himself a large bag and had come-with under beggar's disguise and prepared so about that all should appear as he had then food that he cast in the-bag because that opening its was up by mouth his under goat-beard.	Thorleif now disguised himself as a beggar and wore a goat's beard, he also took a large bag which he kept under the disguise, and it was prepared so that everyone would think that he ate the food that he put into the bag, because the opening was up by his mouth under the goat's beard.
Síðan tekr hann hœkjr tvœr og var broddr niðr úr hvorri, fer nú þar til er hann kemr á Hlaðir.	Afterwards took he crutches two and were spikes down out-of each, travelled now there until that he came to Lade.	Afterwards he also took two crutches with spikes on the ends, and travelled until he came to Lade.
Þat var aðfangskveld jóla í þann tíma er jarl var kominn í sœti og mart stórmenni er jarl hafði at sér boðið til jólaveislunnar.	It was midwinter-evening Yule at that time when the-earl was coming to sit and many great-men that the-earl had that he invited to yule-feast.	It was the midwinter evening of Yule, when the earl was coming to sit, and there were many great men that the earl had invited to the Yule feast.

The Tale of Thorlief the Earl's Poet (Old Norse)

Old Norse	Literal	English
Karl gengr greiðlega inn í höllina en er hann kemr inn stumrar hann geysimjǫk og fellr fast á hœkjurnar og snýr til annarra stafkarla og sest niðr utarlega í hálminn.	The-old-man went quickly in to the-hall and when he came in stumbled he exceedingly-much and fell close had the-crutches and turned to other beggars and sat down out-lying of the-straw.	The old man went quickly into the hall, and when he came in, he stumbled and fell heavily on his crutches, then turned to the other beggars and sat down at the edge of the straw.
Hann var nokkuð bœginn við stafkarla og heldr harðleikinn en þeir þoldu illa er hann lét ganga á þeim stafina.	He was somewhat troubled with beggars and rather rough and they endured badly that he let go to them sticks.	He was irritable with the beggars and quite rough, and they were not happy with being knocked by his sticks.
Hrukku þeir undan og varð af þessu hark og háreysti svo at heyrði um alla höllina.	Drew they back and became of this noise and commotion so that heard about all the-hall.	They drew back and this caused noise and commotion so that all who were in the hall heard.
En er jarl verðr þessa var spyr hann hvat valdi óhljóði þessu.	Then when the-earl became this was asked he what controlled unsoundly this.	Then when the earl was aware of this, he asked what caused this din.
Honum er sagt at stafkarl einn sé sá þar kominn at svo sé illr og úrigr at ekki láti ógert.	He was said that beggar one himself saw there coming that so being bad and unruly that not had undone.	He was told that a beggar had been seen who was so bad and unruly that he stopped at nothing.
Jarl bat kalla hann fyrir sig og svo var og gert.	Earl asked call-to him before him him and so was and done.	The earl asked him to be called before him, and so it was done.
En er karl kom fyrir jarl hafði hann mjǫk stutt um kvaðningar.	And when the-old-man came before the-earl had he much short about greeting.	And when the old man came before the earl, he greeted him shortly.
Jarl spurði hann at nafni, œtt og óðali.	Earl asked him of name, ancestry and estate.	The earl asked him his name, his ancestry, and his estate.
"Óvant er nafn mitt herra at eg heiti Níðungr Gjallandason og kynjaðr úr Syrgisdölum af Svíþjóð hinni köldu.	"Not-lacking is name mine lord that i named Nidung Son-of-gjallandi and descended from Syrgsdalir in Sweden the cold.	"Not lacking is my name, lord, for I am named Nidung son of Gjallandi and descended from Syrgsdalir in Sweden the cold.
Er eg kallaðr Níðungr hinn nákvœmi.	Am i called Nidung the pernickety.	I am called Nidung the pernickety.
Hefi eg víða farið og marga höfðingja heim sótt.	Have i widely travelled and many chieftains' homes sought.	I have travelled widely and sought many chieftains' homes.

The Tale of Thorlief the Earl's Poet (Old Norse)

Old Norse	Literal	English
Gerist eg nú gamall mjǫk svo at trautt má eg aldr minn segja sakir elli og óminnis.	Becoming i now old much so that scarcely may i age mine say with-conviction age of amnesia.	I am now becoming so old that scarcely may I say my age with conviction because of amnesia.
Hefi eg mikla spurn af höfðingskap yðrum og harðfengi, visku og vinsældum, lagasetning og lítillæti, örleik og allri atgervi".	Have i much learned of lordship yours and toughness, wisdom and popularity, legislation and humility, generosity and all deeds".	I have learned much of your lordship and toughness, wisdom and popularity, legislation and humility, and your generosity in all deeds".
"Hví ertu svo harðúðigr og illr viðskiptis frá því sem aðrir stafkarlar?"	"Why are-you so harsher and ill behaved from therefore as other beggars?"	"Why are you so much harsher and badly behaved than the other beggars?"
Hann svarar:	He answered:	He answered:
"Hvat er örvænt um þann sem alls gengr andvana nema víls og vesaldar og ekki hefir þat er þarf og lengi legið úti á mörkum og skógum þó at sá verði œfr við ellina og allt saman en vanr áðr sœmd og sœllífi af hinum dýrstum höfðingjum en vera nú hataðr af hverjum þorpara lítils verðum".	"What is desperation about than as all going destitution taken advantage and wretchedness and not having that which needed and long laying out in marshes and forests though that so become angry with age and all together that experienced before honour and blessed-life of other dearest chieftains but becoming now hated of each peasant little worth".	"What is desperation about other than always going in destitution, taken advantage of by wretchedness, not having what is needed, laying for a long time in the marshes and forests, though becoming so angry with age, when altogether before having experienced a blessed life of the dearest chieftains, but becoming now hated by every peasant of little worth".
Jarl mælti:	The-earl spoke:	The earl spoke:
"Ertu nokkr íþróttamaðr karl er þú segist þó með höfðingjum verið hafa?"	"Are-you anything excellent-man old-man that you say though with chieftains became have?"	"Are you excellent at anything, old man, as you say you have been with chieftains?"
Karl svarar þat megi vera þó at nokkuð hafi til þess haft verið	The-old-man answered that may be though that somewhat have until this have been	The old man answered that it may be something like that:
"þá er eg var á ungum aldri.	"then when i was of young age.	"then when I was young in age.
Komi at því sem mælt er, at hverjum karli kemr at örverpi.	Comes to therefore as said is, to each man comes to decrepitude.	But it comes, as they say, decrepitude to each and every man.

The Tale of Thorlief the Earl's Poet (Old Norse)

Old Norse	Literal	English
Er þat og talat at seigt er svöngum at skruma.	Is that also told that tough from hunger to swagger.	It is also said that it is difficult to swagger when hungry.
Mun eg og ekki við yðr skruma herra nema þér látið gefa mér at eta því at svo dregr at mér af elli, svengd og þorsta at víst eigi fœ eg staðið uppi lengr.	Should i also not with you show-off lord unless you let give me to eat because that so drawn that i-am of age, hungry and thirsty and know not can i stand up for-long.	I can't show off to you, lord, unless you give me something to eat, because I am so drawn and with age, hungry and thirsty, and I do not know how long I can stand up for.
Er slíkt harðla óhöfðinglegt at spyrja ókunna menn í hvern heim en hugsa eigi hvat mönnum hentar því at allir eru með því eðli skapaðir at bœði þurfa át og drykkju".	It-is such hardly chieftain-like to ask unknown people into one's home but think not what peoples' requirements because that all are with therefore nature shaped that both need eat and drink".	It us hardly chieftain-like to ask strangers into one's home but not think about his requirements, because we are all shaped by nature to need both food and drink".
Jarl skipaði at honum skyldi gefa kost sœmilega sem honum þarfaði.	The-earl arranged that he should give food properly as he needed.	The earl arranged that he should be given food properly as he needed.
Var og svo gert.	Was also so done.	This was done.
En er karl kom undir borð tekr hann greiðlega til matar og ryðr diska þá alla er nœstir honum voru og hann náði til svo at þjónustumenn urðu at sœkja kost í annan tíma.	Then the old-man came up-to the-tables took he promptly to food and cleared plates then all that nearest him were and he caught to so the servants became to sake provide for a-second time.	Then the old man came up to the tables, and he promptly took the food and cleared all the plates that were nearest to him, forcing the servants to provide a second helping.
Tók karl nú öngu ófreklegar til matar en fyrr.	Took the-old-man now not un-eagerly to food then before.	The old man was not just as eager as before.
Sýndist öllum sem hann œti en hann kastaði reyndar í hítina þá er fyrr var getið.	Seemed-to all that he ate but he cast actually in the-bag then as before was told-of.	It seemed to everyone that he ate, but the food was actually in the bag, as was told before.
Hlógu menn nú fast at karli þessum.	Laughed people now closely at the-old-man this.	People focused on the old man, and laughed.
Þjónustumenn töluðu at bœði vœri at hann vœri mikill og miðdigr enda gœti hann mikið etið.	Servants told that both were that he was great and broad-waist and got he much to-eat.	The servants said that he was both tall, and with a broad waist, and he could eat a lot.
Karl gaf sér ekki at því og gerði sem áðr.	The-old-man gave himself not that then and did as before.	The old man did not react, and did as before.

The Tale of Thorlief the Earl's Poet (Old Norse)

Old Norse	Literal	English
# 5	# 5	# 5
En er ofan voru drykkjuborð gekk Níðungr karl fyrir jarl og mælti:	When that over were drinking-tables went Nidung the-old-man before the-earl and spoke:	When the drinking tables were removed, the old man Nidung went to the earl and spoke:
"Hafið þér nú þökk fyrir herra en þó eigið þér illa þjónustumenn er allt gera verr en þér segið fyrir.	"Have you now thanks for lord but though own you bad servants that all done worst than you said before.	"You have now my thanks, lord, but you have bad servants that did everything worse than you ordered.
En nú vildi eg at þér sýnduð mér lítillæti herra og hlýdduð kvæði því er eg hefi ort um yðr".	But now wish i that to-you give-performance me a-little lord and listen-to poem because that i have worded about you".	But now I wish to give you a performance of my poem that I have composed about you".
Jarl mælti:	The-earl spoke:	The earl spoke:
"Hefir þú nokkuð fyrr kvæði ort um höfðingja?"	"Have you any before poems worded about chieftains?"	"Have you composed any poems about chieftains before?"
"Satt er þat herra",	"True is that lord",	"That is true, lord",
kvat hann.	said he.	he said.
Jarl mælti:	The-earl spoke:	The earl spoke:
"Búið þar komi at gömlum orðskvið, at þat er oft gott er gamlir kveða, og flyttu fram kvæðið karl en vér munum til hlýða".	"Done there comes that old proverb, that it is often good what old-man recites, and move forward poem old-man and we shall to listen".	"Done there is the proverb, that it is often good what an old man recites, so come forward with the poem, old man, and we shall listen".
Þá hefr karl upp kvæðið og kveðr framan til miðs og þykir jarli lof í hverri vísu og finnr at þar er getið og í framaverka Eiríks sonar hans.	Then had the-old-man upped the-poem and said in-front-of the middle and thought the-earl praise in each verse and found that there was told-of and in previous-deeds Erik's son his.	Then the old man began the poem and recited it to the middle, and the earl thought that he heard praise in each verse, and found that there were tales told about his son Erik.

The Tale of Thorlief the Earl's Poet (Old Norse)

Old Norse	Literal	English
En er á leið kvæðið þá bregðr jarli nokkuð undarlega við at óværi og kláði hleypr svo mikill um allan búkinn á honum og einna mest um þjóin at hann mátti hvergi kyrr þola og svo mikil býsn fylgdi þessum óværa at hann lét hrífa sér með kömbum þar sem þeim kom at.	But as it passed the-poem then tricked the-earl something strange from a restlessness and itching ran so much about all body of him and only most about thighs that he may each sit-still endure and so much strangeness followed this restlessness that he had scratched himself with combs there as they came to.	But as the poem continued, the earl was tricked into feeling a strange restlessness and an itching that ran all over his body, especially around his thighs so that he could hardly sit still, this uneasiness was so strange that he had scratched himself with combs wherever he could.
En þar sem þeim kom eigi at lét hann taka strigadúk og ríða á þrjá knúta og draga tvo menn milli þjóanna á sér.	Then there as they could not that had he taken sack-cloth and rose in three knots and drew two men between thighs for him.	Where he could not reach, he took a sack cloth and made three knots in it, and two men dragged it between his thighs for him.
Nú tók jarli illa at geðjast kvæðið og mælti:	Now took the-earl ill that liking the-poem and spoke:	Now the earl took badly to the poem and spoke:
"Kann þinn heljarkarl ekki betr at kveða því at mér þykir þetta eigi síðr heita mega níð en lof og lát þú um batna ella tekr þú gjöld fyrir".	"Can you hellish-old-man not better to say because that to-me seems this not less call may abuse than praise and let you about better or take you repayment for".	"Can you not recite something better you hellish old man, because it seems to me more like abuse than praise, and make it better or you will be repaid for it".
Karl hét góðu um og hóf þá upp vísr og heita Þokuvísr og standa í miðju Jarlsníði og er þetta upphaf at:	The-old-man promised improvement about and began then up verses and named Fog-verses and stood in middle-of The-earl's-abuse and was this beginning this:	The old man promised improvement and then began verses named Fog Verses, which are in the middle of the Earl's Abuse, and the beginning was this:
Þoku dregr upp hið ytra, *él festist hið vestra,* *mökkr mun náms, af nökkvi,* *naðrbings kominn hingat.*	Fog draws up then outside, blizzard grips the west, thick-clouds shall take, of the-ship, dragon comes here.	Fog draws up then outside, a blizzard grips the west, thick clouds shall take, of the-ship, the dragon comes here.
En er hann hafði úti Þokuvísr þá var myrkt í höllinni.	When that he had finished Fog-verses then was dark in the-hall.	When he had finished the Fog Verses, it was dark in the hall.
Og er myrkt er orðið í höllinni tekr hann aftr til Jarlsníðs.	And was dark was become in the-hall took he returning to Earl's-abuse.	And when it became dark in the hall, he began the Earl Abuse verses again.

The Tale of Thorlief the Earl's Poet (Old Norse)

Old Norse	Literal	English
Og er hann kvat hinn efsta og síðasta þriðjung þá var hvert járn á gangi þat er í var höllinni án manna völdum og varð þat margra manna bani.	And as he spoke the upper and last third then was each iron-weapon from moved it that in was the-hall without man's doing and became that many people dead.	And has he recited the third and last part, then each iron weapon that as in the hall moved without man's doing, and many men became dead.
Jarl féll þá í óvit en karl hvarf þá í brott at luktum dyrum og óloknum lásum.	The-earl fell then into unconsciousness but the-old-man disappeared then to away that shut doors and undone locks.	The earl then fell into unconsciousness, but the old man disappeared away through shut doors and undone locks.
En eftir afliðið kvæðið minnkaði myrkrið og gerði bjart í höllinni.	Then after following the-poem decreased the-darkness and it-was bright in the-hall.	Then following after the poem the darkness decreased, and it was bright again in the hall.
Jarl raknaði við og fann at honum hafði nær gengið níðið.	The-earl recovered from and found that to-him had near gone the-abuse.	The earl recovered and found that the abuse had come quite close to him.
Sá þá og vegsummerki at af var rotnat skegg allt af jarli og hárið öðrum megin reikar og kom aldrei upp síðan.	Saw then also evidence that off was decayed beard all of the-earl and hair other side parting and came never up since.	He also saw evidence of this, because his beard had decayed, along with the hair on one side of his parting, and it never came back.
Nú lætr jarl ræsta höllina og eru hinu dauðu út bornir.	Now had the-earl cleared the-hall and they-were the dead out carried.	Now the earl had the hall cleared and the dead were carried out.
Þykist hann nú vita at þetta mun Þorleifr verið hafa en karl engi annar og mun launat þykjast hafa honum mannalát og fjártjón.	Thought he now knew that this must Thorleif been had the old-man none other and should repay considered had he manslaughter and financial-loss.	He thought that he knew that the old man must have been none other than Thorleif, and that this was repayment for the manslaughter and his financial loss.
Liggr jarl nú í þessum meinlætum allan þenna vetr og mikið af sumrinu.	Laid the-earl now from this malignance all the winter and most of the-summer.	This malignance laid the earl low for all of the winter and most of the summer.

6

Þat er af Þorleifi at segja at hann snýst til ferðar suðr til Danmerkr og hefir þat til leiðarnests sér sem hann ginnti af þeim í höllinni.	It was of Thorleif to say that he turned to travel south to Denmark and had it to food his as he tricked from them in the-hall.	As for Thorleif, he set to travel south to Denmark, and for his provisions he had the food that he had tricked from them in the hall.

The Tale of Thorlief the Earl's Poet (Old Norse)

Old Norse	Literal	English
En hversu lengi sem hann hefir á leið verið þá létti hann eigi sinni ferð fyrr en hann kom á fund Sveins konungs og tók hann við honum fegins hendi og spurði hann at ferðum sínum en Þorleifr sagði allt sem farið hafði.	Then however long as he had to journey made then relief he not his travel before that he came to find Svein the-king and received he with him relieved hands and asked he of journey his and Thorleif said all which gone had.	Then however long the journey was to be made, he had no relief in his travel until he came to find king Svein, and he received him well with relieved hands, and asked him of his journey, and Thorleif said how all had gone.
Konungr svarar:	The-king answered:	The king answered:
"Nú mun eg lengja nafn þitt og kalla þig Þorleif jarlaskáld".	"Now should i lengthen name yours and call you Thorleif Earl's-Poet".	"Now I should lengthen your name and call you Thorleif the Earl's Poet".
Þá kvat konungr vísu:	Then said the-king verse:	Then the king said a verse:
Grenndi Þorleifr Þrœnda þengils hróðr fyr drengjum, hafa ólítið ýtar jarls níð borið víða. Njörðr réð vestan virðum vellstœri brag fœra brot lands galt gœti grálega leóns báru.	Slendered Thorleif The-Tronds' the-prince renown before the-fellows, had no-little out the-earl's abuse carried widely. Njord ruled west worthiness well-sized poetry brought away lands repaid got malice the-lion's carried.	Thorleif slendered the Tronds the prince's renown before the fellows, had no-little out the earl's abuse carried widely. Njord ruled the western worth well-sized poetry brought away lands repaid got for the lion's malice carried.
Þorleifr sagði konungi at hann fýstist út til Íslands og beiddi konung orlofs at fara þegar at vori.	Thorleif told the-king that he desired out-from to Iceland and asked the-king vacations to travel there in the-spring.	Thorleif told the king that he wished to travel out to Iceland and asked the king leave to travel there in the spring.
En konungr sagði svo vera skyldu "vil eg gefa þér skip í nafnfesti með mönnum og reiða og þvílíkri áhöfn sem þér þarfast".	Then the-king said so be-it should "wish i to-give you a-ship in name-giving with people and transport and accordingly-like crew as you need".	The king said that it would be so, "I wish to give you a ship as a name-gift, with people and transport and crew as you need".
Nú er Þorleifr þar um veturinn í góðu yfirlœti en at vordögum býr hann skip sitt og lét í haf og byrjaði vel og kom skipi sínu við Ísland í á þá er Þjórsá heitir.	Now was Thorleif there about winter in good favour and of spring-days prepared he ship his and had to sea and began well and came ship his to Iceland in river then was Thjorsa named.	Thorleif was there for the winter in great favour, and at the beginning of spring he prepared his ship and put to sea, and began well and his ship came to Iceland, into the river that was named Thjorsa.

The Tale of Thorlief the Earl's Poet (Old Norse)

Old Norse	Literal	English
Þat segja menn at Þorleifr kvæntist um haustið og fengi þeirrar konu er Auðr hét og væri Þórðar dóttir er bjó í Skógum undir Eyjafjöllum, gilds bónda og stórauðigs, kominn af ætt Þrasa hins gamla.	It is-said people that Thorleif got-married about autumn and got there a-wife who Aud was-named and was Thord daughter that lived in Skogar under Eyjafjoll-Mountains, strong farmer and great-wealth, came of descendents Thrasi the old.	People say that Thorleif got married in the autumn and had a wife who was named Aud, and she was the daughter of Thord of Skogar under the Eyjafjoll mountains, who was a successful and wealthy farmer, descended from Thrasi the old.
Auðr var kvenskörungr mikill.	Aud was noble-woman much.	Aud was very much a noble woman.
Þorleifr sat um veturinn í Skógum en um vorið eftir keypti hann land at Höfðabrekku í Mýdal og bjó þar síðan.	Thorleif sat about winter in Skogar but about spring afterwards bought he land at Hofdabrekka in Myrdal-Valley and settled there since.	Thorleif spent the winter in Skogar, but the following spring he bought land at Hofdabrekka in the Myrdal valley and settled thereafter.

7

Old Norse	Literal	English
En nú er þar til at taka er Hákon jarl er, at honum batnaði hins mesta meinlætis en þat segja sumir menn at hann yrði aldrei samr maðr og áðr og vildi jarl nú gjarna hefna Þorleifi þessar smánar ef hann gæti, heitir nú á fulltrúa sína, Þorgerði Hörgabrúði og Irpu systr hennar, at reka þann galdr út til Íslands at Þorleifi ynni at fullu og færir þeim miklar fórnir og gekk til fréttar.	But now is there to from take that Hakon the-earl was, that he bettered his most malignancy but that said some people that he became never the-same man of before and wished the-earl now gladly avenge Thorleif this humiliation if he could, called now on delegates his, Thorgerd Horgabrudi and Irpu sister hers, to drive then sorcery out to Iceland to Thorleif win-over that full and carried them much sacrifices and got to omens.	Now to take to the Earl Hakon, he mostly recovered from this malignancy, but some people said that he was never the same man as before, and the earl now wished to gladly avenge Thorleif of this humiliation if he could, he called on his delegates, Thorgerd Horgabrudi and her sister Irpu, to drive sorcery out to Iceland to defeat Thorleif fully, and he carried them many offerings and got omens.

The Tale of Thorlief the Earl's Poet (Old Norse)

Old Norse	Literal	English
En er hann fékk þá frétt er honum líkaði lét hann taka einn rekabút og gera úr trémann og með fjölkynngi og atkvœðum jarls en tröllskap og fítonsanda þeirra systra lét hann drepa einn mann og taka úr hjartat og láta í þenna trémann og fœrðu síðan í föt og gáfu nafn og kölluðu Þorgarð og mögnuðu hann með svo miklum fjandans krafti at hann gekk og mœlti við menn, komu honum síðan í skip og sendu hann út til Íslands þess erindis at drepa Þorleif jarlaskáld.	And when he got then omens that he liked had he taken a drift-wood and made of wooden-man and with witchcraft and songs earls and witchcraft and magic there sisters had he kill one man and taken out heart and had in this wooden-man and brought afterwards to clothing and gave name and called Thorgard and power he with so much devil's power that he walked and talked with people, came to-him afterwards to a-ship and sent him out to Iceland this errand to kill Thorleif Earl's-Poet.	And when he got the omens that he liked, he took some drift wood and made a wooden man, and with his witchcraft and songs, and with the magic of his sisters, he had a man killed to take his heart and place in the wooden man, and afterwards brought clothing and gave him a name and called him Thorgard, and with the strong power of the devil he walked and talked with people, he was put on a ship and sent to Iceland on an errand to kill Thorleif the Earl's poet.
Gyrti Hákon hann atgeir þeim er hann hafði tekið úr hofi þeirra systra og Hörgi hafði átt.	Equipped Hakon him a-halberd then that he had taken out-of temple theirs sisters and Horgi had belonged.	Hakon gave him a halberd that he had taken out of the temple that belonged to his sisters at Horgi.
Þorgarðr kom út til Íslands í þann tíma er menn voru á alþingi.	Thorgard came out to Iceland in that time that men were in assembly.	Thorgard came to Iceland at the time when people were at the assembly.
Þorleifr jarlaskáld var á þingi.	Thorleif Earl's-Poet was at assembly.	Thorleif's the Earl's Poet was at the assembly.
Þat var einn dag at Þorleifr gekk frá búð sinni er hann sá at maðr gekk vestan yfir Öxará.	It was one day that Thorleif went from booth his when he saw that a-man walked from-the-west over Oxara.	One day Thorleif went from his booth and saw a man walking from the west over the Oxara river.
Sá var mikill vexti og illslegr í bragði.	Saw was large grown and evil-like in movement.	He saw that he was large and evil looking in his movement.
Þorleifr spyr þenna mann at heiti.	Thorleif asked this man of name.	Thorleif asked this man his name.
Hann nefndist Þorgarðr og kastaði þegar kaldyrðum at Þorleifi en er Þorleifr heyrði þat œtlaði hann at bregða sverðinu konungsnaut er hann var gyrðr með en í þessu bili lagði Þorgarðr atgeirnum á Þorleifi miðjum og í gegnum hann.	He was-named Thorgard and cast straightaway cold-bloodedly to Thorleif and when Thorleif heard this intended he to draw the-sword king's-gift that he was equipped-with with but in this moment laid Thorgard halberd to Thorleif's middle and in through him.	He said that his name was Thorgard and looked at him cold-bloodedly, and when Thorleif heard this, he intended to draw the sword that king Svein had given to him, but in that moment, Thorgard laid his halberd through his middle.

The Tale of Thorlief the Earl's Poet (Old Norse)

Old Norse	Literal	English
En er hann fékk lagið hjó hann til Þorgarðs en hann steyptist í jörðina niðr svo at í iljarnar var at sjá.	Then when he got laid struck he to Thorgard then he disappeared into the-earth down so that for soles-of-the-feet was to see.	Then when he was hit, he struck at Thorgard, but he had disappeared down into the earth so that only the soles of his feet could be seen.
Þorleifr snaraði at sér kyrtilinn og kvat vísu:	Thorleif twisted about himself tunic and spoke verse:	Thorleif twisted his tunic about him and spoke a verse:
Hvarf hinn hildardjarfi, hvat varð af Þorgarði? villumaðr á velli, vígdjarfr refilstiga.	Disappeared the courageous-warrior, what became of Thorgard villain in the-fields, slaying-warrior mysterious-path.	The courageous warrior disappeared, what became of Thorgard? the villain in the fields, the slaying warrior's mysterious path.
Farið hefir Gautr at grjóti gunnelds hinn fjölkunni, síðan mun hann í helju hvílast stund og mílu.	Gone has Odin to rocks battle-fire the skilled-in-magic, after shall he in Hel rest awhile and mile.	Odin has gone to the rocks, battle-fired the skills in magic, after shall be in Hel and rest awhile a mile.
Þá gekk Þorleifr heim til búðar sinnar og sagði mönnum þenna atburð og þótti öllum mikils um vert um þenna atburð.	Then went Thorleif home to booth his and told people these events and thought all much about had-been about these events.	Thorleif went back to his booth and told people of these events, and people thought much about these events.
Síðan varpar Þorleifr frá sér kyrtlinum og féllu þá út iðrin og lét Þorleifr þar líf sitt við góðan orðstír og þótti mönnum þat allmikill skaði.	Afterwards threw Thorleif from himself tunic and fell then out bowels and laid Thorleif there life his with good fame and thought people that all-great harm.	Afterwards Thorleif threw off his tunic and his bowels spilled out, and he laid his life there with good fame, and all people thought that this was a great harm.
Þóttust nú allir vita at Þorgarðr þessi hafði engi verið annar en galdr og fjölkynngi Hákonar jarls.	Thought now all certainly that Thorgard this had none been other than sorcery and witchcraft Hakon's the-earl.	They thought that it was certain that this Thorgard had been none other than the sorcery and witchcraft of Earl Hakon.
Síðan var Þorleifr heygðr.	Afterwards was Thorleif buried.	Afterwards Thorleif was buried.
Haugr hans stendr norðr af lögréttu og sést hann enn.	Mound his stood north of law-assembly and seen he was.	His mound stood north of the law assembly and could be seen from there.

The Tale of Thorlief the Earl's Poet (Old Norse)

Old Norse	Literal	English
Bræðr hans voru á þingi er þetta var tíðinda og gerðu útferð Þorleifs sœmilega og erfðu hann at fornum sið en Ásgeir faðir þeirra var þá litlu andaðr.	Brothers his was at assembly when this was news and made funeral Thorleif's fair and inherited he the ancient traditions as Asgeir father theirs was then recently died.	His brothers were at the assembly when this became news, and they gave Thorleif a fair funeral feast according to the ancient traditions that his father Asgeir had when he recently died.
Síðan fóru menn heim af þingi og fréttust þessi tíðindi nú víða um Ísland og þóttu mikils verð.	Afterwards went people home from assembly and reported this news now widely about Iceland and thought a-great price.	Afterwards people went home from the assembly and reported this news widely about Iceland, and everyone thought it a great cost.

8

Sá maðr bjó þá á Þingvelli er Þorkell hét.	So a-man lived then at Thingvellir who-was Thorkell named.	So there was a man who lived that Thingvellir and was named Thorkell.
Hann var auðigr maðr at ganganda fé og hafði jafnan hœgt í búi.	He was wealthy man as went cattle and had equally comfortable in farm.	He was a wealth man with regard to cattle, and had a comfortable farm.
Engi var hann virðingamaðr.	None was he man-of-high-rank.	He was not a man of high rank.
Sauðamaðr hans hét Hallbjörn og var kallaðr hali.	Shepherd his named Hallbjorn and was called Hali.	He shepherd was named Hallbjorn but people called him Hali (Tail).
Hann vandist oftlega til at koma á haug Þorleifs og svaf þar um nœtr og hélt þar nálœgt fé sínu.	He did often to that came to mound Thorleif's and slept there about night and held there close cattle his.	He often came to Thorleif's mound and slept there through the night and held his cattle close there.
Kemr honum þat jafnan í hug at hann vildi geta ort lof kvœði nokkurt um haugbúann og talar þat jafnan er hann liggr á hauginum en sakir þess at hann var ekki skáld og hann hafði þeirrar listar eigi fengið fékk hann ekki kveðið og komst aldrei lengra áfram fyrir honum um skáldskapinn en hann byrjaði svo:	Came he that equally in thoughts that he wished get words praise poem some about the-mound-dweller and said that usually when he lay about the-mound but for-the-sake this that he was not poet and he had there art not got went he not poem but came never longer not-further for him about poetry that he began so:	Thoughts often came to him that he wished to compose words of praise about the mound dweller, and he usually said so when he lay about the mound, but because he was not a good poet and did not have the gift, he never managed to compose anything longer than the beginning:
Hér liggr skáld.	Here lies a-poet.	Here lies a poet.

The Tale of Thorlief the Earl's Poet (Old Norse)

Old Norse	Literal	English
En meira gat hann ekki kveðið.	Then more could he not put-to-words.	Then he could not put more to words.
Þat var eina nátt sem oftar at hann liggr á hauginum og hefir hina sömu iðn fyrir stafni ef hann gœti aukið nokkuð lof um haugbúann.	It was one night as often that he laid about the-mound and had then same craft for staves if he got increase some praise about the-mound-dweller.	One night as usual he was lying on the mound and was still trying to craft some verses and write any more in praise about the mound dweller.
Síðan sofnar hann og eftir þat sér hann at opnast haugurinn og gengr þar út maðr mikill vexti og vel búinn.	Afterwards slept he and after that saw he that open the-mound and went there out a-man great grown and well prepared.	Then he fell asleep and after that he saw that the mound opened, and a large man came out, and he was well dressed.
Hann gekk upp á hauginn at Hallbirni og mælti:	He went up to the-mound to Hallbjorn and spoke:	He went up to the mound and said to Hallbjorn:
"Þar liggr Hallbjörn og vildir þú fást í því sem þér er ekki lánat, at yrkja lof um mig og er þat annaðhvort at þér verðr lagið í þessi íþrótt og munt þú þat af mér fá meira en vel flestum mönnum öðrum og er þat vœnna at svo verði ella þarftu ekki í þessu at brjótast lengr.	"There lies Hallbjorn and wish you get with therefore which you are not gifted, that compose praise about me and is that either-way that you become have of this skilled and shall you that of me have more than well most people others and is that good that so becomes or need not of this to break longer.	"There you lie, Hallbjorn, and you would like to catch something not in your power, to compose praise about me, and either you will become skilled and you can get this from me more than others, as is likely to happen, or else there is no need for you to continue any longer.
Skal eg nú kveða fyrir þér vísu og ef þú getr numið vísuna og kannt hana þá er þú vaknar þá munt þú verða þjóðskáld og yrkja lof um marga höfðingja og mun þér í þessi íþrótt mikið lagið verða".	Shall i now speak before you verse and if you can take verse and know it then when you awake then shall you become skilled-poet and compose praise about many chieftains and should you in this skilled much have become".	I shall now speak a verse for you, and if you can take this verse and know it, then when you awake, you shall become a skilled poet and compose praise about many chieftains, and you shall have become much skilled in this".
Síðan togar hann á honum tunguna og kvat vísu þessa:	Afterwards pulled he of his tongue and spoke verse this:	Then he pulled his tongue and spoke this verse:
Hér liggr skáld þat er skálda	Here lies poet that is of-poets	Here lies a poet that is of all poets
skörungr var mestr at flestu.	leading was the-greatest of the-most.	the leading, he was the greatest of the most.
Naddveiti frá eg nýtan	Provided-knowing from i am-able	I hear that he was able
níð Hákoni smíða.	abuse of-Hakon created.	to craft abuse of Hakon.

The Tale of Thorlief the Earl's Poet (Old Norse)

Old Norse	Literal	English
Áðr gat engr né síðan annarra svo manna, frægt hefir orðið þat fyrðum, férán lokið hánum.	After got none nor afterwards others so people, fame had words that warriors, plunder end his.	None before or after, of so many other people, had fame of words that warriors ended his plunder.
"Nú skaltu svo hefja skáldskapinn at þú skalt yrkja lofkvæði um mig þá er þú vaknar og vanda sem mest bœði hátt og orðfæri og einna mest kenningar".	"Now shall so begin poetry that you shall compose praise-words about me then when you awake and care that most both high and vocabulary and only the-best kennings".	"Now you shall begin your poetry that you shall compose words of praise about me, then when you awake, take care that it is both high in vocabulary and the best kennings".
Síðan hverfr hann aftr í hauginn og lýkst hann aftr en Hallbjörn vaknar og þykist sjá á herðar honum.	Afterwards turned he back into the-mound and closed he returned then Hallbjorn awoke and thought saw of shoulders his.	Afterwards he turned back into the mound and it closed behind him, then Hallbjorn awoke and thought he saw his shoulders.
Síðan kunni hann vísuna og fór síðan til byggða heim með fé sitt eftir tíma og sagði þenna atburð.	Afterwards knew he verse and travelled since to settlement home with wealth his after time and said then events.	Afterwards he remembered the verse and then went back to the farm with his flock after a time and told of these events.
Orti Hallbjörn síðan lofkvæði um haugbúann og var hið mesta skáld og fór utan fljótlega og kvat kvæði um marga höfðingja og fékk af þeim miklar virðingar og góðar gjafir og græddi af því stórfé, og gengr af honum mikil saga bæði hér á landi og útlendis þó at hún sé hér eigi rituð.	Words Hallbjorn since praise-words about the-mound-dweller and was then the-best poet and travelled out soon and spoke poems about many chieftains and got of them much honour and good gifts and profit of therefore great-wealth, and went of him much stories both here about the-land and other-lands though that it being here not written.	Hallbjorn composed since words of praise about the mound dweller and was the best poet, and he frequently travelled abroad and composed poems about many chieftains and received from them much honour and good gifts from them, and his wealth increased, and there went many stories about him both in Iceland and abroad, but they are not written down here.
En frá brœðrum Þorleifs er þat at segja at nœsta sumar eftir andlát hans fóru þeir utan, Ólafr völubrjótr og Helgi hinn frækni, og ætluðu til hefnda eftir bróðr sinn.	Then from brothers Thorlief's was it to say that next summer after death his travelled they out, Olaf knuckle-breaker and Helgi the brave, and supposed to revenge after brother theirs.	Then to Thorleif's brothers to say that the next summer after his death day, Olaf knuckle-breaker and Helgi the brave travelled out and intended to get revenge for their brother.
En þeim varð eigi lagið þá enn at standa yfir höfuðsvörðum Hákonar jarls því at hann hafði þá enn eigi öllu illu því fram farið sem honum varð lagið sér til skammar og skaða.	But they were not laid then but to stand over head-skin Hakon's the-earl because that he had then but not all evil such from going as he was laid to-him to shame and damage.	But they were not yet fated to have Earl Hakon's scalp, because he had not yet done all of the evil which was destined for his shame and harm.

The Tale of Thorlief the Earl's Poet (Old Norse)

Old Norse	Literal	English
En þó brenndu þeir mörg hof fyrir jarlinum og gerðu honum margan fjárskaða í ránum og hervirki er þeir veittu honum og margri annarri óspekt.	But though burned they many temples for the-earl and did to-him many wealth-damage in robbery and plundering that they granted him and many other disturbances.	But they managed to burn many of the earl's temples, and did much to damage his wealth with robbery and plundering, and they granted him many other disturbances.
Og lýkr hér frá Þorleifi at segja.	And ends here from Thorleif to say.	And this is the end of what there is to say about Thorleif.

Word List (Old Norse to English)

Old Norse	English
A, a	
aðfangskveld	midwinter-evening
aðrar	other
aðrir	other, others
af	from, in, of, off
afliðið	following
aftr	after, back, returned, returning
afturreka	back-driven
aldr	age
aldrei	never
aldri	age
alfari	for-good
alla	all
allan	all
allir	all
allmikill	all-great
allri	all
alls	all
allt	all
alþingi	assembly
andaðr	died
andar	soul
andlát	death
andvana	destitution
annaðhvort	either-way
annan	a-second
annar	another, other
annarra	other, others
annarri	other
annars	another's
at	a, about, and, as, at, for, from, in, it, of, that, the, then, this, to
atburð	events
atburðir	events
atgeir	a-halberd
atgeirnum	halberd
atgervi	deeds
atgervimaðr	accomplished-man
atkvœðum	songs
auðigr	wealthy
Auðr	Aud (name)
aukið	increase
austr	east
Á, á	
á	about, at, for, from, had, in, it, of, on, river, that, this, to
áðr	after, before, return
áfram	not-further
áhöfn	crew
án	without
ánauð	enslavement
Ásgeir	Asgeir (name)
Ásgeiri	Asgeir (name)
ásjá	assistance
ástfóstr	foster-care
ásum	poles
át	eat
átján	eighteen
átt	belonged, had
áttu	had
B, b	
báðir	both
bani	dead
báru	carried
bat	asked, bid, invited
batna	better
batnaði	bettered
báts	boats
beiddi	asked
beiddist	asked
bekkjunauta	bench-fellows
betr	better
biðr	asked
bili	moment
binda	bound, tied-up
bindr	bound
bjart	bright

Word List (Old Norse to English)

Old Norse	English
bjó	lived, prepared, settled
blekkir	deceived
Blönduósi	Blonduos (place)
blygðar	shame
boðið	invited
bœði	both
bœginn	troubled
böggva	the-mauler
bölvaðra	cursed
bónda	farmer
borð	the-tables
borið	carried
bornir	carried
bráðlega	quickly
brag	poetry
bragði	movement
branda	swords
bregða	draw
bregðr	tricked
Brekku	Brekka (place)
brenna	burned, burnt
brenndu	burned
brjótast	break
broddr	spikes
bróðr	brother
brœðr	brothers
brœðrum	brothers
brot	away
brott	away
búð	booth
búðanna	booths
búðar	booth
búi	farm
búið	done, settled
búinn	prepared
búkinn	body
burt	away
byggða	settlement
býr	prepared
byrjaði	began
byrjar	fair-wind
býsn	strangeness

D, d

Old Norse	English
dag	day
daginn	the-day
dálegra	harmful
Danmerkr	Denmark (place)
dauðu	dead
diska	plates
dœmt	deem
dögum	days
dökkri	dark
dóttir	daughter
draga	drew
drápu	phrases
dregr	drawn, draws
drekktr	drowned
drengjum	the-fellows
drengr	men
drepa	kill
drykkju	drink
drykkjuborð	drinking-tables
dýflissu	dungeon
dýrstum	dearest
dyrum	doors

E, e

Old Norse	English
eða	either, or
eðli	nature
ef	if
efnilegir	promising
efsta	upper
eftir	after, afterwards
eftirmáls	after-the-case
eg	i, if
eiga	not
eigi	not
eigið	own
eign	owning
eina	a, one
einn	a, one
einna	only
Eiríks	Erik's (name)
ekki	not
ella	or
elli	age

Word List (Old Norse to English)

Old Norse	English
ellina	age
elsti	eldest
en	and, as, but, than, that, the, then, when
enda	and, end
engi	none
Englandi	England (place)
engr	none
enn	but, was
er	am, are, as, from, has, is, it-is, that, the, was, what, when, which, who, who-was
erfðu	inherited
erindis	errand
ertu	are-you
eru	are, they-were, we-are
eta	eat
etið	to-eat
Eyjafjöllum	Eyjafjoll-Mountains (place)
eymd	misery
eyri	sand

É, é

él	blizzard

F, f

Old Norse	English
fá	get, have
faðir	father
Fagurkinn	Fair-Cheek (name)
fann	found
fara	travel
fararefna	travel-goods
farið	going, gone, travelled
farning	passage
fast	close, closed, closely
fást	get
fé	cattle, wealth
fegins	relieved
fékk	got, went
félaga	companions
féll	fell
fellr	fell
féllu	fell
fengi	got
fengið	caught, got
fer	travelled, went
férán	plunder
ferð	travel
ferðar	travel
ferðum	journey
fertuga	forty
festist	grips
fíl	elephant
finnr	found
fítonsanda	magic
fjandans	devil's
fjárhlut	fee-lot, financial-share
fjárskaða	wealth-damage
fjártjón	financial-loss
fjölkunni	skilled-in-magic
fjölkynngi	witchcraft
fjölmenni	following-men
fleira	more
flestu	the-most
flestum	most
fljótasta	soonest
fljótlega	soon
flutt	performed
flytja	to-carry
flyttu	move
föðr	father
fœ	can, get
fœra	bring, brought
fœrðu	brought
fœrir	carried
fór	travelled, went
fornfrœði	ancient-ways
fórnir	sacrifices
fornlegum	ancient-ways
fornum	ancient
forsmáðr	shamed
fóru	travelled, went
förunauta	companions
fóstra	foster-father
fóstri	fostered

Word List (Old Norse to English)

Old Norse	English
föt	clothing
frá	from
fram	forward, from
framan	in-front-of
framaverka	previous-deeds
framleiðslu	causing
frásagnar	from-told
frétt	omens
fréttar	omens
fréttist	sought
fréttust	reported
frœðum	instruction
frœgt	fame
frœkni	brave
frœnda	kinsmen
fullkomið	full-coming
fulltingi	assistance
fulltrúa	delegates
fullu	full
fund	find, meet
fylgdi	followed
fylgt	followed
fyr	before
fyrðum	warriors
fyrir	before, before him, for
fyrr	before
fyrst	first
fýsi	desire
fýstist	desired

G, g

Old Norse	English
gáði	cared
gaf	gave
gáfu	gave
gáir	care
galdr	sorcery
galt	repaid
gamall	old
gamla	old
gamlir	old-man
ganga	go, went
ganganda	went
gangi	moved
Gáseyri	Gaseyri (place)
gat	could, got
Gautr	Odin (name)
geðjast	liking
gefa	give, to-give
gegnum	through
geitarskegg	goat-beard
geitarskegginu	goat-beard
gekk	got, walked, went
gengið	gone
gengr	going, went
ger	made
gera	done, made
gerði	did, had-done, it-was
gerðist	happened
gerðu	did, made
gerist	becoming
gerningum	witchcraft
gert	done
gervi	character
gervilegr	talented
gervina	disguise
geta	get
getið	told-of
getr	can, get
geysimjǫk	exceedingly-much
giftu	luck
gildr	capable
gilds	strong
gíman	opening
ginnti	tricked
gjafir	gifts
gjalda	repay
gjallandason	son-of-gjallandi
gjarna	gladly
gjöld	repayment
glögglega	clearly
goða	the-chieftain
góða	food
góðan	good
góðar	good
goði	chieftain
góðu	good, improvement
gœti	could, got
göldrum	magical-arts
gömlum	old

Word List (Old Norse to English)

Old Norse	English
góss	belongings
gott	good
grálega	malice
gramr	warrior
greiðlega	promptly, quickly
grenndi	slendered
grjóti	rocks
grœddi	profit
guðníðingskapr	idol-worship
Guðs	God (name)
gulls	of-gold
gunnelds	battle-fire
gyrðr	equipped-with
gyrti	equipped

H, h

Old Norse	English
haf	sea
hafa	had, have
hafði	had
hafi	have
hafið	have
haft	have
Hákon	Hakon (name)
Hákonar	Hakon (name), Hakon's (name)
hákoni	of-Hakon
halda	hold
hálf	half
Hali	Hali (name)
Hallbirni	Hallbjorn (name)
Hallbjörn	Hallbjorn (name)
hálminn	the-straw
hana	it
hann	he, him
hans	he, his
hánum	his
harðfengi	toughness
harðla	hardly
harðleikinn	rough
harðúðigr	harsher
háreysti	commotion
hárið	hair
hark	noise
háseta	first-mate
hásetum	crew
hataðr	hated
hátt	high
háttum	custom
haug	mound
haugbúann	the-mound-dweller
hauginn	the-mound
hauginum	the-mound
haugr	mound
haugurinn	the-mound
haustið	autumn
hefi	have
hefir	had, has, have, having
hefja	begin
hefna	avenge
hefnda	revenge
hefr	had
hegningartíminn	punishment-time
heim	home, homes
heita	call, named, promise
heiti	name, named
heitir	called, named
heldr	rather
Helgi	Helgi (name)
heljarkarl	hellish-old-man
Helju	Hel (place)
hélt	held
hendi	hands
hengja	hanged
hennar	hers, its
hentar	requirements
hentugri	more-convenient
hér	here
herðar	shoulders
herra	lord
hervirki	plundering
hét	named, promised, was-named
heygðr	buried
heyrði	heard
heyrðu	heard
heyrið	hear
heyrt	heard
hið	the, then
hildardjarfi	courageous-warrior

214

Word List (Old Norse to English)

Old Norse	English
himins	heaven's
hina	then
hingat	here
hinn	the, those
hinni	the
hins	his, the
hinu	the
hinum	other
hít	bag
hítina	the-bag
hitti	met
hjartat	heart
hjó	struck
Hlaðajarl	Earl-Of-Lade (name)
Hlaðajarls	Earl-Of-Lade (name)
Hlaðir	Lade (place)
hleypr	ran
Hlöðum	Lade (place)
hlógu	laughed
hlýða	listen, to-hear
hlýdduð	listen-to
hœgt	comfortable, possible
hœkjr	crutches
hœkjurnar	the-crutches
hof	temples
hóf	began
Höfðabrekku	Hofdabrekka (place)
höfðingja	chieftains, chieftains'
höfðingjum	chieftains
höfðingskap	lordship
hofi	temple
höfuðsvörðum	head-skin
höfum	have
höllina	the-hall
höllinni	the-hall
honum	he, he-had, him, his, to-him
Hörgabrúði	Horgabrudi (name)
Hörgi	Horgi (place)
hríð	awhile
hrífa	scratched
hring	a-ring
hróðr	renown
hrollir	shivering
hrukku	drew
hug	thoughts
hugr	heart
hugsa	think
hún	it, she
hvarf	disappeared
hvat	what
hver	who
hverfr	turned
hvergi	each
hverjum	each, who's
hvern	one's
hverri	each
hversu	however, how-so
hvert	each
hví	why
hvílast	rest
hvorri	each
hvort	whether

I, i

Old Norse	English
iðn	craft
iðrin	bowels
iljarnar	soles-of-the-feet
illa	bad, badly, ill
illr	bad, ill
illslegr	evil-like
illu	evil
inn	in
Irpu	Irpu (name)

Í, í

Old Norse	English
í	about, at, for, from, in, into, of, to, with
Ísland	Iceland (place)
Íslandi	Iceland (place)
Íslands	Iceland (place)
íþrótt	skilled
íþrótta	skills
íþróttamaðr	excellent-man
íþróttir	skilled
ítri	high-born

Word List (Old Norse to English)

Old Norse	English

J, j

Old Norse	English
jafnan	equally, usually
jarl	earl, the-earl
Jarlaskáld	Earl's-Poet (name)
jarli	earl, the-earl
jarlinn	the-earl
jarlinum	the-earl
jarls	earls, the-earl, the-earl's
jarlsníði	the-earl's-abuse
jarlsníðs	earl's-abuse
járn	iron-weapon
Jóla	Yule (name)
jólaveislunnar	yule-feast
jörðina	the-earth
Jóta	Jutland (place)

K, k

Old Norse	English
kaldyrðum	cold-bloodedly
kalla	call, called, call-to
kallaðr	called
kann	can
kannt	know
Karl	Karl (name), old-man, the-old-man
karli	man, the-old-man
kastaði	cast
kaupir	bought
kaupmönnum	trading-men
kaupslagar	bargaining
kaupstaðinn	market-town
kaupunauta	customers
kaupunautar	customers
kemr	came, comes
kenna	teach
kenndr	known
kenningar	kennings
keypti	bought
kláði	itching
Klaufa	Klaufi (name)
knarrar	merchant-ships, of-the-ship
knúta	knots
kol	the-coals
köld	cold
köldu	cold
köldum	cold
kölluðu	called
kolum	coals
kom	came, come, could
koma	came, come, come-with
komast	come
kömbum	combs
komi	comes
kominn	came, comes, coming
komst	came
komu	came
kona	a-woman, wife, woman
Konrvísr	Woman-Verses (name)
konu	a-wife
konung	the-king
konungi	the-king
konungr	the-king
konungs	the-king
konungsnaut	king's-gift
kost	food, provide
krafti	power
krókóttum	devious
kunni	knew
kvaddi	greeted
kvaðningar	greeting
kvala	torment
kvat	said, spoke
kveða	recites, say, speak
kveðið	poem, put-to-words, spoken
kveðr	said
kveldið	evening
kvenskörungr	noble-woman
kvœði	poem, poems
kvœðið	poem, the-poem
kvœðislaunum	poem's-reward
kvœntist	got-married
kyndugskap	cunning
kynferði	kinsmen-origins

Word List (Old Norse to English)

Old Norse	English
kynjaðr	descended
kynstrum	strange
kyrr	sit-still
kyrtilinn	tunic
kyrtlinum	tunic

L, l

Old Norse	English
lagasetning	legislation
lagði	had, laid
lagið	have, laid
lánat	gifted
land	land, the-land
landi	the-land
lands	lands
lásum	locks
lát	let
láta	allow, had
láti	had
látið	let
laun	secrecy
launat	repay
legið	laying
leið	journey, passed
leiðarnests	food
leitaði	sought
lengi	long
lengja	lengthen
lengr	for-long, longer
lengra	longer
leóns	the-lion's
lét	had, laid, let
létti	relief
leysa	solve
líf	life
lífsdaga	life-days
lífstíma	lifetime
liggr	laid, lay, lies
líkaði	liked
líkama	body
líkar	like
linnir	stopped
listar	art
lítillœti	a-little, humility
lítils	little

Old Norse	English
lítinn	little
litlu	recently
Ljótólfi	Ljotolf (name)
Ljótólfr	Ljotolf (name)
Ljótólfs	Ljotolf (name)
ljótu	ghastly
lœtr	had, left
lof	praise
lofaði	praised
lofkvœði	praise-words
lögréttu	law-assembly
lokið	end
luktum	shut
lýkr	ends
lýkst	closed

M, m

Old Norse	English
má	may
maðr	a-man, man
mál	matter
mann	man
manna	man's, men, people
mannalát	manslaughter
manni	people
mannillska	man-evil
manninn	people
marga	many
margan	many
margir	many
margkunnandi	many-known
margra	many, much
margri	many
mart	many
matar	food
mátti	may
með	with
mega	may
megi	may
megin	side
meinlœtis	malignancy
meinlœtum	malignance
meir	more
meira	more
menn	men, people

Word List (Old Norse to English)

Old Norse	English
mér	i-am, me, to-me
mest	most, the-best
mesta	most, the-best
mesti	most
mestr	the-greatest
miðdigr	broad-waist
Miðfirði	Midfjord (place)
Miðfjarðar-Skeggja	Midfjorder-Skeggi (name)
miðju	middle-of
miðjum	middle
miðs	middle
mig	me, shall-i
mikið	most, much
mikil	much
mikill	great, large, much
mikils	a-great, much
mikinn	much
mikla	much
miklar	much
miklum	much
milli	between
mílu	mile
minn	mine
minnkaði	decreased
mislíkaði	misliked
missa	miss
mitt	mine
mjǫk	much
móðr	mother
móðrbróðr	mother's-brother
mælt	said
mælti	spoke, talked
mögnuðu	power
mökkr	thick-clouds
mönnum	men, people, peoples'
mörg	many
mörgum	many
morguninn	morning
mörk	a-mark
mörkum	marshes
mun	must, shall, should
mundi	would
mundu	would
munn	mouth
munt	shall
munuð	shall, should
munum	shall
Mýdal	Myrdal-Valley (place)
myrkrið	the-darkness
myrkt	dark

N, n

Old Norse	English
naddveiti	provided-knowing
náði	caught
naðrbings	dragon
nafn	name
nafnfesti	name-giving
nafni	name
nákvæmi	pernickety
nálægt	close
nam	took
náms	take
nátt	night
náttúra	nature
né	nor
nefndist	was-named
nema	except, taken, unless
níð	abuse
níðið	the-abuse
niðr	down
Níðungr	Nidung (name)
nítján	nineteen
Njörðr	Njord (name)
nœr	near
nœsta	next
nœstir	nearest
nœtr	night
nokkr	anything
nokkuð	any, some, something, somewhat
nokkura	some
nokkurar	some
nokkurt	some
nökkvi	the-ship
norðr	north
Noreg	Norway (place)
Noregs	Norway (place)
nóttina	the-night
nú	now

Word List (Old Norse to English)

Old Norse	English
numið	take
nýtan	am-able

O, o

Old Norse	English
ofan	over
ofanverðum	the-uppermost
ofléttlega	willingly
oft	often
oftar	often
oftlega	often
og	also, and, but, of
opnast	open
orð	words
orðfœri	vocabulary
orðið	become, words
orðskvið	proverb
orðstír	fame
orlof	leave
orlofs	vacations
ort	worded, words
orti	words
oss	us, we

Ó, ó

Old Norse	English
óbœtilegs	un-redeemable
óðali	estate
ófreklegar	un-eagerly
ógert	undone
ógladdist	un-gladdened
ógleði	un-gladness
ógleðr	un-glad
óhljóði	unsoundly
óhöfðinglegt	chieftain-like
ókunna	unknown
Ólafr	Olaf (name)
Ólafs	Olaf's (name)
ólítið	no-little
óloknum	undone
óminnis	amnesia
óspekt	disturbances
óvant	not-lacking
óvinarins	the-enemy's
óvit	unconsciousness
óvœra	restlessness
óvœri	restlessness

Ö, ö

Old Norse	English
öðlings	noble
öðrum	other, others
öldu	wave
öllu	all
öllum	all, of-all
önga	none
öngu	not
örleik	generosity
örverpi	decrepitude
örvœnt	desperation
Öxará	Oxara (place)

Œ, œ

Old Norse	English
œfr	angry
œrnri	merry
œti	ate, had
œtlaði	intended
œtluðu	supposed
œtt	ancestors, ancestry, descendents
œvintýr	adventure

P, p

Old Norse	English
peninga	money

R, r

Old Norse	English
ráðum	advice
raknaði	recovered
ránum	robbery
Rauðfeldr	Red-Cloak (name)
Rauði	Red (name)
réð	ruled
refilstiga	mysterious-path

Word List (Old Norse to English)

Old Norse	English
reiða	transport
reikar	parting
reka	drive
rekabút	drift-wood
Reykjum	Reykir (place)
reyndar	actually
ríða	rose
ríkr	powerful
rís	rose
rituð	written
roðið	reddened
röðla	wheel
rœðr	hired
rœndi	robbed
rœsta	cleared
rotnat	decayed
ryðja	cleared
ryðr	cleared

S, s

Old Norse	English
sá	saw, so
saga	stories
sagði	said, told
sagðr	said
sagt	said
sakir	for-the-sake, sake, with-conviction
saman	together
samr	the-same
samsœtis	banquet
sannlega	truly
sat	sat
satt	true
sauðamaðr	shepherd
sé	being, himself, see
segðu	say-you
segið	said
segir	said
segist	say
segja	is-said, said, say
seigt	tough
selja	to-sell
sem	as, that, what, which
sendu	sent
sér	for-himself, he, he-himself, him, himself, his, saw, to-him
sest	sat
sést	seen
sið	traditions
síðan	after, afterwards, since
síðasta	last
síðr	less
sig	him
sigldu	sailed
sína	himself, his
sinn	his, theirs
sinna	his
sinnar	his
sinni	himself, his
síns	his
sínu	his
sínum	his
sitt	his
sjá	saw, see
sjálfráða	ourselves-decide
skaða	damage
skaði	harm
skal	shall
skáld	a-poet, poet
skálda	of-poets
skaldi	the-poet
skáldskap	poetry
skáldskapinn	poetry
skalt	shall
skaltu	shall, shall-you
skammar	shame
skapaðir	shaped
skegg	beard
Skeggi	Skeggi (name)
Skeggja	Skeggi (name)
skildu	parted
skip	a-ship, ship
skipaði	arranged
skipi	ship
skipið	the-ship
skips	ship, ships
skipti	exchanged
skjóta	launched

Word List (Old Norse to English)

Old Norse	English
skógum	forests, Skogar (place)
skörulega	boldly
skörungr	leading, noble
skruma	show-off, swagger
skyldi	should
skyldr	should
skyldu	should
sléttri	levelled
slíkt	such
slœgða	slyness
smánar	humiliation
smíða	created
snaraði	twisted
snemma	early-age
snýr	turned
snýst	turned
sœkja	sake
sœllífi	blessed-life
sœmd	honour
sœmilega	fair, properly
sœti	sit
sœtis	sit
sofnar	slept
sögðu	said
sögr	sagas
sögu	saga
sölr	sale
sömu	same
son	son
sonar	son
sótt	sought
spurði	asked, learned
spurn	learned
spurt	learned
spyr	asked, asks, learned
spyrja	ask
staðið	stand
stafina	sticks
stafkarl	beggar
stafkarla	beggars
stafkarlar	beggars
stafkarls	as-a-beggar, beggar's
stafni	staves
standa	stand, stood
stef	stave
stendr	stood
steyptist	disappeared
stóð	stood
stóra	large
stórauðigs	great-wealth
stórfé	great-wealth
stórmenni	great-men
stórœttaðr	great-family
strigadúk	sack-cloth
stumrar	stumbled
stund	awhile
stundlegum	temporary
stutt	short
styrk	support
suðr	south
sumar	summer
sumir	some
sumrinu	the-summer
svaf	slept
svara	answered
svarar	answered
Svarfaðardal	Svarfardal (place)
Svarfdœla	Svarfardal (place)
svarri	grave
Sveins	Svein (name)
svengd	hungry
sverð	a-sword
sverðinu	the-sword
Svíþjóð	Sweden (place)
svo	so
svöngum	hunger
sýnast	appear
sýndist	seemed-to
sýnduð	give-performance
syni	sons
Syrgisdölum	Syrgsdalir (place)
systr	sister
systra	sisters

T, t

Old Norse	English
taka	take, taken, took
talar	said
talat	told
tekið	taken

Word List (Old Norse to English)

Old Norse	English
tekr	take, took
tíðinda	news
tíðindi	news
tíðindum	news
til	for, the, to, until
tíma	time
tímir	time
togar	pulled
tók	received, took
töluðu	told
trautt	scarcely
trémann	wooden-man
tröllskap	witchcraft
tunguna	tongue
tvo	two
tvœr	two

Þ, þ

Old Norse	English
þá	then
þakkaði	thanked
þann	than, that, then
þar	them, there
þarf	needed
þarfa	needed
þarfaði	needed
þarfast	need
þarftu	need
þat	it, that, the, this, with
þau	they
þegar	straightaway, there
þeim	them, then, they
þeir	they
þeirra	theirs, there
þeirrar	there
þengils	the-prince
þenna	the, then, these, this, those
þér	to-you, you
þess	this
þessa	this
þessar	this
þessi	this
þessu	this
þessum	this
þetta	this
þig	you
þín	your
þingi	assembly
Þingvelli	Thingvellir (place)
þinn	you
þinna	yours
þinni	yours
þínum	yours
þitt	yours
þjóanna	thighs
þjóðskáld	skilled-poet
þjóin	thighs
þjónustumenn	servants
Þjórsá	Thjorsa (place)
þó	though
þökk	thanks
þoku	fog
Þokuvísr	Fog-verses (name)
þola	endure
þoldu	endured
Þórðar	Thord (name)
Þorgarð	Thorgard (name)
Þorgarði	Thorgard (name)
Þorgarðr	Thorgard (name), Thorgard (name)
Þorgarðs	Thorgard (name)
Þorgerði	Thorgerd (name)
Þórhildr	Thorhild (name)
Þorkell	Thorkell (name)
Þorleif	Thorleif (name)
Þorleifi	Thorleif (name), thorleif's
Þorleifr	Thorleif (name)
þorleifs	thorleif's, Thorleif's (name)
þorpara	peasant
þorsta	thirsty
þótti	thought
þóttist	thought
þóttu	thought
þóttust	thought
Þrándheim	Trondheim (place)
Þrasa	Thrasi (name)
þriðjung	third
þrjá	three

222

Word List (Old Norse to English)

Old Norse	English
Þrœnda	the-Tronds' (name)
þrotnum	waning
þú	you
þunga	heavy
þurfa	need
því	accordingly, because, since, such, then, therefore
þvílíkri	accordingly-like
þykir	seems, thought
þykist	thought
þykjast	considered
þykklega	arrogantly

U, u

Old Norse	English
um	about, at
umráða	about-advice
undan	back, out-of
undarlega	strange
undir	under, up-to
ungum	young
unni	loved
upp	up, upped
upphaf	beginning
uppi	up
urðu	became
utan	out, without
utarlega	out-lying

Ú, ú

Old Norse	English
úr	from, from-out-of, of, out, out-of
úrigr	unruly
út	out, out-from
útferð	funeral
úti	finished, out
útlendis	other-lands
útlœgr	outlaw

V, v

Old Norse	English
vaknar	awake, awoke
vald	power
valdi	controlled
valdið	caused
vanda	care
vandist	did
vandrœði	difficulty
vanr	experienced
var	was, were
varð	became, was, were
varla	scarcely
varning	wares
varninginn	wares
varpar	threw
vegsummerki	evidence, traces
veit	knows
veittu	granted
vel	well
veldr	brought-about
velli	the-fields
vellstœri	well-sized
vér	we
vera	be, becoming, being, be-it, to-be
verð	price
verða	become
verði	become, becomes
verðir	will-be
verðr	became, become
verðugu	honour
verðum	worth
verið	became, been, made
verki	work
verr	worst
vert	had-been
vesaldar	wretchedness
vestan	from-the-west, west
vestr	west
vestra	west
vetr	winter
vetra	winters
veturinn	winter
vexti	grown
við	by, from, to, with
víða	widely
viðskiptis	behaved

Word List (Old Norse to English)

Old Norse	English
vígdjarfr	slaying-warrior
Vík	Vik (place)
víkinni	the-bay
vil	wish
vildi	wish, wished
vildir	wish
viljið	will
viljum	wish, wish-to
villumaðr	villain
víls	advantage
vinsœl	popular
vinsœldum	popularity
virðingamaðr	man-of-high-rank
virðingar	honour
virðum	worthiness
visku	wisdom
vísr	verses
víst	know
vísu	certainly, this-verse, verse
vísuna	verse
vita	certainly, knew, know
vitja	know
vitr	wise
vó	killed
vœnna	good
vœri	was, were
völdum	doing
völubrjótr	knuckle-breaker, knuckle-breaker
von	hope
vonda	wicked
vor	spring
vordögum	spring-days
vori	the-spring
vorið	spring, spring
vort	ours
voru	was, were

Y, y

Old Norse	English
yðr	you, yours
yðrum	yours
yfir	over
yfirlœti	favour
yngsti	youngest
Yngvildi	Yngvild (name)
ynni	win-over
yrði	became
yrkja	compose
ytra	outside

Ý, ý

Old Norse	English
ýmist	either
ýtar	out

Word List (English to Old Norse)

English	Old Norse	English	Old Norse
		are	er, eru
		are-you	ertu
		a-ring	hring
		arranged	skipaði
		arrogantly	þykklega

A, a

English	Old Norse
a	at, eina, einn
about	á, at, í, um
about-advice	umráða
abuse	níð
accomplished-man	atgervimaðr
accordingly	því
accordingly-like	þvílíkri
actually	reyndar
advantage	víls
adventure	œvintýr
advice	ráðum
after	áðr, aftr, eftir, síðan
after-the-case	eftirmáls
afterwards	eftir, síðan
age	aldr, aldri, elli, ellina
a-great	mikils
a-halberd	atgeir
a-little	lítillœti
all	alla, allan, allir, allri, alls, allt, öllu, öllum
all-great	allmikill
allow	láta
also	og
am	er
am-able	nýtan
a-man	maðr
a-mark	mörk
amnesia	óminnis
ancestors	œtt
ancestry	œtt
ancient	fornum
ancient-ways	fornfrœði, fornlegum
and	at, en, enda, og
angry	œfr
another	annar
another's	annars
answered	svara, svarar
any	nokkuð
anything	nokkr
a-poet	skáld
appear	sýnast
art	listar
as	at, en, er, sem
as-a-beggar	stafkarls
a-second	annan
Asgeir (name)	Ásgeir, Ásgeiri
a-ship	skip
ask	spyrja
asked	bat, beiddi, beiddist, biðr, spurði, spyr
asks	spyr
assembly	alþingi, þingi
assistance	ásjá, fulltingi
a-sword	sverð
at	á, at, í, um
ate	œti
Aud (name)	Auðr
autumn	haustið
avenge	hefna
awake	vaknar
away	brot, brott, burt
awhile	hríð, stund
a-wife	konu
awoke	vaknar
a-woman	kona

B, b

English	Old Norse
back	aftr, undan
back-driven	afturreka
bad	illa, illr
badly	illa
bag	hít
banquet	samsœtis
bargaining	kaupslagar
battle-fire	gunnelds
be	vera
beard	skegg

225

Word List (English to Old Norse)

English	*Old Norse*
became	urðu, varð, verðr, verið, yrði
because	því
become	orðið, verða, verði, verðr
becomes	verði
becoming	gerist, vera
been	verið
before	áðr, fyr, fyrir, fyrr
before him	fyrir
began	byrjaði, hóf
beggar	stafkarl
beggars	stafkarla, stafkarlar
beggar's	stafkarls
begin	hefja
beginning	upphaf
behaved	viðskiptis
being	sé, vera
be-it	vera
belonged	átt
belongings	góss
bench-fellows	bekkjunauta
better	batna, betr
bettered	batnaði
between	milli
bid	bat
blessed-life	sœllífi
blizzard	él
Blonduos (place)	Blönduósi
boats	báts
body	búkinn, líkama
boldly	skörulega
booth	búð, búðar
booths	búðanna
both	báðir, bœði
bought	kaupir, keypti
bound	binda, bindr
bowels	iðrin
brave	frœkni
break	brjótast
Brekka (place)	Brekku
bright	bjart
bring	fœra
broad-waist	miðdigr
brother	bróðr
brothers	brœðr, brœðrum

English	*Old Norse*
brought	fœra, fœrðu
brought-about	veldr
buried	heygðr
burned	brenna, brenndu
burnt	brenna
but	en, enn, og
by	við

C, c

English	*Old Norse*
call	heita, kalla
called	heitir, kalla, kallaðr, kölluðu
call-to	kalla
came	kemr, kom, koma, kominn, komst, komu
can	fœ, getr, kann
capable	gildr
care	gáir, vanda
cared	gáði
carried	báru, borið, bornir, fœrir
cast	kastaði
cattle	fé
caught	fengið, náði
caused	valdið
causing	framleiðslu
certainly	vísu, vita
character	gervi
chieftain	goði
chieftain-like	óhöfðinglegt
chieftains	höfðingja, höfðingjum
chieftains'	höfðingja
cleared	rœsta, ryðja, ryðr
clearly	glögglega
close	fast, nálœgt
closed	fast, lýkst
closely	fast
clothing	föt
coals	kolum
cold	köld, köldu, köldum
cold-bloodedly	kaldyrðum
combs	kömbum
come	kom, koma, komast
comes	kemr, komi, kominn

Word List (English to Old Norse)

English	Old Norse
come-with	koma
comfortable	hœgt
coming	kominn
commotion	háreysti
companions	félaga, förunauta
compose	yrkja
considered	þykjast
controlled	valdi
could	gat, gœti, kom
courageous-warrior	hildardjarfi
craft	iðn
created	smíða
crew	áhöfn, hásetum
crutches	hœkjr
cunning	kyndugskap
cursed	bölvaðra
custom	háttum
customers	kaupunauta, kaupunautar

D, d

English	Old Norse
damage	skaða
dark	dökkri, myrkt
daughter	dóttir
day	dag
days	dögum
dead	bani, dauðu
dearest	dýrstum
death	andlát
decayed	rotnat
deceived	blekkir
decreased	minnkaði
decrepitude	örverpi
deeds	atgervi
deem	dœmt
delegates	fulltrúa
Denmark (place)	Danmerkr
descended	kynjaðr
descendents	œtt
desire	fýsi
desired	fýstist
desperation	örvœnt
destitution	andvana
devil's	fjandans
devious	krókóttum
did	gerði, gerðu, vandist
died	andaðr
difficulty	vandrœði
disappeared	hvarf, steyptist
disguise	gervina
disturbances	óspekt
doing	völdum
done	búið, gera, gert
doors	dyrum
down	niðr
dragon	naðrbings
draw	bregða
drawn	dregr
draws	dregr
drew	draga, hrukku
drift-wood	rekabút
drink	drykkju
drinking-tables	drykkjuborð
drive	reka
drowned	drekktr
dungeon	dýflissu

E, e

English	Old Norse
each	hvergi, hverjum, hverri, hvert, hvorri
earl	jarl, jarli
Earl-Of-Lade (name)	Hlaðajarl, Hlaðajarls
earls	jarls
earl's-abuse	jarlsníðs
Earl's-Poet (name)	Jarlaskáld
early-age	snemma
east	austr
eat	át, eta
eighteen	átján
either	eða, ýmist
either-way	annaðhvort
eldest	elsti
elephant	fíl
end	enda, lokið
ends	lýkr
endure	þola
endured	þoldu
England (place)	Englandi

Word List (English to Old Norse)

English	Old Norse
enslavement	ánauð
equally	jafnan
equipped	gyrti
equipped-with	gyrðr
Erik's (name)	Eiríks
errand	erindis
estate	óðali
evening	kveldið
events	atburð, atburðir
evidence	vegsummerki
evil	illu
evil-like	illslegr
exceedingly-much	geysimjǫk
excellent-man	íþróttamaðr
except	nema
exchanged	skipti
experienced	vanr
Eyjafjoll-Mountains (place)	Eyjafjöllum

F, f

English	Old Norse
fair	sœmilega
Fair-Cheek (name)	Fagurkinn
fair-wind	byrjar
fame	frœgt, orðstír
farm	búi
farmer	bónda
father	faðir, föðr
favour	yfirlœti
fee-lot	fjárhlut
fell	féll, fellr, féllu
financial-loss	fjártjón
financial-share	fjárhlut
find	fund
finished	úti
first	fyrst
first-mate	háseta
fog	þoku
Fog-verses (name)	Þokuvísr
followed	fylgdi, fylgt
following	afliðið
following-men	fjölmenni
food	góða, kost, leiðarnests, matar

English	Old Norse
for	á, at, fyrir, í, til
forests	skógum
for-good	alfari
for-himself	sér
for-long	lengr
for-the-sake	sakir
forty	fertuga
forward	fram
foster-care	ástfóstr
fostered	fóstri
foster-father	fóstra
found	fann, finnr
from	á, af, at, er, frá, fram, í, úr, við
from-out-of	úr
from-the-west	vestan
from-told	frásagnar
full	fullu
full-coming	fullkomið
funeral	útferð

G, g

English	Old Norse
Gaseyri (place)	Gáseyri
gave	gaf, gáfu
generosity	örleik
get	fá, fást, fœ, geta, getr
ghastly	ljótu
gifted	lánat
gifts	gjafir
give	gefa
give-performance	sýnduð
gladly	gjarna
go	ganga
goat-beard	geitarskegg, geitarskegginu
God (name)	Guðs
going	farið, gengr
gone	farið, gengið
good	góðan, góðar, góðu, gott, vœnna
got	fékk, fengi, fengið, gat, gekk, gœti
got-married	kvœntist
granted	veittu

Word List (English to Old Norse)

English	Old Norse	English	Old Norse
grave	svarri	heavy	þunga
great	mikill	he-had	honum
great-family	stórœttaðr	he-himself	sér
great-men	stórmenni	Hel (place)	Helju
great-wealth	stórauðigs, stórfé	held	hélt
greeted	kvaddi	Helgi (name)	Helgi
greeting	kvaðningar	hellish-old-man	heljarkarl
grips	festist	here	hér, hingat
grown	vexti	hers	hennar
		high	hátt
		high-born	ítri
		him	hann, honum, sér, sig
		himself	sé, sér, sína, sinni
		hired	rœðr
		his	hans, hánum, hins, honum, sér, sína, sinn, sinna, sinnar, sinni, síns, sínu, sínum, sitt

H, h

English	Old Norse
had	á, átt, áttu, hafa, hafði, hefir, hefr, lagði, láta, láti, lét, lœtr, œti
had-been	vert
had-done	gerði
hair	hárið
Hakon (name)	Hákon, Hákonar
Hakon's (name)	Hákonar
halberd	atgeirnum
half	hálf
Hali (name)	Hali
Hallbjorn (name)	Hallbirni, Hallbjörn
hands	hendi
hanged	hengja
happened	gerðist
hardly	harðla
harm	skaði
harmful	dálegra
harsher	harðúðigr
has	er, hefir
hated	hataðr
have	fá, hafa, hafi, hafið, haft, hefi, hefir, höfum, lagið
having	hefir
he	hann, hans, honum, sér
head-skin	höfuðsvörðum
hear	heyrið
heard	heyrði, heyrðu, heyrt
heart	hjartat, hugr
heaven's	himins

English	Old Norse
Hofdabrekka (place)	Höfðabrekku
hold	halda
home	heim
homes	heim
honour	sœmd, verðugu, virðingar
hope	von
Horgabrudi (name)	Hörgabrúði
Horgi (place)	Hörgi
however	hversu
how-so	hversu
humiliation	smánar
humility	lítillœti
hunger	svöngum
hungry	svengd

I, i

English	Old Norse
i	eg
i-am	mér
Iceland (place)	Ísland, Íslandi, Íslands
idol-worship	guðníðingskapr
if	ef, eg
ill	illa, illr
improvement	góðu
in	á, af, at, í, inn

Word List (English to Old Norse)

English	Old Norse
increase	aukið
in-front-of	framan
inherited	erfðu
instruction	frœðum
intended	œtlaði
into	í
invited	bat, boðið
iron-weapon	járn
Irpu (name)	Irpu
is	er
is-said	segja
it	á, at, hana, hún, þat
itching	kláði
it-is	er
its	hennar
it-was	gerði

J, j

English	Old Norse
journey	ferðum, leið
Jutland (place)	Jóta

K, k

English	Old Norse
Karl (name)	Karl
kennings	kenningar
kill	drepa
killed	vó
king's-gift	konungsnaut
kinsmen	frœnda
kinsmen-origins	kynferði
Klaufi (name)	Klaufa
knew	kunni, vita
knots	knúta
know	kannt, víst, vita, vitja
known	kenndr
knows	veit
knuckle-breaker	völubrjótr, völubrjótr

L, l

English	Old Norse
Lade (place)	Hlaðir, Hlöðum
laid	lagði, lagið, lét, liggr
land	land
lands	lands
large	mikill, stóra
last	síðasta
laughed	hlógu
launched	skjóta
law-assembly	lögréttu
lay	liggr
laying	legið
leading	skörungr
learned	spurði, spurn, spurt, spyr
leave	orlof
left	lœtr
legislation	lagasetning
lengthen	lengja
less	síðr
let	lát, látið, lét
levelled	sléttri
lies	liggr
life	líf
life-days	lífsdaga
lifetime	lífstíma
like	líkar
liked	líkaði
liking	geðjast
listen	hlýða
listen-to	hlýdduð
little	lítils, lítinn
lived	bjó
Ljotolf (name)	Ljótólfi, Ljótólfr, Ljótólfs
locks	lásum
long	lengi
longer	lengr, lengra
lord	herra
lordship	höfðingskap
loved	unni
luck	giftu

M, m

English	Old Norse
made	ger, gera, gerðu, verið
magic	fítonsanda
magical-arts	göldrum

Word List (English to Old Norse)

English	Old Norse
malice	grálega
malignance	meinlœtum
malignancy	meinlœtis
man	karli, maðr, mann
man-evil	mannillska
man-of-high-rank	virðingamaðr
man's	manna
manslaughter	mannalát
many	marga, margan, margir, margra, margri, mart, mörg, mörgum
many-known	margkunnandi
market-town	kaupstaðinn
marshes	mörkum
matter	mál
may	má, mátti, mega, megi
me	mér, mig
meet	fund
men	drengr, manna, menn, mönnum
merchant-ships	knarrar
merry	œrnri
met	hitti
middle	miðjum, miðs
middle-of	miðju
Midfjord (place)	Miðfirði
Midfjorder-Skeggi (name)	Miðfjarðar-Skeggja
midwinter-evening	aðfangskveld
mile	mílu
mine	minn, mitt
misery	eymd
misliked	mislíkaði
miss	missa
moment	bili
money	peninga
more	fleira, meir, meira
more-convenient	hentugri
morning	morguninn
most	flestum, mest, mesta, mesti, mikið
mother	móðr
mother's-brother	móðrbróðr
mound	haug, haugr
mouth	munn
move	flyttu
moved	gangi
movement	bragði
much	margra, mikið, mikil, mikill, mikils, mikinn, mikla, miklar, miklum, mjǫk
must	mun
Myrdal-Valley (place)	Mýdal
mysterious-path	refilstiga

N, n

English	Old Norse
name	heiti, nafn, nafni
named	heita, heiti, heitir, hét
name-giving	nafnfesti
nature	eðli, náttúra
near	nœr
nearest	nœstir
need	þarfast, þarftu, þurfa
needed	þarf, þarfa, þarfaði
never	aldrei
news	tíðinda, tíðindi, tíðindum
next	nœsta
Nidung (name)	Níðungr
night	nátt, nœtr
nineteen	nítján
Njord (name)	Njörðr
noble	öðlings, skörungr
noble-woman	kvenskörungr
noise	hark
no-little	ólítið
none	engi, engr, önga
nor	né
north	norðr
Norway (place)	Noreg, Noregs
not	eiga, eigi, ekki, öngu
not-further	áfram
not-lacking	óvant
now	nú

O, o

Word List (English to Old Norse)

English	Old Norse	English	Old Norse
Odin (name)	Gautr	parted	skildu
of	á, af, at, í, og, úr	parting	reikar
of-all	öllum	passage	farning
off	af	passed	leið
of-gold	gulls	peasant	þorpara
of-Hakon	hákoni	people	manna, manni, manninn, menn, mönnum
of-poets	skálda		
often	oft, oftar, oftlega		
of-the-ship	knarrar	peoples'	mönnum
Olaf (name)	Ólafr	performed	flutt
Olaf's (name)	Ólafs	pernickety	nákvœmi
old	gamall, gamla, gömlum	phrases	drápu
		plates	diska
old-man	gamlir, karl	plunder	férán
omens	frétt, fréttar	plundering	hervirki
on	á	poem	kveðið, kvœði, kvœðið
one	eina, einn		
one's	hvern	poems	kvœði
only	einna	poem's-reward	kvœðislaunum
open	opnast	poet	skáld
opening	gíman	poetry	brag, skáldskap, skáldskapinn
or	eða, ella		
other	aðrar, aðrir, annar, annarra, annarri, hinum, öðrum	poles	ásum
		popular	vinsœl
		popularity	vinsœldum
other-lands	útlendis	possible	hœgt
others	aðrir, annarra, öðrum	power	krafti, mögnuðu, vald
ours	vort	powerful	ríkr
ourselves-decide	sjálfráða	praise	lof
out	úr, út, utan, úti, ýtar	praised	lofaði
out-from	út	praise-words	lofkvœði
outlaw	útlœgr	prepared	bjó, búinn, býr
out-lying	utarlega	previous-deeds	framaverka
out-of	undan, úr	price	verð
outside	ytra	profit	grœddi
over	ofan, yfir	promise	heita
own	eigið	promised	hét
owning	eign	promising	efnilegir
Oxara (place)	Öxará	promptly	greiðlega
		properly	sœmilega
		proverb	orðskvið
		provide	kost
		provided-knowing	naddveiti
		pulled	togar
		punishment-time	hegningartíminn

P, p

Word List (English to Old Norse)

English	Old Norse
put-to-words	kveðið

Q, q

quickly	bráðlega, greiðlega

R, r

ran	hleypr
rather	heldr
received	tók
recently	litlu
recites	kveða
recovered	raknaði
Red (name)	Rauði
Red-Cloak (name)	Rauðfeldr
reddened	roðið
relief	létti
relieved	fegins
renown	hróðr
repaid	galt
repay	gjalda, launat
repayment	gjöld
reported	fréttust
requirements	hentar
rest	hvílast
restlessness	óvœra, óvœri
return	áðr
returned	aftr
returning	aftr
revenge	hefnda
Reykir (place)	Reykjum
river	á
robbed	rœndi
robbery	ránum
rocks	grjóti
rose	ríða, rís
rough	harðleikinn
ruled	réð

S, s

English	Old Norse
sack-cloth	strigadúk
sacrifices	fórnir
saga	sögu
sagas	sögr
said	kvat, kveðr, mœlt, sagði, sagðr, sagt, segið, segir, segja, sögðu, talar
sailed	sigldu
sake	sakir, sœkja
sale	sölr
same	sömu
sand	eyri
sat	sat, sest
saw	sá, sér, sjá
say	kveða, segist, segja
say-you	segðu
scarcely	trautt, varla
scratched	hrífa
sea	haf
secrecy	laun
see	sé, sjá
seemed-to	sýndist
seems	þykir
seen	sést
sent	sendu
servants	þjónustumenn
settled	bjó, búið
settlement	byggða
shall	mun, munt, munuð, munum, skal, skalt, skaltu
shall-i	mig
shall-you	skaltu
shame	blygðar, skammar
shamed	forsmáðr
shaped	skapaðir
she	hún
shepherd	sauðamaðr
ship	skip, skipi, skips
ships	skips
shivering	hrollir
short	stutt
should	mun, munuð, skyldi, skyldr, skyldu
shoulders	herðar

Word List (English to Old Norse)

English	Old Norse	English	Old Norse
show-off	skruma	stood	standa, stendr, stóð
shut	luktum	stopped	linnir
side	megin	stories	saga
since	síðan, því	straightaway	þegar
sister	systr	strange	kynstrum, undarlega
sisters	systra	strangeness	býsn
sit	sœti, sœtis	strong	gilds
sit-still	kyrr	struck	hjó
Skeggi (name)	Skeggi, Skeggja	stumbled	stumrar
skilled	íþrótt, íþróttir	such	slíkt, því
skilled-in-magic	fjölkunni	summer	sumar
skilled-poet	þjóðskáld	support	styrk
skills	íþrótta	supposed	œtluðu
Skogar (place)	Skógum	Svarfardal (place)	Svarfaðardal, Svarfdœla
slaying-warrior	vígdjarfr	Svein (name)	Sveins
slendered	grenndi	swagger	skruma
slept	sofnar, svaf	Sweden (place)	Svíþjóð
slyness	slœgða	swords	branda
so	sá, svo	Syrgsdalir (place)	Syrgisdölum
soles-of-the-feet	iljarnar		
solve	leysa		
some	nokkuð, nokkura, nokkurar, nokkurt, sumir		

T, t

English	Old Norse	English	Old Norse
something	nokkuð	take	náms, numið, taka, tekr
somewhat	nokkuð	taken	nema, taka, tekið
son	son, sonar	talented	gervilegr
songs	atkvœðum	talked	mœlti
son-of-gjallandi	gjallandason	teach	kenna
sons	syni	temple	hofi
soon	fljótlega	temples	hof
soonest	fljótasta	temporary	stundlegum
sorcery	galdr	than	en, þann
sought	fréttist, leitaði, sótt	thanked	þakkaði
soul	andar	thanks	þökk
south	suðr	that	á, at, en, er, sem, þann, þat
speak	kveða	the	at, en, er, hið, hinn, hinni, hins, hinu, þat, þenna, til
spikes	broddr		
spoke	kvat, mœlti		
spoken	kveðið		
spring	vor, vorið, vorið	the-abuse	níðið
spring-days	vordögum	the-bag	hítina
stand	staðið, standa	the-bay	víkinni
stave	stef	the-best	mest, mesta
staves	stafni	the-chieftain	goða
sticks	stafina		

Word List (English to Old Norse)

English	*Old Norse*	*English*	*Old Norse*
the-coals	kol	*they*	þau, þeim, þeir
the-crutches	hœkjurnar	*they-were*	eru
the-darkness	myrkrið	*thick-clouds*	mökkr
the-day	daginn	*thighs*	þjóanna, þjóin
the-earl	jarl, jarli, jarlinn, jarlinum, jarls	*Thingvellir (place)*	Þingvelli
		think	hugsa
the-earl's	jarls	*third*	þriðjung
the-earl's-abuse	jarlsníði	*thirsty*	þorsta
the-earth	jörðina	*this*	á, at, þat, þenna, þess, þessa, þessar, þessi, þessu, þessum, þetta
the-enemy's	óvinarins		
the-fellows	drengjum		
the-fields	velli		
the-greatest	mestr	*this-verse*	vísu
the-hall	höllina, höllinni	*Thjorsa (place)*	Þjórsá
theirs	sinn, þeirra	*Thord (name)*	Þórðar
the-king	konung, konungi, konungr, konungs	*Thorgard (name)*	Þorgarð, Þorgarði, Þorgarðr, Þorgarðr, Þorgarðs
the-land	land, landi		
the-lion's	leóns	*Thorgerd (name)*	Þorgerði
them	þar, þeim	*Thorhild (name)*	Þórhildr
the-mauler	böggva	*Thorkell (name)*	Þorkell
the-most	flestu	*Thorleif (name)*	Þorleif, Þorleifi, Þorleifr
the-mound	hauginn, hauginum, haugurinn		
		thorleif's	þorleifi, þorleifs
the-mound-dweller	haugbúann	*Thorleif's (name)*	Þorleifs
then	at, en, hið, hina, þá, þann, þeim, þenna, því	*those*	hinn, þenna
		though	þó
		thought	þótti, þóttist, þóttu, þóttust, þykir, þykist
the-night	nóttina		
the-old-man	karl, karli	*thoughts*	hug
the-poem	kvœðið	*Thrasi (name)*	Þrasa
the-poet	skaldi	*three*	þrjá
the-prince	þengils	*threw*	varpar
there	þar, þegar, þeirra, þeirrar	*through*	gegnum
		tied-up	binda
therefore	því	*time*	tíma, tímir
the-same	samr	*to*	á, at, í, til, við
these	þenna	*to-be*	vera
the-ship	nökkvi, skipið	*to-carry*	flytja
the-spring	vori	*to-eat*	etið
the-straw	hálminn	*together*	saman
the-summer	sumrinu	*to-give*	gefa
the-sword	sverðinu	*to-hear*	hlýða
the-tables	borð	*to-him*	honum, sér
the-Tronds' (name)	Þrœnda	*told*	sagði, talat, töluðu
the-uppermost	ofanverðum	*told-of*	getið

Word List (English to Old Norse)

English	Old Norse
to-me	mér
tongue	tunguna
took	nam, taka, tekr, tók
torment	kvala
to-sell	selja
tough	seigt
toughness	harðfengi
to-you	þér
traces	vegsummerki
trading-men	kaupmönnum
traditions	sið
transport	reiða
travel	fara, ferð, ferðar
travel-goods	fararefna
travelled	farið, fer, fór, fóru
tricked	bregðr, ginnti
Trondheim (place)	Þrándheim
troubled	bœginn
truly	sannlega
tunic	kyrtilinn, kyrtlinum
turned	hverfr, snýr, snýst
twisted	snaraði
two	tvo, tvœr
true	satt

U, u

English	Old Norse
unconsciousness	óvit
under	undir
undone	ógert, óloknum
un-eagerly	ófreklegar
un-glad	ógleðr
un-gladdened	ógladdist
un-gladness	ógleði
unknown	ókunna
unless	nema
un-redeemable	óbœtilegs
unruly	úrigr
unsoundly	óhljóði
until	til
up	upp, uppi
upped	upp
upper	efsta
up-to	undir
us	oss

English	Old Norse
usually	jafnan

V, v

English	Old Norse
vacations	orlofs
verse	vísu, vísuna
verses	vísr
Vik (place)	Vík
villain	villumaðr
vocabulary	orðfœri

W, w

English	Old Norse
walked	gekk
waning	þrotnum
wares	varning, varninginn
warrior	gramr
warriors	fyrðum
was	enn, er, var, varð, vœri, voru
was-named	hét, nefndist
wave	öldu
we	oss, vér
wealth	fé
wealth-damage	fjárskaða
wealthy	auðigr
we-are	eru
well	vel
well-sized	vellstœri
went	fékk, fer, fór, fóru, ganga, ganganda, gekk, gengr
were	var, varð, vœri, voru
west	vestan, vestr, vestra
what	er, hvat, sem
wheel	röðla
when	en, er
whether	hvort
which	er, sem
who	er, hver
who's	hverjum
who-was	er
why	hví
wicked	vonda

Word List (English to Old Norse)

English	Old Norse
widely	víða
wife	kona
will	viljið
will-be	verðir
willingly	ofléttlega
win-over	ynni
winter	vetr, veturinn
winters	vetra
wisdom	visku
wise	vitr
wish	vil, vildi, vildir, viljum
wished	vildi
wish-to	viljum
witchcraft	fjölkynngi, gerningum, tröllskap
with	í, með, þat, við
with-conviction	sakir
without	án, utan
woman	kona
Woman-Verses (name)	Konrvísr
wooden-man	trémann
worded	ort
words	orð, orðið, ort, orti
work	verki
worst	verr
worth	verðum
worthiness	virðum
would	mundi, mundu
wretchedness	vesaldar
written	rituð

Y, y

Yngvild (name)	Yngvildi
you	þér, þig, þinn, þú, yðr
young	ungum
youngest	yngsti
your	þín
yours	þinna, þinni, þínum, þitt, yðr, yðrum
Yule (name)	Jóla
yule-feast	jólaveislunnar

The Tale of Thorlief the Earl's Poet (Old Icelandic)

The Tale of Thorlief the Earl's Poet (*Old Icelandic*)

Old Icelandic	Literal	English
1	**1**	**1**
Nú skal segja þann ævintýr er gerðist á ofanverðum dögum Hákonar Hlaðajarls, í hverjum kynstrum, göldrum og gerningum hann varð forsmáður og mjög að verðugu, því að hans mannillska og guðníðingskapur varð mörgum manni til mikils þunga og óbætilegs skaða andar og líkama.	Now shall say then adventure that happened in the-uppermost days Hakon Earl-Of-Lade, about who's strange, magical-arts and witchcraft he was shamed and much to honour, because that he man-evil and idol-worship became many people to much heavy and un-redeemable damage soul and body.	Now shall be told the adventure that happened in the early days of Hakon the earl of Lade, about his strange magic and witchcraft which greatly shamed his honour, because this evil man and his idolatry became a heavy burden to many people, and caused irreparable harm to soul and body.
Varð honum það sem margan tímir að þá er hegningartíminn er kominn er eigi hægt undan að komast því að það er óvinarins náttúra að þann manninn sem hann þykist fullkomið vald á eiga og önga von á til guðs blekkir hann fyrst og blygðar með krókóttum kyndugskap sinna bölvaðra slægða í framleiðslu hans ljótu lífsdaga en að þrotnum hans stundlegum lífstíma verður hann drekktur í dökkri dýflissu dálegra kvala með eymd og ánauð utan enda.	Became to-him that as many time that then was punishment-time was came that not possible out-of to come because that it was the-enemy's nature that then people which he thought full-coming power that not and none hope of to God deceived he first and shame with devious cunning his cursed slyness in causing his ghastly life-days then that waning his temporary lifetime became he drowned in dark dungeon harmful torment with misery and enslavement without end.	It befell him, as it does to many, when the time of punishment came, he could not come out of it, as it was the devil's nature to deceive people who he thinks he has full power over, and who has no hope of God's mercy. First comes shame with devious cunning and cursed slyness, causing a ghastly life, and in the waning of his temporary life, he is drowned in the dark dungeon of harmful torment, with misery and enslavement without end.
2	**2**	**2**
Þá bjó Ásgeir rauðfeldur á Brekku í Svarfaðardal.	Then lived Asgeir Red-Cloak at Brekka in Svarfardal.	Then Asgeir Red-Cloak lived at Brekka in Svafardal.
Hann var ríkur maður og stórættaður.	He was powerful man and great-family.	He was a powerful man from a great family.
Þórhildur hét kona hans.	Thorhild named wife his.	His wife was named Thorhild.
Hún var vitur kona og vinsæl og skörungur mikill.	She was wise woman and popular and noble much.	She was a very wise, popular, and noble woman.

The Tale of Thorlief the Earl's Poet (Old Icelandic)

Old Icelandic	Literal	English
Þau áttu þrjá syni og voru allir efnilegir.	They had three sons and were all promising.	They had three sons, all of whom were promising.
Ólafur hét son þeirra hinn elsti og var kallaður völubrjótur, annar Helgi hinn frækni og koma þeir báðir meir við aðrar sögur en þessa.	Olaf named son theirs the eldest and was called knuckle-breaker, another Helgi the brave and came they both more with other sagas than this.	Their eldest son was named Olaf, who was called 'knuckle-breaker', the second son was called Helgi the brave, and they appear in other sagas than this one.
Þorleifur hét hinn yngsti son þeirra.	Thorleif named the youngest son theirs.	Their youngest son was named Thorleif.
Hann var snemma gildur og gervilegur og hinn mesti atgervimaður um íþróttir.	He was early-age capable and talented and the most accomplished-man at skilled.	He was fully capable at an early age, an accomplished man and skilful.
Hann var skáld gott.	He was a-poet good.	He was a good poet
Hann var á fóstri með Miðfjarðar-Skeggja móðurbróður sínum að Reykjum í Miðfirði þar til er hann var átján vetra gamall.	He was in fostered with Midfjorder-Skeggi mother's-brother his at Reykir in Midfjord there until that he was eighteen winters old.	He was brought up with his uncle Midfjorder-Skeggi at Reykir in Midfjord there until he was eighteen years old.
Skeggi unni mikið Þorleifi og lagði við hann ástfóstur.	Skeggi loved much Thorleif and had with him foster-care.	Skeggi loved Thorleif very much and brought him up with care.
Það töluðu menn að Skeggi mundi fleira kenna Þorleifi í fræðum fornlegum en aðrir mundu vita.	This told people that Skeggi would more teach Thorleif in instruction ancient-ways than others would know.	People said that Skeggi would teach Thorleif more about the ways of magic than others would know.
Þá fór Þorleifur heim til föður síns.	Then went Thorleif home to father his.	Then Thorleif went home to his father.
Hann vó Klaufa böggva með fulltingi Ólafs bróður síns en til eftirmáls eftir Klaufa var Karl hinn rauði og gekk svo fast að að Þorleifur varð útlægur og ger í burt úr Svarfaðardal.	He killed Klaufi the-mauler with assistance Olaf's brother his and to after-the-case after Klaufi was Karl the Red and went so closed it that Thorleif became outlaw and made to away from-out-of Svarfardal.	He killed Klaufi the mauler with the help of his brother Olaf, and in the following legal case was Karl the Red, and so it concluded that Thorleif became an outlaw and banished from Svafardal.
Ljótólfur goði hafði fylgt Yngvildi fagurkinn systur Þorleifs.	Ljotolf chieftain had followed Yngvild Fair-Cheek sister Thorleif's.	Ljotolf the chieftain lived with Yngvild the fair-cheek, Thorleif's sister.

The Tale of Thorlief the Earl's Poet (Old Icelandic)

Old Icelandic	Literal	English
Hann kom Þorleifi í skip á Gáseyri.	He came Thorleif to ship at Gaseyri.	He brought Thorleif to a ship at Gaseyri.
Þorleifur varð afturreka.	Thorleif became back-driven.	But Thorleif was driven back.
Hann var um veturinn á laun ýmist með Ljótólfi goða eða Ásgeiri föður sínum.	He was about winter in secrecy either with Ljotolf the-chieftain or Asgeir father his.	During the winter he was hiding with Ljotolf the chieftain or his father Asgeir.
Nam hann þá að föður sínum marga fornfræði því að hann var sagður margkunnandi.	Took he then to father his many ancient-ways because that he was said many-known.	He then took to learning many of the ancient ways, as it is said that he knew many things.
Var þá Þorleifur nítján vetra.	Was then Thorleif nineteen winters.	Thorleif was then nineteen winters old.
Karl leitaði fast eftir um Þorleif og urðu þar um veturinn margir atburðir, þeir er frásagnar eru verðir sem segir í Svarfdæla sögu.	Karl sought closely after about Thorleif and became there about winter many events, they are from-told are will-be as said in Svarfardal saga.	Karl looked closely for Thorleif, and from there came many events, which are told in Svafardal Saga.
Um vorið eftir fór Þorleifur vestur til Skeggja fóstra síns og frænda og biður hann ásjá og umráða með sér um þessi mál.	About spring after travelled Thorleif west to Skeggi foster-father his and kinsmen and asked him assistance and about-advice with him about this matter.	About the following spring, Thorleif travelled west to Skeggi his foster father and kinsman, and asked for his help and guidance in this matter.
Og með styrk og ráðum Miðfjarðar-Skeggja og Ljótólfs goða fer Þorleifur og kaupir sér skip að kaupmönnum er uppi stóð í Blönduósi og ræður háseta til og fór síðan heim á Brekku og hitti föður sinn og móður og beiddist af þeim fararefna og fékk svo mikinn fjárhlut sem honum þótti sér þarfa og að vordögum lét hann varning sinn til skips binda og fór í brott af Brekku alfari og bað vel fyrir föður sínum og móður og Miðfjarðar-Skeggja fóstra sínum.	And with support and advice Midfjorder-Skeggi and Ljotolf the-chieftain went Thorleif and bought himself a-ship from trading-men that up stood in Blonduos and hired first-mate for and travelled afterwards home to Brekka and met father his and mother and asked of them travel-goods and got so much fee-lot as he thought he-himself needed and to spring-days had he wares his to ship bound and travelled to away from Brekka for-good and bid well for father his and mother and Midfjorder-Skeggi foster-father his.	And with the support and advice of Midfjorder-Skeggi and Ljotolf the chieftain, Thorleif went and bought himself a ship from merchants up in Blonduos, and hired a first mate for it. After that he then travelled home to Brekka and met his father and mother, asking for wares and travel goods, and he got as much money as he thought he needed. In the first days of spring he brought his wares to his ship, bound them up, and travelled away from Brekka once and for all, wishing his father and mother well, and Midfjorder-Skeggi, his foster father.

The Tale of Thorlief the Earl's Poet (Old Icelandic)

Old Icelandic	Literal	English
3	**3**	**3**
Nú lætur Þorleifur í haf og byrjar honum vel og kemur skipi sínu í Vík austur.	Now left Thorleif to sea and fair-wind he-had well and came ship his into Vik east.	Now Thorleif set out to sea and got a fair wind, and his ship came to Vik in the east.
Hákon Hlaðajarl var þá í Víkinni.	Hakon Earl-Of-Lade was then in The-bay.	Hakon was the earl of Lade at Vik.
Þorleifur gekk á land og lét ryðja skip sitt.	Thorleif went to the-land and had cleared ship his.	Thorleif went to land and had is ship unloaded.
Hann hitti jarlinn og kvaddi hann.	He met the-earl and greeted him.	He met the earl and greeted him.
Jarl tók honum vel og spurði hann að nafni, ætt og kynferði en Þorleifur sagði honum.	The-earl received him well and asked him of name, ancestors and kinsmen-origins and Thorleif told him.	The earl received him well and asked his name, ancestry, and origins, and Thorleif told him.
Jarl spurði og margra tíðinda af Íslandi en Þorleifur sagði honum ofléttlega.	The-earl asked of much news of Iceland and Thorleif told him willingly.	The earl asked for much news of Iceland, and Thorleif told him.
Þá sagði jarl:	Then said the-earl:	Then the earl said:
"Svo er orðið Þorleifur að vér viljum hafa sölur af þér og hásetum þínum".	"So has become Thorleif that we wish-to have sale of you and crew yours".	"So it is, Thorleif, that we wish to buy some things from you and your crew".
Þorleifur svarar:	Thorleif answered:	Thorleif answered:
"Vér höfum lítinn varninginn herra en oss eru þó aðrir kaupunautar hentugri og munuð þér láta oss sjálfráða vera að selja þeim góss vort og peninga sem oss líkar".	"We have little wares lord and us we-are though other customers more-convenient and shall you allow us ourselves-decide being for to-sell them belongings ours and money as we like".	"We have little in the way of wares, my lord, and we need more useful customers, and you shall allow us to decide for ourselves who to sell our belongings to as we like".
Jarli þótti hann þykklega svara og mislíkaði orð hans mjög og skildu við svo búið.	Earl thought he arrogantly answered and misliked words his much and parted with so settled.	The earl thought he had answered arrogantly, and disliked his words, and with that they parted.

The Tale of Thorlief the Earl's Poet (Old Icelandic)

Old Icelandic	Literal	English
Þorleifur fór nú til manna sinna og svaf af um nóttina og um morguninn rís hann upp og fer í kaupstaðinn og fréttist fyrir um góða kaupunauta og kaupslagar við þá um daginn.	Thorleif travelled now to men his and slept of about the-night and about morning rose he up and travelled to market-town and sought for about food customers and bargaining with then about the-day.	Thorleif went back to his men and slept through the night, and in the morning he got up and travelled to town and sought good customers, and bargained with them throughout the day.
Og er jarl spurði það fór hann með fjölmenni til skips Þorleifs og lét taka þar menn alla og binda.	And when the-earl learned that travelled he with following-men to ships Thorleif's and had took there men all and tied-up.	And when the earl learned of this, he travelled with his followers to Thorleif's ship and took all the men and had them tied up.
Síðan rændi hann þar fjárhlut öllum og kastaði á sinni eign en lét brenna skipið að köldum kolum.	Afterwards robbed he there financial-share of-all and cast about himself owning and had burnt the-ship to cold coals.	Afterwards he robbed them of all their wealth and took it for himself, and had the ship burnt to coals.
Og eftir þetta lét hann skjóta ásum milli búðanna og lét þar hengja við alla förunauta Þorleifs.	And after this had he launched poles between booths and had them hanged with all companions Thorleif's.	After this he had poles raised between booths and had all of Thorleif's companions hanged.
Síðan fór jarl í brott og hans menn og tók að sér varning þann er Þorleifur hafði átt og skipti upp með sínum mönnum.	Afterwards travelled the-earl to away and his men and took then for-himself wares then that Thorleif had had and exchanged up with his men.	Afterwards the earl went away with his men, taking all the wares and dividing it among his men.
En um kveldið er Þorleifur kom heim og ætlaði að vitja manna sinna sem hann gerði sá hann vegsummerki hversu við hans félaga hafði farið verið og þóttist vita að Hákon jarl mundi þessu vonda verki valdið hafa og spyr nú eftir þessum tíðindum glögglega.	Then about evening when Thorleif came home and intended to know men his what he had-done saw he traces how-so with his companions had gone been and thought certainly that Hakon earl would this wicked work caused had and learned now after this news clearly.	In the evening when Thorleif came home and looked for his men as usual, he saw traces of what had happened with his companions, and thought certainly that Earl Hakon caused this evil deed, and afterwards he learned the full news clearly.
Og er hann hafði þessi tíðindi sannlega spurt þá kvað hann vísu:	And when he had this news truly learned then spoke he this-verse:	And when he learned the news, then he spoke this verse:
Hrollir hugr minn illa. Hefir drengr skaða fengið sé eg á sléttri eyri, svarri, báts og knarrar.	Shivering heart mine badly. Have men damage caught see i this levelled sand, grave, boats and merchant-ships.	My heart shivers badly. Men have caught damage, I see this levelled sand, grave, both ship and boat.

The Tale of Thorlief the Earl's Poet (Old Icelandic)

Old Icelandic	Literal	English
Hinn er upp réð brenna öldu fíl fyrir skaldi, hver veit nema kol knarrar köld fýsi mig gjalda.	Those are up ruled burned wave elephant before the-poet, who knows except the-coals of-the-ship cold desire shall-i repay.	Those that ruled to burn the elephant of the waves, who knows except the coals of the ship cold desire I to repay.

4

Old Icelandic	Literal	English
Svo er sagt að eftir þenna atburð kom Þorleifur sér í skip með kaupmönnum og sigldu suður til Danmerkur og fór hann á fund Sveins konungs og var með honum um veturinn.	So it-is said that after those events came Thorleif himself in a-ship with trading-men and sailed south to Denmark and travelled he to meet Svein the-king and was with him about winter.	It is said that after this Thorleif went on a ship with trading-men and sailed south to Denmark, and he travelled to meet king Svein and stayed with him over the winter.
En er hann hafði þar eigi lengi verið var það einn dag að Þorleifur gekk fyrir konung og beiddi hann hlýða kvæði því er hann hafði ort um hann.	Then when he had there not long been was it one day that Thorleif went before the-king and asked him to-hear poem since that he had worded about him.	Then when he had not long been there, one day Thorleif went before the king and asked hi to hear a poem that he had composed about him.
Konungur spurði hvort hann væri skáld.	The-king asked whether he was a-poet.	The king asked whether he was a poet.
Þorleifur svarar:	Thorleif answered:	Thorleif answered:
"Það er eftir því sem þér viljið dæmt hafa herra er þér heyrið".	"It is after therefore which to-you will deem have lord when you hear".	"That is for you to judge, lord, when you have heard it".
Konungur bað hann þá fram flytja.	The-king asked him then from to-carry.	The king then asked him to perform.
Þorleifur kvað þá fertuga drápu og er þetta stef í:	Thorleif spoke then forty phrases and is this stave in:	Thorleif spoke forty verses and among them is this stave:
Oft með ærnri giftu öðlings himins röðla Jóta gramr hinn ítri Englandi roðið branda.	Often with merry luck noble heaven's wheel Jutland warrior the high-born England reddened swords.	Often with merry luck from noble heaven's wheel the high-born Jutland warrior reddened swords in England.
Konungur lofaði mjög kvæðið og allir þeir er heyrðu og sögðu bæði vel kveðið og skörulega fram flutt.	The-king praised much the-poem and all they who heard and said both well spoken and boldly forward performed.	The king praised the poem very much, and all those who heard it said it was both well spoken and boldly performed.

The Tale of Thorlief the Earl's Poet (Old Icelandic)

Old Icelandic	Literal	English
Konungur gaf Þorleifi að kvæðislaunum hring þann er stóð mörk og það sverð er til kom hálf mörk gulls og bað hann lengi með sér vera.	The-king gave Thorleif to poem's-reward a-ring then was stood a-mark and with a-sword was to come half a-mark of-gold and invited him long with him to-be.	The king gave Thorleif a reward for the poem, a ring that was worth a mark of gold, and a sword worth half a mark of gold, and he invited him to stay with him.
Þorleifur gekk til sætis og þakkaði vel konungi.	Thorleif went to sit and thanked well the-king.	Thorleif took his place and thanked the king well.
Og leið svo fram nokkura hríð og ekki lengi áður en Þorleifur ógladdist svo mjög að hann gáði varla undir drykkjuborð að ganga eða samsætis við sína bekkjunauta.	And passed so from some awhile and not long before that Thorleif un-gladdened so much that he cared scarcely up-to drinking-tables and went either banquet with himself bench-fellows.	And so it passed, and it was not long before Thorleif became so unhappy that he scarcely cared to go to the drinking tables to feast or talk with his bench mates.
Finnur konungur þetta bráðlega og lætur kalla Þorleif fyrir sig og mælti:	Found the-king this quickly and had called Thorleif before him and spoke:	The king soon noticed this and had Thorleif called before him, and asked:
"Hvað veldur ógleði þinni er þú gáir varla að halda háttum við oss?"	"What brought-about un-gladness yours that you care scarcely to hold custom with us?"	"What has brought about your unhappiness, that you hardly keep to our customs?"
Þorleifur svarar:	Thorleif answered:	Thorleif answered:
"Það munuð þér heyrt hafa herra að sá er skyldur að leysa annars vandræði er að spyr".	"That should you heard have lord that so who should to solve another's difficulty who that asks".	"You must have heard, lord, that he who asks another's difficulty should solve it for him".
"Segðu fyrst",	"Say-you first",	"Tell it first",
segir konungur.	said the-king.	said the king.
Þorleifur svarar:	Thorleif answered:	Thorleif answered:
"Eg hefi kveðið vísur nokkurar í vetur er eg kalla Konurvísur er eg hefi ort um Hákon jarl því að jarl er kona kenndur í skáldskap.	"If have poem verses some in winter that i call Woman-Verses that i have worded about Hakon earl because that the-earl is a-woman known in poetry.	"I have composed some verses in the winter, that I call Women Verses, that I composed about Earl Hakon, because the earl is called a woman in poetry.

The Tale of Thorlief the Earl's Poet (Old Icelandic)

Old Icelandic	Literal	English
Nú ógleður mig það herra ef eg fæ eigi orlof af yður að fara til Noregs og færa jarli kvæðið".	Now un-glad me that lord if i get not leave of yours to travel to Norway and bring the-earl the-poem".	I will be unhappy, lord, if I do not get your leave to travel to Norway to bring the earl the poem".
"Þú skalt að vísu fá orlof",	"You shall this certainly get leave",	"You shall certainly have leave",
segir konungur, "og skaltu þó heita oss áður að koma aftur til vor það fljótasta sem þú getur því að vér viljum þín ekki missa sakir íþrótta þinna".	said the-king, "and shall-you though promise us return to come after to spring the soonest as you get therefore that we wish your not miss sake skills yours".	said the king, "and you shall promise to return to us soon after spring, because we do not wish to miss your skills".
Þorleifur hét því og fékk sér nú farning og fór norður í Noreg og linnir eigi fyrr en hann kemur í Þrándheim.	Thorleif promised accordingly and got himself now passage and travelled north to Norway and stopped not before that he came to Trondheim.	Thorleif promised accordingly and now got himself passage to travel north to Norway, and did not stop until he came to Trondheim.
Þá sat Hákon jarl á Hlöðum.	Then sat Hakon earl at Lade.	Then Hakon sat in residence at Lade.
Þorleifur býr sér nú stafkarls gervi og bindur sér geitarskegg og tók sér eina stóra hít og lét koma undir stafkarls gervina og bjó svo um að öllum skyldi sýnast sem hann æti þann kost er hann kastaði í hítina því að gíman hennar var uppi við munn honum undir geitarskegginu.	Thorleif prepared himself now as-a-beggar character and bound himself goat-beard and took himself a large bag and had come-with under beggar's disguise and prepared so about that all should appear as he had then food that he cast in the-bag because that opening its was up by mouth his under goat-beard.	Thorleif now disguised himself as a beggar and wore a goat's beard, he also took a large bag which he kept under the disguise, and it was prepared so that everyone would think that he ate the food that he put into the bag, because the opening was up by his mouth under the goat's beard.
Síðan tekur hann hækjur tvær og var broddur niður úr hvorri, fer nú þar til er hann kemur á Hlaðir.	Afterwards took he crutches two and were spikes down out-of each, travelled now there until that he came to Lade.	Afterwards he also took two crutches with spikes on the ends, and travelled until he came to Lade.
Það var aðfangskveld jóla í þann tíma er jarl var kominn í sæti og mart stórmenni er jarl hafði að sér boðið til jólaveislunnar.	It was midwinter-evening Yule at that time when the-earl was coming to sit and many great-men that the-earl had that he invited to yule-feast.	It was the midwinter evening of Yule, when the earl was coming to sit, and there were many great men that the earl had invited to the Yule feast.

The Tale of Thorlief the Earl's Poet (Old Icelandic)

Old Icelandic	Literal	English
Karl gengur greiðlega inn í höllina en er hann kemur inn stumrar hann geysimjög og fellur fast á hækjurnar og snýr til annarra stafkarla og sest niður utarlega í hálminn.	The-old-man went quickly in to the-hall and when he came in stumbled he exceedingly-much and fell close had the-crutches and turned to other beggars and sat down out-lying of the-straw.	The old man went quickly into the hall, and when he came in, he stumbled and fell heavily on his crutches, then turned to the other beggars and sat down at the edge of the straw.
Hann var nokkuð bæginn við stafkarla og heldur harðleikinn en þeir þoldu illa er hann lét ganga á þeim stafina.	He was somewhat troubled with beggars and rather rough and they endured badly that he let go to them sticks.	He was irritable with the beggars and quite rough, and they were not happy with being knocked by his sticks.
Hrukku þeir undan og varð af þessu hark og háreysti svo að heyrði um alla höllina.	Drew they back and became of this noise and commotion so that heard about all the-hall.	They drew back and this caused noise and commotion so that all who were in the hall heard.
En er jarl verður þessa var spyr hann hvað valdi óhljóði þessu.	Then when the-earl became this was asked he what controlled unsoundly this.	Then when the earl was aware of this, he asked what caused this din.
Honum er sagt að stafkarl einn sé sá þar kominn að svo sé illur og úrigur að ekki láti ógert.	He was said that beggar one himself saw there coming that so being bad and unruly that not had undone.	He was told that a beggar had been seen who was so bad and unruly that he stopped at nothing.
Jarl bað kalla hann fyrir sig og svo var og gert.	Earl asked call-to him before him him and so was and done.	The earl asked him to be called before him, and so it was done.
En er karl kom fyrir jarl hafði hann mjög stutt um kvaðningar.	And when the-old-man came before the-earl had he much short about greeting.	And when the old man came before the earl, he greeted him shortly.
Jarl spurði hann að nafni, ætt og óðali.	Earl asked him of name, ancestry and estate.	The earl asked him his name, his ancestry, and his estate.
"Óvant er nafn mitt herra að eg heiti Níðungur Gjallandason og kynjaður úr Syrgisdölum af Svíþjóð hinni köldu.	"Not-lacking is name mine lord that i named Nidung Son-of-gjallandi and descended from Syrgsdalir in Sweden the cold.	"Not lacking is my name, lord, for I am named Nidung son of Gjallandi and descended from Syrgsdalir in Sweden the cold.
Er eg kallaður Níðungur hinn nákvæmi.	Am i called Nidung the pernickety.	I am called Nidung the pernickety.
Hefi eg víða farið og marga höfðingja heim sótt.	Have i widely travelled and many chieftains' homes sought.	I have travelled widely and sought many chieftains' homes.

The Tale of Thorlief the Earl's Poet (Old Icelandic)

Old Icelandic	Literal	English
Gerist eg nú gamall mjög svo að trautt má eg aldur minn segja sakir elli og óminnis.	Becoming i now old much so that scarcely may i age mine say with-conviction age of amnesia.	I am now becoming so old that scarcely may I say my age with conviction because of amnesia.
Hefi eg mikla spurn af höfðingskap yðrum og harðfengi, visku og vinsældum, lagasetning og lítillæti, örleik og allri atgervi".	Have i much learned of lordship yours and toughness, wisdom and popularity, legislation and humility, generosity and all deeds".	I have learned much of your lordship and toughness, wisdom and popularity, legislation and humility, and your generosity in all deeds".
"Hví ertu svo harðúðigur og illur viðskiptis frá því sem aðrir stafkarlar?"	"Why are-you so harsher and ill behaved from therefore as other beggars?"	"Why are you so much harsher and badly behaved than the other beggars?"
Hann svarar:	He answered:	He answered:
"Hvað er örvænt um þann sem alls gengur andvana nema víls og vesaldar og ekki hefir það er þarf og lengi legið úti á mörkum og skógum þó að sá verði æfur við ellina og allt saman en vanur áður sæmd og sællífi af hinum dýrstum höfðingjum en vera nú hataður af hverjum þorpara lítils verðum".	"What is desperation about than as all going destitution taken advantage and wretchedness and not having that which needed and long laying out in marshes and forests though that so become angry with age and all together that experienced before honour and blessed-life of other dearest chieftains but becoming now hated of each peasant little worth".	"What is desperation about other than always going in destitution, taken advantage of by wretchedness, not having what is needed, laying for a long time in the marshes and forests, though becoming so angry with age, when altogether before having experienced a blessed life of the dearest chieftains, but becoming now hated by every peasant of little worth".
Jarl mælti:	The-earl spoke:	The earl spoke:
"Ertu nokkur íþróttamaður karl er þú segist þó með höfðingjum verið hafa?"	"Are-you anything excellent-man old-man that you say though with chieftains became have?"	"Are you excellent at anything, old man, as you say you have been with chieftains?"
Karl svarar það megi vera þó að nokkuð hafi til þess haft verið	The-old-man answered that may be though that somewhat have until this have been	The old man answered that it may be something like that:
"þá er eg var á ungum aldri.	"then when i was of young age.	"then when I was young in age.
Komi að því sem mælt er, að hverjum karli kemur að örverpi.	Comes to therefore as said is, to each man comes to decrepitude.	But it comes, as they say, decrepitude to each and every man.

The Tale of Thorlief the Earl's Poet (Old Icelandic)

Old Icelandic	Literal	English
Er það og talað að seigt er svöngum að skruma.	Is that also told that tough from hunger to swagger.	It is also said that it is difficult to swagger when hungry.
Mun eg og ekki við yður skruma herra nema þér látið gefa mér að eta því að svo dregur að mér af elli, svengd og þorsta að víst eigi fæ eg staðið uppi lengur.	Should i also not with you show-off lord unless you let give me to eat because that so drawn that i-am of age, hungry and thirsty and know not can i stand up for-long.	I can't show off to you, lord, unless you give me something to eat, because I am so drawn and with age, hungry and thirsty, and I do not know how long I can stand up for.
Er slíkt harðla óhöfðinglegt að spyrja ókunna menn í hvern heim en hugsa eigi hvað mönnum hentar því að allir eru með því eðli skapaðir að bæði þurfa át og drykkju".	It-is such hardly chieftain-like to ask unknown people into one's home but think not what peoples' requirements because that all are with therefore nature shaped that both need eat and drink".	It us hardly chieftain-like to ask strangers into one's home but not think about his requirements, because we are all shaped by nature to need both food and drink".
Jarl skipaði að honum skyldi gefa kost sæmilega sem honum þarfaði.	The-earl arranged that he should give food properly as he needed.	The earl arranged that he should be given food properly as he needed.
Var og svo gert.	Was also so done.	This was done.
En er karl kom undir borð tekur hann greiðlega til matar og ryður diska þá alla er næstir honum voru og hann náði til svo að þjónustumenn urðu að sækja kost í annan tíma.	Then the old-man came up-to the-tables took he promptly to food and cleared plates then all that nearest him were and he caught to so the servants became to sake provide for a-second time.	Then the old man came up to the tables, and he promptly took the food and cleared all the plates that were nearest to him, forcing the servants to provide a second helping.
Tók karl nú öngu ófreklegar til matar en fyrr.	Took the-old-man now not un-eagerly to food then before.	The old man was not just as eager as before.
Sýndist öllum sem hann æti en hann kastaði reyndar í hítina þá er fyrr var getið.	Seemed-to all that he ate but he cast actually in the-bag then as before was told-of.	It seemed to everyone that he ate, but the food was actually in the bag, as was told before.
Hlógu menn nú fast að karli þessum.	Laughed people now closely at the-old-man this.	People focused on the old man, and laughed.
Þjónustumenn töluðu að bæði væri að hann væri mikill og miðdigur enda gæti hann mikið etið.	Servants told that both were that he was great and broad-waist and got he much to-eat.	The servants said that he was both tall, and with a broad waist, and he could eat a lot.
Karl gaf sér ekki að því og gerði sem áður.	The-old-man gave himself not that then and did as before.	The old man did not react, and did as before.

The Tale of Thorlief the Earl's Poet (Old Icelandic)

Old Icelandic	Literal	English

5   5   5

Old Icelandic	Literal	English
En er ofan voru drykkjuborð gekk Níðungur karl fyrir jarl og mælti:	When that over were drinking-tables went Nidung the-old-man before the-earl and spoke:	When the drinking tables were removed, the old man Nidung went to the earl and spoke:
"Hafið þér nú þökk fyrir herra en þó eigið þér illa þjónustumenn er allt gera verr en þér segið fyrir.	"Have you now thanks for lord but though own you bad servants that all done worst than you said before.	"You have now my thanks, lord, but you have bad servants that did everything worse than you ordered.
En nú vildi eg að þér sýnduð mér lítillæti herra og hlýdduð kvæði því er eg hefi ort um yður".	But now wish i that to-you give-performance me a-little lord and listen-to poem because that i have worded about you".	But now I wish to give you a performance of my poem that I have composed about you".
Jarl mælti:	The-earl spoke:	The earl spoke:
"Hefir þú nokkuð fyrr kvæði ort um höfðingja?"	"Have you any before poems worded about chieftains?"	"Have you composed any poems about chieftains before?"
"Satt er það herra",	"True is that lord",	"That is true, lord",
kvað hann.	said he.	he said.
Jarl mælti:	The-earl spoke:	The earl spoke:
"Búið þar komi að gömlum orðskvið, að það er oft gott er gamlir kveða, og flyttu fram kvæðið karl en vér munum til hlýða".	"Done there comes that old proverb, that it is often good what old-man recites, and move forward poem old-man and we shall to listen".	"Done there is the proverb, that it is often good what an old man recites, so come forward with the poem, old man, and we shall listen".
Þá hefur karl upp kvæðið og kveður framan til miðs og þykir jarli lof í hverri vísu og finnur að þar er getið og í framaverka Eiríks sonar hans.	Then had the-old-man upped the-poem and said in-front-of the middle and thought the-earl praise in each verse and found that there was told-of and in previous-deeds Erik's son his.	Then the old man began the poem and recited it to the middle, and the earl thought that he heard praise in each verse, and found that there were tales told about his son Erik.

The Tale of Thorlief the Earl's Poet (Old Icelandic)

Old Icelandic	Literal	English
En er á leið kvæðið þá bregður jarli nokkuð undarlega við að óværi og kláði hleypur svo mikill um allan búkinn á honum og einna mest um þjóin að hann mátti hvergi kyrr þola og svo mikil býsn fylgdi þessum óværa að hann lét hrífa sér með kömbum þar sem þeim kom að.	But as it passed the-poem then tricked the-earl something strange from a restlessness and itching ran so much about all body of him and only most about thighs that he may each sit-still endure and so much strangeness followed this restlessness that he had scratched himself with combs there as they came to.	But as the poem continued, the earl was tricked into feeling a strange restlessness and an itching that ran all over his body, especially around his thighs so that he could hardly sit still, this uneasiness was so strange that he had scratched himself with combs wherever he could.
En þar sem þeim kom eigi að lét hann taka strigadúk og ríða á þrjá knúta og draga tvo menn milli þjóanna á sér.	Then there as they could not that had he taken sack-cloth and rose in three knots and drew two men between thighs for him.	Where he could not reach, he took a sack cloth and made three knots in it, and two men dragged it between his thighs for him.
Nú tók jarli illa að geðjast kvæðið og mælti:	Now took the-earl ill that liking the-poem and spoke:	Now the earl took badly to the poem and spoke:
"Kann þinn heljarkarl ekki betur að kveða því að mér þykir þetta eigi síður heita mega níð en lof og lát þú um batna ella tekur þú gjöld fyrir".	"Can you hellish-old-man not better to say because that to-me seems this not less call may abuse than praise and let you about better or take you repayment for".	"Can you not recite something better you hellish old man, because it seems to me more like abuse than praise, and make it better or you will be repaid for it".
Karl hét góðu um og hóf þá upp vísur og heita Þokuvísur og standa í miðju Jarlsníði og er þetta upphaf að:	The-old-man promised improvement about and began then up verses and named Fog-verses and stood in middle-of The-earl's-abuse and was this beginning this:	The old man promised improvement and then began verses named Fog Verses, which are in the middle of the Earl's Abuse, and the beginning was this:
Þoku dregr upp hið ytra, él festist hið vestra, mökkr mun náms, af nökkvi, naðrbings kominn hingað.	Fog draws up then outside, blizzard grips the west, thick-clouds shall take, of the-ship, dragon comes here.	Fog draws up then outside, a blizzard grips the west, thick clouds shall take, of the ship, the dragon comes here.
En er hann hafði úti Þokuvísur þá var myrkt í höllinni.	When that he had finished Fog-verses then was dark in the-hall.	When he had finished the Fog Verses, it was dark in the hall.
Og er myrkt er orðið í höllinni tekur hann aftur til Jarlsníðs.	And was dark was become in the-hall took he returning to Earl's-abuse.	And when it became dark in the hall, he began the Earl Abuse verses again.

The Tale of Thorlief the Earl's Poet (Old Icelandic)

Old Icelandic	Literal	English
Og er hann kvað hinn efsta og síðasta þriðjung þá var hvert járn á gangi það er í var höllinni án manna völdum og varð það margra manna bani.	And as he spoke the upper and last third then was each iron-weapon from moved it that in was the-hall without man's doing and became that many people dead.	And has he recited the third and last part, then each iron weapon that as in the hall moved without man's doing, and many men became dead.
Jarl féll þá í óvit en karl hvarf þá í brott að luktum dyrum og óloknum lásum.	The-earl fell then into unconsciousness but the-old-man disappeared then to away that shut doors and undone locks.	The earl then fell into unconsciousness, but the old man disappeared away through shut doors and undone locks.
En eftir afliðið kvæðið minnkaði myrkrið og gerði bjart í höllinni.	Then after following the-poem decreased the-darkness and it-was bright in the-hall.	Then following after the poem the darkness decreased, and it was bright again in the hall.
Jarl raknaði við og fann að honum hafði nær gengið níðið.	The-earl recovered from and found that to-him had near gone the-abuse.	The earl recovered and found that the abuse had come quite close to him.
Sá þá og vegsummerki að af var rotnað skegg allt af jarli og hárið öðrum megin reikar og kom aldrei upp síðan.	Saw then also evidence that off was decayed beard all of the-earl and hair other side parting and came never up since.	He also saw evidence of this, because his beard had decayed, along with the hair on one side of his parting, and it never came back.
Nú lætur jarl ræsta höllina og eru hinu dauðu út bornir.	Now had the-earl cleared the-hall and they-were the dead out carried.	Now the earl had the hall cleared and the dead were carried out.
Þykist hann nú vita að þetta mun Þorleifur verið hafa en karl engi annar og mun launað þykjast hafa honum mannalát og fjártjón.	Thought he now knew that this must Thorleif been had the old-man none other and should repay considered had he manslaughter and financial-loss.	He thought that he knew that the old man must have been none other than Thorleif, and that this was repayment for the manslaughter and his financial loss.
Liggur jarl nú í þessum meinlætum allan þenna vetur og mikið af sumrinu.	Laid the-earl now from this malignance all the winter and most of the-summer.	This malignance laid the earl low for all of the winter and most of the summer.

6

Það er af Þorleifi að segja að hann snýst til ferðar suður til Danmerkur og hefir það til leiðarnests sér sem hann ginnti af þeim í höllinni.	It was of Thorleif to say that he turned to travel south to Denmark and had it to food his as he tricked from them in the-hall.	As for Thorleif, he set to travel south to Denmark, and for his provisions he had the food that he had tricked from them in the hall.

The Tale of Thorlief the Earl's Poet (Old Icelandic)

Old Icelandic	Literal	English
En hversu lengi sem hann hefir á leið verið þá létti hann eigi sinni ferð fyrr en hann kom á fund Sveins konungs og tók hann við honum fegins hendi og spurði hann að ferðum sínum en Þorleifur sagði allt sem farið hafði.	Then however long as he had to journey made then relief he not his travel before that he came to find Svein the-king and received he with him relieved hands and asked he of journey his and Thorleif said all which gone had.	Then however long the journey was to be made, he had no relief in his travel until he came to find king Svein, and he received him well with relieved hands, and asked him of his journey, and Thorleif said how all had gone.
Konungur svarar:	The-king answered:	The king answered:
"Nú mun eg lengja nafn þitt og kalla þig Þorleif jarlaskáld".	"Now should i lengthen name yours and call you Thorleif Earl's-Poet".	"Now I should lengthen your name and call you Thorleif the Earl's-Poet".
Þá kvað konungur vísu:	Then said the-king verse:	Then the king said a verse:
Grenndi Þorleifr Þrænda þengils hróðr fyr drengjum, *hafa ólítið ýtar jarls níð borið víða. Njörðr réð vestan virðum vellstæri brag færa brot lands galt gæti grálega leóns báru.*	Slendered Thorleif The-Tronds' the-prince renown before the-fellows, had no-little out the-earl's abuse carried widely. Njord ruled west worthiness well-sized poetry brought away lands repaid got malice the-lion's carried.	Thorleif slendered the Tronds the prince's renown before the fellows, had no-little out the earl's abuse carried widely. Njord ruled the western worth well-sized poetry brought away lands repaid got for the lion's malice carried.
Þorleifur sagði konungi að hann fýstist út til Íslands og beiddi konung orlofs að fara þegar að vori.	Thorleif told the-king that he desired out-from to Iceland and asked the-king vacations to travel there in the-spring.	Thorleif told the king that he wished to travel out to Iceland and asked the king leave to travel there in the spring.
En konungur sagði svo vera skyldu "vil eg gefa þér skip í nafnfesti með mönnum og reiða og þvílíkri áhöfn sem þér þarfast".	Then the-king said so be-it should "wish i to-give you a-ship in name-giving with people and transport and accordingly-like crew as you need".	The king said that it would be so, "I wish to give you a ship as a name-gift, with people and transport and crew as you need".
Nú er Þorleifur þar um veturinn í góðu yfirlæti en að vordögum býr hann skip sitt og lét í haf og byrjaði vel og kom skipi sínu við Ísland í á þá er Þjórsá heitir.	Now was Thorleif there about winter in good favour and of spring-days prepared he ship his and had to sea and began well and came ship his to Iceland in river then was Thjorsa named.	Thorleif was there for the winter in great favour, and at the beginning of spring he prepared his ship and put to sea, and began well and his ship came to Iceland, into the river that was named Thjorsa.

The Tale of Thorlief the Earl's Poet (Old Icelandic)

Old Icelandic	Literal	English
Það segja menn að Þorleifur kvæntist um haustið og fengi þeirrar konu er Auður hét og væri Þórðar dóttir er bjó í Skógum undir Eyjafjöllum, gilds bónda og stórauðigs, kominn af ætt Þrasa hins gamla.	It is-said people that Thorleif got-married about autumn and got there a-wife who Aud was-named and was Thord daughter that lived in Skogar under Eyjafjoll-Mountains, strong farmer and great-wealth, came of descendents Thrasi the old.	People say that Thorleif got married in the autumn and had a wife who was named Aud, and she was the daughter of Thord of Skogar under the Eyjafjoll mountains, who was a successful and wealthy farmer, descended from Thrasi the old.
Auður var kvenskörungur mikill.	Aud was noble-woman much.	Aud was very much a noble woman.
Þorleifur sat um veturinn í Skógum en um vorið eftir keypti hann land að Höfðabrekku í Mýdal og bjó þar síðan.	Thorleif sat about winter in Skogar but about spring afterwards bought he land at Hofdabrekka in Myrdal-Valley and settled there since.	Thorleif spent the winter in Skogar, but the following spring he bought land at Hofdabrekka in the Myrdal valley and settled thereafter.

7

En nú er þar til að taka er Hákon jarl er, að honum batnaði hins mesta meinlætis en það segja sumir menn að hann yrði aldrei samur maður og áður og vildi jarl nú gjarna hefna Þorleifi þessar smánar ef hann gæti, heitir nú á fulltrúa sína, Þorgerði Hörgabrúði og Irpu systur hennar, að reka þann galdur út til Íslands að Þorleifi ynni að fullu og færir þeim miklar fórnir og gekk til fréttar.	But now is there to from take that Hakon the-earl was, that he bettered his most malignancy but that said some people that he became never the-same man of before and wished the-earl now gladly avenge Thorleif this humiliation if he could, called now on delegates his, Thorgerd Horgabrudi and Irpu sister hers, to drive then sorcery out to Iceland to Thorleif win-over that full and carried them much sacrifices and got to omens.	Now to take to the Earl Hakon, he mostly recovered from this malignancy, but some people said that he was never the same man as before, and the earl now wished to gladly avenge Thorleif of this humiliation if he could, he called on his delegates, Thorgerd Horgabrudi and her sister Irpu, to drive sorcery out to Iceland to defeat Thorleif fully, and he carried them many offerings and got omens.

The Tale of Thorlief the Earl's Poet (Old Icelandic)

Old Icelandic	Literal	English
En er hann fékk þá frétt er honum líkaði lét hann taka einn rekabút og gera úr trémann og með fjölkynngi og atkvæðum jarls en tröllskap og fítonsanda þeirra systra lét hann drepa einn mann og taka úr hjartað og láta í þenna trémann og færðu síðan í föt og gáfu nafn og kölluðu Þorgarð og mögnuðu hann með svo miklum fjandans krafti að hann gekk og mælti við menn, komu honum síðan í skip og sendu hann út til Íslands þess erindis að drepa Þorleif jarlaskáld.	And when he got then omens that he liked had he taken a drift-wood and made of wooden-man and with witchcraft and songs earls and witchcraft and magic there sisters had he kill one man and taken out heart and had in this wooden-man and brought afterwards to clothing and gave name and called Thorgard and power he with so much devil's power that he walked and talked with people, came to-him afterwards to a-ship and sent him out to Iceland this errand to kill Thorleif Earl's-Poet.	And when he got the omens that he liked, he took some drift wood and made a wooden man, and with his witchcraft and songs, and with the magic of his sisters, he had a man killed to take his heart and place in the wooden man, and afterwards brought clothing and gave him a name and called him Thorgard, and with the strong power of the devil he walked and talked with people, he was put on a ship and sent to Iceland on an errand to kill Thorleif the Earl's poet.
Gyrti Hákon hann atgeir þeim er hann hafði tekið úr hofi þeirra systra og Hörgi hafði átt.	Equipped Hakon him a-halberd then that he had taken out-of temple theirs sisters and Horgi had belonged.	Hakon gave him a halberd that he had taken out of the temple that belonged to his sisters at Horgi.
Þorgarður kom út til Íslands í þann tíma er menn voru á alþingi.	Thorgard came out to Iceland in that time that men were in assembly.	Thorgard came to Iceland at the time when people were at the assembly.
Þorleifur jarlaskáld var á þingi.	Thorleif Earl's-Poet was at assembly.	Thorleif's the Earl's Poet was at the assembly.
Það var einn dag að Þorleifur gekk frá búð sinni er hann sá að maður gekk vestan yfir Öxará.	It was one day that Thorleif went from booth his when he saw that a-man walked from-the-west over Oxara.	One day Thorleif went from his booth and saw a man walking from the west over the Oxara river.
Sá var mikill vexti og illslegur í bragði.	Saw was large grown and evil-like in movement.	He saw that he was large and evil looking in his movement.
Þorleifur spyr þenna mann að heiti.	Thorleif asked this man of name.	Thorleif asked this man his name.
Hann nefndist Þorgarður og kastaði þegar kaldyrðum að Þorleifi en er Þorleifur heyrði það ætlaði hann að bregða sverðinu konungsnaut er hann var gyrður með en í þessu bili lagði Þorgarður atgeirnum á Þorleifi miðjum og í gegnum hann.	He was-named Thorgard and cast straightaway cold-bloodedly to Thorleif and when Thorleif heard this intended he to draw the-sword king's-gift that he was equipped-with with but in this moment laid Thorgard halberd to Thorleif's middle and in through him.	He said that his name was Thorgard and looked at him cold-bloodedly, and when Thorleif heard this, he intended to draw the sword that king Svein had given to him, but in that moment, Thorgard laid his halberd through his middle.

The Tale of Thorlief the Earl's Poet (Old Icelandic)

Old Icelandic	Literal	English
En er hann fékk lagið hjó hann til Þorgarðs en hann steyptist í jörðina niður svo að í iljarnar var að sjá.	Then when he got laid struck he to Thorgard then he disappeared into the-earth down so that for soles-of-the-feet was to see.	Then when he was hit, he struck at Thorgard, but he had disappeared down into the earth so that only the soles of his feet could be seen.
Þorleifur snaraði að sér kyrtilinn og kvað vísu:	Thorleif twisted about himself tunic and spoke verse:	Thorleif twisted his tunic about him and spoke a verse:
Hvarf hinn hildardjarfi, hvað varð af Þorgarði? villumaðr á velli, vígdjarfr refilstiga.	Disappeared the courageous-warrior, what became of Thorgard? villain in the-fields, slaying-warrior mysterious-path.	The courageous warrior disappeared, what became of Thorgard? the villain in the fields, the slaying warrior's mysterious path.
Farið hefir Gautr að grjóti gunnelds hinn fjölkunni, síðan mun hann í helju hvílast stund og mílu.	Gone has Odin to rocks battle-fire the skilled-in-magic, after shall he in Hel rest awhile and mile.	Odin has gone to the rocks, battle-fired the skills in magic, after shall be in Hel and rest awhile a mile.
Þá gekk Þorleifur heim til búðar sinnar og sagði mönnum þenna atburð og þótti öllum mikils um vert um þenna atburð.	Then went Thorleif home to booth his and told people these events and thought all much about had-been about these events.	Thorleif went back to his booth and told people of these events, and people thought much about these events.
Síðan varpar Þorleifur frá sér kyrtlinum og féllu þá út iðrin og lét Þorleifur þar líf sitt við góðan orðstír og þótti mönnum það allmikill skaði.	Afterwards threw Thorleif from himself tunic and fell then out bowels and laid Thorleif there life his with good fame and thought people that all-great harm.	Afterwards Thorleif threw off his tunic and his bowels spilled out, and he laid his life there with good fame, and all people thought that this was a great harm.
Þóttust nú allir vita að Þorgarður þessi hafði engi verið annar en galdur og fjölkynngi Hákonar jarls.	Thought now all certainly that Thorgard this had none been other than sorcery and witchcraft Hakon's the-earl.	They thought that it was certain that this Thorgard had been none other than the sorcery and witchcraft of Earl Hakon.
Síðan var Þorleifur heygður.	Afterwards was Thorleif buried.	Afterwards Thorleif was buried.
Haugur hans stendur norður af lögréttu og sést hann enn.	Mound his stood north of law-assembly and seen he was.	His mound stood north of the law assembly and could be seen from there.

The Tale of Thorlief the Earl's Poet (Old Icelandic)

Old Icelandic	Literal	English
Bræður hans voru á þingi er þetta var tíðinda og gerðu útferð Þorleifs sæmilega og erfðu hann að fornum sið en Ásgeir faðir þeirra var þá litlu andaður.	Brothers his was at assembly when this was news and made funeral Thorleif's fair and inherited he the ancient traditions as Asgeir father theirs was then recently died.	His brothers were at the assembly when this became news, and they gave Thorleif a fair funeral feast according to the ancient traditions that his father Asgeir had when he recently died.
Síðan fóru menn heim af þingi og fréttust þessi tíðindi nú víða um Ísland og þóttu mikils verð.	Afterwards went people home from assembly and reported this news now widely about Iceland and thought a-great price.	Afterwards people went home from the assembly and reported this news widely about Iceland, and everyone thought it a great cost.

8   8   8

Old Icelandic	Literal	English
Sá maður bjó þá á Þingvelli er Þorkell hét.	So a-man lived then at Thingvellir who-was Thorkell named.	So there was a man who lived that Thingvellir and was named Thorkell.
Hann var auðigur maður að ganganda fé og hafði jafnan hægt í búi.	He was wealthy man as went cattle and had equally comfortable in farm.	He was a wealth man with regard to cattle, and had a comfortable farm.
Engi var hann virðingamaður.	None was he man-of-high-rank.	He was not a man of high rank.
Sauðamaður hans hét Hallbjörn og var kallaður hali.	Shepherd his named Hallbjorn and was called Hali.	He shepherd was named Hallbjorn but people called him Hali (Tail).
Hann vandist oftlega til að koma á haug Þorleifs og svaf þar um nætur og hélt þar nálægt fé sínu.	He did often to that came to mound Thorleif's and slept there about night and held there close cattle his.	He often came to Thorleif's mound and slept there through the night and held his cattle close there.
Kemur honum það jafnan í hug að hann vildi geta ort lof kvæði nokkurt um haugbúann og talar það jafnan er hann liggur á hauginum en sakir þess að hann var ekki skáld og hann hafði þeirrar listar eigi fengið fékk hann ekki kveðið og komst aldrei lengra áfram fyrir honum um skáldskapinn en hann byrjaði svo:	Came he that equally in thoughts that he wished get words praise poem some about the-mound-dweller and said that usually when he lay about the-mound but for-the-sake this that he was not poet and he had there art not got went he not poem but came never longer not-further for him about poetry that he began so:	Thoughts often came to him that he wished to compose words of praise about the mound dweller, and he usually said so when he lay about the mound, but because he was not a good poet and did not have the gift, he never managed to compose anything longer than the beginning:
Hér liggr skáld.	Here lies a-poet.	Here lies a poet.

The Tale of Thorlief the Earl's Poet (Old Icelandic)

Old Icelandic	Literal	English
En meira gat hann ekki kveðið.	Then more could he not put-to-words.	Then he could not put more to words.
Það var eina nátt sem oftar að hann liggur á hauginum og hefir hina sömu iðn fyrir stafni ef hann gæti aukið nokkuð lof um haugbúann.	It was one night as often that he laid about the-mound and had then same craft for staves if he got increase some praise about the-mound-dweller.	One night as usual he was lying on the mound and was still trying to craft some verses and write any more in praise about the mound dweller.
Síðan sofnar hann og eftir það sér hann að opnast haugurinn og gengur þar út maður mikill vexti og vel búinn.	Afterwards slept he and after that saw he that open the-mound and went there out a-man great grown and well prepared.	Then he fell asleep and after that he saw that the mound opened, and a large man came out, and he was well dressed.
Hann gekk upp á hauginn að Hallbirni og mælti:	He went up to the-mound to Hallbjorn and spoke:	He went up to the mound and said to Hallbjorn:
"Þar liggur Hallbjörn og vildir þú fást í því sem þér er ekki lánað, að yrkja lof um mig og er það annaðhvort að þér verður lagið í þessi íþrótt og munt þú það af mér fá meira en vel flestum mönnum öðrum og er það vænna að svo verði ella þarftu ekki í þessu að brjótast lengur.	"There lies Hallbjorn and wish you get with therefore which you are not gifted, that compose praise about me and is that either-way that you become have of this skilled and shall you that of me have more than well most people others and is that good that so becomes or need not of this to break longer.	"There you lie, Hallbjorn, and you would like to catch something not in your power, to compose praise about me, and either you will become skilled and you can get this from me more than others, as is likely to happen, or else there is no need for you to continue any longer.
Skal eg nú kveða fyrir þér vísu og ef þú getur numið vísuna og kannt hana þá er þú vaknar þá munt þú verða þjóðskáld og yrkja lof um marga höfðingja og mun þér í þessi íþrótt mikið lagið verða".	Shall i now speak before you verse and if you can take verse and know it then when you awake then shall you become skilled-poet and compose praise about many chieftains and should you in this skilled much have become".	I shall now speak a verse for you, and if you can take this verse and know it, then when you awake, you shall become a skilled poet and compose praise about many chieftains, and you shall have become much skilled in this".
Síðan togar hann á honum tunguna og kvað vísu þessa:	Afterwards pulled he of his tongue and spoke verse this:	Then he pulled his tongue and spoke this verse:
Hér liggr skáld það er skálda	Here lies poet that is of-poets	Here lies a poet that is of all poets
var mestr að flestu.	was the-greatest of. the-most	he was the greatest of the most.
Naddveiti frá eg nýtan	Provided-knowing from i am-able	I hear that he was able
níð Hákoni smíða.	abuse of-Hakon created.	to craft abuse of Hakon.
Áðr gat engr né síðan	After got none nor afterwards	None before or after,

The Tale of Thorlief the Earl's Poet (Old Icelandic)

Old Icelandic	Literal	English
annarra svo manna, frægt hefir orðið það fyrðum, férán lokið hánum.	others so people, fame had words that warriors, plunder end his.	of so many other people, had fame of words that warriors ended his plunder.
"Nú skaltu svo hefja skáldskapinn að þú skalt yrkja lofkvæði um mig þá er þú vaknar og vanda sem mest bæði hátt og orðfæri og einna mest kenningar".	"Now shall so begin poetry that you shall compose praise-words about me then when you awake and care that most both high and vocabulary and only the-best kennings".	"Now you shall begin your poetry that you shall compose words of praise about me, then when you awake, take care that it is both high in vocabulary and the best kennings".
Síðan hverfur hann aftur í hauginn og lýkst hann aftur en Hallbjörn vaknar og þykist sjá á herðar honum.	Afterwards turned he back into the-mound and closed he returned then Hallbjorn awoke and thought saw of shoulders his.	Afterwards he turned back into the mound and it closed behind him, then Hallbjorn awoke and thought he saw his shoulders.
Síðan kunni hann vísuna og fór síðan til byggða heim með fé sitt eftir tíma og sagði þenna atburð.	Afterwards knew he verse and travelled since to settlement home with wealth his after time and said then events.	Afterwards he remembered the verse and then went back to the farm with his flock after a time and told of these events.
Orti Hallbjörn síðan lofkvæði um haugbúann og var hið mesta skáld og fór utan fljótlega og kvað kvæði um marga höfðingja og fékk af þeim miklar virðingar og góðar gjafir og græddi af því stórfé, og gengur af honum mikil saga bæði hér á landi og útlendis þó að hún sé hér eigi rituð.	Words Hallbjorn since praise-words about the-mound-dweller and was then the-best poet and travelled out soon and spoke poems about many chieftains and got of them much honour and good gifts and profit of therefore great-wealth, and went of him much stories both here about the-land and other-lands though that it being here not written.	Hallbjorn composed since words of praise about the mound dweller and was the best poet, and he frequently travelled abroad and composed poems about many chieftains and received from them much honour and good gifts from them, and his wealth increased, and there went many stories about him both in Iceland and abroad, but they are not written down here.
En frá bræðrum Þorleifs er það að segja að næsta sumar eftir andlát hans fóru þeir utan, Ólafur völubrjótur og Helgi hinn frækni, og ætluðu til hefnda eftir bróður sinn.	Then from brothers Thorleif's was it to say that next summer after death his travelled they out, Olaf knuckle-breaker and Helgi the brave, and supposed to revenge after brother theirs.	Then to Thorleif's brothers to say that the next summer after his death day, Olaf knuckle-breaker and Helgi the brave travelled out and intended to get revenge for their brother.
En þeim varð eigi lagið þá enn að standa yfir höfuðsvörðum Hákonar jarls því að hann hafði þá enn eigi öllu illu því fram farið sem honum varð lagið sér til skammar og skaða.	But they were not laid then but to stand over head-skin Hakon's the-earl because that he had then but not all evil such from going as he was laid to-him to shame and damage.	But they were not yet fated to have Earl Hakon's scalp, because he had not yet done all of the evil which was destined for his shame and harm.

The Tale of Thorlief the Earl's Poet (Old Icelandic)

Old Icelandic	Literal	English
En þó brenndu þeir mörg hof fyrir jarlinum og gerðu honum margan fjárskaða í ránum og hervirki er þeir veittu honum og margri annarri óspekt.	But though burned they many temples for the-earl and did to-him many wealth-damage in robbery and plundering that they granted him and many other disturbances.	But they managed to burn many of the earl's temples, and did much to damage his wealth with robbery and plundering, and they granted him many other disturbances.
Og lýkur hér frá Þorleifi að segja.	And ends here from Thorleif to say.	And this is the end of what there is to say about Thorleif.

Word List (Old Icelandic to English)

Old Icelandic	English

A, a

að	a, about, and, as, at, for, from, in, it, of, that, the, then, this, to
aðfangskveld	midwinter-evening
aðrar	other
aðrir	other, others
af	from, from, in, of, of, off
afliðið	following
aftur	after, back, returned, returning
afturreka	back-driven
aldrei	never
aldri	age
aldur	age
alfari	for-good
alla	all, all
allan	all
allir	all
allmikill	all-great
allri	all
alls	all
allt	all, all
alþingi	assembly
andaður	died
andar	soul
andlát	death
andvana	destitution
annaðhvort	either-way
annan	a-second
annar	another, other
annarra	other, others
annarri	other
annars	another's
atburð	events
atburðir	events
atgeir	a-halberd
atgeirnum	halberd
atgervi	deeds
atgervimaður	accomplished-man
atkvæðum	songs

Old Icelandic	English
auðigur	wealthy
Auður	Aud (name), Aud (name)
aukið	increase
austur	east

Á, á

á	about, at, for, from, had, in, it, of, on, river, that, this, to
áðr	after
áður	before, return
áfram	not-further
áhöfn	crew
án	without
ánauð	enslavement
Ásgeir	Asgeir (name)
Ásgeiri	Asgeir (name)
ásjá	assistance
ástfóstur	foster-care
ásum	poles
át	eat
átján	eighteen
átt	belonged, had
áttu	had

Æ, æ

æfur	angry
ærnri	merry
æti	ate, had
ætlaði	intended
ætluðu	supposed
ætt	ancestors, ancestry, descendents
ævintýr	adventure

B, b

bað	asked, bid, invited
báðir	both

260

Word List (Old Icelandic to English)

Old Icelandic	English
bæði	both
bæginn	troubled
bani	dead
báru	carried
batna	better
batnaði	bettered
báts	boats
beiddi	asked
beiddist	asked
bekkjunauta	bench-fellows
betur	better
biður	asked
bili	moment
binda	bound, tied-up
bindur	bound
bjart	bright
bjó	lived, prepared, settled
blekkir	deceived
Blönduósi	Blonduos (place)
blygðar	shame
boðið	invited
böggva	the-mauler
bölvaðra	cursed
bónda	farmer
borð	the-tables
borið	carried
bornir	carried
bráðlega	quickly
bræðrum	brothers
bræður	brothers
brag	poetry
bragði	movement
branda	swords
bregða	draw
bregður	tricked
Brekku	Brekka (place)
brenna	burned, burnt
brenndu	burned
brjótast	break
broddur	spikes
bróður	brother
brot	away
brott	away
búð	booth
búðanna	booths

Old Icelandic	English
búðar	booth
búi	farm
búið	done, settled
búinn	prepared
búkinn	body
burt	away
byggða	settlement
býr	prepared
byrjaði	began
byrjar	fair-wind
býsn	strangeness

D, d

dæmt	deem
dag	day
daginn	the-day
dálegra	harmful
Danmerkur	Denmark (place)
dauðu	dead
diska	plates
dögum	days
dökkri	dark
dóttir	daughter
draga	drew
drápu	phrases
dregr	draws
dregur	drawn
drekktur	drowned
drengjum	the-fellows
drengr	men
drepa	kill
drykkju	drink
drykkjuborð	drinking-tables
dýflissu	dungeon
dýrstum	dearest
dyrum	doors

E, e

eða	either, or
eðli	nature
ef	if
efnilegir	promising

Word List (Old Icelandic to English)

Old Icelandic	English
efsta	upper
eftir	after, afterwards
eftirmáls	after-the-case
eg	i, if
eiga	not
eigi	not
eigið	own
eign	owning
eina	a, one
einn	a, one
einna	only
Eiríks	Erik's (name)
ekki	not
ella	or
elli	age
ellina	age
elsti	eldest
en	and, as, but, than, that, the, then, when
enda	and, end
engi	none
Englandi	England (place)
engr	none
enn	but, was
er	am, are, as, from, has, is, it-is, that, the, was, what, when, which, who, who-was
erfðu	inherited
erindis	errand
ertu	are-you
eru	are, they-were, we-are
eta	eat
etið	to-eat
Eyjafjöllum	Eyjafjoll-Mountains (place)
eymd	misery
eyri	sand

É, é

él	blizzard

F, f

Old Icelandic	English
fá	get, have
faðir	father
fæ	can, get
færa	bring, brought
færðu	brought
færir	carried
Fagurkinn	Fair-Cheek (name)
fann	found
fara	travel
fararefna	travel-goods
farið	going, gone, travelled
farning	passage
fast	close, closed, closely
fást	get
fé	cattle, wealth
fegins	relieved
fékk	got, went
félaga	companions
féll	fell
féllu	fell
fellur	fell
fengi	got
fengið	caught, got
fer	travelled, went
férán	plunder
ferð	travel
ferðar	travel
ferðum	journey
fertuga	forty
festist	grips
fíl	elephant
finnur	found
fítonsanda	magic
fjandans	devil's
fjárhlut	fee-lot, financial-share
fjárskaða	wealth-damage
fjártjón	financial-loss
fjölkunni	skilled-in-magic
fjölkynngi	witchcraft
fjölmenni	following-men
fleira	more
flestu	the-most
flestum	most
fljótasta	soonest

Word List (Old Icelandic to English)

Old Icelandic	English
fljótlega	soon
flutt	performed
flytja	to-carry
flyttu	move
föður	father
fór	travelled, went
fornfræði	ancient-ways
fórnir	sacrifices
fornlegum	ancient-ways
fornum	ancient
forsmáður	shamed
fóru	travelled, went
förunauta	companions
fóstra	foster-father
fóstri	fostered
föt	clothing
frá	from
fræðum	instruction
frægt	fame
frækni	brave
frænda	kinsmen
fram	forward, from
framan	in-front-of
framaverka	previous-deeds
framleiðslu	causing
frásagnar	from-told
frétt	omens
fréttar	omens
fréttist	sought
fréttust	reported
fullkomið	full-coming
fulltingi	assistance
fulltrúa	delegates
fullu	full
fund	find, meet
fylgdi	followed
fylgt	followed
fyr	before
fyrðum	warriors
fyrir	before, before him, for
fyrr	before
fyrst	first
fýsi	desire
fýstist	desired

G, g

Old Icelandic	English
gáði	cared
gæti	could, got
gaf	gave
gáfu	gave
gáir	care
galdur	sorcery
galt	repaid
gamall	old
gamla	old
gamlir	old-man
ganga	go, went
ganganda	went
gangi	moved
Gáseyri	Gaseyri (place)
gat	could, got
Gautr	Odin (name)
geðjast	liking
gefa	give, to-give
gegnum	through
geitarskegg	goat-beard
geitarskegginu	goat-beard
gekk	got, walked, went
gengið	gone
gengur	going, went
ger	made
gera	done, made
gerði	did, had-done, it-was
gerðist	happened
gerðu	did, made
gerist	becoming
gerningum	witchcraft
gert	done
gervi	character
gervilegur	talented
gervina	disguise
geta	get
getið	told-of
getur	can, get
geysimjög	exceedingly-much
giftu	luck
gilds	strong
gildur	capable
gíman	opening

Word List (Old Icelandic to English)

Old Icelandic	English
ginnti	tricked
gjafir	gifts
gjalda	repay
gjallandason	son-of-gjallandi
gjarna	gladly
gjöld	repayment
glögglega	clearly
goða	the-chieftain
góða	food
góðan	good
góðar	good
goði	chieftain
góðu	good, improvement
göldrum	magical-arts
gömlum	old
góss	belongings
gott	good
græddi	profit
grálega	malice
gramr	warrior
greiðlega	promptly, quickly
grenndi	slendered
grjóti	rocks
guðníðingskapur	idol-worship
Guðs	God (name)
gulls	of-gold
gunnelds	battle-fire
gyrður	equipped-with
gyrti	equipped

H, h

Old Icelandic	English
hægt	comfortable, possible
hækjur	crutches
hækjurnar	the-crutches
haf	sea
hafa	had, have
hafði	had
hafi	have
hafið	have
haft	have
Hákon	Hakon (name)
Hákonar	Hakon (name), Hakon's (name)
hákoni	of-Hakon
halda	hold
hálf	half
Hali	Hali (name)
Hallbirni	Hallbjorn (name)
Hallbjörn	Hallbjorn (name)
hálminn	the-straw
hana	it
hann	he, him
hans	he, his
hánum	his
harðfengi	toughness
harðla	hardly
harðleikinn	rough
harðúðigur	harsher
háreysti	commotion
hárið	hair
hark	noise
háseta	first-mate
hásetum	crew
hataður	hated
hátt	high
háttum	custom
haug	mound
haugbúann	the-mound-dweller
hauginn	the-mound
hauginum	the-mound
haugur	mound
haugurinn	the-mound
haustið	autumn
hefi	have
hefir	had, has, have, having
hefja	begin
hefna	avenge
hefnda	revenge
hefur	had
hegningartíminn	punishment-time
heim	home, homes
heita	call, named, promise
heiti	name, named
heitir	called, named
heldur	rather
Helgi	Helgi (name)
heljarkarl	hellish-old-man
Helju	Hel (place)
hélt	held

264

Word List (Old Icelandic to English)

Old Icelandic	English
hendi	hands
hengja	hanged
hennar	hers, its
hentar	requirements
hentugri	more-convenient
hér	here
herðar	shoulders
herra	lord
hervirki	plundering
hét	named, promised, was-named
heygður	buried
heyrði	heard
heyrðu	heard
heyrið	hear
heyrt	heard
hið	the, then
hildardjarfi	courageous-warrior
himins	heaven's
hina	then
hingað	here
hinn	the, those
hinni	the
hins	his, the
hinu	the
hinum	other
hít	bag
hítina	the-bag
hitti	met
hjartað	heart
hjó	struck
Hlaðajarl	Earl-Of-Lade (name)
Hlaðajarls	Earl-Of-Lade (name)
Hlaðir	Lade (place)
hleypur	ran
Hlöðum	Lade (place)
hlógu	laughed
hlýða	listen, to-hear
hlýdduð	listen-to
hof	temples
hóf	began
Höfðabrekku	Hofdabrekka (place)
höfðingja	chieftains, chieftains'
höfðingjum	chieftains
höfðingskap	lordship
hofi	temple
höfuðsvörðum	head-skin
höfum	have
höllina	the-hall
höllinni	the-hall
honum	he, he-had, him, his, to-him
Hörgabrúði	Horgabrudi (name)
Hörgi	Horgi (place)
hríð	awhile
hrífa	scratched
hring	a-ring
hróðr	renown
hrollir	shivering
hrukku	drew
hug	thoughts
hugr	heart
hugsa	think
hún	it, she
hvað	what
hvarf	disappeared
hver	who
hverfur	turned
hvergi	each
hverjum	each, who's
hvern	one's
hverri	each
hversu	however, how-so
hvert	each
hví	why
hvílast	rest
hvorri	each
hvort	whether

I, i

Old Icelandic	English
iðn	craft
iðrin	bowels
iljarnar	soles-of-the-feet
illa	bad, badly, ill
illslegur	evil-like
illu	evil
illur	bad, ill
inn	in
Irpu	Irpu (name)

Word List (Old Icelandic to English)

Old Icelandic	English

Í, í

í	about, at, for, from, in, into, of, to, with
Ísland	Iceland (place)
Íslandi	Iceland (place)
Íslands	Iceland (place)
íþrótt	skilled
íþrótta	skills
íþróttamaður	excellent-man
íþróttir	skilled
ítri	high-born

J, j

jafnan	equally, usually
jarl	earl, the-earl
Jarlaskáld	Earl's-Poet (name)
jarli	earl, the-earl
jarlinn	the-earl
jarlinum	the-earl
jarls	earls, the-earl, the-earl's
jarlsníði	the-earl's-abuse
jarlsníðs	earl's-abuse
járn	iron-weapon
Jóla	Yule (name)
jólaveislunnar	yule-feast
jörðina	the-earth
Jóta	Jutland (place)

K, k

kaldyrðum	cold-bloodedly
kalla	call, called, call-to
kallaður	called
kann	can
kannt	know
Karl	Karl (name), old-man, the-old-man
karli	man, the-old-man
kastaði	cast
kaupir	bought
kaupmönnum	trading-men
kaupslagar	bargaining
kaupstaðinn	market-town
kaupunauta	customers
kaupunautar	customers
kemur	came, comes
kenna	teach
kenndur	known
kenningar	kennings
keypti	bought
kláði	itching
Klaufa	Klaufi (name)
knarrar	merchant-ships, of-the-ship
knúta	knots
kol	the-coals
köld	cold
köldu	cold
köldum	cold
kölluðu	called
kolum	coals
kom	came, come, could
koma	came, come, come-with
komast	come
kömbum	combs
komi	comes
kominn	came, comes, coming
komst	came
komu	came
kona	a-woman, wife, woman
konu	a-wife
konung	the-king
konungi	the-king
konungs	the-king
konungsnaut	king's-gift
konungur	the-king
Konurvísur	Woman-Verses (name)
kost	food, provide
krafti	power
krókóttum	devious
kunni	knew
kvað	said, spoke
kvaddi	greeted
kvaðningar	greeting

Word List (Old Icelandic to English)

Old Icelandic	English
kvæði	poem, poems
kvæðið	poem, the-poem
kvæðislaunum	poem's-reward
kvæntist	got-married
kvala	torment
kveða	recites, say, speak
kveðið	poem, put-to-words, spoken
kveður	said
kveldið	evening
kvenskörungur	noble-woman
kyndugskap	cunning
kynferði	kinsmen-origins
kynjaður	descended
kynstrum	strange
kyrr	sit-still
kyrtilinn	tunic
kyrtlinum	tunic

L, l

Old Icelandic	English
lætur	had, left
lagasetning	legislation
lagði	had, laid
lagið	have, laid
lánað	gifted
land	land, the-land
landi	the-land
lands	lands
lásum	locks
lát	let
láta	allow, had
láti	had
látið	let
laun	secrecy
launað	repay
legið	laying
leið	journey, passed
leiðarnests	food
leitaði	sought
lengi	long
lengja	lengthen
lengra	longer
lengur	for-long, longer
leóns	the-lion's

Old Icelandic	English
lét	had, laid, let
létti	relief
leysa	solve
líf	life
lífsdaga	life-days
lífstíma	lifetime
liggr	lies
liggur	laid, lay, lies
líkaði	liked
líkama	body
líkar	like
linnir	stopped
listar	art
lítillæti	a-little, humility
lítils	little
lítinn	little
litlu	recently
Ljótólfi	Ljotolf (name)
Ljótólfs	Ljotolf (name)
Ljótólfur	Ljotolf (name)
ljótu	ghastly
lof	praise
lofaði	praised
lofkvæði	praise-words
lögréttu	law-assembly
lokið	end
luktum	shut
lýkst	closed
lýkur	ends

M, m

Old Icelandic	English
má	may
maður	a-man, man
mælt	said
mælti	spoke, talked
mál	matter
mann	man
manna	man's, men, men, people
mannalát	manslaughter
manni	people
mannillska	man-evil
manninn	people
marga	many

Word List (Old Icelandic to English)

Old Icelandic	English
margan	many
margir	many
margkunnandi	many-known
margra	many, much
margri	many
mart	many
matar	food
mátti	may
með	with
mega	may
megi	may
megin	side
meinlætis	malignancy
meinlætum	malignance
meir	more
meira	more
menn	men, people
mér	i-am, me, to-me
mest	most, the-best
mesta	most, the-best
mesti	most
mestr	the-greatest
miðdigur	broad-waist
Miðfirði	Midfjord (place)
Miðfjarðar-Skeggja	Midfjorder-Skeggi (name)
miðju	middle-of
miðjum	middle
miðs	middle
mig	me, shall-i
mikið	most, much
mikil	much
mikill	great, large, much
mikils	a-great, much
mikinn	much
mikla	much
miklar	much
miklum	much
milli	between
mílu	mile
minn	mine
minnkaði	decreased
mislíkaði	misliked
missa	miss
mitt	mine
mjög	much

Old Icelandic	English
móður	mother
móðurbróður	mother's-brother
mögnuðu	power
mökkr	thick-clouds
mönnum	men, people, peoples'
mörg	many
mörgum	many
morguninn	morning
mörk	a-mark
mörkum	marshes
mun	must, shall, should
mundi	would
mundu	would
munn	mouth
munt	shall
munuð	shall, should
munum	shall
Mýdal	Myrdal-Valley (place)
myrkrið	the-darkness
myrkt	dark

N, n

Old Icelandic	English
naddveiti	provided-knowing
náði	caught
naðrbings	dragon
nær	near
næsta	next
næstir	nearest
nætur	night
nafn	name
nafnfesti	name-giving
nafni	name
nákvæmi	pernickety
nálægt	close
nam	took
náms	take
nátt	night
náttúra	nature
né	nor
nefndist	was-named
nema	except, taken, unless
níð	abuse
níðið	the-abuse
Níðungur	Nidung (name)

Word List (Old Icelandic to English)

Old Icelandic	English
niður	down
nítján	nineteen
Njörðr	Njord (name)
nokkuð	any, some, something, somewhat
nokkur	anything
nokkura	some
nokkurar	some
nokkurt	some
nökkvi	the-ship
norður	north
Noreg	Norway (place)
Noregs	Norway (place)
nóttina	the-night
nú	now
numið	take
nýtan	am-able

O, o

Old Icelandic	English
ofan	over
ofanverðum	the-uppermost
ofléttlega	willingly
oft	often
oftar	often
oftlega	often
og	also, and, but, of
opnast	open
orð	words
orðfæri	vocabulary
orðið	become, words
orðskvið	proverb
orðstír	fame
orlof	leave
orlofs	vacations
ort	worded, words
orti	words
oss	us, we

Ó, ó

Old Icelandic	English
óbætilegs	un-redeemable
óðali	estate
ófreklegar	un-eagerly
ógert	undone
ógladdist	un-gladdened
ógleði	un-gladness
ógleður	un-glad
óhljóði	unsoundly
óhöfðinglegt	chieftain-like
ókunna	unknown
Ólafs	Olaf's (name)
Ólafur	Olaf (name)
ólítið	no-little
óloknum	undone
óminnis	amnesia
óspekt	disturbances
óværa	restlessness
óværi	restlessness
óvant	not-lacking
óvinarins	the-enemy's
óvit	unconsciousness

Ö, ö

Old Icelandic	English
öðlings	noble
öðrum	other, others
öldu	wave
öllu	all
öllum	all, of-all
önga	none
öngu	not
örleik	generosity
örvænt	desperation
örverpi	decrepitude
Öxará	Oxara (place)

P, p

Old Icelandic	English
peninga	money

R, r

Old Icelandic	English
ráðum	advice
ræður	hired
rændi	robbed
ræsta	cleared

Word List (Old Icelandic to English)

Old Icelandic	English
raknaði	recovered
ránum	robbery
Rauðfeldur	Red-Cloak (name)
Rauði	Red (name)
réð	ruled
refilstiga	mysterious-path
reiða	transport
reikar	parting
reka	drive
rekabút	drift-wood
Reykjum	Reykir (place)
reyndar	actually
ríða	rose
ríkur	powerful
rís	rose
rituð	written
roðið	reddened
röðla	wheel
rotnað	decayed
ryðja	cleared
ryður	cleared

S, s

Old Icelandic	English
sá	saw, so
sækja	sake
sællífi	blessed-life
sæmd	honour
sæmilega	fair, properly
sæti	sit
sætis	sit
saga	stories
sagði	said, said, told
sagður	said
sagt	said
sakir	for-the-sake, sake, with-conviction
saman	together
samsætis	banquet
samur	the-same
sannlega	truly
sat	sat
satt	true
sauðamaður	shepherd
sé	being, himself, see
segðu	say-you
segið	said
segir	said
segist	say
segja	is-said, said, say
seigt	tough
selja	to-sell
sem	as, that, what, which
sendu	sent
sér	for-himself, he, he-himself, him, himself, his, saw, to-him
sest	sat
sést	seen
sið	traditions
síðan	after, afterwards, since
síðasta	last
síður	less
sig	him
sigldu	sailed
sína	himself, his
sinn	his, theirs
sinna	his
sinnar	his
sinni	himself, his
síns	his
sínu	his
sínum	his
sitt	his
sjá	saw, see
sjálfráða	ourselves-decide
skaða	damage
skaði	harm
skal	shall
skáld	a-poet, poet
skálda	of-poets
skaldi	the-poet
skáldskap	poetry
skáldskapinn	poetry
skalt	shall
skaltu	shall, shall-you
skammar	shame
skapaðir	shaped
skegg	beard
Skeggi	Skeggi (name)

Word List (Old Icelandic to English)

Old Icelandic	English
Skeggja	Skeggi (name)
skildu	parted
skip	a-ship, ship
skipaði	arranged
skipi	ship
skipið	the-ship
skips	ship, ships
skipti	exchanged
skjóta	launched
skógum	forests, Skogar (place)
skörulega	boldly
skörungur	noble
skruma	show-off, swagger
skyldi	should
skyldu	should
skyldur	should
slægða	slyness
sléttri	levelled
slíkt	such
smánar	humiliation
smíða	created
snaraði	twisted
snemma	early-age
snýr	turned
snýst	turned
sofnar	slept
sögðu	said
sögu	saga
sögur	sagas
sölur	sale
sömu	same
son	son
sonar	son
sótt	sought
spurði	asked, learned
spurn	learned
spurt	learned
spyr	asked, asks, learned
spyrja	ask
staðið	stand
stafina	sticks
stafkarl	beggar
stafkarla	beggars
stafkarlar	beggars
stafkarls	as-a-beggar, beggar's
stafni	staves
standa	stand, stood
stef	stave
stendur	stood
steyptist	disappeared
stóð	stood
stóra	large
stórættaður	great-family
stórauðigs	great-wealth
stórfé	great-wealth
stórmenni	great-men
strigadúk	sack-cloth
stumrar	stumbled
stund	awhile
stundlegum	temporary
stutt	short
styrk	support
suður	south
sumar	summer
sumir	some
sumrinu	the-summer
svaf	slept
svara	answered
svarar	answered
Svarfaðardal	Svarfardal (place)
Svarfdæla	Svarfardal (place)
svarri	grave
Sveins	Svein (name)
svengd	hungry
sverð	a-sword
sverðinu	the-sword
Svíþjóð	Sweden (place)
svo	so
svöngum	hunger
sýnast	appear
sýndist	seemed-to
sýnduð	give-performance
syni	sons
Syrgisdölum	Syrgsdalir (place)
systra	sisters
systur	sister

T, t

Word List (Old Icelandic to English)

Old Icelandic	English
taka	take, taken, took
talað	told
talar	said
tekið	taken
tekur	take, took
tíðinda	news
tíðindi	news
tíðindum	news
til	for, the, to, until
tíma	time
tímir	time
togar	pulled
tók	received, took
töluðu	told
trautt	scarcely
trémann	wooden-man
tröllskap	witchcraft
tunguna	tongue
tvær	two
tvo	two

Þ, þ

Old Icelandic	English
þá	then
það	it, that, the, this, with
þakkaði	thanked
þann	than, that, then
þar	them, there
þarf	needed
þarfa	needed
þarfaði	needed
þarfast	need
þarftu	need
þau	they
þegar	straightaway, there
þeim	them, then, they
þeir	they
þeirra	theirs, there
þeirrar	there
þengils	the-prince
þenna	the, then, these, this, those
þér	to-you, you
þess	this
þessa	this
þessar	this
þessi	this
þessu	this
þessum	this
þetta	this
þig	you
þín	your
þingi	assembly
Þingvelli	Thingvellir (place)
þinn	you
þinna	yours
þinni	yours
þínum	yours
þitt	yours
þjóanna	thighs
þjóðskáld	skilled-poet
þjóin	thighs
þjónustumenn	servants
Þjórsá	Thjorsa (place)
þó	though
þökk	thanks
þoku	fog
Þokuvísur	Fog-verses (name)
þola	endure
þoldu	endured
Þórðar	Thord (name)
Þorgarð	Thorgard (name)
Þorgarði	Thorgard (name)
Þorgarðs	Thorgard (name)
Þorgarður	Thorgard (name)
Þorgerði	Thorgerd (name)
Þórhildur	Thorhild (name)
Þorkell	Thorkell (name)
Þorleif	Thorleif (name)
Þorleifi	Thorleif (name), thorleif's
Þorleifr	Thorleif (name)
þorleifs	thorleif's, Thorleif's (name)
Þorleifur	Thorleif (name), Thorleif (name)
þorpara	peasant
þorsta	thirsty
þótti	thought
þóttist	thought

Word List (Old Icelandic to English)

Old Icelandic	English
þóttu	thought
þóttust	thought
Þrænda	the-Tronds' (name)
Þrándheim	Trondheim (place)
Þrasa	Thrasi (name)
þriðjung	third
þrjá	three
þrotnum	waning
þú	you
þunga	heavy
þurfa	need
því	accordingly, because, since, such, then, therefore
þvílíkri	accordingly-like
þykir	seems, thought
þykist	thought
þykjast	considered
þykklega	arrogantly

U, u

Old Icelandic	English
um	about, at
umráða	about-advice
undan	back, out-of
undarlega	strange
undir	under, up-to
ungum	young
unni	loved
upp	up, upped
upphaf	beginning
uppi	up
urðu	became
utan	out, without
utarlega	out-lying

Ú, ú

Old Icelandic	English
úr	from, from-out-of, of, out, out-of
úrigur	unruly
út	out, out-from
útferð	funeral
úti	finished, out
útlægur	outlaw
útlendis	other-lands

V, v

Old Icelandic	English
vænna	good
væri	was, were
vaknar	awake, awoke
vald	power
valdi	controlled
valdið	caused
vanda	care
vandist	did
vandræði	difficulty
vanur	experienced
var	was, were
varð	became, was, were
varla	scarcely
varning	wares
varninginn	wares
varpar	threw
vegsummerki	evidence, traces
veit	knows
veittu	granted
vel	well
veldur	brought-about
velli	the-fields
vellstæri	well-sized
vér	we
vera	be, becoming, being, be-it, to-be
verð	price
verða	become
verði	become, becomes
verðir	will-be
verðugu	honour
verðum	worth
verður	became, become
verið	became, been, made
verki	work
verr	worst
vert	had-been
vesaldar	wretchedness
vestan	from-the-west, west
vestra	west

Word List (Old Icelandic to English)

Old Icelandic	English
vestur	west
vetra	winters
vetur	winter
veturinn	winter
vexti	grown
við	by, from, to, with
víða	widely
viðskiptis	behaved
vígdjarfr	slaying-warrior
Vík	Vik (place)
víkinni	the-bay
vil	wish
vildi	wish, wished
vildir	wish
viljið	will
viljum	wish, wish-to
villumaðr	villain
víls	advantage
vinsæl	popular
vinsældum	popularity
virðingamaður	man-of-high-rank
virðingar	honour
virðum	worthiness
visku	wisdom
víst	know
vísu	certainly, this-verse, verse
vísuna	verse
vísur	verses
vita	certainly, knew, know
vitja	know
vitur	wise
vó	killed
völdum	doing
völubrjótur	knuckle-breaker
von	hope
vonda	wicked
vor	spring
vordögum	spring-days
vori	the-spring
vorið	spring
vort	ours
voru	was, were

Y, y

Old Icelandic	English
yðrum	yours
yður	you, yours
yfir	over
yfirlæti	favour
yngsti	youngest
Yngvildi	Yngvild (name)
ynni	win-over
yrði	became
yrkja	compose
ytra	outside

Ý, ý

Old Icelandic	English
ýmist	either
ýtar	out

Word List (English to Old Icelandic)

Word List (English to Old Icelandic)

English	Old Icelandic
# A, a	
a	að, eina, einn
about	á, að, í, um
about-advice	umráða
abuse	níð
accomplished-man	atgervimaður
accordingly	því
accordingly-like	þvílíkri
actually	reyndar
advantage	víls
adventure	ævintýr
advice	ráðum
after	áðr, aftur, eftir, síðan
after-the-case	eftirmáls
afterwards	eftir, síðan
age	aldri, aldur, elli, ellina
a-great	mikils
a-halberd	atgeir
a-little	lítillæti
all	alla, alla, allan, allir, allri, alls, allt, allt, öllu, öllum
all-great	allmikill
allow	láta
also	og
am	er
am-able	nýtan
a-man	maður
a-mark	mörk
amnesia	óminnis
ancestors	ætt
ancestry	ætt
ancient	fornum
ancient-ways	fornfræði, fornlegum
and	að, en, enda, og
angry	æfur
another	annar
another's	annars
answered	svara, svarar
any	nokkuð
anything	nokkur
a-poet	skáld
appear	sýnast
are	er, eru
are-you	ertu
a-ring	hring
arranged	skipaði
arrogantly	þykklega
art	listar
as	að, en, er, sem
as-a-beggar	stafkarls
a-second	annan
Asgeir (name)	Ásgeir, Ásgeiri
a-ship	skip
ask	spyrja
asked	bað, beiddi, beiddist, biður, spurði, spyr
asks	spyr
assembly	alþingi, þingi
assistance	ásjá, fulltingi
a-sword	sverð
at	á, að, í, um
ate	æti
Aud (name)	Auður, Auður
autumn	haustið
avenge	hefna
awake	vaknar
away	brot, brott, burt
awhile	hríð, stund
a-wife	konu
awoke	vaknar
a-woman	kona
# B, b	
back	aftur, undan
back-driven	afturreka
bad	illa, illur
badly	illa
bag	hít
banquet	samsætis
bargaining	kaupslagar
battle-fire	gunnelds
be	vera
beard	skegg

Word List (English to Old Icelandic)

English	*Old Icelandic*
became	urðu, varð, verður, verið, yrði
because	því
become	orðið, verða, verði, verður
becomes	verði
becoming	gerist, vera
been	verið
before	áður, fyr, fyrir, fyrr
before him	fyrir
began	byrjaði, hóf
beggar	stafkarl
beggars	stafkarla, stafkarlar
beggar's	stafkarls
begin	hefja
beginning	upphaf
behaved	viðskiptis
being	sé, vera
be-it	vera
belonged	átt
belongings	góss
bench-fellows	bekkjunauta
better	batna, betur
bettered	batnaði
between	milli
bid	bað
blessed-life	sællífi
blizzard	él
Blonduos (place)	Blönduósi
boats	báts
body	búkinn, líkama
boldly	skörulega
booth	búð, búðar
booths	búðanna
both	báðir, bæði
bought	kaupir, keypti
bound	binda, bindur
bowels	iðrin
brave	frækni
break	brjótast
Brekka (place)	Brekku
bright	bjart
bring	færa
broad-waist	miðdigur
brother	bróður
brothers	bræðrum, bræður

English	*Old Icelandic*
brought	færa, færðu
brought-about	veldur
buried	heygður
burned	brenna, brenndu
burnt	brenna
but	en, enn, og
by	við

C, c

call	heita, kalla
called	heitir, kalla, kallaður, kölluðu
call-to	kalla
came	kemur, kom, koma, kominn, komst, komu
can	fæ, getur, kann
capable	gildur
care	gáir, vanda
cared	gáði
carried	báru, borið, bornir, færir
cast	kastaði
cattle	fé
caught	fengið, náði
caused	valdið
causing	framleiðslu
certainly	vísu, vita
character	gervi
chieftain	goði
chieftain-like	óhöfðinglegt
chieftains	höfðingja, höfðingjum
chieftains'	höfðingja
cleared	ræsta, ryðja, ryður
clearly	glögglega
close	fast, nálægt
closed	fast, lýkst
closely	fast
clothing	föt
coals	kolum
cold	köld, köldu, köldum
cold-bloodedly	kaldyrðum
combs	kömbum
come	kom, koma, komast
comes	kemur, komi, kominn

276

Word List (English to Old Icelandic)

English	Old Icelandic
come-with	koma
comfortable	hægt
coming	kominn
commotion	háreysti
companions	félaga, förunauta
compose	yrkja
considered	þykjast
controlled	valdi
could	gæti, gat, kom
courageous-warrior	hildardjarfi
craft	iðn
created	smíða
crew	áhöfn, hásetum
crutches	hækjur
cunning	kyndugskap
cursed	bölvaðra
custom	háttum
customers	kaupunauta, kaupunautar

D, d

English	Old Icelandic
damage	skaða
dark	dökkri, myrkt
daughter	dóttir
day	dag
days	dögum
dead	bani, dauðu
dearest	dýrstum
death	andlát
decayed	rotnað
deceived	blekkir
decreased	minnkaði
decrepitude	örverpi
deeds	atgervi
deem	dæmt
delegates	fulltrúa
Denmark (place)	Danmerkur
descended	kynjaður
descendents	ætt
desire	fýsi
desired	fýstist
desperation	örvænt
destitution	andvana
devil's	fjandans
devious	krókóttum
did	gerði, gerðu, vandist
died	andaður
difficulty	vandræði
disappeared	hvarf, steyptist
disguise	gervina
disturbances	óspekt
doing	völdum
done	búið, gera, gert
doors	dyrum
down	niður
dragon	naðrbings
draw	bregða
drawn	dregur
draws	dregr
drew	draga, hrukku
drift-wood	rekabút
drink	drykkju
drinking-tables	drykkjuborð
drive	reka
drowned	drekktur
dungeon	dýflissu

E, e

English	Old Icelandic
each	hvergi, hverjum, hverri, hvert, hvorri
earl	jarl, jarli
Earl-Of-Lade (name)	Hlaðajarl, Hlaðajarls
earls	jarls
earl's-abuse	jarlsníðs
Earl's-Poet (name)	Jarlaskáld
early-age	snemma
east	austur
eat	át, eta
eighteen	átján
either	eða, ýmist
either-way	annaðhvort
eldest	elsti
elephant	fíl
end	enda, lokið
ends	lýkur
endure	þola
endured	þoldu
England (place)	Englandi

Word List (English to Old Icelandic)

English	Old Icelandic
enslavement	ánauð
equally	jafnan
equipped	gyrti
equipped-with	gyrður
Erik's (name)	Eiríks
errand	erindis
estate	óðali
evening	kveldið
events	atburð, atburðir
evidence	vegsummerki
evil	illu
evil-like	illslegur
exceedingly-much	geysimjög
excellent-man	íþróttamaður
except	nema
exchanged	skipti
experienced	vanur
Eyjafjoll-Mountains (place)	Eyjafjöllum

F, f

English	Old Icelandic
fair	sæmilega
Fair-Cheek (name)	Fagurkinn
fair-wind	byrjar
fame	frægt, orðstír
farm	búi
farmer	bónda
father	faðir, föður
favour	yfirlæti
fee-lot	fjárhlut
fell	féll, féllu, fellur
financial-loss	fjártjón
financial-share	fjárhlut
find	fund
finished	úti
first	fyrst
first-mate	háseta
fog	þoku
Fog-verses (name)	Þokuvísur
followed	fylgdi, fylgt
following	afliðið
following-men	fjölmenni
food	góða, kost, leiðarnests, matar

English	Old Icelandic
for	á, að, fyrir, í, til
forests	skógum
for-good	alfari
for-himself	sér
for-long	lengur
for-the-sake	sakir
forty	fertuga
forward	fram
foster-care	ástfóstur
fostered	fóstri
foster-father	fóstra
found	fann, finnur
from	á, að, af, af, er, frá, fram, í, úr, við
from-out-of	úr
from-the-west	vestan
from-told	frásagnar
full	fullu
full-coming	fullkomið
funeral	útferð

G, g

English	Old Icelandic
Gaseyri (place)	Gáseyri
gave	gaf, gáfu
generosity	örleik
get	fá, fæ, fást, geta, getur
ghastly	ljótu
gifted	lánað
gifts	gjafir
give	gefa
give-performance	sýnduð
gladly	gjarna
go	ganga
goat-beard	geitarskegg, geitarskegginu
God (name)	Guðs
going	farið, gengur
gone	farið, gengið
good	góðan, góðar, góðu, gott, vænna
got	fékk, fengi, fengið, gæti, gat, gekk
got-married	kvæntist
granted	veittu

Word List (English to Old Icelandic)

English	Old Icelandic
grave	svarri
great	mikill
great-family	stórættaður
great-men	stórmenni
great-wealth	stórauðigs, stórfé
greeted	kvaddi
greeting	kvaðningar
grips	festist
grown	vexti

H, h

English	Old Icelandic
had	á, æti, átt, áttu, hafa, hafði, hefir, hefur, lætur, lagði, láta, láti, lét
had-been	vert
had-done	gerði
hair	hárið
Hakon (name)	Hákon, Hákonar
Hakon's (name)	Hákonar
halberd	atgeirnum
half	hálf
Hali (name)	Hali
Hallbjorn (name)	Hallbirni, Hallbjörn
hands	hendi
hanged	hengja
happened	gerðist
hardly	harðla
harm	skaði
harmful	dálegra
harsher	harðúðigur
has	er, hefir
hated	hataður
have	fá, hafa, hafi, hafið, haft, hefi, hefir, höfum, lagið
having	hefir
he	hann, hans, honum, sér
head-skin	höfuðsvörðum
hear	heyrið
heard	heyrði, heyrðu, heyrt
heart	hjartað, hugr
heaven's	himins

English	Old Icelandic
heavy	þunga
he-had	honum
he-himself	sér
Hel (place)	Helju
held	hélt
Helgi (name)	Helgi
hellish-old-man	heljarkarl
here	hér, hingað
hers	hennar
high	hátt
high-born	ítri
him	hann, honum, sér, sig
himself	sé, sér, sína, sinni
hired	ræður
his	hans, hánum, hins, honum, sér, sína, sinn, sinna, sinnar, sinni, síns, sínu, sínum, sitt
Hofdabrekka (place)	Höfðabrekku
hold	halda
home	heim
homes	heim
honour	sæmd, verðugu, virðingar
hope	von
Horgabrudi (name)	Hörgabrúði
Horgi (place)	Hörgi
however	hversu
how-so	hversu
humiliation	smánar
humility	lítillæti
hunger	svöngum
hungry	svengd

I, i

English	Old Icelandic
i	eg
i-am	mér
Iceland (place)	Ísland, Íslandi, Íslands
idol-worship	guðníðingskapur
if	ef, eg
ill	illa, illur
improvement	góðu
in	á, að, af, í, inn

Word List (English to Old Icelandic)

English	Old Icelandic
increase	aukið
in-front-of	framan
inherited	erfðu
instruction	fræðum
intended	ætlaði
into	í
invited	bað, boðið
iron-weapon	járn
Irpu (name)	Irpu
is	er
is-said	segja
it	á, að, hana, hún, það
itching	kláði
it-is	er
its	hennar
it-was	gerði

J, j

journey	ferðum, leið
Jutland (place)	Jóta

K, k

Karl (name)	Karl
kennings	kenningar
kill	drepa
killed	vó
king's-gift	konungsnaut
kinsmen	frænda
kinsmen-origins	kynferði
Klaufi (name)	Klaufa
knew	kunni, vita
knots	knúta
know	kannt, víst, vita, vitja
known	kenndur
knows	veit
knuckle-breaker	völubrjótur

L, l

Lade (place)	Hlaðir, Hlöðum
laid	lagði, lagið, lét, liggur
land	land
lands	lands
large	mikill, stóra
last	síðasta
laughed	hlógu
launched	skjóta
law-assembly	lögréttu
lay	liggur
laying	legið
learned	spurði, spurn, spurt, spyr
leave	orlof
left	lætur
legislation	lagasetning
lengthen	lengja
less	síður
let	lát, látið, lét
levelled	sléttri
lies	liggr, liggur
life	líf
life-days	lífsdaga
lifetime	lífstíma
like	líkar
liked	líkaði
liking	geðjast
listen	hlýða
listen-to	hlýdduð
little	lítils, lítinn
lived	bjó
Ljotolf (name)	Ljótólfi, Ljótólfs, Ljótólfur
locks	lásum
long	lengi
longer	lengra, lengur
lord	herra
lordship	höfðingskap
loved	unni
luck	giftu

M, m

made	ger, gera, gerðu, verið
magic	fítonsanda
magical-arts	göldrum
malice	grálega

Word List (English to Old Icelandic)

English	Old Icelandic
malignance	meinlætum
malignancy	meinlætis
man	karli, maður, mann
man-evil	mannillska
man-of-high-rank	virðingamaður
man's	manna
manslaughter	mannalát
many	marga, margan, margir, margra, margri, mart, mörg, mörgum
many-known	margkunnandi
market-town	kaupstaðinn
marshes	mörkum
matter	mál
may	má, mátti, mega, megi
me	mér, mig
meet	fund
men	drengr, manna, manna, menn, mönnum
merchant-ships	knarrar
merry	ærnri
met	hitti
middle	miðjum, miðs
middle-of	miðju
Midfjord (place)	Miðfirði
Midfjorder-Skeggi (name)	Miðfjarðar-Skeggja
midwinter-evening	aðfangskveld
mile	mílu
mine	minn, mitt
misery	eymd
misliked	mislíkaði
miss	missa
moment	bili
money	peninga
more	fleira, meir, meira
more-convenient	hentugri
morning	morguninn
most	flestum, mest, mesta, mesti, mikið
mother	móður
mother's-brother	móðurbróður
mound	haug, haugur
mouth	munn
move	flyttu
moved	gangi
movement	bragði
much	margra, mikið, mikil, mikill, mikils, mikinn, mikla, miklar, miklum, mjög
must	mun
Myrdal-Valley (place)	Mýdal
mysterious-path	refilstiga

N, n

English	Old Icelandic
name	heiti, nafn, nafni
named	heita, heiti, heitir, hét
name-giving	nafnfesti
nature	eðli, náttúra
near	nær
nearest	næstir
need	þarfast, þarftu, þurfa
needed	þarf, þarfa, þarfaði
never	aldrei
news	tíðinda, tíðindi, tíðindum
next	næsta
Nidung (name)	Níðungur
night	nætur, nátt
nineteen	nítján
Njord (name)	Njörðr
noble	öðlings, skörungur
noble-woman	kvenskörungur
noise	hark
no-little	ólítið
none	engi, engr, önga
nor	né
north	norður
Norway (place)	Noreg, Noregs
not	eiga, eigi, ekki, öngu
not-further	áfram
not-lacking	óvant
now	nú

O, o

Word List (English to Old Icelandic)

English	*Old Icelandic*	*English*	*Old Icelandic*
Odin (name)	Gautr	*passed*	leið
of	á, að, af, af, í, og, úr	*peasant*	þorpara
of-all	öllum	*people*	manna, manni, manninn, menn, mönnum
off	af		
of-gold	gulls		
of-Hakon	hákoni	*peoples'*	mönnum
of-poets	skálda	*performed*	flutt
often	oft, oftar, oftlega	*pernickety*	nákvæmi
of-the-ship	knarrar	*phrases*	drápu
Olaf (name)	Ólafur	*plates*	diska
Olaf's (name)	Ólafs	*plunder*	férán
old	gamall, gamla, gömlum	*plundering*	hervirki
		poem	kvæði, kvæðið, kveðið
old-man	gamlir, karl		
omens	frétt, fréttar	*poems*	kvæði
on	á	*poem's-reward*	kvæðislaunum
one	eina, einn	*poet*	skáld
one's	hvern	*poetry*	brag, skáldskap, skáldskapinn
only	einna		
open	opnast	*poles*	ásum
opening	gíman	*popular*	vinsæl
or	eða, ella	*popularity*	vinsældum
other	aðrar, aðrir, annar, annarra, annarri, hinum, öðrum	*possible*	hægt
		power	krafti, mögnuðu, vald
		powerful	ríkur
		praise	lof
other-lands	útlendis	*praised*	lofaði
others	aðrir, annarra, öðrum	*praise-words*	lofkvæði
ours	vort	*prepared*	bjó, búinn, býr
ourselves-decide	sjálfráða	*previous-deeds*	framaverka
out	úr, út, utan, úti, ýtar	*price*	verð
out-from	út	*profit*	græddi
outlaw	útlægur	*promise*	heita
out-lying	utarlega	*promised*	hét
out-of	undan, úr	*promising*	efnilegir
outside	ytra	*promptly*	greiðlega
over	ofan, yfir	*properly*	sæmilega
own	eigið	*proverb*	orðskvið
owning	eign	*provide*	kost
Oxara (place)	Öxará	*provided-knowing*	naddveiti
		pulled	togar
		punishment-time	hegningartíminn
		put-to-words	kveðið

P, p

parted	skildu
parting	reikar
passage	farning

Q, q

Word List (English to Old Icelandic)

English	Old Icelandic
quickly	bráðlega, greiðlega

R, r

English	Old Icelandic
ran	hleypur
rather	heldur
received	tók
recently	litlu
recites	kveða
recovered	raknaði
Red (name)	Rauði
Red-Cloak (name)	Rauðfeldur
reddened	roðið
relief	létti
relieved	fegins
renown	hróðr
repaid	galt
repay	gjalda, launað
repayment	gjöld
reported	fréttust
requirements	hentar
rest	hvílast
restlessness	óværa, óværi
return	áður
returned	aftur
returning	aftur
revenge	hefnda
Reykir (place)	Reykjum
river	á
robbed	rændi
robbery	ránum
rocks	grjóti
rose	ríða, rís
rough	harðleikinn
ruled	réð

S, s

English	Old Icelandic
sack-cloth	strigadúk
sacrifices	fórnir
saga	sögu
sagas	sögur
said	kvað, kveður, mælt, sagði, sagði, sagður, sagt, segið, segir, segja, sögðu, talar
sailed	sigldu
sake	sækja, sakir
sale	sölur
same	sömu
sand	eyri
sat	sat, sest
saw	sá, sér, sjá
say	kveða, segist, segja
say-you	segðu
scarcely	trautt, varla
scratched	hrífa
sea	haf
secrecy	laun
see	sé, sjá
seemed-to	sýndist
seems	þykir
seen	sést
sent	sendu
servants	þjónustumenn
settled	bjó, búið
settlement	byggða
shall	mun, munt, munuð, munum, skal, skalt, skaltu
shall-i	mig
shall-you	skaltu
shame	blygðar, skammar
shamed	forsmáður
shaped	skapaðir
she	hún
shepherd	sauðamaður
ship	skip, skipi, skips
ships	skips
shivering	hrollir
short	stutt
should	mun, munuð, skyldi, skyldu, skyldur
shoulders	herðar
show-off	skruma
shut	luktum
side	megin
since	síðan, því

Word List (English to Old Icelandic)

English	Old Icelandic	English	Old Icelandic
sister	systur	strange	kynstrum, undarlega
sisters	systra	strangeness	býsn
sit	sæti, sætis	strong	gilds
sit-still	kyrr	struck	hjó
Skeggi (name)	Skeggi, Skeggja	stumbled	stumrar
skilled	íþrótt, íþróttir	such	slíkt, því
skilled-in-magic	fjölkunni	summer	sumar
skilled-poet	þjóðskáld	support	styrk
skills	íþrótta	supposed	ætluðu
Skogar (place)	Skógum	Svarfardal (place)	Svarfaðardal, Svarfdæla
slaying-warrior	vígdjarfr	Svein (name)	Sveins
slendered	grenndi	swagger	skruma
slept	sofnar, svaf	Sweden (place)	Svíþjóð
slyness	slægða	swords	branda
so	sá, svo	Syrgsdalir (place)	Syrgisdölum
soles-of-the-feet	iljarnar		
solve	leysa		
some	nokkuð, nokkura, nokkurar, nokkurt, sumir		

T, t

English	Old Icelandic
something	nokkuð
somewhat	nokkuð
son	son, sonar
songs	atkvæðum
son-of-gjallandi	gjallandason
sons	syni
soon	fljótlega
soonest	fljótasta
sorcery	galdur
sought	fréttist, leitaði, sótt
soul	andar
south	suður
speak	kveða
spikes	broddur
spoke	kvað, mælti
spoken	kveðið
spring	vor, vorið
spring-days	vordögum
stand	staðið, standa
stave	stef
staves	stafni
sticks	stafina
stood	standa, stendur, stóð
stopped	linnir
stories	saga
straightaway	þegar

English	Old Icelandic
take	náms, numið, taka, tekur
taken	nema, taka, tekið
talented	gervilegur
talked	mælti
teach	kenna
temple	hofi
temples	hof
temporary	stundlegum
than	en, þann
thanked	þakkaði
thanks	þökk
that	á, að, en, er, sem, það, þann
the	að, en, er, hið, hinn, hinni, hins, hinu, það, þenna, til
the-abuse	níðið
the-bag	hítina
the-bay	víkinni
the-best	mest, mesta
the-chieftain	goða
the-coals	kol
the-crutches	hækjurnar
the-darkness	myrkrið
the-day	daginn

Word List (English to Old Icelandic)

English	*Old Icelandic*	*English*	*Old Icelandic*
the-earl	jarl, jarli, jarlinn, jarlinum, jarls	Thingvellir (place)	Þingvelli
the-earl's	jarls	think	hugsa
the-earl's-abuse	jarlsníði	third	þriðjung
the-earth	jörðina	thirsty	þorsta
the-enemy's	óvinarins	this	á, að, það, þenna, þess, þessa, þessar, þessi, þessu, þessum, þetta
the-fellows	drengjum		
the-fields	velli		
the-greatest	mestr	this-verse	vísu
the-hall	höllina, höllinni	Thjorsa (place)	Þjórsá
theirs	sinn, þeirra	Thord (name)	Þórðar
the-king	konung, konungi, konungs, konungur	Thorgard (name)	Þorgarð, Þorgarði, Þorgarðs, Þorgarður
the-land	land, landi	Thorgerd (name)	Þorgerði
the-lion's	leóns	Thorhild (name)	Þórhildur
them	þar, þeim	Thorkell (name)	Þorkell
the-mauler	böggva	Thorleif (name)	Þorleif, Þorleifi, Þorleifr, Þorleifur, Þorleifur
the-most	flestu		
the-mound	hauginn, hauginum, haugurinn	thorleif's	þorleifi, þorleifs
the-mound-dweller	haugbúann	Thorleif's (name)	Þorleifs
then	að, en, hið, hina, þá, þann, þeim, þenna, því	those	hinn, þenna
		though	þó
		thought	þótti, þóttist, þóttu, þóttust, þykir, þykist
the-night	nóttina		
the-old-man	karl, karli	thoughts	hug
the-poem	kvæðið	Thrasi (name)	Þrasa
the-poet	skaldi	three	þrjá
the-prince	þengils	threw	varpar
there	þar, þegar, þeirra, þeirrar	through	gegnum
		tied-up	binda
therefore	því	time	tíma, tímir
the-same	samur	to	á, að, í, til, við
these	þenna	to-be	vera
the-ship	nökkvi, skipið	to-carry	flytja
the-spring	vori	to-eat	etið
the-straw	hálminn	together	saman
the-summer	sumrinu	to-give	gefa
the-sword	sverðinu	to-hear	hlýða
the-tables	borð	to-him	honum, sér
the-Tronds' (name)	Þrænda	told	sagði, talað, töluðu
the-uppermost	ofanverðum	told-of	getið
they	þau, þeim, þeir	to-me	mér
they-were	eru	tongue	tunguna
thick-clouds	mökkr	took	nam, taka, tekur, tók
thighs	þjóanna, þjóin	torment	kvala

Word List (English to Old Icelandic)

English	Old Icelandic
to-sell	selja
tough	seigt
toughness	harðfengi
to-you	þér
traces	vegsummerki
trading-men	kaupmönnum
traditions	sið
transport	reiða
travel	fara, ferð, ferðar
travel-goods	fararefna
travelled	farið, fer, fór, fóru
tricked	bregður, ginnti
Trondheim (place)	Þrándheim
troubled	bæginn
truly	sannlega
tunic	kyrtilinn, kyrtlinum
turned	hverfur, snýr, snýst
twisted	snaraði
two	tvær, tvo
true	satt

U, u

English	Old Icelandic
unconsciousness	óvit
under	undir
undone	ógert, óloknum
un-eagerly	ófreklegar
un-glad	ógleður
un-gladdened	ógladdist
un-gladness	ógleði
unknown	ókunna
unless	nema
un-redeemable	óbætilegs
unruly	úrigur
unsoundly	óhljóði
until	til
up	upp, uppi
upped	upp
upper	efsta
up-to	undir
us	oss
usually	jafnan

V, v

English	Old Icelandic
vacations	orlofs
verse	vísu, vísuna
verses	vísur
Vik (place)	Vík
villain	villumaðr
vocabulary	orðfæri

W, w

English	Old Icelandic
walked	gekk
waning	þrotnum
wares	varning, varninginn
warrior	gramr
warriors	fyrðum
was	enn, er, væri, var, varð, voru
was-named	hét, nefndist
wave	öldu
we	oss, vér
wealth	fé
wealth-damage	fjárskaða
wealthy	auðigur
we-are	eru
well	vel
well-sized	vellstæri
went	fékk, fer, fór, fóru, ganga, ganganda, gekk, gengur
were	væri, var, varð, voru
west	vestan, vestra, vestur
what	er, hvað, sem
wheel	röðla
when	en, er
whether	hvort
which	er, sem
who	er, hver
who's	hverjum
who-was	er
why	hví
wicked	vonda
widely	víða
wife	kona
will	viljið
will-be	verðir

Word List (English to Old Icelandic)

English	Old Icelandic
willingly	ofléttlega
win-over	ynni
winter	vetur, veturinn
winters	vetra
wisdom	visku
wise	vitur
wish	vil, vildi, vildir, viljum
wished	vildi
wish-to	viljum
witchcraft	fjölkynngi, gerningum, tröllskap
with	í, með, það, við
with-conviction	sakir
without	án, utan
woman	kona
Woman-Verses (name)	Konurvísur
wooden-man	trémann
worded	ort
words	orð, orðið, ort, orti
work	verki
worst	verr
worth	verðum
worthiness	virðum
would	mundi, mundu
wretchedness	vesaldar
written	rituð

Y, y

English	Old Icelandic
Yngvild (name)	Yngvildi
you	þér, þig, þinn, þú, yður
young	ungum
youngest	yngsti
your	þín
yours	þinna, þinni, þínum, þitt, yðrum, yður
Yule (name)	Jóla
yule-feast	jólaveislunnar

A Word Comparison of Old Norse and Old Icelandic Words

A Word Comparison of Old Norse and Old Icelandic Words

Old Norse	Old Icelandic	English	Old Norse	Old Icelandic	English
áðr	áður	before	brœðr	bræður	brothers
áðr	áður	return	brœðrum	bræðrum	brothers
aftr	aftur	after	Danmerkr	Danmerkur	Denmark (place)
aftr	aftur	back	dœmt	dæmt	deem
aftr	aftur	returned	dregr	dregur	drawn
aftr	aftur	returning	drekktr	drekktur	drowned
aldr	aldur	age	fellr	fellur	fell
andaðr	andaður	died	finnr	finnur	found
ástfóstr	ástfóstur	foster-care	föðr	föður	father
at	að	a	fœ	fæ	can
at	að	about	fœ	fæ	get
at	að	and	fœra	færa	bring
at	að	as	fœra	færa	brought
at	að	at	fœrðu	færðu	brought
at	að	for	fœrir	færir	carried
at	að	from	fornfrœði	fornfræði	ancient-ways
at	að	in	forsmáðr	forsmáður	shamed
at	að	it	frœðum	fræðum	instruction
at	að	of	frœgt	frægt	fame
at	að	that	frœkni	frækni	brave
at	að	the	frœnda	frænda	kinsmen
at	að	then	galdr	galdur	sorcery
at	að	this	gengr	gengur	going
at	að	to	gengr	gengur	went
atgervimaðr	atgervimaður	accomplished-man	gervilegr	gervilegur	talented
atkvœðum	atkvæðum	songs	getr	getur	can
auðigr	auðigur	wealthy	getr	getur	get
Auðr	Auður	Aud (name)	geysimjǫk	geysimjög	exceedingly-much
austr	austur	east	gildr	gildur	capable
bat	bað	asked	gœti	gæti	could
bat	bað	bid	gœti	gæti	got
bat	bað	invited	grœddi	græddi	profit
betr	betur	better	guðníðingskapr	guðníðingskapur	idol-worship
biðr	biður	asked	gyrðr	gyrður	equipped-with
bindr	bindur	bound	harðúðigr	harðúðigur	harsher
bœði	bæði	both	hataðr	hataður	hated
bœginn	bæginn	troubled	haugr	haugur	mound
bregðr	bregður	tricked	hefr	hefur	had
broddr	broddur	spikes	heldr	heldur	rather
bróðr	bróður	brother			

A Word Comparison of Old Norse and Old Icelandic Words

Old Norse	Old Icelandic	English
heygðr	heygður	buried
hingat	hingað	here
hjartat	hjartað	heart
hleypr	hleypur	ran
hœgt	hægt	comfortable
hœgt	hægt	possible
hœkjr	hækjur	crutches
hœkjurnar	hækjurnar	the-crutches
hvat	hvað	what
hverfr	hverfur	turned
illr	illur	bad
illr	illur	ill
illslegr	illslegur	evil-like
íþróttamaðr	íþróttamaður	excellent-man
kallaðr	kallaður	called
kemr	kemur	came
kemr	kemur	comes
kenndr	kenndur	known
Konrvísr	Konurvísur	Woman-Verses (name)
konungr	konungur	the-king
kvat	kvað	said
kvat	kvað	spoke
kveðr	kveður	said
kvenskörungr	kvenskörungur	noble-woman
kvœði	kvæði	poem
kvœði	kvæði	poems
kvœðið	kvæðið	poem
kvœðið	kvæðið	the-poem
kvœðislaunum	kvæðislaunum	poem's-reward
kvœntist	kvæntist	got-married
kynjaðr	kynjaður	descended
lánat	lánað	gifted
launat	launað	repay
lengr	lengur	for-long
lengr	lengur	longer
liggr	liggur	laid
liggr	liggur	lay
liggr	liggur	lies
lítillœti	lítillæti	a-little
lítillœti	lítillæti	humility
Ljótólfr	Ljótólfur	Ljotolf (name)
lœtr	lætur	had
lœtr	lætur	left
lofkvœði	lofkvæði	praise-words
lýkr	lýkur	ends
maðr	maður	a-man
maðr	maður	man
meinlœtis	meinlætis	malignancy
meinlœtum	meinlætum	malignance
miðdigr	miðdigur	broad-waist
mjǫk	mjög	much
móðr	móður	mother
móðrbróðr	móðurbróður	mother's-brother
mœlt	mælt	said
mœlti	mælti	spoke
mœlti	mælti	talked
nákvœmi	nákvæmi	pernickety
nálœgt	nálægt	close
niðr	niður	down
Níðungr	Níðungur	Nidung (name)
nœr	nær	near
nœsta	næsta	next
nœstir	næstir	nearest
nœtr	nætur	night
nokkr	nokkur	anything
norðr	norður	north
óbœtilegs	óbætilegs	un-redeemable
œfr	æfur	angry
œrnri	ærnri	merry
œti	æti	ate
œti	æti	had
œtlaði	ætlaði	intended
œtluðu	ætluðu	supposed
œtt	ætt	ancestors
œtt	ætt	ancestry
œtt	ætt	descendents
œvintýr	ævintýr	adventure
ógleðr	ógleður	un-glad
Ólafr	Ólafur	Olaf (name)
orðfœri	orðfæri	vocabulary
örvœnt	örvænt	desperation

A Word Comparison of Old Norse and Old Icelandic Words

Old Norse	Old Icelandic	English
óværa	óværa	restlessness
óværi	óværi	restlessness
Rauðfeldr	Rauðfeldur	Red-Cloak (name)
ríkr	ríkur	powerful
rœðr	ræður	hired
rœndi	rændi	robbed
rœsta	ræsta	cleared
rotnat	rotnað	decayed
ryðr	ryður	cleared
sagðr	sagður	said
samr	samur	the-same
samsœtis	samsætis	banquet
sauðamaðr	sauðamaður	shepherd
síðr	síður	less
skörungr	skörungur	noble
skyldr	skyldur	should
slœgða	slægða	slyness
sœkja	sækja	sake
sœllífi	sællífi	blessed-life
sœmd	sæmd	honour
sœmilega	sæmilega	fair
sœmilega	sæmilega	properly
sœti	sæti	sit
sœtis	sætis	sit
sögr	sögur	sagas
sölr	sölur	sale
stendr	stendur	stood
stórœttaðr	stórættaður	great-family
suðr	suður	south
Svarfdœla	Svarfdæla	Svarfardal (place)
systr	systur	sister
talat	talað	told
tekr	tekur	take
tekr	tekur	took
þat	það	it
þat	það	that
þat	það	the
þat	það	this
þat	það	with
Þokuvísr	Þokuvísur	Fog-verses (name)
Þorgarðr	Þorgarður	Thorgard (name)
Þórhildr	Þórhildur	Thorhild (name)
Þorleifr	Þorleifur	Thorleif (name)
Þrœnda	Þrænda	the-Tronds' (name)
tvœr	tvær	two
úrigr	úrigur	unruly
útlœgr	útlægur	outlaw
vandrœði	vandræði	difficulty
vanr	vanur	experienced
veldr	veldur	brought-about
vellstœri	vellstæri	well-sized
verðr	verður	became
verðr	verður	become
vestr	vestur	west
vetr	vetur	winter
vinsœl	vinsæl	popular
vinsœldum	vinsældum	popularity
virðingamaðr	virðingamaður	man-of-high-rank
vísr	vísur	verses
vitr	vitur	wise
vœnna	vænna	good
vœri	væri	was
vœri	væri	were
völubrjótr	völubrjótur	knuckle-breaker
yðr	yður	you
yðr	yður	yours
yfirlœti	yfirlæti	favour

www.ingramcontent.com/pod-product-compliance
Lightning Source LLC
Chambersburg PA
CBHW051401070526
44584CB00023B/3248